Blackstone's Guide to the
EMPLOYMENT
RELATIONS ACT 1999

Charles Barrow
Steve Blunt
Steve Gibbons
Isabel Manley
Nick Rose

**BLACKSTONE
PRESS LIMITED**

Published by
Blackstone Press Limited
Aldine Place
London
W12 8AA

Sales enquiries and orders
Telephone +44-(0)-20-8740-2277
Facsimile +44-(0)-20-8743-2292
e-mail: sales@blackstone.demon.co.uk
website: www.blackstonepress.com

ISBN 1 84174 125 6
© C. Barrow, S. Blunt, S. Gibbons, I. Manley, N. Rose 2001
First published 2001

500 562 466

British Library Cataloguing in Publication Data
A catalogue record for this book is available from the British Library

Typeset in 10/12pt Times by Montage Studios Limited, Tonbridge, Kent
Printed and bound in Great Britain by Antony Rowe Limited,
Chippenham and Reading

Contents

1 Introduction

1.1 Industrial and legal background   1.2 The White Paper: *Fairness at Work*
1.3 Key features of the Act   1.4 Compliance with the Human Rights Act 1998

PART 1   INDIVIDUAL RIGHTS

2 Unfair Dismissal

2.1 Qualification period   2.2 Agreements to exclude unfair dismissal rights
2.3 Indexation of compensation   2.4 Compensatory award limit   2.5 Additional
and special awards   2.6 Industrial action dismissals

3 Maternity and Parental Rights

3.1 Introduction   3.2 Maternity rights   3.3 Parental leave   3.4 Time off to assist
dependants   3.5 Discrimination and the new rights

4 Part-time Workers

4.1 Introduction   4.2 The scope of the Regulations   4.3 Less favourable treatment
4.4 The comparator   4.5 Right to receive a written statement of reasons for less
favourable treatment   4.6 Unfair dismissal and the right not to be subjected to a
detriment   4.7 Complaint to an employment tribunal   4.8 Miscellaneous matters   4.9 Summary and conclusions

application by the CAC   10.9 'Admissibility' requirements for applications   10.10
Withdrawal and notice to cease consideration of the application   10.11 Determina-
tion of the appropriate bargaining unit   10.12 Validity of application   10.13
Automatic recognition

Preface

This book is intended to be a clear, comprehensive and authoritative guide to the Employment Relations Act 1999 — an extensive and wide ranging statute which makes fundamental changes to many areas of collective and individual employment law. The Act is the product of a bid by the Labour Government to develop a 'third way' in industrial and employment policy — by bestowing 'fairness not favours' to trade unions and workers and by promoting 'partnership' at the workplace. Although it may be doubted whether all the provisions have this effect, it is evident that the Act represents a significant advance in employment protection for individuals, enhances trade union rights and as such is a major departure from previous government policy.

Many of the provisions of the Act are of a complex nature and so it is inevitable that any explanation of value will be of a detailed nature. Yet we have attempted to provide an appraisal of the legal significance of the Act and it's subordinate legislation, by reference to it's likely practical impact and have sought to identify difficulties that may arise in the future.

Finally, thanks is due to Heather Saward and Sarah McGuire at Blackstone for their patience whilst awaiting the manuscript and for their help in the process of producing this text. Steve Blunt would also like to thank Nick Elwell-Sutton for his assistance in providing background research.

The law is stated as at 1 January 2001.

Table of Cases

Table of Statutes

Table of Secondary Legislation

Table of Codes of Practice

Abbreviations

ACAS	Advisory, Conciliation and Arbitration Service
CAC	Central Arbitration Committee
CBI	Confederation of British Industry
CO	Certification Officer
CPUIA	Commissioner for Protection against Unlawful Industrial Action
CROTUM	Commissioner for the Rights of Trade Union Members
EAT	Employment Appeal Tribunal
EPCA	Employment Protection (Consolidation) Act 1978
ILO	International Labour Organisation
JNB	joint negotiating body
para./paras	paragraph/paragraphs
QIP	qualified independent person
reg.	regulation
s./ss.	section/sections
SMP	statutory maternity pay
TUC	Trades Union Congress
TULR(C)A	Trade Union and Labour Relations (Consolidation) Act 1992

Chapter 1
Introduction

1.1 INDUSTRIAL AND LEGAL BACKGROUND

The Employment Relations Act 1999 is the Labour Government's first attempt at major reform of individual and collective employment law. It is intended to be the 'industrial relations settlement . . . for the remainder of this Parliament' and '. . . will promote the best of modern employment practices, encouraging a culture of fairness and trust in the workplace coupled with rights and responsibilities' (Stephen Byers, Secretary of State for Trade and Industry, House of Commons Second Reading, 9 February 1999, coll. 134 and 131). By seeking to develop a new 'partnership' culture between employers and trade unions, the Act represents a departure from the 'restrictive' and deregulatory policy of prior Conservative regimes and from the 'social contract' and corporatist approach of the Labour administrations of the 1970s.

At the time of the last Labour Government (1974–1979), industrial and employment policy was informed by the conclusions of the Royal Commission on Trade Unions and Employers' Associations (the Donovan Commission). The Commission's core recommendation was that Britain's industrial malaise could only be cured by the strengthening of the industrial relations framework through encouraging and fostering the model of centralised collective bargaining. As a consequence the Trade Union and Labour Relations Act 1974 and the Employment Protection Act 1975 introduced a comprehensive package of legal measures to help develop and underpin collective bargaining. There was legal support for the strengthening of trade union organisation through the provision of specific rights for members and officials; for example, to take time off to engage in industrial relations duties, to participate in trade union activities and the right not to be discriminated against or dismissed for such participation. Collective 'props' to bargaining were introduced which provided unions with rights to recognition, consultation and information for bargaining purposes. At the individual level a 'floor of rights' was provided — such as maternity pay, guaranteed pay on lay-off — via the incorporation of statutory implied terms into the individual employment contract. Procedures were also introduced for imposing minimum terms on employers in poorly unionised industries, and the first race and sex discrimination legislation was enacted.

The *quid pro quo* for the provision of these collective and individual benefits was union cooperation in the drive to conquer inflation by the moderation of wage demands — known as the 'social contract'. Although Government pay policy was initially successful in the private sector, where self-financing productivity deals were often struck, serious conflict arose in the public sector. Coordinated industrial action in the winter of 1978–79 in the public sector, the so-called 'winter of discontent', paved the way for the election of a Conservative administration in the General Election of May 1979 and heralded a change in attitudes towards employee and trade union rights.

Both economic and legal strategies were employed to curb the perceived excesses of union power. Management of the economy was achieved through the application of monetarist economic policy, based on the control of the money supply and the primacy of the free market. This resulted in profound changes to the industrial structure and the organisation of work, which stimulated severe unemployment throughout the 1980s, a decline in centralised collective bargaining arrangements and a consequent loss of union membership (from over 12 million in 1978 to under 8 million in 1997) — all contributing to a weakened union movement, with limited influence on the national stage and less ability to represent members' interests effectively at the workplace.

In addition to the effects of market forces, statutory initiatives revolutionised the legal relationship between workers, unions and employers. Legal policies designed to limit trade union activity were developed, taking into account the lessons learnt from the failure of the Industrial Relations Act 1971 (where a regime of all-embracing legal regulation of union activities was imposed by the Heath Government), eventually defeated by coordinated trade union action. Accordingly, Conservative strategy from 1979 was, instead, to implement restrictive laws on a gradual 'step-by step' basis, passing new Acts of Parliament almost every two years (from 1980 to 1993) to create a comprehensive legal regime of some complexity to control the internal and external affairs of trade unions. Legislation constrained trade union autonomy over internal elections, financial issues, political expenditure, the admission, discipline and expulsion of members and, by reforming the operation of the immunities, limited a trade union's ability to take strike action and to represent its membership during workplace disputes.

Distaste for labour market regulation was not, however, manifested by the wholesale dismantling of legislative protection for the individual, partly due to the requirements of European Community law. Yet in those spheres where European legal rights were absent, employment protection legislation was amended considerably. For instance, the qualifying period for bringing an unfair dismissal complaint was increased in 1979 from six months to one year and then further increased in 1985 to two years; protection for employees dismissed while engaged in industrial action was heavily restricted; and the power of Wages Councils to set minimum remuneration throughout low pay industries was first limited in 1986 and then abolished in 1993. The Fair Wages Resolution of 1891 (re-affirmed by Parliament in subsequent years), which introduced the notion of the state as a 'model employer', requiring contractors to adhere to certain minimum terms and conditions, was rescinded in 1983.

1.2   THE WHITE PAPER: *FAIRNESS AT WORK*

It is against this industrial and legal background that the Labour Government issued their White Paper on employment rights — *Fairness at Work* (Cm 3968) — developed after almost a year of extensive consultation with trade union and employer representatives and published in May 1998. Many trade unionists had looked to the new administration to repeal the bulk of the Conservative trade union legislation and to re-instate a comprehensive framework of employment rights at the individual and collective level. However, the Prime Minister made it apparent in his foreword to the White Paper that the essential elements of the existing trade union legislation would remain, as he sought to 'draw a line under the issue of industrial relations law': 'There will be no going back. The days of strikes without ballots, mass picketing, closed shops and secondary action are over. Even after the changes we propose, Britain will have the most lightly regulated labour market of any leading economy in the world.'

The introductory chapters of the White Paper ('Building Prosperity' and 'Modern Business at Work') further emphasised that the focus of Labour's industrial and economic policy would be on the development of competitive businesses and the enhancement of wealth creation through encouragement of the enterprise economy. In this context employment relationships based on conflict at the workplace were incompatible with efficiency in the labour market and the pursuit of greater business competitiveness. Rather than old conflict, new partnerships at work need to be properly developed and managed so as to enhance company performance and profitability, leading to a strong economy and national prosperity.

It was the Government's view that effective partnerships at work, a flexible and efficient workforce and competitive industries can be built only where there is fairness in the workplace. Therefore, to ensure the just treatment of employees and unions in order to promote fruitful partnerships at work, the White Paper proposed a framework of measures that would underpin effective working relationships and invited views on a range of other employment issues. The proposals were grouped under three broad headings: (i) individual rights, (ii) collective rights, and (iii) family friendly policies. The main recommendations included:

- reducing the qualifying period for claiming unfair dismissal from two years to one year
- abolishing the upper limit on compensation awards in unfair dismissal cases
- introducing a statutory right to trade union recognition 'where a majority of the relevant workforce wishes it'
- allowing individuals dismissed for taking part in lawfully organised industrial action the right to make an unfair dismissal claim
- giving employees the right to be accompanied in grievance and disciplinary proceedings

- making it unlawful to discriminate by omission on grounds of trade union membership and prohibiting the 'blacklisting' of trade unionists
- reducing the qualifying period for extended maternity leave from two years to one year
- increasing the length of basic maternity leave from 14 to 18 weeks
- implementing the EC Directive on Parental Leave, which gives all parents the right to three months' parental leave, and introducing the right to time off for urgent family reasons.

Following a further period of consultation (with the CBI, TUC and other interested parties), the Secretary of State announced the Government's decisions 'on the key outstanding issues' on 17 December 1998 (Hansard HC, written answers, coll. 692–693). When the Bill was published in January 1999, it was apparent that the Government had taken account of some of the concerns expressed by employers' representatives. For example, the upper limit on unfair dismissal compensation was not abolished but raised from £12,000 to £50,000; the right for employees to claim unfair dismissal while on official strike was restricted to the first eight weeks of a dispute; and the provisions on recognition were essentially as set out in the White Paper but with some important refinements (in particular more stringent numerical tests were introduced) for the Central Arbitration Committee (CAC) to apply when considering a union application.

1.3   KEY FEATURES OF THE ACT

The Employment Relations Bill was introduced in the House of Commons on 27 January 1999. Although there were some substantive changes to the original Bill, most were of a technical nature initiated by Government representatives without affecting the essential principles and thrust of the Bill.

The Act, which received the Royal Assent on 27 July 1999, introduces wholly new measures and amends existing provisions in current legislation (particularly sections in the Trade Union and Labour Relations (Consolidation) Act (TULR(C)A) 1992 and the Employment Rights Act 1996). It will have a gradual impact as the commencement of its provisions has been phased in from the period between the Royal Assent and late 2000 — in order for unions and business to prepare for the changes in employment law and practice. Additionally, the detail underpinning many of the major provisions of the Act is contained in regulations and Codes of Practice, issued only after further consultation and coinciding with the enforcement of the relevant provision.

1.3.1   Trade union recognition

One of the most contentious measures in the Act is the new trade union recognition law. The recognition provisions are contained in Schedule 1 to the 1999 Act, which incorporates a new Schedule A1 into the TULR(C)A 1992. The basic principle behind the introduction of the statutory trade union recognition procedure, was made clear by Mr Michael Wills, Minister for Small Firms, Trade and Industry, during the Committee Stage of the Bill: 'If a majority of workers want to be represented by a trade union in collective bargaining, they should have the right to be so represented' (Hansard HC, Standing Committee E, 16 March 1999, col. 346). The principle is simple enough to state, and the Government hope and expect that most employers and unions will approach it in that light. The legislation is drafted so as to encourage the parties to reach agreement, and it is the Government's view that 'only the most recalcitrant employer or trade union will fail to reach agreement on one of the many occasions that the Schedule offers' (Mr Michael Wills, Minister for Small Firms, Trade and Industry, Hansard HC, Standing Committee E, 16 March 1999, col. 346). Nevertheless, while the principle is simple, the actual operation of the procedure — in those few cases involving recalcitrant employers and trade unions — is not, running as it does to over 40 pages of the Act.

To initiate the process a union's request for recognition must first be made to the relevant employer, in writing and identifying the proposed bargaining unit over which recognition is sought. The parties then have ten working days to agree recognition and the bargaining unit. The employer can accept the request, reject it outright or agree to negotiate. If, after a 20-day negotiation period, there is still no agreement, the union may apply to the CAC to determine the claim. If the union has over 50 per cent membership at the workplace, the CAC must grant automatic recognition, unless the CAC believes that a ballot should be held on the grounds of 'good industrial relations' or where there is evidence that a significant number of members do not want the union to conduct collective bargaining on their behalf. If the union does not have at least 50 per cent membership then a ballot will not be held unless the CAC is satisfied that at least 10 per cent of the relevant bargaining unit are union members and a majority would be likely to favour recognition. The CAC must not accept more than one application for the same or overlapping bargaining groups of workers, and must not proceed with joint applications unless unions are likely to cooperate so as to ensure stable collective bargaining arrangements.

Once it is clear that the applicant union has attained the necessary membership targets and the bargaining unit has been agreed between the parties or determined by the CAC (where the parties fail to agree), the balloting process commences. The CAC appoints a 'Qualified Independent Person' to conduct the ballot, which must be held within 20 days of his or her appointment and may be by post or held at the workplace. During the balloting period employers must comply with the duty to cooperate generally with the union and independent person, must give the union access to all the relevant workers (details of this duty are contained in a new ACAS Code) and provide all required information to the CAC. On completion of the ballot, recognition will be granted where the union achieves a simple majority of those who voted and at least 40 per cent of those eligible to vote.

Once a declaration of recognition has been made the parties then have a 30-day period (which may be extended by agreement) in which to agree the method to conduct collective bargaining. If there is a failure to agree, either party may apply to the CAC for assistance. Should there still be a failure to agree the CAC will impose a 'model method', which will be legally enforceable by an order for specific performance. All workers participating in the recognition process have protection against detriment, dismissal and selection for redundancy, whether they supported recognition or actively canvassed against it.

Where, after a declaration of recognition, either party believes that the original bargaining unit is no longer appropriate, an application to the CAC may be made for the determination of a new bargaining unit. The application must not be accepted unless it is clear to the CAC that there is *prima facie* evidence that the original unit is no longer appropriate. The parties must first attempt to agree the new bargaining unit. If this is not possible, the CAC may establish a new unit and then must initiate the same inquiries (as above) as to levels of support and undertake the same balloting process.

1.3.2 Derecognition

A derecognition procedure may be initiated by an employer or a group of workers three years from the date on which the CAC issued a declaration of recognition and imposed a method of collective bargaining, or from the parties' agreement of method. At the employer's request the process effectively mirrors that which is undertaken when a union serves a recognition request to an employer. Where a group of workers applies for derecognition (such as where a non-independent union is presently recognised), similarly there is a ballot procedure and an extended period of negotiation to encourage voluntary derecognition.

1.3.3 Right of workers to be accompanied at grievance and disciplinary hearings

Another new provision introduced by the 1999 Act is the right of workers to be accompanied at grievance hearings (defined as a complaint relating to the performance of a legal duty by an employer) and disciplinary hearings (defined as a hearing that could result in the administration of a formal warning or some other action against the worker). The right to be accompanied extends to a trade union representative or co-worker of a worker's choice, who will have the right to be heard and to confer with the worker. The right will operate by reference to a new ACAS Code of Practice on Disciplinary and Grievance Procedures. This will mean that for the first time a trade union official will be entitled to enter an employer's premises to represent a union member, if the member so requests, even where the trade union is not recognised.

1.3.4 Industrial action

The Act also changes aspects of the law relating to industrial action. The obligation on unions to disclose (to employers) the individual names of union members who are to be balloted has been ended. The balloting procedure regarding separate workplace ballots, and where there are multi-employer ballots, has been simplified and the rules on entitlement to vote and on inducing members to take action have been clarified. The validity of the industrial action ballot has been extended from beyond the four-week period to up to eight weeks, subject to agreement between the employer(s) and union. Employees who engage in official industrial action will have automatic unfair dismissal protection for the first eight weeks of a dispute. Thereafter dismissal will be fair only if the employer has taken all reasonable steps to try to resolve the dispute. As proposed in the White Paper, measures to prohibit the 'blacklisting' of union members (aimed at preventing them from finding work) have been included in the Act, and the law on discrimination at the workplace on union grounds has been amended to make discrimination by omission unlawful in the same way as discrimination by a positive act, so closing that 'loophole' revealed by the House of Lords judgment in the cases of *Associated Newspapers Ltd* v *Wilson* and *Associated British Ports* v *Palmer* [1995] IRLR 258.

1.3.5 'Family friendly' policies

The Act puts into effect all the White Paper proposals on 'family friendly' policies (implementing the Parental Leave and Part-time Work Directives). Maternity leave is extended to 18 weeks to align it with statutory pay for this period and the notice arrangements for maternity leave have been simplified. Additional maternity leave will run from the end of the 18-week maternity leave period for up to 29 weeks.

Terms and conditions of employment (except those relating to remuneration) will now expressly continue during extended maternity absence, and the rights to extended maternity absence are available after one year's service. Furthermore, new parental leave rights (up to three months' unpaid leave for both mothers and fathers to be taken while the child is under eight) are provided, and include the right to return to a previous job and protection against dismissal or detriment for exercising the leave entitlement. Three months' unpaid adoption leave is also provided, as is a right to reasonable time off for family emergencies (to care for immediate family members or those who reasonably rely upon the employee for assistance). Regulations have also been issued under the Act detailing new rights for part-time workers.

1.3.6 Miscellaneous provisions

The Act also gives the Secretary of State power to extend a wide range of existing employment rights to categories of workers who may not technically qualify as 'employees', e.g., agency workers, contract workers and some who are self-employed. In addition to the cap on unfair dismissal awards having been increased to £50,000 and the qualification limit reduced to one year's service, it will also no longer be possible for employees on fixed-term contracts to waive their right to claim unfair dismissal, although clauses waiving rights to redundancy payments will continue to be lawful. The Act also includes various amendments to the law on employment agencies, abolishes the offices of the Trade Union Commissioners and includes many miscellaneous provisions on, amongst others, the rights of national security employees, enforcement of the national minimum wage legislation and the dismissal of school staff.

1.4   COMPLIANCE WITH THE HUMAN RIGHTS ACT 1998

During the Second Reading of the 1999 Act Stephen Byers, the Secretary of State for Trade and Industry, made the requisite statement, under section 19 of the Human Rights Act 1998, that in his view the provisions of the Employment Relations Act 1999 were compatible with the European Convention on Human Rights (introduced into UK law by the Human Rights Act 1998).

Employers may beg to differ as they could well have legitimate concerns that the application of the recognition law may in certain situations be in breach of their Article 6 rights to a fair hearing (in the determination of civil rights and obligations); such as in the limited circumstances where decisions of the Central Arbitration Committee (which have an impact on an employer's civil obligations to recognise and bargain with unions) are taken without employer representation.

It is not anticipated, however, that the Secretary of State's opinion will be challenged by workers or their representatives as, in general terms, the provisions of the 1999 Act do not curtail individual or union rights but enhance employment protection and so are unlikely to be in breach of European Convention standards. The real question, rather, that arises in the context of employment issues and human rights, is whether the major features of collective and individual employment law that have been left unreformed by the Act are compatible with Convention safeguards.

For example, at the collective level, the Conservative legislation intervening in trade union internal affairs has not been repealed by the 1999 Act. It could be argued that elements of that law — such as the control over trade union rights to discipline members — is incompatible with Article 11 of the Convention (on Freedom of Association). Strasbourg authorities such as *Cheall* v *UK* (1986) 8 EHRR 74 and *Johansson* v *Sweden* (1990) 65 DR 202 hold that an individual has no right inherent in Article 11 to be admitted, or not excluded from their union and that unions must be free to decide, in accordance with their rules, questions concerning admission to or expulsion from a union (unless this power was clearly abused by arbitrary or unreasonable action which resulted in exceptional hardship for the individual). State interference with the right of the union to administer their own internal membership affairs is thus incompatible with the Convention, unless it is justified (under Article 11(2)) as 'necessary in a democratic society … for the protection of the rights and freedoms of others'. According to the Strasbourg jurisprudence for a constraint to be 'necessary in a democratic society' depends on whether the restriction meets a 'pressing social need' and if it goes no further than is absolutely necessary to meet that need — i.e., it is 'a strictly proportionate response to the legitimate objective pursued'.

A challenge to the law on expulsion and discipline (ss. 60–65 and s. 174 of TULR(C)A 1992) would require the Government to defend legislative provisions which grant individuals an absolute right to belong to and remain a member of a trade union and which protects them from nearly all disciplinary action, even where it is clear the individual is acting against the union's interests. An argument that this blanket unqualified protection is justifiable by reference to the Strasbourg principles outlined above is unlikely to be sustained. In an era of reduced union power where exclusion or discipline by a union has little material effect on a member's livelihood there are no 'pressing social needs' (of the magnitude signified by the legislation) that requires state interference. Even if some limited protection is required on exceptional grounds (such as where an employee of an emergency service is disciplined or expelled for refusing to strike on grounds of conscience) the legislative response is clearly disproportionate to the aims that may be legitimately pursued — thus offending against the principle of proportionality.

The Article 11 provision specifically provides individuals with the right to membership of a trade union '... for the protection of his interests'. The European case law (see for example, *National Union of Belgian Police* v *Belgium* (1975) 1 EHRR 578) has indicated that members of a trade union have a right (in order for their interests to be protected) for their trade union to make representations on their behalf. The provisions of the 1999 Act on recognition and the right to be accompanied clearly satisfy this relatively low level of protection. However, it is also the case that legislation that permits victimisation where an individual insists on his or her rights to trade union representation or which permits discrimination between trade unions that cannot be objectively justified (Article 11 read in conjunction with Article 14) is in violation of the Convention (see, for example, *Schmidt & Dahlstorm* v *Sweden* (1976) 1 EHRR 632).

Although the UK has legislation (ss. 146 and 152 TULR(C)A 1992) protecting workers from victimisation on union grounds this protection has been limited by the House of Lords interpretation of these statutory provisions in *Wilson* and *Palmer* (1995) IRLR 258 and by a Conservative legislative amendment to s. 146 TULR(C)A 1992. Their combined effect is to permit discrimination against union members where differential payments are made to employees to induce them to relinquish their union membership and their right to trade union representation and collective bargaining. The 1999 Act has clearly dealt with one aspect of the House of Lords judgment by providing that discrimination or victimisation by omission (as well as by act) is now actionable but has arguably not neutralised effectively the other elements of the *Wilson* and *Palmer* decision and has not repealed the restrictive statutory amendment to s. 146 permitting discrimination by an employer between union and non-union members in certain circumstances (see chapter 7 for further details). This continuing state of affairs may well be contrary to case law interpretations of Article 11. Indeed the relevant unions in the *Wilson* and *Palmer* cases (although prior to the passage of the 1999 Act) have lodged a claim with the Strasbourg institutions that has been declared 'admissible' with judgment by the European Court of Human Rights expected later in 2001.

Other collective matters that may be the subject of action in the courts include a challenge to the extent of legislative control over strike action, little of which has been repealed or amended by the 1999 Act (see *Gustafsson* v *Sweden* (1996) 22 EHRR 409 on the legitimacy of strike action in order to protect the occupational interests of members). Additional Articles that may be cited include Article 10 on freedom of expression that may have a relevance to a claim (in conjunction with Article 11 on freedom of assembly) that picketing laws are too restrictive of this freedom.

At the individual level Article 8 may well prove to be the most fruitful source of case law. This Article guarantees respect for an individual's private and family life, home and correspondence. The concept of private life covers a person's physical and moral security and sexual life (including sexual orientation; *Smith & Grady* v *UK* (1999) 29 EHRR 493). Interferences with a worker's 'private life' whilst at work include, CCTV and other forms of workplace surveillance, a ban on personal relationships at work, the application of a dress code, applying a detriment to an individual on grounds of sexual orientation or activity. Not all these interferences would be actionable (for example, see *Kara* v *UK* (1999) EHRLR 232 where a dress code was held not to be incompatible with Article 8). However, it is apparent that any detriment applied to an individual on grounds of their sexuality (including sexual orientation) is arguably a breach of Article 8 and in addition, any less favourable treatment by comparison with heterosexual employees, is a violation of Article 14 (the non discrimination Article) taken in conjunction with Article 8. (see the EAT judgment in *MacDonald* v *Ministry of Defence* (19/9/00, No. 121/00).

All of these issues and many others not considered here await adjudication in the future. Whether an expansion in collective and individual employment rights beyond those provided by the 1999 Act materialises will depend on the attitude of the domestic courts to the Convention and Strasbourg authorities. If Human Rights Act litigation does identify areas of weakness in employment protection many of the matters outlined above may have to be included as a matter of priority in a future Employment Bill.

PART 1

INDIVIDUAL RIGHTS

Chapter 2
Unfair Dismissal

2.1   QUALIFICATION PERIOD

The right to submit a claim for unfair dismissal has always been subject to a length of service qualification. Originally, under the Industrial Relations Act 1971, this was set at two years. This was reduced during the period of the Labour Government (1974–1979), first to one year and then to six months. Under more recent Conservative regimes the service qualification was increased in stages back to two years' continuous employment.

In the White Paper, *Fairness at Work* (Cm 3968), the Government considered the two-year qualifying period for an unfair dismissal qualification to be a barrier to labour mobility, due to the perceived reluctance of employees to move jobs within the first two years of employment and so lose unfair dismissal protection. Despite business hostility, the proposal in the White Paper to reduce the qualifying period from two years to one year was given legislative effect by the Unfair Dismissal and Statement of Reasons for Dismissal (Variation of Qualifying Period) Order 1999 (SI 1999 No. 1436), applicable to all dismissals occurring on or after 1 June 1999.

2.2   AGREEMENTS TO EXCLUDE UNFAIR DISMISSAL RIGHTS

One controversial aspect of unfair dismissal law has, for some time, been the ability of an employer and employee to agree that the employee will waive his or her right to claim unfair dismissal; or, for that matter, claim a redundancy payment. Essentially, this option was available in the case of an employee who was employed under a fixed-term contract for more than one year; and under a fixed-term contract of more than two years in the case of waiving redundancy payments.

The logic behind these waiver provisions is that they provide employers with the option to take on employees for a fixed time to work on short-term tasks without any fear of unfair dismissal claims. However, there was a concern, expressed in the White Paper, that 'some employees are obliged to accept fixed-term contracts and to waive these employment rights for open-ended jobs', thus denying them statutory employment protection.

The Employment Relations Act 1999, s. 18(1) (which repeals s. 197(1) and (2) of the Employment Rights Act 1996) removes the possibility of waiving rights, but only in relation to unfair dismissal — the option remains in contracts for a fixed term of more than two years to exclude rights to a redundancy payment. This means that anyone who has more than one year's service can claim unfair dismissal regardless of the fact that he or she is employed under a fixed-term contract. All specific protection against waiver clauses that previously applied (for certain shop workers and those individuals who could claim automatic unfair dismissal) is repealed, no longer being necessary.

The amendments take effect in the following way: the repeal of s. 197(1) and (2) applies in relation to any dismissal where the effective date of termination occurs on or after 25 October 1999. However, there is an exception to this where the agreement to exclude unfair dismissal rights was concluded prior to 25 October 1999 and the non-renewal of contract occurred after this date, or, if there was a renewal, the last renewal took place before 25 October 1999. These provisions are contained in Schedule 1, para. 2 of the Employment Relations Act 1999 (Commencement No. 2 and Transitional and Saving Provisions) Order 1999 (SI 1999 No. 2830). What this appears to mean is, for example, that if an employee entered into a fixed-term contract of, say, five years in early 1999 and that contract contained a waiver clause, that waiver will be valid.

2.3   INDEXATION OF COMPENSATION

Until the coming into force of the relevant provisions of the Employment Relations Act 1999, the Secretary of State was under an obligation (under s. 208 of the Employment Rights Act 1996) to review the level of employment protection payments (including the limit on the basic and compensatory awards for unfair dismissal) and the limit on a week's pay for statutory purposes, and to decide whether or not to increase the award. Over the years the Secretary of State has, on several occasions, declined to raise the limits and they have consistently failed to keep pace either with inflation, or with average earnings.

The amendments made by s. 34 of the Employment Relations Act 1999 mean, however, that in future the various statutory limits on payment will be adjusted every year by a process of index linking, with the relevant index figure being the retail prices index in September each year. Section 34(2) provides that the Secretary of State shall make an order as soon as practical after the publication of the September figure, increasing or (in the unlikely instance of price deflation) reducing the following:

- the limit on guarantee payments provided for by s. 31(1) of the Employment Rights Act 1996
- the minimum amount of the unfair dismissal basic award provided for by s. 120(1) of the Employment Rights Act 1996
- the limit on the unfair dismissal compensatory award provided for by s. 124(1) of the Employment Rights Act 1996

- the maximum amount payable to employees in relation to their rights on insolvency under s. 186(1)(a) and (b) of the Employment Rights Act 1996
- the maximum amount of a week's pay for various employment rights calculations, as provided for by s. 227(1) of the Employment Rights Act 1996
- the minimum amount of a basic award for trade union related dismissals, as defined by s. 156(1) of TULR(C)A 1992
- limits on payments for the breach of the right to membership of a trade union as contained in s. 176(6) of TULR(C)A 1992.

2.4   COMPENSATORY AWARD LIMIT

Section 34(4) of the 1999 Act specifically introduces a figure of £50,000 (into s. 124(1) of the Employment Rights Act 1996) as the new limit on compensatory awards applicable in respect of any dismissal that takes effect on or after 25 October 1999. This is an increase on the previous limit of £12,000 and is a compromise from the Government's first suggestion in the *Fairness at Work* White Paper that they would remove the limit altogether. This proposal was met with considerable hostility from the business sector, and the Government chose instead to impose a much higher limit, rather than abolishing it outright.

There are likely to be few cases that will be affected by the £50,000 limit. The manner in which an employee's loss is calculated is normally based on the employee's immediate loss of earnings; an assessment of his or her future loss of earnings; any expenses incurred as a result of the dismissal; loss of statutory employment rights and loss of pension rights. The reality of calculating awards in this way is that awards are rarely that high. This is in many ways due to the fact that there is normally a limitation on lost future earnings, as a result either of the principles of mitigation or of the fact that an employee has a new job by the time the tribunal reaches a decision.

In certain cases the 1999 Act (by virtue of s. 37) has, however, abolished the limit on compensatory awards altogether. These are where:

(a)   the dismissal is for a reason connected with health and safety matters within the meaning of ss. 100 and 105(3) of the Employment Rights Act 1996; or

(b)   the dismissal is for making a protected disclosure (see ss. 103A and 105(6A) of the Employment Rights Act 1996) under the Public Interest Disclosure Act 1998. For the calculation of compensation, see the Public Interest Disclosure (Compensation) Regulations 1999 (SI 1999 No. 1548).

2.5   ADDITIONAL AND SPECIAL AWARDS

When an employment tribunal finds that an employee has been unfairly dismissed, it is open to the tribunal to make an order that the employee should be re-employed or reinstated. If such an order is not complied with, the tribunal will award compensation for the dismissal in the normal way and also could make an additional award of 13–26 weeks' pay, or, if the dismissal involves discrimination on the grounds of sex, race or disability, 26–52 weeks' pay.

Prior to the Employment Relations Act amendments there were also certain circumstances in which a tribunal could make a 'special' award, i.e. where employees had been dismissed because of their membership or non-membership of a trade union, or because of their trade union activities, or because of certain activities carried out as an employee representative or occupational pension scheme trustee, or because they had taken certain types of action on health and safety grounds. Section 33 of the Employment Relations Act 1999 repeals the relevant sections that provided for the making of a special award. This does not mean that the sums payable to employees, over and above normal compensatory principles, are not available. Section 33(2) amends s. 117(3)(b) of the Employment Rights Act 1996, replacing the 'special' awards with the 'additional' award increased to 26–52 weeks' pay in all cases. These provisions apply to dismissals that take effect on or after 25 October 1999.

These amendments simplify the law. They will make some differences, although they will affect only a few cases per year. The most obvious is where an employee requests reinstatement or re-engagement after dismissal for trade union reasons, or other specified circumstances, and the tribunal does not order it. In such cases the employee would previously have received up to 104 weeks' pay under the special award, and he or she would have received up to 156 weeks' pay where the tribunal made the award and the employer refused to comply. Now the employee would receive up to 52 weeks' pay in either case.

2.6   INDUSTRIAL ACTION DISMISSALS

Over the years one of the more controversial aspects of unfair dismissal law has related to the dismissal of those workers who are taking part in a strike or in other forms of industrial action. The way in which these employees were treated became one of the central manoeuvres in the game of political football that was conducted between the two main political parties in the 1970s and 1980s.

The first point to make is that workers who are taking part in a strike — or most other forms of industrial action — will be in breach of their contracts of employment: see, for example, *Ticehurst and Thompson* v *British Telecommunications plc* [1992] IRLR 219, where the Court of Appeal held that it is an implied term of a contract of employment that the employee will serve the employer faithfully within the terms of the contract. In the Court's view, that term was breached when, as part of the union's campaign to withdraw goodwill, a manager deliberately exercised the judgement and discretion with which she was entrusted in such a way as to disrupt her employer's business. Where an employee is in fundamental breach of contract an employer is perfectly entitled, at common law, to dismiss the employee. While this common law position has been established for some time, there has been substantial statutory change with regard to the extent to which an employee is entitled to be protected by the provisions of unfair dismissal law if he or she is dismissed.

2.6.1 Background

The original position (as enacted in the 1970s) was that employees who were taking strike action would have the right to claim unfair dismissal unless all employees taking that action had been dismissed and none had been selectively re-engaged. This position was slightly amended in the 1980s so as to provide that the employer could selectively re-engage employees after a grace period of three months and still retain an effective immunity from the dismissed employees having a right to claim unfair dismissal.

The Employment Act 1990 introduced a new regime whereby a distinction was drawn between official and unofficial industrial action. The earlier basic scheme — whereby all employees have to be dismissed with no selectivity — was retained in relation to official action; but the ability to dismiss selectively, with no employee having the right to claim unfair dismissal, was introduced in relation to unofficial action. The distinction between official and unofficial is still relevant to the position after the introduction of the measures contained in the Employment Relations Act 1999 and is discussed further below.

In the light of some high-profile examples where employers used the ability to dismiss all of their workforce in order effectively to break a strike, leaving the employees without any legal recourse, the Labour Party in opposition committed itself to amending the legislation on the dismissal of those taking industrial action. While the continued employment of those taking unofficial action was at the total whim of their employer, those taking official industrial action could find that even though their union had gone through the inordinately complex balloting and notification procedures required by the TULR(C)A 1992, employees participating in this lawful action could still be collectively dismissed without recourse to law. This state of affairs had also been consistently criticised by the International Labour Organisation (ILO) Committee on Freedom of Association and Committee of Experts as being in breach of ILO Convention 87. For example, in the 1994 General Survey on freedom of association and collective bargaining, at para. 139, the UK legislation was criticised on the basis that 'sanctions were frequently inadequate when strikers were singled out through some measures taken by the employer ... and that this raised a particularly serious issue in the case of dismissal if workers could only obtain damages and not their reinstatement'. The Committee of Experts had suggested that legislation should be introduced to 'provide for genuine protection ... otherwise the right to strike would be devoid of content'.

2.6.2 Key provisions

The key legislative change in this area is brought about by Schedule 5 to the 1999 Act and, in the main, involves the introduction of a new s. 238A into the TULR(C)A

1992. Essentially, this section introduces a new category of automatically unfair dismissal for the purposes of Part X of the Employment Rights Act 1996. The rules apply in circumstances where the protected industrial action commenced on or after 24 April 2000.

A dismissal will be unfair by virtue of s. 238A if the reason, or if there was more than one reason, the principal reason, for the dismissal is that the employee took 'protected' industrial action (defined in s. 238A(1) as an act or a series of acts the employee is induced to commit by an act which, by virtue of s. 219, is not actionable in tort) and:

(a)   the dismissal takes place within eight weeks beginning with the day on which the employee started to take protected industrial action (s. 238A(3)); or

(b)   the dismissal takes place after the eight-week period, and the employee had stopped taking protected industrial action before the end of the period (s. 238A(4)); or

(c)   the dismissal takes place after the end of the eight-week period, the employee had not stopped taking part in industrial action before the end of that period, and the employer has not taken such procedural steps as would have been reasonable for the purposes of resolving the dispute to which the protected industrial action relates (s. 238A(5)).

When determining whether or not an employer has taken such steps as are referred to in s. 238A(5), s. 238A(6) states that the tribunal should have regard to:

(a)   whether the employer or a union have complied with procedures established by any applicable collective or other agreement;

(b)   whether the employer or a union offered or agreed to commence or resume negotiations after the start of the protected industrial action;

(c)   whether the employer or union unreasonably refused, after the start of the protected industrial action, a request for conciliation services to be used;

(d)   whether the employer or a union unreasonably refused, after the start of the protected industrial action, a request that mediation services be used in relation to procedures to be adopted for the purposes of resolving the dispute.

Section 238A(7) specifically states that, when considering the above matters, the tribunal should have no regard to the merits of the dispute.

What this new statutory provision means is that when an employee is dismissed by reason of the fact that he or she is taking part in a strike or other industrial action, and that action is both supported by the union (in the sense that is official, under the terms of the TULR(C)A 1992) and lawful (in the sense that the action is such that the trade union is protected by the immunity in tort law for inducing it), then it will be automatically unfair to dismiss the employee in three separate circumstances. These are:

(a)   where the dismissal takes effect before the end of an eight-week period beginning with the commencement of the action;

(b)   where the dismissal does take effect after the end of the eight-week period, but the employee stopped taking part in the action before the end of the period;

(c)   potentially much more controversially, where the action has continued for a period of time beyond the eight weeks and the dismissal also takes place after this time has elapsed, and the employer has not taken such legal steps as would have been reasonable for the purposes of resolving the dispute.

The four categories of issues that the tribunal has to take into account in determining the reasonableness of the employer's actions in relation to the third category of dismissals are set out above in s. 238A(6). The question that necessarily arises is how tribunals will determine such cases. The cases that will test this part of the law are inevitably going to be those that arise from protracted disputes, and therefore will be cases where both parties have a vested interest in ensuring that the dispute continues until they achieve an appropriate resolution. However, the nature of the steps which the tribunal must consider in relation to the reasonableness of the employer's actions are necessarily procedural, with the tribunal not being expected to judge the reasonableness of the dispute itself. This was reinforced by a statement by the Minister of State, Department of Trade and Industry, in the House of Commons, that the 'test of fairness is whether an employer has taken all reasonable procedural steps to resolve the dispute' (House of Commons, Standing Committee E debates, 9 March 1999).

Of the issues that the tribunal will have to determine when considering a claim under s. 238A, the first clear fact is that it will have to determine the legality of the action by reference to the TULR(C)A 1992. This will be necessary in order to determine whether the action amounts to 'protected' industrial action. This will involve a consideration of a number of factors, ranging from whether the action is in furtherance or pursuance of a trade dispute, whether the union has gone through the appropriate balloting and notification procedures, and whether there are factors such as unlawful picketing activities which take the action outside the bounds of lawfulness. This may have been determined by earlier High Court proceedings, in which case the tribunal will be bound by the principles of *res judicata*. However, it is not difficult to conceive of circumstances in which these issues have not been previously litigated, and tribunals have to delve into areas of legal interpretation that were previously the preserve of the superior courts in injunctive proceedings.

One other issue that a tribunal will have to consider when adjudicating on a claim brought under the new s. 238A is whether the employee was actually dismissed *by reason* of his or her participation in industrial action. If there is some other reason for the dismissal then it will be the pre-existing law on unfair dismissal contained in s. 238 and not s. 238A that will apply. Therefore, there may be instances where an employee is taking part in officially organised industrial action where he or she is dismissed, say, for misconduct. In such circumstances the first thing to consider will be whether the employment tribunal has jurisdiction to hear the claim at all. In most instances it probably will, as the dismissal is likely to be selective (one can presume that most non-selective, mass sackings in the course of industrial action are likely to be for a reason connected to the industrial action).

There may be another set of circumstances in which the original law under s. 238 is still relevant, even though the case appears to fall within s. 238A at first sight. This is where the employer demonstrates that the dismissal takes effect after the end of the eight-week period, and the tribunal decides that the employer had taken all reasonable steps to resolve the dispute. In such circumstances it would still be open to an employee who had been selectively dismissed while taking industrial action to lodge a claim. This was confirmed by the Minister of State during the Committee Stage of the Bill in the Commons, when he explained that:

> The rights under section 238 of the 1992 Act will apply when the employer has complied with proposed new section 238A, but still dismisses or re-engages employees selectively. In those circumstances, employees can still apply to a tribunal to determine whether they have been dismissed unfairly, even though the employer has taken all reasonable steps to resolve the dispute. That will ensure that employers do not victimise union activists or strike leaders. It is a sensible additional protection. At the end of the eight-week period, an employer who sought to resolve the dispute reasonably might take individual action against those involved in the dispute. That cannot be fair, and it is why we have included the proposal. (House of Commons, Standing Committee E debates, 9 March 1999)

Patently, one of the key distinctions that will have to be drawn is between unofficial and official action, with employees who take the former having next to no rights, while those taking the latter will have the specific protections afforded by s. 238A. In short, all action that an employee participates in will be classified as unofficial action unless:

(a)   he or she is a member of a trade union and the action is authorised or endorsed by that union; or

(b)   he or she is not a member of a trade union but there are among those taking part in the industrial action members of a trade union by which the action has been authorised or endorsed.

Whether action is authorised or endorsed is governed by s. 20 of TULR(C)A 1992, which states that a wide category of union officials can endorse the action, including the principal executive committee; the president; the general secretary; any committee of the union constituted in accordance with the rules; any official, whether employed or not (which can include a shop steward); and any group of persons of which any official was a member. Section 21 covers the situation when the action is no longer official because the union has repudiated it by sending individual statements to all employees. Section 238A(8) specifically states that if an employee continues to take industrial action the day after the union's repudiation, the entitlement to claim unfair dismissal under s. 238A is lost.

2.6.3   Specific provisions on remedies and hearings

Where a dismissal has been found to be unfair by virtue of TULR(C)A 1992, s. 238A, there are some specific provisions dealing with the powers of the employment tribunal in relation to remedies. A new s. 239(4) of the Employment Rights Act 1996 provides that there shall be no order of reinstatement or re-engagement made until after the end of the protected industrial action involved in the dispute. Further, there is a power for the Secretary of State to make regulations to provide that hearings of claims under s. 238A may be adjourned or renewed, or for the holding of a pre-hearing review. Thus, the first effect of these provisions will be absolutely to prohibit the issuing of an order for reinstatement or re-engagement during industrial action. Secondly, a tribunal will be given the power to prevent a claim from even being argued during the duration of the industrial action.

One could question the public policy arguments surrounding such provisions. A criticism of industrial action dismissals in the past has been that the employer has been able effectively to destroy the morale of the workers involved in the strike action by dismissing large numbers. The fact that the employees could, in theory, claim unfair dismissal often made very little difference, as the potential hearing and remedy were some time after the conclusion of the action. The fact that the tribunal will be able to choose not to hear the claim until sometime after the dispute is over, and is absolutely prohibited from making an order putting the workers back into their jobs, could mean that the practical effects of these new legal rights in the heat of a serious industrial dispute are negligible.

However, the logic behind the provisions was explained by the Minister of State during the Committee Stage of the then Bill before the Commons, when he stated that:

> ... it would be wrong for tribunals to issue reinstatement orders while action is still being taken. That might lead to absurd situations whereby tribunals issued orders to employers to reinstate people who did not want to work. Employers might be required to pay additional compensation ... if they failed to abide by such orders, even though the workers involved were still on strike. We have made provision to allow tribunals to consider applications for unfair dismissal while industrial action is still proceeding, but not to consider applications for reinstatement or re-engagement until the end of the dispute.

On the question of holding pre-hearing reviews, the Minister suggested that the Government would 'want tribunals to conduct pre-hearing reviews in all cases when requested. If the tribunal gives an early opinion on the merits of unfair dismissal cases, it should help to stimulate negotiations to settle the dispute. For example, if an employer had an early indication that the case for unfair dismissal was strong, it might change his or her willingness to negotiate a settlement with the union on the underlying trade dispute' (House of Commons, Standing Committee E debates, 9 March 1999).

Chapter 3
Maternity and Parental Rights

3.1 INTRODUCTION

This chapter deals with those parts of the Employment Relations Act 1999 that give certain rights to leave for family related reasons. These include changes to existing maternity rights, and the introduction of parental leave and time off for emergencies involving dependants.

'Family friendly' measures were a major element of the employment rights White Paper, *Fairness at Work* (Cm 3968). It recognised the conflicting pressures that exist between work and parental responsibilities and the consequent need for measures that assist employees to balance work and family commitments. Most of the initiatives signposted in the White Paper owe their origins to European Community law, and the Parental Leave Directive (96/34/EC) in particular. The new provisions are contained in ss. 7–9 and Schedule 4 of the Employment Relations Act 1999 (which, for the most part, amend the Employment Rights Act 1996), and in the Maternity and Parental Leave etc. Regulations 1999 (SI 1999 No. 3312) and the Schedules thereto.

It ought to be noted that a Green Paper, Work and Parents: Competitiveness and Choice was published on 7 December 2000 as part of the DTI's review of maternity pay and parental leave. Thus many of these new provisions described below may well be superseded by additional amendments if legislation is enacted once the consultation period comes to an end (7 March 2001). The Green Paper states that a central aim of Government policy is to increase the participation of parents in the labour market by providing greater support at the time of a child's birth and incentives to encourage flexible working practices around family commitments. Options canvassed for opinion in the Green Paper include:

- introducing paid paternity leave
- extending the period of paid and unpaid maternity leave
- increasing the minimum rate of maternity pay
- permitting parents the right to work reduced hours
- further simplifying existing rules on maternity leave and pay
- increasing the rights of parents of adoptive and disabled children.

3.2 MATERNITY RIGHTS

Statutory maternity rights in the UK were first introduced at the time of the last Labour Government (1974–1979). The Employment Protection Act 1975 granted mothers who were employees and who had sufficient qualifying service, the right to return to work after a period of 40 (mostly unpaid) weeks' leave and limited protection from unfair dismissal. These basic minimal rights were much extended when the UK Government introduced legislation in 1993 to comply with the Pregnant Workers Directive (92/85/EEC). The provisions (providing, amongst others, 14 weeks' maternity leave regardless of length of service, the right to return to the same job and the automatic right not to be unfairly dismissed for a reason connected to pregnancy or maternity) came into force in October 1994, provided the minimum required by the Directive and were the subject of some criticism because they were complex and difficult to understand. The reforms introduced by the 1999 Act simplify and streamline the complex procedural rules for taking leave and significantly strengthen the existing rights.

Schedule 4, Part I of the Employment Relations Act 1999 replaces the maternity provisions previously contained in Part VIII of the Employment Rights Act 1996. The new Part VIII (ss. 71–75) confers the framework of the rights, with the Maternity and Parental Leave etc. Regulations 1999 (see Appendix 2) supplying the details of implementation. Some of the original provisions are retained without substantive alteration, although all the maternity provisions have new, less complex and more intelligible procedural rules. The Act alters the terminology of maternity leave: the statutory minimum period without service qualification becomes 'ordinary maternity leave' (new s. 71 of the Employment Rights Act 1996); longer leave for which a minimum period of service is required becomes 'additional maternity leave' (new s. 73 of the Employment Rights Act 1996); and the prohibition on work immediately after birth becomes 'compulsory maternity leave' (new s. 72 of the Employment Rights Act 1996).

3.2.1 Ordinary maternity leave

This will apply to all women employees, regardless of length of service, whose babies are due from the week beginning 30 April 2000. It will give them an entitlement to at least 18 weeks' leave. This is an increase from the previous 14 weeks and matches the 18-week period for statutory maternity pay (SMP).

The new s. 71(1) of the Employment Rights Act 1996 gives an employee the right to be absent from work during the ordinary maternity leave period, provided she satisfies prescribed conditions outlined in the Maternity and Parental Leave etc. Regulations 1999. Regulation 4 states what notification is required. It is simpler than before, primarily because such notice does not have to be *in writing* unless the employer requests it. However, entitlement to leave is still dependent on notice. The Regulations require that the worker informs her employer of her pregnancy at least 21 days (or as soon as reasonably practicable) before the commencement of leave, of the date of the expected week of childbirth and the date upon which she wishes to start ordinary maternity leave. If requested, she must produce a medical certificate (reg. 4(1)(b)) and put the notification in writing (reg. 4(2)). Regulation 4(3) deals with the situation where the woman's maternity leave has been automatically triggered by her absence due to sickness within the six-week period before the expected week of childbirth. The notification is required to be provided 'as soon as reasonably practicable' and, again, will have to be in writing if requested by the employer.

The new s. 71(4) of the Employment Rights Act 1996, read along with reg. 9, deals with contractual obligations. An employee has the right to the benefit of terms and conditions as if she had not been absent and the right to return to the job in which she was employed before her absence. In other words, her contract continues during the ordinary maternity leave period. The new s. 71(5) states that terms and conditions of employment includes matters connected to an employee's employment *whether or not* they arise under the contract. This seems to cover occasional non-contractual benefits. The section goes on specifically to *exclude* remuneration (s. 71(5)(b)). Regulation 9 clarifies this further, as 'only sums payable by way of wages or salary are to be treated as remuneration'. In short, it would seem that the only benefit which a women on maternity leave is not entitled to receive is wages or salary. This will mean that pension payments, holiday leave and seniority rights will be maintained, as will any entitlement to a company car and, possibly, profit-related pay or gifts in kind.

3.2.2 Additional maternity leave

The new s. 73 of the Employment Rights Act 1996 and reg. 5 makes some changes to what used to be called extended maternity absence. They still give women the right to a total of up to 40 weeks' leave (11 weeks before the birth and up to 29 after), but employees can now qualify after one year's service with the employer, compared to two years previously (now matching the qualifying period for ordinary unfair dismissal).

The notification requirements are the same as those for ordinary maternity leave (see above), although reg. 12 imposes a requirement that the returning employee should, within 21 days of receiving a request from her employer as to when she will return (the request should not be made earlier than 21 days before the end of *ordinary maternity leave*), respond in writing stating the date of birth and whether she intends to return to work after additional maternity leave. The consequences of a woman failing to respond is that she will lose her right to claim that she has been automatically unfairly dismissed. Depending on the circumstances, she may still be able to claim under the ordinary unfair dismissal principles contained in s. 98 of the Employment Rights Act 1996.

It should be noted that the old provision allowing an employer to postpone the return of a woman on extended maternity leave has been removed. The only circumstances in which an employer can now postpone the return of a woman from ordinary or additional maternity leave are set out under reg. 11. This deals with the situation where a woman wishes to return before the end of maternity leave. Under reg. 11(1), she is required to give 21 days' notice (not necessarily in writing) of the intended day of return. If she fails to do so, an employer can postpone her return to ensure that the 21-day notice period is observed (provided the date does not fall after the end of the relevant maternity leave period).

3.2.3   Compulsory maternity leave

The new s. 72 of the Employment Rights Act 1996 re-introduces a prohibition on work for two weeks after the day of childbirth on health and safety grounds (replacing the Maternity (Compulsory Leave) Regulations 1994 (SI 1994 No. 2479)). It is important to note that this is a ban on *work*, not simply on returning to work, so that during this period women should not be asked to work at home, just to make one or two phone calls or anything else connected to work. The provisions put the onus on the employer not to permit a woman to work during the compulsory leave period. It is a criminal offence for employers to contravene this prohibition, and they will be liable on summary conviction to a fine not exceeding level 2 on the standard scale. It will be a defence for the employer if the breach of the provision was not intentional.

3.2.4   Pay and other benefits during leave

3.2.4.1   Statutory pay
Some, but not all, employees will be entitled to SMP, depending on their National Insurance contributions record and whether they have earned wages at or above the lower earnings limit for the benefit.

To qualify for SMP an employee must have worked for a continuous period of 26 weeks before the 15th week before the expected date of childbirth (note 15th not 11th as the qualifying period for additional maternity leave) *and* have earned on average at least the lower earnings limit (currently around £50 per week). SMP is paid at 90 per cent of average weekly pay for six weeks, and for 12 weeks at the SMP flat rate of £60.20 (from April 2000). SMP is paid by the employer who can recover most of it from National Insurance payments.

Those employees not entitled to SMP may be entitled to maternity allowance, which also depends upon the contributions record. There are two levels of payment of maternity allowance, currently £59.55 and £51.70. It is paid by the Benefits Agency.

Both SMP and maternity allowance can be paid only to employees who are absent from work. If a woman is not entitled to either SMP or maternity allowance, the Benefits Agency will check her entitlements to incapacity benefit and income support.

3.2.4.2   Contractual pay
It may be that the contract of employment specifically requires the employer to pay some wages or salary to women on maternity leave, usually for a certain number of

weeks. If the contract is silent on this point, the position regarding ordinary maternity leave is as explained at 3.2.1, i.e. that the contract of employment continues throughout that period and, consequently, every woman on ordinary maternity leave should receive benefits under the contract, excluding wages or salary. Examples of terms from which a woman should continue to benefit from include a company car, mobile phone and health club membership (see Department of Trade and Industry, *Maternity Rights — A Guide for Employers and Employees*).

Even more significant is the change whereby certain contractual terms also continue during the additional leave period (thus partially resolving the previous uncertainty as to the status of the employment contract during extended maternity leave — see *Kwik Save Stores Ltd* v *Greaves* [1998] ICR 848 and *Halfpenny* v *IGE Medical Systems* [1999] IRLR 177). Regulation 17, of the Maternity and Parental Leave etc. Regulations, specifies the contractual terms that continue throughout the additional leave period, which includes the implied term of trust and confidence, other terms and conditions relating to notice of termination, redundancy compensation and disciplinary or grievance procedures, and implied and express confidentiality and competition clauses. Therefore, unless agreed otherwise, employees are not entitled during the additional leave period to the full benefit of their terms and conditions as they are during the ordinary leave period, neither are they entitled to remuneration. Thus, for example, an employee may be entitled to keep the company car for up to 18 weeks, but not for the whole of the additional leave period of up to 29 weeks after the birth.

3.2.5　The right to return to work

Section 71(4)(c) of the Employment Rights Act 1996 states that after ordinary maternity leave a women is entitled to return to the job in which she was employed before her absence. She is further entitled to the same job 'on terms and conditions not less favourable than those which would have applied if she had not been absent' (s. 71(7)(b)). Where 'it is not practicable by means of redundancy for her employer to continue to employ her under her existing contract of employment', she is entitled to be offered any other appropriate vacancy (Maternity and Parental Leave etc. Regulations 1999, reg. 10). Women returning from additional maternity leave are entitled to the same job, or, if that is not reasonably practicable, to 'another job which is both suitable for her and appropriate for her to do in the circumstances' on not less favourable terms and conditions (reg. 18(3)(5)). Should the employee be made redundant during leave, the provisions in reg. 10 apply (see above).

3.2.6　Protection against detriment, dismissal and discrimination

The Employment Rights Act 1996, s. 99, already contains protection against dismissal, making it automatically unfair to dismiss an employee because she was pregnant, had given birth to a child or taken maternity leave.

Section 9 of the Employment Relations Act 1999 amends the 1996 Act to include a new right (s. 47C) not to be subjected to a detriment by any act, or any deliberate failure to act, for a reason which relates to pregnancy, childbirth or maternity, ordinary, compulsory or additional maternity leave. Maternity and Parental Leave etc. Regulations 19 and 20 expand on this section by detailing the circumstances in which an employee is protected, and by including an act or failure to act on the part of an employer as amounting to a detriment. Protection against dismissal and detriment is forfeited, though, if a woman does not comply with the notice requirements set out in reg. 12(1), i.e. to reply within 21 days to an employer's request in writing (made not earlier than 21 days before the end of ordinary maternity leave) of the date of birth of the child and her date of return.

It should also be noted that any less favourable treatment of a woman connected with pregnancy will be also be direct sex discrimination under s. 1(1)(a) of the Sex Discrimination Act 1975. This is now settled law after the question was raised over a number of years, culminating in the judgment of the European Court of Justice in *Webb* v *EMO Air Cargo (UK) Ltd* [1994] IRLR 482. That case made it clear that dismissal of a woman because of pregnancy would amount to automatic direct sex discrimination and that no comparator male is needed as pregnancy is a characteristic unique to women (see also *Brown* v *Rentokil Ltd* [1998] IRLR 445).

In some cases there may also be arguments that a woman has been indirectly discriminated against, for instance, in attempting to return to work on a part-time basis. Section 1(1)(b) of the Sex Discrimination Act 1975 provides that where an employer has applied a requirement or condition to both men and women and the proportion of women who can comply is considerably smaller than the proportion of men, and that requirement is to a woman's detriment, it will be unlawful unless the employer can justify the requirement. A number of cases have been argued on this basis with mixed success. It has been held that insisting on full-time work is a requirement or condition (*Home Office* v *Holmes* [1984] IRLR 299). It is not usually necessary to prove by statistics that fewer women with child care responsibilities will be able to work full time (again, see *Home Office* v *Holmes*) as tribunals are used to making commonsense judgments on these questions. Similarly, it is very likely to be accepted that the requirement is to a woman employee's detriment, and so the usual difficulty for a woman trying to show indirect sex discrimination on these grounds will be whether the employer can justify the requirement. Much will depend here on the nature of the business and the work done by the employee. The employer will have to justify the requirement (to work full time) by showing a real need, appropriate and necessary for the business at the time of the alleged discrimination.

Although the Employment Relations Act 1999 makes no changes to discrimination law, the Act's provisions are important because they encourage the notion that the requirements of work should be balanced with the needs of family life. That attitude may begin to affect how tribunals decide whether an employer has been able to justify a full-time work requirement.

3.3   PARENTAL LEAVE

3.3.1   Introduction

The right to parental leave results from the implementation of the EU Parental Leave Directive (96/34/EC) by Schedule 4, Part I to the Employment Relations Act 1999. New ss. 76–80 of the Employment Rights Act 1996 were introduced, providing power for the Secretary of State to make regulations regarding the application of the Directive and specifying a particular enforcement procedure. The requirements of the Directive are thus now effected by Part III of the Maternity and Parental Leave etc. Regulations 1999. The Regulations apply to employees who have completed one year's service with their employer. They enable parents of children born or adopted on or after 15 December 1999 to take unpaid leave for up to 13 weeks in the first five years to care for their child. The restriction on the right to leave to care for children born before 15 December 1999 has been the subject of a judicial review challenge by the TUC and of a complaint to the European Commission. In May 2000, the High Court referred to the European Court of Justice the issue of whether the denial of parental leave to parents of children born before that date was a breach of the Directive. (See *R* v *Secretary of State for Trade and Industry ex parte Trade Unions Congress* (2000) IRLR 565)

In the Directive and the Department of Trade and Industry consultation document (*Parental and Maternity Leave*, URN 99/1043, August 1999) it was anticipated that 'workforce' collective agreements would be made to enhance and develop the minimum standards in the Regulations and outline industry-appropriate qualification and procedural requirements. Thus s. 81 of the Employment Rights Act 1996 provides for workforce agreements to have effect in place of the Regulations. Schedule 1 to the Regulations sets out the elements which need to be satisfied for a valid workforce agreement, including that it should be in writing, last for a period not exceeding five years, that it should be signed by elected employee representatives or a majority of employees, and that employees have received copies. An agreement applying less favourable terms than those outlined in the Regulations will be invalid. Parties may, of course, agree better terms and ones that might fit the specific needs of particular industries.

The Regulations specify that, in the absence of a collective workforce agreement, default provisions as outlined in Schedule 2 will apply. These provisions provide a minimum standard covering predominantly procedural matters relating to notice to be given to an employer, postponement of leave and minimum and maximum periods of leave.

3.3.2   Qualifying conditions

Regulation 13(1)(a) and (b) of the 1999 Regulations provide that in order to qualify for parental leave an employee (note, not a 'worker') must have at least one year's continuous service and have, or expect to have, 'responsibility' for a child.

Regulation 13(2) explains the circumstances in which an employee will be deemed to have the necessary responsibility. That is, where the employee:

(a)   is a parent named on the birth certificate of a child born on or after 15 December 1999 who is also under five years old; or

(b)   has adopted a child on or after 15 December 1999 under 18 years old; or

(c)   has 'parental responsibility' under the Children Act 1989 or the Children (Scotland) Act 1995 for a child born on or after 15 December 1999 who is under five years old.

Under the Children Act 1989, birth mothers always have parental responsibility, as does a birth father named on the birth certificate even if the parents do not live together. Non-parents can acquire parental responsibility by an application to court if they acquire a residence order under the Children Act — an application can be granted by consent. This means that step-parents (married or unmarried) will *not* be deemed to have responsibility for a child under the Regulations without a formal application to court. However, parents do not have to be living with the child to have parental responsibility, so that parents in separated families will still have rights under the Regulations.

3.3.3   Extent of the entitlement

Regulation 13(1) states that an employee is entitled to 'be absent from work on parental leave for the purpose of caring for that child'. The 1999 Regulations do not provide a mechanism whereby an employer can check if this is the true purpose of the leave, although the employer may refuse the request on that basis.

Regulation 14 provides that an employee who satisfies the qualifying conditions is entitled to 13 weeks' leave for each child (including multiple births, i.e. for twins a parent would be entitled to a total of 26 weeks). A week's leave is that which equals the period an employee is normally required to work (reg. 14(2)). This means that, for example, a part-time employee working three days per week will be entitled to $13 \times 3 = 39$ days for each child. If the working week varies, an average over 52 weeks should be used (reg. 14(3)).

3.3.4   Parents of disabled and adopted children

Regulation 15 contains special rules regarding parental leave entitlement for parents of disabled and adopted children. These state that leave cannot be taken after the child's fifth birthday (effectively covering children more than four years old) *unless*:

(a)   the child is entitled to a disability living allowance, in which case the entitlement ceases after the child's eighteenth birthday; or

(b)   the child was placed for adoption with the employee, in which case the fifth anniversary of the date of placement or the eighteenth birthday (whichever is earlier) is the cut-off date for leave.

3.3.5 Requirements under the default scheme

The default scheme restricts the right to take leave to employees complying with requests from their employer for evidence of entitlement and the proper giving of notice (1999 Regulations, Schedule 2, paras 1–5). If the employer requests it, the employee should provide proof of the child's date of birth and of the employee's parental responsibility.

The notice provisions require that the employee gives 21 days' notice (not necessarily in writing). Where the request is from a father in respect of leave around the time of childbirth, notice must be given 21 days before the expected week of childbirth. Where the request is from an employee adopting a child, notice must be 21 days before the week in which the placement is expected to occur, or as soon as reasonably practicable.

Under Schedule 2, para. 6, an employer may postpone leave for up to six months if he 'considers that the operation of his business would be unduly disrupted if the employee took leave during the period identified in [the] notice'. The employer must give notice in writing stating the reason for postponement no later than seven days after the employee's notice, and specify dates when leave can be taken. This entitlement to postpone does not apply to immediate childbirth or adoption leave.

Employees are entitled to take minimum leave of one week up to a maximum of four weeks per year (unless the child is in receipt of disability living allowance, in which case leave of shorter periods than a week is permitted).

Employers do not have to keep records, although many will want to do so to ensure administrative efficiency and to avoid disputes over entitlement. Employers can make enquiries of previous employers if they need information on the amount of leave taken, as the entitlement exists over five years and employees may well move jobs in that time. Note that employees who change jobs will have to re-qualify by working for one year with the new employer.

3.3.6 Remedies

Section 80 of the Employment Rights Act 1996 provides that employees have the right to complain to an employment tribunal if their employer unreasonably postpones or attempts to prevent them from taking leave. The usual time limit of three months in which to submit a claim is applied (unless it was not reasonably practicable for the complaint to be made within that time limit) and the tribunal may make a declaration and award compensation to the level the tribunal considers just and equitable, 'having regard to the employer's behaviour and any loss sustained by the employee which is attributable to the matters complained of (s. 80(3) and (4), Employment Rights Act 1996).

Apart from these specific provisions, the protections outlined in 3.2 above for women who have taken additional maternity leave (the continuation of certain terms and conditions of employment except remuneration, the right to return to the same job as before, or, if that is not reasonably practicable, to a similar job, and protection from detriment and dismissal) also apply to men and women taking parental leave.

Regulations 19 and 20 cover protection from detriment and unfair dismissal for employees taking maternity leave, parental leave and time off for dependants. The provisions for all are identical. Dismissal for a reason connected to the taking or seeking to take parental leave is automatically unfair under s. 99(3)(c) of the Employment Rights Act 1996, and an employee has the right not to be subjected to a detriment under s. 47C(2)(c) of the 1996 Act. Complaints are made to an employment tribunal with the usual time limit of three months applying.

3.3.7 Pay and other benefits during leave

As there is no statutory right to pay and the contract continues but for the right to pay, the only circumstances in which employees would be paid for parental leave would be if there were express agreement on this in a workforce or collective agreement, by individual negotiation or custom and practice. The Department of Trade and Industry's booklet *Parental Leave — A Guide for Employers and Employees*, suggests that income support can be paid during periods of leave. However, this is only for those on a very low income with savings under £8,000. Anyone with a partner in work would not be entitled. There are also conditions about the amount of leave (which fit broadly into the fallback scheme) and that the claimant should have been receiving another low-income benefit before taking leave. It may also be possible for the jobseeker's allowance and other benefits such as council tax and housing benefit to be paid, but again these are means tested and strict conditions have to be met. For the majority of employees any parental leave they take will be unpaid, and it is therefore not clear how many will avail themselves of this right.

3.4 TIME OFF TO ASSIST DEPENDANTS

This new right also emanates from the EU Parental Leave Directive (96/34/EC). Originally, the intention was to implement the Directive using the same method as for parental leave, i.e. by way of regulations (supplemented, where applicable, by workforce agreements). However, after fierce criticism of the over-use of regulation-making powers this was abandoned. The new provisions are found solely by reference to primary legislation. Section 8 of and Schedule 4, Part II to the Employment Relations Act 1999 insert two new provisions into the Employment Rights Act 1996 — s. 57A (time off for dependants) and s. 57B (complaint to employment tribunal).

3.4.1 Definition of dependant

Section 57A(3) of the 1996 Act defines a dependant as a spouse, a child, a parent and 'a person who lives in the same household as the employee, otherwise than by reason of being his employee, tenant, lodger or boarder'. This would seem to include same sex partners and siblings living together, for instance, but not those with whom the employee has a commercial relationship. Section 57A(4) and (5) add that dependants are also those who reasonably rely on the employee for assistance when they fall ill or are injured, or those who reasonably rely on the employee to make arrangements for care when ill or injured (including mental injury or illness: s. 57A(6)). This may extend to neighbours or friends, but note the requirement that the reliance must be reasonable (see 3.4.2 below). In the Department of Trade and Industry publication, *Time off for Dependants — A Guide for Employers and Employees*, a dependant is described as:

> the partner, child or parent of the employee, or someone who lives with the employee as part of their family. For example, this could be an elderly aunt or grandparent who lives in the household. It does not include tenants or boarders living in the family home, or someone who lives in the household as an employee, for example, a live-in housekeeper.

3.4.2   Entitlement to time off

Section 57A(1) of the 1996 Act provides that an employee (note that the right, like that to parental leave, applies only to employees):

> ... is entitled to be permitted by his employer to take a *reasonable* amount of time off during the employee's working hours in order to take action which is *necessary*—
>
>   (a)   to provide assistance on an occasion when a dependant falls ill, gives birth or is injured or assaulted,
>
>   (b)   to make arrangements for the provision of care for a dependant who is ill or injured,
>
>   (c)   in consequence of the death of a dependant,
>
>   (d)   because of the unexpected disruption or termination of arrangements for the care of a dependant, or
>
>   (e)   to deal with an incident which involves a child of the employee and which occurs unexpectedly in a period during which an educational establishment which the child attends is responsible for him. (emphasis added)

The question arises as to what would be a 'reasonable' time and what action would be considered 'necessary' in specific circumstances? In some workplaces there may be collective agreements detailing circumstances and time frames that are 'reasonable' in that particular workplace.

Although there may be disputes about the detail of the circumstances that should attract leave, it is evident that the right is really limited to emergency and urgent situations that were not envisaged and are unexpected. Employees will have to convince their employers (and any employment tribunal hearing a complaint) that the event or incident was not one they knew or should have known about before the situation arose. A planned hospital stay or the ending of childcare arrangements where notice has been given would seem not to be covered, although there is no reason why they should not be covered by the right to parental leave. Other domestic emergencies, like a flooding washing machine or burglary, are not covered, even though it is often the case that reasonable employers do allow some time off in these circumstances.

The DTI booklet mentioned in 3.4.1 above suggests that where a child is ill, one or two days' leave to make longer-term arrangements is reasonable: 'The employee is not entitled to take two weeks' leave to look after a sick child.' The Guide further hopes that employer and employee will seek to resolve their differences though the normal grievance procedures. The problem with that may well be that the emergency will almost certainly be over by the time the question is resolved by a grievance procedure (with the employee possibly exercising his or her new right to be accompanied (see Chapter 6)). The Guide rather unhelpfully points out: 'Otherwise, it will be up to an employment tribunal to resolve what is reasonable'.

The Government's view of how the provisions might operate was put by Lord Sainsbury of Turville during debate at the Report Stage of the Bill in the House of Lords:

Let me spell out what the [right] is intended to cover. We intend the right to apply where a dependant becomes sick or has an accident, or is assaulted, including where the victim is distressed rather than physically injured. It provides for reasonable time off, if an employee suffers a bereavement of a family member, to deal with the consequences of that bereavement, such as making funeral arrangements, as well as to take time off to attend the funeral.

Employees will be able also to take time off in the event of the unexpected absence of the carer, where the person is a dependant of the employee. So if the childminder or nurse does not turn up, the employee will be able to sort things out without fearing reprisals at work.

Employees may have to take time off to attend to a problem arising at their children's school or during school hours — for example, if the child has been involved in a fight, where the child is distressed, or if the child has committed a serious misdemeanour which could lead to expulsion. Again, the provision will secure their right to do so. (HL Report 8 July 1999, col. 1085)

Section 57A(2) of the 1996 Act further limits the right to those employees who have informed their employer 'as soon as reasonably practicable' of the reason for the absence and for how long they expect to be absent. The need to tell the employer the expected length of absence does not apply where employees cannot explain the reason for absence until they return to work.

The statutory right to time off for dependants does not contain any express provision in relation to pay — thus, *prima facie*, it is unpaid. Some employees who already have these rights may have an express term dealing with this, and many will have gained the right to payment for short amounts of time off through custom and practice.

3.4.3 Remedies

Section 57B of the 1996 Act gives an aggrieved employee the right to complain to an employment tribunal 'that his employer has unreasonably refused to permit him to take time off as required by section 57A'. There is the usual three-month time limit from the date when the refusal occurred, with the tribunal having the power to make a declaration and award compensation, such compensation to be that which is just and equitable in all the circumstances having regard to the employer's default and any loss of the employee which is attributable to the refusal.

Furthermore, the employee is protected against being subjected to a detriment by s. 47C of the Employment Rights Act 1996 (inserted by Schedule 4 to the Employment Relations Act 1999). This has been considered at 3.2.6 and 3.3.6 above in relation to maternity and parental leave, the protection being identical for all the 'family friendly' rights so far discussed — maternity leave, parental leave and time off for dependants. Schedule 4 to the Employment Relations Act 1999 has also amended s. 99 of the 1996 Act, to include dismissal for a reason connected to time off under s. 57A as automatically unfair.

3.5 DISCRIMINATION AND THE NEW RIGHTS

All the rights discussed above — maternity and parental leave and time off for dependants — have the potential also to have an impact in the area of unlawful discrimination. This has been mentioned in relation to pregnancy and maternity at 3.2.6 above; where the jurisprudence of the ECJ has taken us to a point where almost all less favourable treatment on those grounds would constitute sex discrimination. It is also often the case that indirect sex discrimination can be proved when mothers' work patterns affect their ability to care for their children (see *London Underground Ltd* v *Edwards (No. 2)* [1998] IRLR 364, CA). It is not the place in this chapter, which concentrates on the changes brought about by the Employment Relations Act 1999, to set out any more detail on this point, but readers should be aware that sex discrimination arguments may well arise in the context of employees having difficulty enforcing the rights outlined above. The Government hopes that male employees, especially fathers, will take advantage of the new rights, but it remains the case that tribunals are aware that most childcare and dependant care is carried out by women and that any refusal to allow them to exercise rights may arguably be sex discrimination.

Chapter 4
Part-time Workers

4.1   INTRODUCTION

Part-time workers (who have been overwhelmingly female) have previously been able to secure equal employment rights only by the application of equal treatment legislation (e.g., through equal pay and indirect discrimination laws). The EU Part-time Work Directive (97/81/EC) provides part-time workers with a more direct route by which to secure parity with full-time workers. The provisions in the Directive (adopted under the Agreement on Social Policy procedure) arise from a 'framework agreement' made by the 'social partners' at European level, that is, by the employers' organisations and trade unions. The Directive sets out general principles and minimum requirements, leaving the detailed implementation to national governments and their employers' and employees' organisations. However, its clear purpose is to 'establish a general framework for the elimination of discrimination against part-time workers and assist the development of opportunities for part-time working on a basis acceptable to employers and workers'.

The UK Government was under a responsibility to implement the Directive by April 2000. In order to do so, s. 19 of the Employment Relations Act 1999 gave power to the Secretary of State to make regulations:

for the purpose of securing that persons in part-time employment are treated, for such purposes and to such extent as the regulations may specify, no less favourably than persons in full-time employment.

Section 19(2) and (3) elaborate on what the regulations may contain, including:

(a)   specifying the classes of person who are in part-time and full-time employment;

(b)   defining the circumstances in which part-timers are treated less favourably;

(c)   creating criminal offences for certain breaches of the regulations;

(d)   conferring civil jurisdiction on the employment tribunal and Employment Appeal Tribunal; and

(e) providing for the provision of collective agreements to have effect in place of the regulations.

The section also provides the Secretary of State with general powers to amend relevant legislation, including the Employment Rights Act 1996, and to make any provision 'which appears ... to be necessary or expedient ... for the purpose of implementing Council Directive 97/81/EC'.

Section 20 of the 1999 Act gives power to the Secretary of State to issue a Code of Practice containing guidance for the purpose of, amongst other things, eliminating discrimination against part-time workers, and which:

(a) is admissible in evidence in proceedings before an employment tribunal; and

(b) shall be taken into account by an employment tribunal in any case in which it appears to the tribunal to be relevant (s. 20(4)).

In pursuance of the powers provided under s. 19 of the 1999 Act, draft Regulations were published for consultation during January 2000. After a raft of critical responses (including criticism of the Regulations' reference to employees rather than to all workers, the narrow definition of a part-time employee, the failure to allow a hypothetical comparison with a full-time employee and the failure to publish a Code of Practice under s. 20) the Regulations were substantially amended, although not all of the points of criticism have been addressed.

The final draft — the Part-time Workers (Prevention of Less Favourable Treatment) Regulations 2000 (SI 2000 No. 1551) (see appendix 3) — was laid before Parliament on 3 May and came into force on 1 July 2000. Although the Code of Practice has still not been published, the Government have issued a number of useful documents, including *Notes to the Part-time Work Regulations*, *Compliance Guidance* and *Best Practice Guidance*, which may well not have any direct legal effect but which will almost certainly be referred to in proceedings. Reference will be made to these documents at appropriate points throughout the chapter.

4.2 THE SCOPE OF THE REGULATIONS

The Government appear to have responded to criticism that the draft Regulations only covered 'employees' (thus excluding the most vulnerable workers who often have 'casual' or 'self-employed' status assigned to them) as the final Regulations apply to 'workers' as well.

Regulation 1 deals with the interpretation of both 'employee' and 'worker'. This is necessary as some parts of the Regulations apply only to employees (for instance, the right not to be unfairly dismissed). The definitions of both terms are virtually identical to those contained in s. 230 of the Employment Rights Act 1996:

(2)   In these Regulations—

...

employee means an individual who has entered into or works under or (except where a provision of these Regulations otherwise requires) where the employment has ceased, worked under a contract of employment;

...

worker means an individual who has entered into or works under or (except where a provision of these Regulations otherwise requires) where the employment has ceased, worked under—

(a)   a contract of employment; or

(b)   any other contract, whether express or implied and (if it is express) whether oral or in writing, whereby the individual undertakes to do or perform personally any work or services for another party to the contract whose status is not by virtue of the contract that of a client or customer of any profession or business undertaking carried on by the individual.

Where a point of disagreement arises as to whether a particular individual is a worker or an employee, there is a large body of case law to assist. The well-known tests of control, integration and mutuality of obligation may need to be considered and each case will turn on its own facts arising from oral evidence and any documents (see the discussion of the tests of employment status in chapter 6 at 6.3). Otherwise, unless someone is very clearly working 'on his own account', he will almost certainly fit the definition of 'worker'.

Regulation 2 defines 'full-time worker', 'part-time worker' and 'comparable full-time worker', all of which definitions are necessary for the purpose of the rest of the Regulations which make unlawful less favourable treatment of part-time workers.

A 'full-time worker' is one who is 'paid wholly or in part by reference to the time he works and, having regard to the custom and practice of the employer in relation to workers employed by the worker's employer under the same type of contract, is identifiable as a full-time worker' (reg. 2(1)).

A 'part-time worker' is one who is 'paid wholly or in part by reference to the time he works and, having regard to the custom and practice of the employer in relation to workers employed by the worker's employer under the same type of contract, is not identifiable as a full-time worker' (reg. 2(2)). A part-time worker is thus anyone who is not full-time by reference to the *custom and practice* of that particular employer. This is necessary because full-time hours vary (roughly between 35 and 40 hours) between industries and sectors. Essentially, a part-time member of staff is someone who works fewer hours than others in that particular workplace. Often the statement of employment particulars will specify the normal weekly hours of full-time workers, and other documentation may well state that a worker or employee is full- or part-time.

The meaning of 'comparable full-time worker' is discussed in 4.4 below.

4.3   LESS FAVOURABLE TREATMENT

The core right contained in reg. 5 reads as follows:

5.—(1)   A part-time worker has the right not to be treated by his employer less favourably than the employer treats a comparable full-time worker—

(a)   as regards the terms of his contract; or

(b)   by being subjected to any other detriment by any act, or deliberate failure to act, of his employer.

The reason for the less favourable treatment must be that the worker is part-time, and it must not be justified on objective grounds. In determining whether a part-time worker has been treated less favourably than a comparable full-timer, the *pro rata* principle (where pay or other benefits are provided at a proportionate rate) should be ordinarily applied.

4.4   THE COMPARATOR

Because one of the key concepts of the Regulations is less favourable treatment, it is also necessary to find a 'comparator', that is, a worker or employee who has been treated more favourably (i.e., better) than the complainant. For this reason reg. 2(4) provides:

(4)   A full-time worker is a comparable full-time worker in relation to a part-time worker if, at the time when the treatment that is alleged to be less favourable to the part-time worker takes place—

(a)   both workers are—

(i)   employed by the same employer under the same type of contract, and

(ii)   engaged in the same or broadly similar work having regard, where relevant, to whether they have a similar level of qualification, skills and experience; and

(b)   the full-time worker works or is based at the same establishment as the part-time worker or, where there is no full-time worker working or based at that establishment who satisfies the requirements of sub-paragraph (a), works or is based at a different establishment and satisfies those requirements.

In order to complain of less favourable treatment, then, a worker must identify a full-time worker (not another part-time worker) working for the same employer, either at the same establishment or doing at least broadly similar work, and under the *same type of contract*. Regulation 2(3) specifies that certain workers and employees will be regarded as being employed under *different types of contract* for these purposes. These include fixed-term and apprenticeship contracts as well as 'any other description of worker that it is reasonable for the employer to treat differently from other workers on the ground that workers of that description have a different type of contract' (reg. 2(3)(f)). No guidance is given on this, but it is expected the employers will have to show good evidence that the workers are employed under different types of contract where there is less favourable treatment of a part-time worker.

Regulations 3 and 4 cover the situation where full-time workers become part-time, and allow a comparison to be made with the workers' own treatment while full-time.

All part-time workers who were previously working full-time can also compare themselves to other full-time workers as in reg. 2. In the case of workers returning after an absence to work part-time, the right not to be treated less favourably applies only if the return was within 12 months (reg. 4(1)(b)).

4.5   RIGHT TO RECEIVE A WRITTEN STATEMENT OF REASONS FOR LESS FAVOURABLE TREATMENT

The provision of this right is an attempt to assist internal dispute resolution. Presumably, the Government hope that bringing the matter to the employer's attention in this way will help remedy the problem 'in house' and make it clear to the employee whether the matter is worth pursuing at a tribunal. Regulation 6 entitles a worker (who believes his employer may have infringed a reg. 5 right and who has requested in writing a written statement) to receive such a statement within 21 days. There is no formal remedy, but the failure to provide such a statement or to provide one that is evasive or equivocal, can lead a tribunal to draw inferences of less favourable treatment. The right does not apply to employees who wish to complain of dismissal, who have the right to written reasons for dismissal under s. 92 of the Employment Rights Act 1996.

4.6   UNFAIR DISMISSAL AND THE RIGHT NOT TO BE SUBJECTED TO A DETRIMENT

Regulation 7 of the 2000 Regulations protects *employees* against unfair dismissal where the dismissal is for a reason connected to the bringing of proceedings or actions under the Regulations (listed at reg. 7(3)). Such a dismissal is automatically unfair for the purposes of Part X of the Employment Rights Act 1996. *Workers* (which includes employees) are protected from being subjected to a detriment by any act or failure to act where the reasons or grounds are those listed at reg. 7(3). These reasons or grounds include where the worker has: (i) brought proceedings against the employer, (ii) alleged that the employer has infringed the Regulations, (iii) requested a written statement of reasons, (iv) given evidence or information in connection with proceedings, (v) done anything under the Regulations to the employer or another person, or (vi) refused or proposed to refuse to forgo a right conferred by the Regulations, or (vii) if the employer believes or suspects any of the above. These rights are lost where the complaint relates to an allegation that the employer infringed the Regulations or that the employer believed or suspected that the worker intended to do any of the acts mentioned, and the allegation made by the worker is false and not made in good faith (reg. 7(4)).

4.7   COMPLAINT TO AN EMPLOYMENT TRIBUNAL

Any complaint must be made within three months (six months for the armed forces) beginning with the date of the less favourable treatment or detriment. In common with other discrimination claims, that time limit will run from the date of the last of the acts or failures to act (reg. 8(2)). Regulation 8(4) specifies how the date will be calculated in particular circumstances. In common with other forms of discrimination, the tribunal can consider an out of time claim if it considers it is just and equitable to do so. Unusually, reg. 8(6) states that it is for the employer to show the reason for the less favourable treatment or detriment when a complaint is made.

Regulation 8(7) sets out the remedies available to tribunals where they find the complaint well-founded. A tribunal can take any of the following steps as it considers just and equitable:

- a declaration as to the rights of the complainant
- ordering compensation
- recommending action by the employer within a specified period for the purpose of obviating or reducing the adverse effect on the complainant of any matter to which the complaint relates.

If the matter concerns less favourable treatment in respect of the terms of an occupational pension scheme, the steps listed above cannot be taken if they relate to a period more than two years before the date of the complaint.

As far as compensation is concerned, the amount shall be such as the tribunal considers just and equitable in all the circumstances having regard to the infringement, including any expenses and the loss of any benefit (reg. 8(9) and (10)). A reg. 5 infringement (less favourable treatment) cannot include a sum for injury to feelings, and the usual principles of the duty to mitigate apply (reg. 8(11) and (12)). The tribunal has power under reg. 8(13) to reduce compensation by such proportion as it considers just and equitable where it finds the act was to any extent caused or contributed to by the complainant. Lastly, the tribunal has the unusual power in reg. 8(14) to increase compensation where the employer has failed to comply with a recommendation.

4.8   MISCELLANEOUS MATTERS

Part III of the Part-time Workers (Prevention of Less Favourable Treatment) Regulations 2000 deals with amendments to primary legislation and vicarious liability. Regulation 11 specifies that liability falls upon an employer for anything done in the course of employment by a worker of his, whether the employer knew or approved of it. Liability also extends to agents with the authority of the employer. An employer does have a defence under reg. 11(3) if it can be shown that such steps as were reasonably practicable were taken to prevent the worker from doing the act or acts of that description.

Part IV of the Regulations makes it clear that Crown employees and those in the armed forces (except some members of the reserve forces) are subject to these rights, although armed forces personnel must comply with special procedures in order to benefit from the Regulations. Other employment covered includes House of Lords and House of Commons staff and members of the police service. Daily fee-paid judicial officers are not covered under reg. 17.

Lastly, the Schedule to the 2000 Regulations makes consequential amendments to the Employment Tribunals Act 1996 and the Employment Rights Act 1996.

4.9 SUMMARY AND CONCLUSIONS

To re-cap, the worker has to show that he or she works part-time, that there is a full-time worker employed by the same employer under the same type of contract who has received more favourable treatment, either in the terms of the contract or through an act (or failure to act), which would constitute a detriment to the part-time worker (for instance, access to training), and that the reason for the treatment was that the worker was part-time and the employer cannot justify it objectively.

For example, consider the situation where an employer runs a computer-training course on a day when the part-time worker does not usually work. Assuming the worker satisfies the requirement to identify a comparator, the next consideration would be to consider whether the act is to the detriment of the worker, whether he or she was denied the opportunity to train because he or she worked part-time, and whether it can be justified.

The *Compliance Guidance* issued by the Department of Trade and Industry gives us some assistance:

> Access to training is essential if part-time workers are to work effectively, and employers are to make the most of their staff . . . denying part-time workers access to training will obviously be less favourable treatment . . . to comply with the law employers should not exclude part-time staff from training simply because they work part-time. (*Compliance Guidance*, p. 10)

Similarly, the *Best Practice Guidance* says (at p. 19): 'Employers should look at whether their training is arranged in a way which is inconvenient for part-time workers . . . Employers should ensure that the needs of part-time workers are given proper weight when the structure, time and location of training is being planned.' Although each case will be decided on its particular facts, it can be seen that the employer in the example above is vulnerable to a claim unless it can show objective reasons for the failure to include the worker on the training course. Guidance Notes issued with the Regulations remind employers that to be justifiable, the less favourable treatment has to: (i) achieve a legitimate objective, for example a genuine business objective; (ii) be necessary to achieve that objective; and (iii) be an appropriate way to achieve that objective'.

Although the Regulations do not spell out those aspects of the working relationship where less favourable treatment could be found, the Explanatory Notes and *Compliance Guidance* specifically mention pay, overtime, contractual sick and maternity pay, occupational pensions, training, holidays and career breaks, redundancy and health insurance and mortgage subsidies as areas where part-time workers must be treated no less favourably.

Although these Regulations provide extensive protection, their impact may be limited because previous legislation and case law have led to a reduction in discrimination against part-time workers. Challenges under sex discrimination and European legislation on the basis of the greater proportion of women being in part-time work have led to moves towards equality of treatment. However, the Regulations apply equally to men and women workers, and the guidance from the Government makes it clear that employers will have to consider their arrangements so that they do not adversely affect part-time workers of either sex. This should lead to better terms and conditions for all workers, especially those with family responsibilities who predominantly make up the bulk of the part-time labour market.

Chapter 5
Miscellaneous Provisions

5.1   EXTENSION OF EMPLOYMENT PROTECTION RIGHTS

Over recent years there has been some concern that particular categories of employment — whether casual workers, the nominally self-employed or temporary workers — were being used by unscrupulous employers to avoid employment protection legislation. One of the suggestions in *Fairness at Work*, White Paper (Cm 3968) was to consult over the possibility of giving the Secretary of State power to extend coverage of some or all of the existing employment rights to those who work in 'atypical' employment.

This proposal was taken up and enacted in the 1999 Act. By virtue of s. 23 of the Employment Relations Act 1999, the Secretary of State is given a wide-ranging power to extend (by statutory instrument) a range of employment rights to individuals who are presently not protected by legislation. The rights in question are any right conferred on an individual against an employer under or by virtue of any of the following:

- the Trade Union and Labour Relations (Consolidation) Act 1992
- the Employment Rights Act 1996
- the Employment Relations Act 1999
- any statutory instruments made under s. 2(2) of the European Communities Act 1992.

These rights include all the key employment rights — to claim unfair dismissal, maternity leave, various rights to time off and rights in relation to redundancy and insolvency. It is noticeable that the anti-discrimination legislation is not included in the list, the scope of which may be effectively 'extended' by an order made under s. 23. One presumes that this is because the anti-discrimination legislation already covers a wider group of individuals than the other forms of employment legislation.

By virtue of s. 23(4), the Secretary of State has a number of options in order to provide the specified rights to a wider group of workers. Any order issued under the section may:

(a)   provide that individuals are to be treated as parties to workers' contracts or contracts of employment;

(b)   make provision as to who are to be regarded as the employers of individuals;

(c)   make provision which has the effect of modifying the operation of any right as conferred on individuals by the order;

(d)   include such consequential, incidental or supplementary provisions as the Secretary of State thinks fit.

The key definitional issue that it is assumed will be dealt with by any order made under the section, is whether the relevant pieces of employment legislation cover the wider category of 'workers' or only 'employees'. For example, the right to claim unfair dismissal applies only to employees, while the new rules on working time cover the much wider category of workers.

The Explanatory Notes to the Act state:

> ... the Government considers it desirable to clarify the coverage of the legislation and to reflect better the considerable diversity of working relationships in the modern labour market. Currently, significant numbers of economically active individuals — including for example many home workers and agency workers — are either uncertain whether they qualify or else clearly fail to qualify, for most if not all employment rights ... The Government envisages using this power to ensure that all workers other than the genuinely self-employed enjoy the minimum standards of protection that the legislation is intended to provide, and that none are excluded simply because of technicalities relating to the type of contract or other arrangement under which they are engaged.

However, as yet, the power to extend employment protection has not been utilised; neither have the Government so far initiated a consultation exercise, as would be expected prior to enactment.

5.2   EMPLOYMENT AGENCIES

Schedule 7, para. 2 to the 1999 Act gives the Secretary of State wide-ranging powers to make amending and additional regulations under s. 5(1) of the Employment Agencies Act 1973 in order to control abuses of the system. Examples in the Act of matters that may be the subject of regulations include:

(a)   preventing employment agencies from entering into contracts with workers that have a term permitting the charging of workers for finding them work;

(b)   restricting the ability of employment agencies and businesses to make payment conditional on completion of additional work;

(c)   restricting employment agencies and businesses from unilaterally varying terms of contracts negotiated with workers; and

(d) restricting employment agencies and businesses from imposing terms on employers (such as financial charges) that prevent or discourage them from dealing directly with workers supplied to them.

In addition, Schedule 7, para. 3 amends s. 6(1) of the 1973 Act, strengthening the prohibition on employment agencies or businesses charging persons seeking work for their services. Paragraph 4 extends the range of premises that may be entered by inspectors and details the records or documents that may be scrutinised, copied and seized, and provides that information obtained under the compulsory powers in the 1973 Act may be disclosed for the purposes of *any* criminal proceedings under the 1973 Act or any other offence. Paragraph 5 lengthens the time limit for prosecutions under the 1973 Act and provides for costs to be awarded to the Secretary of State. Paragraph 7 amends the definition of 'employment agency' by substituting the word 'persons' for 'workers' in the text, so ensuring that the definition of employment agency activity includes the supply of services to companies as well as individuals.

5.3   AMENDMENTS TO THE TRANSFER OF UNDERTAKINGS (PROTECTION OF EMPLOYMENT) REGULATIONS 1981

The Government's intention is to bring forward a new version of the Transfer of Undertakings (Protection of Employment) Regulations 1981 (SI 1981 No. 1794). The main reason behind the amendments to the Regulations was the issuing of an amended Acquired Rights Directive in 1998 (Council Directive 98/50, amending Council Directive 77/187). There are a number of changes that arise from the new Directive, but in general all that they represent is a codification of the existing case law on transfers as developed by the European Court of Justice.

However, it is clear that the Government intend to produce amendment regulations that may go beyond the obligations required by European law, such as by clarifying the definition of a transfer of an undertaking (particularly in the context of contracted out services) and by clarifying the position with regard to pension entitlements (at least in relation to the entitlement to pension contributions). Due to question marks over whether the Secretary of State has the power to legislate by way of secondary legislation in relation to matters that are beyond the specific Community obligation (see, for example, the Divisional Court judgment in *R* v *Secretary of State for Trade and Industry ex parte UNISON and ors* [1996] ICR 1003), the Employment Relations Act 1999 contains a provision that provides that in these circumstances the Secretary of State can introduce legislation by virtue of a statutory instrument.

Section 38 of the 1999 Act applies only where an obligation arises under European law, and permits the Secretary of State to initiate measures in order to protect an employee's rights on the transfer of an undertaking. It provides the Secretary of State with the powers to extend the protection in the 1981 Regulations to those employees who may not actually be covered by the scope of the Acquired Rights Directive. For example, taking the issue of the contacting out of services, the Regulations could provide that all employees are covered, regardless of the vagaries of European law and its interpretation.

While it is not clear whether the Government will choose to adopt a more expansive approach to the protection afforded to employees in relation to a transfer of an undertaking, s. 38 does mean that any extension of rights may be introduced by way of a statutory instrument without the need to bring forward primary legislation.

5.4 AMENDMENTS TO THE NATIONAL MINIMUM WAGE ACT 1998

Section 22 of the 1999 Act inserts a new s. 44A into the National Minimum Wage Act 1998, excluding members of charitable religious communities from the scheme of the Act.

Section 39 of the 1999 Act creates a new enforcement provision, providing that information (relating to a failure to pay the minimum wage) obtained by officials of the Inland Revenue while carrying out their official duties may be shared with national minimum wage inspectors.

5.5 GUARANTEE PAYMENTS

As a result of the changes to the method of up-rating awards, there have had to be minor amendments in relation to the review and up-rating of guarantee payments. At present s. 31(2)–(4) of the Employment Rights Act 1996 provides that guarantee payments are payable in respect of five days of lay-off in any three-month period. Previously, the Secretary of State would review both the limit on such payments and the duration of the payments. Section 35 of the 1999 Act simply amends the 1996 Act so that there is no longer an obligation to review the limit on guarantee payments, but an enabling power is provided to vary the time periods set out in s. 31(2)–(4).

5.6 DISMISSAL OF SCHOOL STAFF

Section 40 of the Employment Relations Act 1999 amends procedural provisions relating to the dismissal of school staff on fixed-term contracts under the School Standards and Framework Act 1998, so ensuring that they reflect the reduction in the qualifying period for unfair dismissal to one year.

5.7 NATIONAL SECURITY EMPLOYEES

Schedule 8 to the 1999 Act introduces numerous reforms to the employment protection regime that applies to national security employees. In particular, the right of access of employees of the intelligence and security services to employment tribunals is improved and new enforcement procedures created, subject to the inevitable limitations where it is believed that national security will be compromised.

5.8   JURISDICTIONAL CHANGES

Section 196 of the Employment Rights Act 1996 provided that employees who worked ordinarily outside Great Britain under their contracts of employment were excluded from unfair dismissal and other employment protection legislation. Section 32(3) of the 1999 Act has repealed that section, thus providing that jurisdictional questions before employment tribunals in unfair dismissal and other cases are to be determined solely by existing conflict of law principles. Mr Michael Wills, the Minister for Small Firms, Trade and Industry, explained the reasoning behind the change:

> ... Repealing that section has a number of significant advantages. It extends employment rights to employees temporarily working in Great Britain and thus facilitates the implementation of the Posting of Workers Directive (96/71/EC), which otherwise would require further regulations later this year. It also means that people who may have worked for some years in the UK, but who are nevertheless excluded from claiming under the Employment Rights Act 1996, will be able to rely on the protection of our legislation, as should be the case. The recent case of *Carver* v *Saudi Arabian Airlines* [1999] IRLR 370 demonstrates the need for this provision.
>
> I do not claim that the amendment will have dramatic effects in practice — few cases arise, and the additional costs to employers will be minimal. Nevertheless it takes forward an important principle and modernises and simplifies our legislation. The position of mariners is special, and special provisions apply to them at present under sections 196 and 199. The amendment ensures that their position is unchanged. (Hansard HC vol. 336, col. 31)

PART 2
COLLECTIVE RIGHTS

Chapter 6
The Individual Right to Representation

6.1   INTRODUCTION

Sections 10 to 15 of the Employment Relations Act 1999 introduce a new right for workers in the UK to be accompanied at disciplinary or grievance hearings by a trade union official or a fellow worker. The sections came into force on 4 September 2000. The Government's reasoning behind the provisions was made clear in *Fairness at Work*:

> Most employers treat people fairly, but a minority do not. The law should protect employees from intimidation, and assist those who might have difficulties in representing themselves. (Cm 3968, para. 4.28)

Prior to the 1999 Act, the only obligation on employers to allow accompaniment stemmed from the ACAS Code of Practice on Disciplinary Practice and Procedures in Employment, the previous version of which came into effect on 5 February 1998. Paragraph 10(g) stated that employers' disciplinary procedures should 'give individuals the right to be accompanied by a trade union representative or by a fellow employee of their choice'. A new and fully revised Code of Practice on Disciplinary and Grievance Procedures came into effect with the new accompaniment provisions. The new Code (see Appendix 4) includes detailed guidance on the new rights of accompaniment.

While a Code of Practice is not, of itself, legally binding, it is taken into account by employment tribunals in determining whether an employer has acted reasonably in dismissing an employee (see, for instance, *Lock* v *Cardiff Railway Co. Ltd* [1998] IRLR 358). The refusal to afford representation could disadvantage an employer in unfair dismissal proceedings, particularly where the refusal is not in accordance with the employer's own internal procedures.

Representation by trade union officials has, in the past, been an issue only where a trade union is recognised by the employer. Depending on the applicable procedures, lay union representatives are usually involved in the early stages, perhaps with the facility for a full-time union official to appear on appeal. Where a trade union is not recognised, it has been common practice for an employer to refuse an employee representation by a union official. If an employee is entitled to accompaniment at all, perhaps under an internal disciplinary procedure, it is usually restricted to a fellow employee.

The new Act's provisions will, for the first time, allow a trade union official to enter the employer's premises to represent a union member, if the member so requests, even where a trade union (or that particular union) is not recognised. If the employer fails to accede to the request made by a worker (which need not be made in writing), a tribunal award of up to two weeks' wages (at the statutory maximum, currently £230 per week from February 2000) can be made against the employer. Perhaps of greater significance for employers, however, is the high probability that tribunals will view a refusal of accompaniment as a central factor in determining the fairness of a dismissal if that refusal is in breach of the statutory right.

Until recently, the chances of an unfair dismissal claim being successful seemed further increased by the questioning of the long-standing 'reasonable responses' test, applied when considering the reasonableness of the employer's decision to dismiss. This test obliges the tribunal to consider whether the decision to dismiss falls within the band of reasonable responses that a reasonable employer should have adopted. The test was criticised by Morison J in the EAT decision of *Haddon* v *Van den Burgh Foods Ltd* [1999] IRLR 672, as posing a danger of fairness being determined 'by reference to the extreme'. The EAT preferred the Court of Appeal's approach in *Gilham and others* v *Kent County Council* [1985] IRLR 18 to the earlier comments of Lord Denning in *British Leyland UK Ltd* v *Swift* [1981] IRLR 91 and Browne-Wilkinson J's comments in the EAT decision of *Iceland Frozen Foods Ltd* v *Jones* [1982] IRLR 439.

The test favoured by the EAT in *Haddon* was more favourable to tribunal applicants as it required greater consideration of the dismissal and its fairness from the employee's perspective. As Morison J stated of the past application of the 'reasonable responses' test: '... a combination of the judicial embellishment upon the statute has led tribunals to adopt a perversity test of reasonableness and to depress the chances of success for applicants' (para. 30).

The decision in *Haddon* soon thereafter received the enthusiastic support of the Scottish EAT in the case of *Wilson* v *Ethicon* [2000] IRLR 5. But the story does not end there. The new President of the EAT, Lindsay J, in *Midland Bank* v *Madden* [2000] IRLR 288, challenged the approach taken in *Haddon* in some important respects. While *Haddon* was not appealed, the decision in *Madden* recently reached the Court of Appeal, which firmly reinstated the 'reasonable responses' test and criticised the approach of Morison J in *Haddon* as an unwarranted departure from binding authority (see *Foley* v *Post Office* and *HSBC Bank plc (formerly Midland Bank plc)* v *Madden* [2000] IRLR 827). Leave to appeal to the House of Lords was refused.

6.2   THE CONNECTION TO TRADE UNION RECOGNITION

It is certain that trade unions will see the new right of accompaniment as complimentary to the new statutory right of recognition provided under s. 1 and

Schedule 1 to the 1999 Act. One reason for the steady decline in trade union membership and collective bargaining over the last 20 years has been the ease with which hostile or ambivalent employers have been able to prevent trade union members enjoying the membership benefits of professional representation in the workplace. It has proved difficult for trade unions to recruit on the basis only of fringe benefits such as financial services and legal support. Trade unions have often been frustrated in their attempts to build membership to a critical mass as part of a thrust for recognition.

The new right to accompaniment will allow trade unions for the first time to promote professional representation as a sound reason for workers to join a trade union even though the union does not enjoy recognition. The benefit of professional trade union representation is likely to be seen as a distinct advantage when compared to the assistance of a fellow, untrained and inexperienced employee. The new right could provide trade unions with the necessary platform to increase membership numbers within workplaces towards the levels required to trigger an application for statutory recognition.

Detailed consideration is given below to the definition and scope of grievance and disciplinary hearings during which the new rights will apply. But what if the employer does not have any formal grievance or disciplinary procedures? Many smaller employers do not. It has been stated in both the Explanatory Notes to the Bill and to the Act that nothing in the new Act will compel an employer to introduce a formal procedure where one does not already exist (paras 152 and 193 respectively). However, s. 3 of the Employment Rights Act 1996 obliges employers employing 20 or more employees to inform them of any disciplinary or grievance procedures that might be applicable, including the identity of an individual to whom appeals on disciplinary matters or grievances should be addressed. Even those employing fewer than 20 must still advise employees of the identity of the person to whom grievances should be addressed and the manner in which any such grievance should be made. Furthermore, case law indicates that *all* employees enjoy an implied term in their contracts that the employer must deal reasonably with grievances raised by the employee (see *W. A. Goold (Pearmak) Ltd* v *McConnell and another* [1995] IRLR 516). This has been described as an implied contractual grievance procedure existing within all employees' contracts. If, faced with this contractual obligation, the employer holds a meeting to deal with a grievance, the employee will enjoy the right to be accompanied provided the grievance raised concerns the performance of a duty by the employer.

The restriction of the right of accompaniment to those grievances concerning the performance of a duty, was made clear by the Government from the outset of the *Fairness at Work* proposals. Ian McCartney MP, Minister of State at the Department of Trade and Industry, stated to the House of Commons Standing Committee that only grievances concerning 'statutory or contractual rights' would trigger the right to be accompanied (Hansard HC Standing Committee E, 25 February 1999). This is further reflected in the new ACAS Code of Practice on Disciplinary and Grievance Procedures, which came into effect on 4 September 2000. It is stated that 'grievances arising out of day to day friction between fellow workers' are unlikely to concern a legal duty and thereby trigger the right of accompaniment, unless the friction develops into harassment or bullying (para. 55). Moreover, a request for a pay rise to which the worker is not already contractually entitled will also fall short, unless it concerns an equal pay claim or where a refusal might be otherwise discriminatory. Similarly, a grievance registered following the rejection of a promotion request by a worker is unlikely to attract the right of accompaniment unless it concerns, say, the application of a contractual grading or promotion exercise, or has discriminatory consequences. In short, for the right of accompaniment to be available, the grievance must be linked to a duty incumbent on the employer, emanating from a common law or statutory duty of care or the contract of employment.

Despite this apparently authoritative opinion from the revised ACAS Code, another view has been expressed based on the actual wording of s. 13(5) of the new Act. This activates the right to accompaniment with reference to a 'hearing that concerns the performance of a duty by the employer'. Note that no reference is made to 'legal duty'. Accordingly, it is at least arguable that a breach of a 'duty' to follow the terms of a collective agreement, for example, might trigger the right of accompaniment for anyone who objects and wishes to raise the matter as a grievance. This approach might be supported by the specific reference to 'legal obligations' in the whistleblowing provisions (see Employment Rights Act 1996, s. 43B(1)(b)), suggesting that the Government could have referred to 'legal duty' but chose not to do so. This is a point very likely to be tested.

In respect of disciplinary meetings, the coverage seems somewhat wider than for grievance hearings. As Mr McCartney stated, in the same Committee session referred to above:

> Employers can take many forms of disciplinary action. They can suspend, dismiss, demote, relocate or fine. They can also issue a formal warning or simply put a note on a worker's file. . . . A note on a file can have a significant impact on employees and so we believe that the right to be accompanied should be available.

The new ACAS Code of Practice states that the right of accompaniment is not expected to apply in respect of a meeting where no action will be taken against the employee or worker. This might involve a 'one to one' talk with a supervisor or manager, for example. If any action follows from it, however, even a short note on the individual's personnel file, the right of accompaniment will apply.

6.3   WHO CAN SEEK ACCOMPANIMENT?

Only a 'worker' may rely on the right to be accompanied. Section 13(1) of the 1999 Act defines a 'worker' as an individual as described in s. 230(3) of the Employment Rights Act 1996 (see 6.3.1), an agency worker, a home worker, a person in Crown employment or a person employed in Parliament.

The extension of rights to 'workers' rather than 'employees', and therefore beyond the present limits of protection for rights such as unfair dismissal and redundancy payments, is a trend to which the present Government seem firmly committed. The Working Time Regulations 1998 (SI 1998 No. 1833: reg. 2(1)) apply to 'workers' using the same wording as s. 230(3) of the 1996 Act. Similarly, the Minimum Wage Act 1998, s. 54(3). Furthermore, s. 23 of the 1999 Act allows the Secretary of State to make provision for other statutory rights to be conferred on 'workers' rather than 'employees'. This will be the subject of further consultation in 2001. The Government have expressed the intention that basic statutory rights should not be restricted only to those who enjoy contracts of employment, but should apply to everyone who works for someone else (*Fairness at Work*, para. 3.18 and Explanatory Notes to the Act, para. 232).

6.3.1 Worker status

Section 230(3) of the Employment Rights Act 1996 defines a 'worker' as:

> ... an individual who has entered into or works under (or where the employment has ceased, worked under)—
> (a)   a contract of employment, or
> (b)   any other contract, whether express or implied and (if it is express) whether oral or in writing, whereby the individual undertakes to do or perform personally any work or services for another party to the contract whose status is not by virtue of the contract that of a client or customer of any profession or business undertaking carried on by the individual ...

Section 230(2) defines those working under a contract of employment as those with a contract of service or apprenticeship, whether express or implied, and (if it is express) whether oral or in writing.

In the following explanation of the definition of 'worker' the author is indebted to Gwyneth Pitt and John Fairhurst for their analysis of the same subject in *Blackstone's Guide to the Working Time Regulations*, published in 1998.

The definition of 'worker' is wider in scope than the definition of an 'employee'. It occupies the grey area between 'employee' and 'self-employed'. The former certainly falls within the definition, the latter does not. The genuinely self-employed will be excluded from worker status as they do not enjoy a *personal* relationship with the hirer of their services. However, the outcome is not always clear-cut. In *Lane* v *Shire Roofing* [1995] IRLR 493, CA, an individual roofing contractor who worked on a 'payment by job basis' with his own equipment was still confirmed as an employee by the Court of Appeal. It should be borne in mind, however, that this was a personal injury case and did not concern the statutory definition in an employment context.

Some guidance might be found here by an examination of previous decisions made under other legislation that has endowed rights on a wider group of the workforce than just employees. The Industrial Relations Act 1971, the Sex Discrimination Act 1975, the Race Relations Act 1976 and, more recently, the Disability Discrimination

Act 1995, all apply not only to employees but also to others under a contract 'of service or of apprenticeship or a contract personally to do any work'.

In *Mirror Group Newspapers* v *Gunning* [1986] IRLR 27, CA, the question of the dominant purpose of the contract was held to be the relevant test. In that case, an allegation of unlawful sex discrimination was made when a newspaper company refused to allow the daughter of her deceased father to take over the area distribution of the newspaper. For the claim to be successful, it was necessary to show that the distributorship came within the definition of 'employment' in s. 82(1) of the 1975 Act. The employment tribunal and EAT found that it did. However, the Court of Appeal disagreed. The tribunal should have considered: (i) whether there was an obligation by one contracting party to execute *personally* any work or labour; and (ii) whether that was the *dominant purpose* of the contract. On the facts, this latter requirement was not satisfied, and the applicant's claim failed.

One case considered by the Court of Appeal in *Gunning* was that of *Broadbent* v *Crisp* [1974] ICR 248, which dealt with the definition of 'worker' under the Industrial Relations Act 1971. In that case the central issue was whether the contractual relationship was governed more by the requirement that the individual perform the service himself or herself rather than the individual being free to delegate performance to another. If the former, the individual would be a worker: if the latter, he or she would not. As Sir Hugh Griffiths stated in the decision of the NIRC:

No one test will be conclusive, but if the personality of the contracting party is found to be of importance in the formation of the contract it is a strong pointer towards the conclusion that his personal performance of the contractual obligations is envisaged by the contract. (p. 225A)

In this context, it is perhaps possible to see what was meant when it was stated in the *Fairness at Work* White Paper that these basic rights should be available to all who work for another person, but not to those who are genuinely individually self-employed (para. 3.18). If evidence indicates that an *individual* was hired, he or she will be a worker, or perhaps even an employee. If evidence shows that the hirer engaged a service provider only to carry out a specific task, without any reference to the personal, that service provider will be self-employed. The central factor in the equation is the obligation on the individual to render personal service.

Another recent decision of the Court of Appeal has confirmed this general approach. In *Express & Echo Publications Ltd* v *Tanton* [1999] IRLR 367, CA, Mr Tanton was engaged as a driver on an ostensibly self-employed basis. His contract stated: 'In the event that the contractor is unable or unwilling to perform the services personally, he shall arrange at his own expense entirely for another suitable person to perform the service.' Mr Tanton refused to sign it but continued to work in accordance with its terms, even, on occasion, using a substitute driver. He later brought a claim to an employment tribunal complaining that he had not been provided with a written statement of particulars, thereby seeking to confirm his employee status. The employment tribunal chairman concluded that the factors pointing to Mr

Tanton being an employee outweighed the factors which pointed to self-employed status. The EAT dismissed the employer's appeal on the ground that it raised no arguable point of law. However, the Court of Appeal ruled that the ability to provide a substitute was 'inherently inconsistent' with employee status. A contract of employment must necessarily contain an obligation on the part of the employee to provide services personally as an 'irreducible minimum'. The Court of Appeal concluded that Mr Tanton must, on the facts of the case, have been a self-employed contractor. As such, it seems to rule out the possibility that he might have been a worker within the statutory definition (though, of course, the matter was not directly addressed). A slightly more flexible approach was subsequently taken in *Macfarlane and another* v *Glasgow City Council* [2000] IRLR 7.

6.3.2   Casual workers

Those potentially most at risk of being excluded from important statutory rights are casual workers. There are two problems here for such workers; one legal and one practical. First, like Mr Tanton, they might be found to be self-employed. Secondly, even if they can avoid the substitution clause that tripped up Mr Tanton (and that may become more popular in temporary employment contracts as a result), they are often engaged on a succession of short contracts as required. They do not enjoy a global or umbrella contract that maintains the relationship between periods of work. Most workers falling into this category are also excluded from disciplinary or grievance procedures, making the right of accompaniment irrelevant.

These weaknesses in respect of casual workers were amply demonstrated in the recent decision of the House of Lords in the case of *Carmichael* v *National Power* [2000] IRLR 43, HL. Two female tour guides were engaged to show visitors round the two Blythe power stations. Their contracts referred to their employment being 'on a casual as required basis'. They requested a statement of the essential terms of the contract of employment under s. 11 of the Employment Rights Act 1996; and, being refused, both submitted applications to an employment tribunal in the following terms:

> I have been employed since 9 March 1989 and I regularly work in excess of 25 hours per week. The respondent pays my tax and insurance contribution. I am provided with a uniform and I have full use of company vehicles for business use. I work for no other employer and I am not entitled to send along a substitute to perform my duties. I therefore claim that I am entitled to a contract of employment.

The employment tribunal found that their case foundered 'on the rock of absence of mutuality'. In other words, when not working as tour guides as required, they did not enjoy an ongoing contractual relationship with the employer. Instead they were party to a series of successive *ad hoc* contracts.

The tribunal made this decision on the basis of (i) the language of the documentation, (ii) the way in which the relationship had operated, and (iii) the evidence from the parties as to how it had been understood. The EAT refused to interfere with the decision of the employment tribunal and the tour guides appealed to the Court of Appeal.

The Court of Appeal (by a majority, Kennedy LJ dissenting) overturned the tribunal decision and held that the relationship did indeed involve the necessary 'mutuality of obligation' (see *Nethermere (St Neots) Ltd* v *Gardiner* [1984] IRLR 240, CA, and *O'Kelly* v *Trusthouse Forte* [1983] IRLR 369). Ward LJ stated:

> There was mutuality because there was an obligation to accept and perform some reasonable amount of work for the power station who were to make reasonable allocation of the work between the guides whom they had engaged. (para. 81)

In other words, the facts showed an implied contractual obligation on the company to offer work as available, and on the tour guides to accept that work. Despite being employed on zero-hours contracts, working only as required, the women were found to be employees under a global contract of mutuality. Indeed, Chadwick LJ went so far as to say that, on the facts of the case, it would be 'wholly artificial' for the applicants to be treated as independent contractors. National Power appealed to the House of Lords, the decision being delivered on 18 November 1999.

It had been hoped that the House of Lords would take the opportunity to carry out a full review of the case law and lay down firm guidance for the lower courts. Rather disappointingly, however, their Lordships did not do so. In finding for National Power and overturning the decision of the Court of Appeal, the Lord Chancellor, in delivering a very short lead judgment, reinstated the decision of the employment tribunal as the 'correct approach'. In the absence of any firm and clear lead from the House of Lords, the comprehensive dissenting judgment of Kennedy LJ in the Court of Appeal (with which the Lord Chancellor agreed) would now seem to represent the leading authority on the present state of the law in this area.

While the question of whether the tour guides might be classed as 'workers' was not addressed for obvious reasons, it seems very likely that this would be the case, at least for the duration of each separate '*ad hoc*' contract. This, of course, re-emphasises the practical difficulties of a right to accompaniment where the worker is offered only a succession of short duration separate contracts.

First, the employer can decide whether such a worker is to be subject to disciplinary or grievance procedures at all. The two tour guides in *Carmichael* were specifically excluded from such procedures by National Power. The likelihood elsewhere is that such workers will now be omitted even if they were not before. Neither can workers rely on an implied obligation that the employer will deal reasonably with grievances which might require the holding of a meeting at which accompaniment can be requested. The implied term to deal reasonably with grievances established in the case of *W. A. Goold (Pearmak) Ltd* v *McConnell and another* (see 6.2 above) applies only to employees, stemming from the statutory right to receive contractual information in s. 3 of the 1996 Act. The House of Lords has now made clear that casual workers like Mrs Carmichael are unlikely to be employees and, as such, are unlikely to gain much benefit from the new rights of accompaniment.

Even if casual workers are fortunate enough to be expressly subject to grievance and disciplinary procedures, there seems little to prevent an employer terminating an *ad hoc* contract (perhaps prematurely) *before* a disciplinary or grievance matter has been resolved with a meeting that might allow the right to accompaniment. Moreover, the worker could not challenge this decision because, not being an employee, he or she would not be able to claim unfair dismissal.

One might then look at the protection from being subjected to any detriment under s. 12 of the 1999 Act. However, the ability to claim unfair dismissal under s. 12(3) applies only when the principal reason for dismissal is that the worker 'exercised or sought to exercise' the right to be accompanied, postpone or to accompany another. If the worker is not 'required or invited by his employer' (s. 10(1)) to a hearing, it seems that the right to be accompanied will not apply and dismissal will not be an issue.

Lastly, will casual workers (or relatively secure employees for that matter) really insist on the right to be accompanied when faced with an employer openly hostile to trade unions and/or the idea of accompaniment generally? It is important to note that the worker must request accompaniment to trigger the right. The employer need not volunteer the information. Will workers even want to take the chance and test the views of their employer in the real world? Even if they are fortunate enough to enjoy the right of accompaniment, casual workers like Mrs Carmichael, surviving from contract to contract, day to day, might consider a request for accompaniment by a trade union official as a potentially serious career-limiting move.

6.3.3 Apprentices and trainees

Apprentices certainly enjoy 'worker' status. Section 230(2) of the Employment Rights Act 1996 defines those with a contract of employment as including apprentices. For more on the definition of 'apprentice', see the recent Court of Appeal decision in *Edmunds* v *Lawson QC and others* [2000] IRLR 391, in which a decision of the High Court that a pupil barrister was an apprentice, and thereby qualified for the statutory minimum wage, was overturned.

Trainees, as opposed to apprentices, on the other hand, are unlikely to be found to be party to a contract of employment. In *Wiltshire Police Authority* v *Wynn* [1980] ICR 649, CA, it was held the where the primary object of the relationship was that of training, there was no contract of service at all. This view was supported for non-apprentices by the Court of Appeal in *Edmunds* (above).

Faced with the same difficulty in the Working Time Regulations 1998 (SI 1998 No. 1833), and for avoidance of doubt, the Government introduced reg. 42, which specifically provided that those engaged in training contracts would be protected. This avoided difficulties such as those evident in *Daley* v *Allied Suppliers Ltd* [1983] IRLR 14, EAT. In this case, Miss Daley was a trainee on a Youth Opportunities Programme who made a complaint to an employment tribunal that she had suffered racial discrimination. The tribunal held that they could not hear her complaint since she was not 'employed' by the company within the meaning of the Act. She appealed against the decision.

Section 78 of the Race Relations Act 1976 defines 'employment' as employment under a contract of service or apprenticeship, or a contract personally to execute any work or labour. Miss Daley argued that she was employed by the company within the meaning of the Act and was entitled to have her complaint heard.

The EAT supported the decision of the employment tribunal. It was held that even if a contract did exist, it was a contract for the training of the applicant, not a contract of employment or a 'contract personally to execute any work or labour' within the meaning of s. 78. The primary purpose of the contract was not to establish a relationship of employer and employee, but to enable the applicant to acquire certain skills and experience.

As the definition of 'employee' in the Race Relations Act 1976 is similar to the definition of 'worker' in the Working Time Regulations 1998, the logic of including reg. 42 is clear. No such similar provision is provided in s. 13 of the 1999 Act in respect of the right of accompaniment, and it must be doubtful whether trainees (who are not apprentices) will fall within the definition of 'worker' for these purposes.

6.3.4 Agency workers

Section 13(1)(b) of the Employment Relations Act 1999 specifically identifies 'an agency worker' as a worker for the purposes of the right to accompaniment. Under s. 13(2), the right is available when an individual (the agency worker) is supplied by an agent to carry out work for another (the principal), even though it might not give rise to a contract falling within s. 230(3) of the 1996 Act. Provided the contractual relationship is not one in which the agency worker is providing professional or business services to a client on his own account, the right to representation will apply as if there was a contractual relationship between the worker and *either* the agent *or* the principal. Thus, an agency worker can claim the right to be represented at a grievance or disciplinary meeting arranged by the agency or the principal.

6.3.5 Home workers

Section 13(1)(c) of the 1999 Act applies the protection of ss. 10–12 to any 'home worker', which is defined in s. 13(3) as an individual who enters into a contract for work to be carried out other than under the employer's control or management. Provided the contractual relationship is not one in which the home worker is working as part of his or her own business or professional undertaking, the person providing the work will be the employer for the purposes of the right to be accompanied.

6.4   DEFINITION OF DISCIPLINARY OR GRIEVANCE HEARING

6.4.1   Accompaniment and disciplinary hearings

Section 13(4) of the 1999 Act defines a disciplinary hearing as any hearing that could result in:

(a)   the administration of a formal warning to a worker by his employer;

(b)   the taking of some other action in respect of a worker by his employer; or

(c)   the confirmation of a warning issued or some other action taken.

The scope of coverage is relatively wide-ranging. During the passage of the Bill through the House of Lords, Lord Simon of Highbury, speaking on behalf of the Government, attempted to clarify the provision in the Bill when he stated, 'it is not our intention to permit accompaniment at hearings without the immediate threat of disciplinary action' (HL Debs, 16 June 1999, col. 336). It is this important distinction that is likely to determine the right to be accompanied. Is it an informal chat, or something leading to formal action against the worker? As Lord Simon went on to say, 'counselling interviews and exploratory talks are excluded' (col. 337). If there is some element of formality present, however, even a note on the worker's file, then it is likely to be enough to trigger the right to accompaniment (see quote from Ian McCartney MP, at 6.2 above).

In the course of formal disciplinary proceedings, it might occur to an employer to side-step the need for a disciplinary interview altogether, thereby avoiding the need for accompaniment. The sanction of a formal letter of warning might be issued where dismissal is not thought imminent. This would be unwise if the sanction might in future be used to justify dismissal in the event of repeat behaviour. Dismissal connected to a previous disciplinary sanction issued without the employee being given the opportunity to state his or her case will increase the chances of a finding of unfair dismissal. The employer will not be in compliance with the new ACAS Code of Practice on Disciplinary and Grievance Procedures.

Compliance with the ACAS Code is an important factor in determining the fairness of a dismissal. In *Lock* v *Cardiff Railway Co. Ltd* [1998] IRLR 358, Morison J, presiding in the EAT, emphasised the respect with which employment tribunals should regard the provisions of the Code, even though the parties themselves might not make reference to it. Paragraph 10(f) of the old Code provided that employers should 'provide for individuals to be informed of the complaints against them and to be given an opportunity to state their case before decisions are reached'. The new Code now includes similar advice in para. 9.

In *McLaren* v *National Coal Board* [1988] IRLR 215, the Court of Appeal highlighted the importance of ensuring that employees are given a proper hearing before dismissal, even in the most extreme of circumstances — in that case during the 'warfare' of a major industrial dispute. Without such a hearing, a dismissal will almost always be unfair.

While an employer is undoubtedly wise to tread carefully on matters of accompaniment when dealing with employees who might claim unfair dismissal, it might not be thought to apply to non-employees who are not able to claim unfair dismissal. If an individual cannot make such a claim, an employer might feel less concerned. This might induce a employer to avoid disciplinary hearings and simply issue warning letters. It should be noted, however, that the Government have reserved the right under s. 23 of the new Act to introduce regulations to allow those satisfying the wider definition of 'workers' to claim unfair dismissal.

Lastly, it is worth taking note of the wording of s. 13(4)(c), quoted above. This was introduced as an amendment during the passage of the Bill through Parliament. It ensures that the right of accompaniment is available during hearings at which a disciplinary decision is being challenged on appeal (see HL Debs, 16 June 1999, col. 336).

6.4.2   Accompaniment and grievance hearings

Reference was made at 6.2 above to the Government's intention to restrict the right to accompaniment in grievance hearings unless the grievance issue concerns a legal duty (in contract, statute or tort). In the Committee Stage debates in the House of Commons and the House of Lords, Ministers made it clear that it was not the intention that individuals should enjoy the right to be accompanied in grievance hearings on trivial matters.

Section 13(5) of the 1999 Act states:

(5)   For the purposes of section 10 a grievance hearing is a hearing which concerns the performance of a duty by the employer in relation to a worker.

While as noted above, no reference is actually made in the subsection to 'legal duty', the definition seems to fit reasonably well with the Government's restrictive interpretation which is further reflected in the new Code of Practice. Grievances arising out of day-to-day friction between workers are unlikely to cause a breach of the employer's duty. If such friction extends to bullying or harassment, it is likely to involve a breach as it concerns the employer's legal duty of care. In short, the right is most likely to apply to grievances concerning allegations of a breach of contractual terms and conditions or contractual procedures (express or implied), or allegations that the employer has breached a statutory or common law obligation.

By apparently excluding non-legal matters (which as explained above is not necessarily certain) from the accompaniment provisions, the Government have resisted a definition of 'grievance hearing' that might have allowed workers to pursue pseudo collective matters by raising individual grievances. For instance, where a trade union was not recognised, union activists might have tried to raise individual grievances on matters such as improving pay and conditions and, in so doing, insist that a trade union official accompany them. The individual grievance might then have been widened to apply to all workers employed.

Reference was made at 6.2 to the case of *W. A. Goold (Pearmak) Ltd* v *McConnell and another* [1995] IRLR 516. This case might be of interest to those employers who do not have a formal grievance procedure within which an employee might ask to be accompanied. While it has been stated by Government representatives that the new provisions will not enforce disciplinary or grievance procedures where they do not already exist, the absence of formal grievance procedures will not necessarily allow an employer to avoid the provisions.

In 1992, Mr McConnell and a colleague attempted to raise the issue of a change in sales practices which had resulted in them sustaining a reduction in commission earnings. Despite several attempts to register their grievances with the managing director and chairman, they were unsuccessful in getting the matter resolved. Eventually they left and claimed constructive dismissal. An employment tribunal concluded that the employer's failure to establish and implement a grievance procedure amounted to a serious breach of the employees' contracts of employment. The tribunal also found the employees to have been unfairly dismissed. The employer appealed to the EAT. The EAT dismissed the appeal. Morison J stated:

> Parliament considered that good industrial relations requires employers to provide their employees with a method of dealing with grievances in a proper and timeous fashion. . . . That being so, the industrial tribunal was entitled, in our judgement, to conclude that there was an implied term in the contract of employment that the employers would reasonably and promptly afford a reasonable opportunity to their employees to obtain redress of any grievance they may have. (para. 11)

An employer's attempt to avoid an employee's right of accompaniment because of the absence of a formal grievance procedure is likely to be defeated by the fact that all employers are obliged to deal with the grievances of their employees fairly or be in breach of contract. In other words, an implied contractual grievance procedure is always available (to employees rather than workers). If the employer holds a meeting to deal with the grievance, the employee will enjoy the right to be accompanied provided the grievance raised concerns the performance of a legal duty by the employer, as explained above.

Ironically, the facts in *McConnell* seem to suggest that the applicants would *not* have enjoyed the statutory right to be accompanied on the basis of the grievance raised. Mr McConnell and his colleague complained of their declining commission payments which were related to a change in sales practice. The changed practice was apparently accepted as lawful. It is therefore difficult to see a breach by the employer of a duty that would have triggered the right to accompaniment.

It is also noticeable that in the original Employment Relations Bill, a disciplinary or grievance hearing was specifically defined by clause 14(4) as a hearing 'held in the course of a disciplinary or grievance procedure established or adopted by the employer'. This definition was dropped in the course of the passage of the Bill and did not find its way into s. 13(4) and (5) of the final Act. It is quite arguable, therefore, that the intention of the legislators was to focus the right of accompaniment on the nature and substance of any meeting or hearing that actually takes place, rather than on whether a hearing takes place under a formal procedure. Again, this leads to the conclusion that wise employers would be well-advised to err on the side of caution and allow the right of accompaniment in all but the most trivial of circumstances.

6.5 RIGHT TO BE ACCOMPANIED

6.5.1 Scope of the individual right

Section 10 of the 1999 Act provides the basic right to be accompanied during grievance and disciplinary hearings. Section 10(1) states:

(1) This section applies where a worker—
(a) is required or invited by his employer to attend a disciplinary or grievance hearing, and
(b) reasonably requests to be accompanied at the hearing.

There are two points of interest here. First, the worker must *ask* to be accompanied. The employer need not tell the worker of the right. This means that the worker, if he or she wants a trade union representative to attend, must tell the employer of his or her trade union membership. Considering that the right is intended to introduce fair procedures into areas uninhabited by trade unions, and where employers might well be hostile to trade unions, workers might think twice before identifying themselves as union members.

Secondly, the parameters of a 'reasonable request' are unclear. It raises the prospect of an employer challenging the worker's request for accompaniment because the subject to which it relates is insufficiently serious. Those seeking guidance on the point from the new Code of Practice on Disciplinary and Grievance Procedures will be disappointed. Its only advice is, 'It will be for the Courts to decide what is reasonable in all the circumstances' (para. 56). Until case law is available on the point, therefore, employers would be wise to allow accompaniment where requested in all marginal cases. The alternative is to run the risk of potentially costly tribunal claims.

Once the worker makes the request, s. 10(2) states that the employer 'must permit' the worker to be accompanied at the subsequent hearing by a single companion who:

(a) is chosen by the worker and is within s. 10(3);
(b) is to be permitted to address the hearing (but not to answer questions on behalf of the worker); and
(c) is to be permitted to confer with the worker during the hearing.

Section 10(3) provides the statutory definition of the person who can accompany the worker. This can be a union official employed by the union as defined in s. 119 of the TULR(C)A 1992, an official (not employed) who is 'reasonably certified' by the union as having the necessary experience and training to act as a worker's companion at a hearing, or, lastly, another of the employer's workers. A lawyer is not permitted unless he or she falls into one of the above categories.

Interestingly, the new ACAS Code of Practice provides some guidance where the person seeking accompaniment is a member of a union other than that recognised by the employer:

> . . . where a trade union is recognised in a workplace it is good practice for an official from that union to be selected to accompany the worker at a hearing. (para. 58)

While this proposal might be put to the worker, s. 10(2)(a) of the Act is clear in stating that the worker has the final say as to the identity of the companion. Indeed, to be fair to those who drafted the new Code, this is made clear earlier in para. 58. If the worker is a member of a union that is not recognised by the employer, he or she may choose a companion from his or her own union. If this is refused, a tribunal claim might follow.

Section 119 of the TULR(C)A 1992 defines a union official as an officer of the union, branch or section, or a person elected or appointed under the rules of the union to represent members. The Explanatory Notes to the 1999 Act make it clear that there is no intention by Government to place a duty on a trade union to provide a companion (para. 193). Whether to provide a companion and who to send (provided the person is an 'official' as defined) is purely a matter for the trade union (as made clear in para. 59 of the new Code).

6.5.2 Postponement of a hearing

Section 10(4) of the 1999 Act allows for the hearing to be postponed should the worker's chosen companion not be available at the time proposed for the hearing by the employer. Provided the worker proposes an alternative time that satisfies the terms of s. 10(5), the employer *must* postpone the hearing. If the employer does not postpone, and proceeds without the worker being allowed his or her chosen companion, it will be treated as a refusal, possibly leading to a tribunal claim for compensation.

An alternative time proposed by the worker must be reasonable and fall before the end of a period of five working days beginning with the first working day after the date proposed by the employer. For example, if a manager speaking to a worker on Monday proposes a meeting at 2 pm on Friday, the worker could postpone the meeting (should the chosen representative not be available) to a date not later than the following Friday. This might be put further back should Christmas Day, Good Friday or a bank holiday fall within the five working days period.

Employers might be wary of workers seeking to delay proceedings on the pretext that their chosen union official is not available. This might well lead to employers seeking written confirmation of the union official's non-availability before agreeing to postpone the original date.

6.5.3   Fellow workers as companions

Should a worker requested to attend a relevant hearing not be a member of a trade union, or choose not to be accompanied by a trade union official, he or she might choose instead to be accompanied by a fellow worker. Section 10(6) of the 1999 Act obliges an employer to allow a fellow worker chosen as a companion time off with full pay during working hours to attend such a hearing with the worker. Such rights are in accordance with ss. 168(3) and (4), 169 and 171 to 173 of the TULR(C)A 1992. These give the same rights to time off as apply to bone fide union officials and allow a reasonable amount of paid time off work to carry out the relevant duties. A right of complaint to an employment tribunal is available (to be made within three months of the date of the failure) if the employer fails to allow adequate time off. This will to include time off to prepare for the hearing in discussion with the worker concerned. Section 168(3) of the 1992 Act states that:

> (3)   The amount of time off which an employee is to be permitted to take under this section and the purposes for which, the occasions on which and any conditions subject to which time off may be so taken are those that are reasonable in all the circumstances having regard to any relevant provisions of a Code of Practice issued by ACAS.

Paragraph 61 of the new ACAS Code of Practice on Disciplinary and Grievance Procedures is clear in stating:

> A worker who has been requested to accompany a colleague employed by the same employer and has agreed to do so is entitled to take a reasonable amount of paid time off to fulfil this responsibility. The time off should not only cover the hearing but should allow a reasonable amount of time off for the accompanying person to familiarise themselves with the case and confer with the worker before and after the hearing.

6.6   REMEDIES FOR NON-COMPLIANCE BY THE EMPLOYER

Section 11 of the 1999 Act provides a remedy against an employer who has 'failed or threatened to fail' to allow the right of accompaniment under s. 10(2) or to postpone proceedings under s. 10(4). Just the *threat* of a refusal to allow these statutory rights could result in a successful tribunal claim, even if the disciplinary matter or grievance is later withdrawn without a hearing.

A complaint must be made to an employment tribunal before the end of a period of three months beginning with the date of the failure or threatened failure. This can be extended, at the discretion of the tribunal, if it was not reasonably practicable for the application to be presented in time.

If an employment tribunal finds a complaint well founded, it can make an award of compensation to the worker not exceeding two weeks' pay. This will be subject to the maximum week's pay limits within s. 227(1) of Employment Rights Act 1996, which is currently £230 (from 1 February 2000).

6.7 RIGHT NOT TO BE SUBJECTED TO DETRIMENT

Section 12 of the 1999 Act provides protection from victimisation suffered by a worker who has exercised a right to be accompanied or postpone a hearing, or who has sought to accompany another. Interestingly, the protection from victimisation is available to those who accompany, or seek to accompany, another whether or not it concerns a fellow worker of the same employer or of another employer (s. 12(1)(b)). Time off with pay is not available to those who represent another employer's worker.

Individuals who believe themselves to have been subjected to such a detriment, up to and including dismissal, must apply to an employment tribunal within three months of the alleged act by the employer. This period can be extended at the discretion of the tribunal. The normal 12-month qualifying period or upper age limit restriction for unfair dismissal claims will not apply to such applications courtesy of s. 12(4).

Victimisation resulting in dismissal is dealt with by s. 12(3). If the reason or principal reason for the dismissal is that the employee exercised the right to be accompanied or postpone a hearing or accompany another (whether or not of the same employer), the dismissal will be automatically unfair for the purposes of Part X of the Employment Rights Act 1996.

Section 12(6) of the 1999 Act extends the scope of Part II of Chapter X (unfair dismissal provisions) in the 1996 Act so that the unfair dismissal protection ordinarily available only to employees is also made available to those falling within the wider definition of 'worker' claiming under s. 12(3).

Section 12(5) allows workers to claim a rarely used injunctive remedy when dismissed for requesting the right to be accompanied, seeking a postponement or seeking to accompany another. Interim relief has applied in the past only to trade union or certain health and safety dismissals. If interim relief is granted, employment is continued pending the outcome of the full tribunal hearing. There are two essential hurdles to clear before it can apply:

(a)   While the complainant can apply for interim relief before dismissal (as defined in the Employment Rights Act 1996, s. 95), he or she cannot apply for it later than seven days after the effective date of termination.

(b)   The tribunal must be convinced that the substantive claim is likely to succeed at a subsequent full hearing.

If the employer is unwilling to reinstate the applicant, the tribunal can make an order for the continuation of the applicant's contract (including full pay and benefits) until the full hearing when reinstatement can be considered as a final remedy.

Chapter 7
Discrimination Against Trade Union Members in the Workplace

7.1 INTRODUCTION

Prior to coming to power in the General Election in May 1997, the Labour Party had already formulated many of its ideas for reform in employment law that were to establish the basis of the subsequent *Fairness at Work* White Paper. In the 1996 Labour Party document *Building Prosperity — Flexibility, Efficiency and Fairness at Work*, it was stated:

> One of the individual entitlements we propose should be the choice whether or not to join a trade union. If [employees] choose to do so, they will have an entitlement not to be discriminated against by their employer. (p. 5)

The cause of this concern was the decision of the House of Lords in the cases of *Associated Newspapers Ltd* v *Wilson* and *Associated British Ports* v *Palmer and others* [1995] IRLR 258, HL. The joint decision opened the way for employers to discriminate against trade union members, by omission if not by an overt act. Employers were found to be acting lawfully if they offered financial benefits only to those who agreed to enter new individual contracts and not to those who wished to remain on collectively agreed terms.

Following victory in the General Election in May 1997, the new Labour Government introduced the *Fairness at Work* White Paper. This stated:

> The Government believes that such discrimination is contrary to its commitment to ensuring individuals are free to choose whether or not to join a trade union . . . The Government therefore proposes to make it unlawful to discriminate by omission on grounds of trade union membership, non-membership or activities. (para. 4.25)

7.2   *WILSON* AND *PALMER*: LEGISLATIVE HISTORY

7.2.1   Introduction of protective legislation

The history of the legislation outlawing discrimination against trade union members played a significant part in the majority decision of the House of Lords in *Wilson* and *Palmer*.

Protective legislation was first enacted in the Industrial Relations Act 1971. Section 5 made it unlawful for an employer to 'discriminate against' a worker on union grounds. The 1971 Act was repealed by the Trade Union and Labour Relations Act 1974, which continued the protection against unfair dismissal on union grounds only. It did not, however, provide specific protection against victimisation on union grounds by a detriment or action short of dismissal.

Protection against action short of dismissal was re-introduced by the Employment Protection Act 1975, s. 53 being the direct ancestor of the present law. The provisions of the 1974 and 1975 Act were consolidated into the Employment Protection (Consolidation) Act (EPCA) 1978. Section 53 of the 1975 Act became s. 23 of the EPCA 1978. Section 23 was then consolidated into s. 146 of the TULR(C)A 1992, where it remains today. It was itself amended on 25 October 1999 by Schedule 2 of the 1999 Act. Before the most recent amendments, s. 146(1) stated:

(1)   An employee has the right not to have action short of dismissal taken against him as an individual by his employer for the purpose of—
(a)   preventing or deterring him from being or seeking to become a member of an independent trade union, or penalising him for doing so,
(b)   preventing or deterring him from taking part in the activities of an independent union at an appropriate time, or penalising him for doing so, or
(c)   compelling him to be or become a member of any trade union or of a particular trade union or of one of a number of particular trade unions.

7.2.2   *Wilson* and *Palmer*: EAT

In *Associated Newspapers* v *Wilson* [1992] IRLR 440, EAT, the applicant was a journalist for the *Daily Mail*, a member of the National Union of Journalists and father of chapel. Prior to 1989, the union was recognised by the employers for collective bargaining purposes, and terms and conditions of employment were negotiated with the union and set out in a 'house agreement'. In 1989, the employers gave notice that they were terminating the agreement and introducing a system of individual contracts. Those who agreed to new contracts were given a 4.5 per cent additional pay increase. All but 15 of the 173 journalists signed the new contracts and received the increase. As David Wilson did not sign, he did not receive it.

Mr Wilson complained to an industrial tribunal, alleging a breach of his rights under s. 23(1)(a) of the EPCA 1978 (worded similarly to s. 146 above). The tribunal held that the employer's action in derecognising the union did not itself fall within

s. 23 because it was not action taken against the employee as an individual. However, the tribunal upheld his complaint concerning the failure to pay the 4.5 per cent increase, concluding that it was an action taken against Mr Wilson and that the employer's ultimate purpose was to deter individual journalists from remaining members of the union. The employers appealed to the Employment Appeal Tribunal (EAT).

By a majority decision, the EAT allowed the appeal. While they held that the offer of a salary increase only to those accepting new contracts was action taken against the employees as individuals, the employer's *purpose* (from the preamble to s. 23(1)(a) of the 1978 Act) was to end collective bargaining and not to deter the journalists from retaining union membership. Because the journalists were free to retain their membership, the action could not be said to deter union membership or penalise employees because of it.

In answer to Mr Wilson's arguments that besides the 4.5 per cent relative salary reduction, he had indeed been deprived of the use of union services such as negotiation on terms and conditions and individual representation in disciplinary or grievance matters, Wood J stated:

> If this submission is correct, the collective agreement could never have been terminated without an employer incurring some form of liability. The legislature envisaged that derecognition was an option open to an employer. (para. 61)

In *Associated British Ports* v *Palmer and others* [1993] IRLR 63, EAT, the employees worked at the port of Southampton. They were members of the National Union of Rail, Maritime and Transport Workers, which was recognised for collective bargaining purposes.

The company had promoted a policy of offering 'personal contracts' to employees in place of collectively negotiated terms and conditions since 1988. At first such contracts were offered only to non-manual workers and were accepted by the majority. Encouraged by their success, the company decided to offer personal contracts to manual workers.

In 1991, the manual workers were offered a substantial pay rise if they agreed to accept personal contracts and relinquish their right to union representation. The few who refused continued to be employed under their existing contracts and the employers carried on negotiations with the union on their behalf. The negotiated pay rise was considerably less than that given to those who accepted personal contracts, leaving Mr Palmer some £30 a week worse off. Mr Palmer and others submitted industrial tribunal applications claiming action short of dismissal contrary to s. 23(1)(a) of the EPCA 1978.

The industrial tribunal concluded that although the employers honestly believed that their purpose was to increase flexibility, the reality indicated that their purpose was to penalise the few who would not give up union representation. In other words, the employers had 'confused purpose with objective'. If their purpose were to be successful (persuading the employees to abandon union membership), they would achieve their objective (flexibility). This was the position even though nothing prevented the employees from maintaining their union membership and enjoying the benefits of continued representation (though this was later withdrawn).

The employers appealed to the EAT, arguing that once the tribunal had accepted the employer's honest belief as to the purpose of their actions, it was not open to it to substitute its own perceived purpose. Moreover, even if the employer's purpose had been to penalise those who refused to sign the personal contracts, they had not acted in breach of s. 23(1)(a) as they had not penalised the employees for being *individual* members of a trade union.

In another majority decision, the EAT allowed the employer's appeal. First, after accepting evidence from the employers that their purpose was to achieve greater flexibility, the tribunal was not entitled to conclude that, in reality, their purpose was to penalise. A tribunal either accepted the employer's evidence on its purpose or it did not. Wood J then went on to consider the interrelationship between 'reason', 'purpose' and 'means'.

An employer's purpose must be contrasted with the means by which it is achieved and the collateral results that may be caused. In Mr Palmer's case, the evidence indicated that flexibility was the actual purpose of the employer's action, and they had chosen the only means of achieving that purpose.

Even if this were wrong, however, the employer's actions would still not have constituted a breach of s. 23(1)(a). Action had not been taken against Mr Palmer for being a member of an independent trade union. The right of an employee to be represented by his union could not be implied in the phrase 'being a member'. Neither was there a basis for such a general proposition in the decision in *Discount Tobacco and Confectionery Ltd* v *Armitage* [1990] IRLR 15, EAT (see 7.2.3 below). As those affected by the actions of the employer still had the right to maintain their union membership, s. 23(1) had not been breached.

7.2.3 *Discount Tobacco and Confectionery Ltd* v *Armitage*

The EAT carefully considered the *Armitage* case in its decision in *Palmer*. The case was also the subject of detailed consideration in the Court of Appeal and House of Lords (see 7.2.4 and 7.2.6).

Mrs Armitage was employed as a manager of one of her employer's shops from February 1988. In May, she wrote to the company asking for a written statement of her terms and conditions of employment, to which she did not receive a reply. She asked her union official to write to the company. She was then sent a statement immediately, but very soon thereafter she was dismissed.

The company argued that the dismissal was on the grounds of capability, while Mrs Armitage claimed that she had been dismissed because of her trade union membership contrary to s. 58 of the EPCA 1978 which protected against unfair dismissal on grounds of trade union membership (now TULR(C)A 1992, s. 152). An industrial tribunal found her to have been unfairly dismissed and the employer appealed to the EAT.

The employer argued a distinction between membership of the union, on the one hand, and seeking the services of a union officer on the other. Just because the dismissal might have been connected with her request for union assistance, it did not mean it was because of her union membership. The two issues were divorced.

The EAT found a clear connection between union membership and making use of the services of the union. Indeed, utilising the services of a union was an 'outward and visible manifestation of trade union membership' (para. 13). Knox J went on:

> Were it not so, the scope of s. 58(1)(a) would be reduced almost to vanishing point, since it would only be just the fact that a person was a member of a union, without regard to the consequences of that membership, that would be the subject matter of that statutory provision and, it seems to us, that to construe that paragraph so narrowly would really be to emasculate the provision altogether. (para. 14)

The EAT in *Palmer*, however, could not accept that the *Armitage* decision supported the existence of a statutory right for a union member to have his or her terms and conditions of employment dealt with only via his or her trade union.

7.2.4   *Wilson* and *Palmer*: Court of Appeal

Wilson and *Palmer* were considered together when the employees' appeals reached the next stage ([1993] IRLR 336, CA). The Court of Appeal decided firmly in favour of the employees, reinstating both industrial tribunal decisions. Both tribunals were perfectly entitled to find that the employers' purpose in offering financial incentives to employees to sign personal contracts and forgo union representation was to deter employees from remaining members of a union and/or to penalise them for so doing, contrary to s. 23(1)(a) of the EPCA 1978.

The Court of Appeal also expressed support for the approach taken by the EAT in *Armitage* (see 7.2.3). It was not correct to argue that there could be no breach of s. 23(1)(a) if the employee's right to remain a union member was unaffected by the employer's actions. *Armitage* was 'unquestionably correct', and a tribunal was entitled to find that an employee was dismissed or otherwise penalised for being a union member if the employer's action affected the relationship between the union and its member.

Neither did the Court of Appeal agree with the distinction drawn in the EAT by Wood J in *Palmer*, between the 'reason' or the 'purpose' of the employer in taking an action, on the one hand, and the 'means' by which that purpose was to be achieved, on the other. As Dillon LJ stated:

> I have no doubt that the purpose of Associated British Ports in offering extra pay to those employees who signed the new personal contracts was to persuade the employees to abandon union representation by making personal contracts so attractive that, as it was put by Miss Brenda Dean — the dissentient member of the Employment Appeal Tribunal — the union would 'wither on the vine'. (para. 22)

Turning to the case of *Wilson*, the industrial tribunal had erred in deciding that changes in terms and conditions of employment following the derecognition of the union amounted to action taken against employees as individuals. Since the terms applied equally to all employees, they could not be regarded as action taken against any one of them as individuals. Nevertheless, the tribunal was still entitled to find that the employer's ultimate purpose was so to reduce the power of the union as to negate it totally and thus to deter individual employees from being members of the union contrary to s. 23(1)(a) of the 1978 Act.

Dillon LJ concluded by making an important practical point of which, as will be discussed at 7.3 below, the Labour Government might have taken more note when they drafted the 1999 provisions:

> ... this decision does not dispute an employer's right to derecognise a union and make changes in consequence in the terms and conditions of the employee's employment. The employer only enters a potential danger area if he offers a douceur to employees who will support his policy, which is to be withheld from those who are not prepared to support it. (para. 69)

The Court in its decision was not challenging the rights of an employer to derecognise a trade union and/or introduce personal contracts *per se*. An employer was free to do so, provided it did not offer a sweetener to employees to give up their collectively agreed terms and, probably, eventually their trade union membership.

7.2.5 The Government's response to the Court of Appeal

The Conservative Government's response to the Court of Appeal's decision was swift. Within five days of the decision, and even before it was in print, Viscount Ullswater had introduced in the House of Lords three new subsections to s. 148 of the 1992 TULR(C)A by way of late amendments to the Trade Union Reform and Employment Rights Act 1993. The main amendment was to introduce a new s. 148(3). The provision, which is not repealed by the 1999 Act, remains an area of contention between the new Labour Government and the trade unions, as will be seen below. Section 148(3) stated:

> (3)   In determining what was the purpose for which action was taken by the employer against the complainant in a case where—
>
>   (a)   there is evidence that the employer's purpose was to further a change in his relationship with all or any class of his employees, and
>
>   (b)   there is also evidence that his purpose was one falling within section 146, the tribunal shall regard the purpose mentioned in paragraph (a) (and not the purpose mentioned in paragraph (b)) as the purpose for which the employer took the action, unless it considers that the action was such as no reasonable employer would take having regard to the purpose mentioned in paragraph (a).

Section 148(3) had the immediate effect of overturning the decision of the Court of Appeal in *Wilson* and *Palmer* when the amendment came into effect at the end of August 1993. If an employer were to discriminate against trade union members (by either action or omission, as it was thought then) with the intention of implementing a different system of employee relations (such as the introduction of personal contracts instead of collective bargaining), the discrimination would be disregarded unless wholly disproportionate.

Meanwhile, the *Wilson* and *Palmer* case rumbled on when the employers were successful in persuading the House of Lords to overturn the Court of Appeal's refusal to grant leave to appeal.

7.2.6   *Wilson* and *Palmer*: House of Lords

Before looking at the decision of the House of Lords, two essential points should be noted. First, the House of Lords were examining only s. 23 of EPCA 1978 as the operative section at the time of the employers' acts. No reference was made to s. 146 of TULR(C)A 1992. The importance of this will soon become clear.

Secondly, it was not argued by the employers before the industrial tribunals, EAT or Court of Appeal that an omission might be other than an act for the purposes of s. 23(1). The reason for this was undoubtedly the decision of the Court of Appeal in *Ridgway and Fairbrother* v *National Coal Board* [1987] IRLR 80, CA.

The *Ridgway* decision was clear authority that an omission was to be considered as an act under s. 23. The majority of the Court of Appeal (Nicholls and Bingham LJJ) held that an omission becomes unlawful only if the employer acts with a prohibited purpose such as to prevent, deter or penalise the employee for being, or not being, a trade unionist. In stating that 'an omission need be no more than a failure or neglect to act', Bingham LJ (para. 106) indicated clearly, and logically, that the *purpose* was to be the central limiting factor and not the omission itself. However, the House of Lords in *Wilson* and *Palmer* were not to be convinced in a decision that was described as 'a major blow to freedom of association in the UK' (Michael Rubinstein's editorial [1995] IRLR 229).

7.2.6.1   *Point 1: Could an omission be an act?*

Lord Bridge, giving the lead judgment in the decision, examined the context of s. 23 and s. 153(1) of EPCA 1978 with great care. The relevant part of s. 153(1) stated:

> In this Act, except so far as the context otherwise requires—
> 'act' and 'action' each includes omission and references to doing an act or taking action shall be construed accordingly . . .

After consideration of this section, Lord Bridge then moved on to s. 23(1) and the relevant part, 'every employee shall have the right not to have action (short of dismissal) taken against him'. As it was not possible grammatically to read 'omission' into this phrase without substantial recasting, it was necessary to examine the legislative history of these provisions and the context in which they were drafted.

The Industrial Relations Act 1971 had been clear that an 'action' included a refusal or failure to act (s. 167). It had also been an act of discrimination to withhold benefits (s. 5(4)). It continued to be the case that an action included an omission to act in the Trade Union and Labour Relations Act 1974 (s. 30(1)). Section 53 of the Employment Protection Act 1975, however, was silent on the issue of withholding benefits. Despite this, at least one industrial tribunal was still able to find that a failure to allow union representation was an act for the purposes of s. 53 (see *Cheall* v *Vauxhall Motors Ltd* [1979] IRLR 253).

In 1978, s. 53 of the 1975 Act became s. 23 of EPCA 1978. Section 153(1) of the 1978 Act stated that, 'except so far as the context otherwise requires', an act includes an omission to act. The EAT held that withholding a benefit provided to others constituted taking action for the purposes of s. 23 (see *Carlson* v *Post Office* [1981] IRLR 158, in which the EAT found that a refusal to provide a car parking space on union grounds was an act under s. 23).

Then, in 1986, the Court of Appeal confirmed that a failure to pay a wage increase to members of a particular trade union, as against another, was an act under s. 23, in the important decision of *Ridgway and Fairbrother* v *National Coal Board* [1987] IRLR 80, CA.

From this background, Lord Bridge noted that the Employment Protection Act 1975 had not included the definition within s. 153(1). This was the case even though both previous definitions, in the 1971 and 1974 Acts, had stated that an action was to include a refusal or failure to act. When s. 53 of the 1975 Act was being drafted, the wording and extent of protection from previous Acts must have been in the draftsman's mind. The fact that omissions or failures to act had not been specifically protected must have been deliberate.

The 1975 and 1974 Acts were consolidated into the EPCA 1978. The immediate predecessor of s. 153(1) of the EPCA 1978 was s. 30(1) of the 1974 Act. It was not replicated anywhere in the Employment Protection Act 1975. As s. 53 of the 1975 Act had become s. 23 of the EPCA 1978: '... there was no question of applying any definition giving an extended meaning of the word "action" in the context in which we now have to construe it' (para. 9).

Citing *Beswick* v *Beswick* [1968] AC 58, Lord Bridge reminded the House that a consolidating Act of Parliament is not capable of being amended relative to the Acts from which it derives. Thus, if the definition of 'action' in s. 153 of the EPCA 1978 were to be read into s. 23(1), a consolidating Act would have 'substantially altered the pre-existing law'. Accordingly, it was not possible to interpret s. 23(1) so as to apply it to an omission to act. On this point, Lord Bridge thought the decision of the Court of Appeal in *Ridgway* must be overruled.

Lord Keith agreed with this textual and historical approach, as did Lord Browne-Wilkinson, though somewhat hesitantly:

> I reach the conclusion with great regret since, in my view, it leaves an undesirable lacuna in the legislation protecting employees against victimisation. (para. 27)

Keith Ewing has referred to Lord Bridge's efforts in examining this point as a 'brilliant example of grammatical pedantry', leading to the 'singular triumph of the clever mind at the expense of the big picture' ((1999) ILJ, vol. 28, p. 287).

Lord Lloyd and Lord Slynn could not agree with the majority view. In their view the Court of Appeal in *Ridgway* was correct. They thought the words of the Act 'clear and unambiguous' and that they should be given effect according to their meaning. There were no grounds to resolve the point by reference to legislative history.

It has been submitted that the logic of Lord Bridge's analysis of the legislative history is flawed; and, in any event, is not applicable to s. 146(1) of the 1992 Act as it might have been to s. 23(1) of the 1978 Act. The General Editor of *Harvey on Industrial Relations and Employment Law*, Bryn Perrins, has suggested that the logic of the analysis is open to question (see N.682–683).

Lord Bridge had suggested that there was 'no question' of giving an extended meaning to s. 23(1) and that both the draftsman and relevant Parliamentary Committee must have been so satisfied. But, Perrins argues, there was some (albeit limited) authority for the view that s. 53 of the 1975 Act did indeed include omissions. Such a decision was reached in the industrial tribunal case of *Cheall v Vauxhall Motors* (above). At least one experienced tribunal had challenged Lord Bridge's assertion that there was 'no question' of s. 53 being given that extended meaning. As such, it is at least as possible that the draftsman and Parliamentary Committee also made the same assumption.

Secondly, and perhaps more convincingly, Perrins argues that the logic of Lord Bridge's arguments would not similarly apply to the 1992 Act. This is because there could have been no doubt when TULR(C)A 1992 passed through Parliament that s. 23 of the EPCA 1978 covered omissions, and that this would have been in the minds of the draftsman and the relevant Parliamentary Committee. After all, there was a unanimous decision from the Court of Appeal in *Ridgway* on that very point, which had not been questioned at that stage. Therefore, using Lord Bridge's own logic, s. 146(1) of the 1992 Act must include an omission to act even without the Government's recent amendments.

In implementing Schedule 2 of the 1999 Act, however, the Government were obviously taking no chances, and s. 146 has been comprehensively amended to overturn the House of Lords' decision that omissions to act are outside the coverage of the provision.

7.2.6.2   Point 2: the purpose of the employer's actions?

Perhaps surprisingly, having allowed the employers' appeals, the House of Lords then went on to explore the possibilities if they were wrong on the first point of their decision. Lord Bridge stated that there was no need to go into the issue in great detail, but thought it appropriate to offer some 'observations' on the issue.

The majority view of the House of Lords was that the employers' purpose in withholding pay increases from those who refused to give up collective bargaining was not to deter membership of the union or penalise them under s. 23(1)(a). The employer's purpose in *Wilson* was to change the system of employee relations from collective bargaining to individual agreements. In *Palmer*, it was to achieve greater flexibility generally. Lord Browne-Wilkinson opposed this view expressed by Lord Bridge, though without explanation.

This inevitably put the House of Lords onto a collision course with the EAT's decision in *Discount Tobacco Ltd* v *Armitage* (7.2.3 above) which had been supported by the Court of Appeal in *Palmer*. This provided authority for the proposition that membership of a union was essentially the same as making use of the essential services of that union. Lord Bridge avoided declaring *Armitage* as fundamentally wrong. Instead, he declared the EAT's decision as authority only in that it might allow an inference to be drawn, on the facts of the case:

> ... that [Mrs Armitage] had been dismissed because the employers resented the fact that she had invited the union to intervene on her behalf. In this narrow context the reasoning of Knox J may have been a legitimate means of refuting a particular argument advanced by counsel for the employers. (para. 23)

Armitage did not, Lord Bridge declared, establish a general proposition in law that membership is to be equated with using the essential services of the union.

This undoubtedly raises the question as to whether the decision in *Armitage* remains good law. Despite the fact that Lord Bridge was expressing only 'observations', they are likely to be given some weight by tribunals. The EAT subsequently reviewed the authorities in *Speciality Care plc* v *Pachela* [1996] IRLR 248, a claim alleging dismissal for reasons of trade union membership. In *Pachela*, it was held that *Armitage* was unquestionably correct on its facts. It was the unanimous decision of the Court of Appeal in *Wilson* and *Palmer* on a material part of the decision but was the subject of *obiter* comments only in the House of Lords. Moreover, Lord Bridge did not question the correctness of the decision on its facts. Clark J summarised that should a tribunal be asked to decide whether particular action had been taken by an employer by reason of trade union membership, the tribunal should consider not only the fact of the applicant joining the union, but also:

> ... whether the introduction of union representation into the employment relationship had led the employer to dismiss the employee. Tribunals should answer that question robustly, based on their findings as to what really caused the dismissal in the mind of the employer. (para. 39)

7.3   GOVERNMENT POLICY AND THE 1999 ACT

7.3.1   Omissions

The Labour Government came to power in 1997 committed to overturning at least the first limb of the House of Lords' decision that an omission could not be an act of discrimination. The consequent amendments in Schedule 2 of the 1999 Act concentrate heavily on the 'omission' question by amending ss. 146–150 of the TULR(C)A. For instance, the new s. 146(1) reads (amendment in italics):

> (1)   An employee has the right not to *be subjected to any detriment as an individual by any act, or any deliberate failure to act, by his employer if the act or failure takes place* for the purpose of—
>
> (a)   preventing or deterring him from being or seeking to become a member of an independent trade union, or penalising him for doing so,
>
> (b)   preventing or deterring him from taking part in the activities of an independent union at an appropriate time, or penalising him for doing so, or
>
> (c)   compelling him to be or become a member of any trade union or of a particular trade union or of one of a number of particular trade unions.

Amendments are made to the other relevant sections in a similar vein, making it absolutely clear that an omission will be considered as an act for the purposes of the protection. In this respect, the first limb of the decision of the House of Lords is well and truly overturned.

7.3.2   Employer's purpose

The second limb of the House of Lords decision has proved more problematical for the Labour Government. The amendments in Schedule 2 are insufficient in themselves to overturn the possible effects of the 'observations' made by Lord Bridge on the purpose of the employer's actions (though see *Pachela* at 7.2.6.2 above). Even if their Lordships had decided that an omission was an act for the purposes of s. 23(1) of the 1978 Act, they would still have found against the employees on the question of the purpose of the employers' actions which, they held, was not directed against union membership rights.

The Government have reserved the right to address this potential problem through the power to introduce regulations by way of s. 17 of the 1999 Act. The intention of the Government was indicated in the Committee Stage of the passage of the Bill. In response to questions on the intended effects of the new regulations, the Minister for Small Firms, Trade and Industry, Michael Wills MP, stated:

> We propose to make it unfair to dismiss workers or subject them to other detriment because they refuse to accept a contract on terms that differ from those applicable to them under a collective agreement.
>
> Workers will be regarded as having had action short of dismissal taken against them if they are punished or subject to any detriment because of their refusal to accept a contract of different terms. Detriment could take several forms, perhaps a block on promotion for those who refuse to give up the terms of a collective agreement, the withholding of discretionary benefits if the employer chooses to award such benefits to those who have accepted contracts differing from the collective agreement, or the allocation of workers who refuse to give up terms of

collective agreement to less favourable duties or locations. (Hansard HC Standing Committee E, 18 March 1999)

This comment was made, however, in rather confused circumstances. The Minister preceded the answer by agreeing with concerns expressed by Conservative Members that the provisions should not be introduced by secondary legislation. He announced the Government's intention to change this. He went on: 'I hope Conservative Members will welcome the Government's intention to table substantive provisions to replace the power in clause 16 [now s. 17] on Report.'

At this relatively late stage in the passage of the Bill, therefore (only three months before the Bill received Royal Assent), the Government had firm plans to replace the power to introduce regulations under what became s. 17 by a specific substantive provision in the 1999 Act. For whatever reason, most probably lack of time, it did not happen. It is therefore unclear whether the Government's expressed intentions in respect of the proposed primary legislation will be unchanged within the context of new regulations. If future regulations mirror the expressed intention of the Minister, it would appear that concerns surrounding the second limb of the House of Lords decision might be unfounded. But are the Government free to introduce regulations to outlaw 'any detriment', as the Minister suggested?

The Government accepted a Conservative amendment in the House of Lords to what became s. 17, moved by Baroness Miller of Hendon. This was accepted, in all probability, due to the lack of time to introduce the anticipated substantive provisions. The amendment became s. 17(4) of the 1999 Act and reads:

(4)   The payment of higher wages or higher rates of pay or overtime or the payment of any signing on or other bonuses or the provision of other benefits having a monetary value to other workers employed by the same employer shall not constitute a detriment to any worker not receiving the same or similar payments or benefits within the meaning of subsection (1)(a) of this section so long as—
(a)   there is no inhibition in the contract of employment of the worker receiving the same from being the member of any trade union, and
(b)   the said payments of higher wages or rates of pay or overtime or bonuses or the provision of other benefits are in accordance with the terms of a contract of employment and reasonably relate to services provided by the worker under that contract.

Baroness Miller made it clear in moving the amendment that its intention was to allow employers and workers to agree changes in the *monetary* terms of contracts without them being classed as an unlawful detriment. This, she stated, was in line with the Government's intentions expressed in para. 4.20 and Annex 1, para. viii of the *Fairness at Work* White Paper. She did not mention, however, that these comments in the White Paper were made in the context of the statutory recognition proposals and not protection from discrimination against trade unionists.

Baroness Miller explained that her amendment was limited to improvements in financial benefits:

> It does not permit an employer to refuse to promote the dissenting worker ... it does not permit the employer to give to the dissenting employee all the worst tasks or worse places of work ... It does not permit the employer to harass or wrongly dismiss the dissenting worker. (HL Debs, 16 June 1999, col. 357)

While this might be correct, the wording of the section is not restricted to, 'extra money, and just money' as Baroness Miller submitted. The wording of s. 17(4) also includes 'other benefits having a monetary value'. Not only would this allow different rates of pay between those on individual contracts and those covered by the terms of a collective agreement, but it would seem also to apply similarly to fringe benefits such as pensions, medical insurance, or even preferential parking spaces.

Such differences in pay and benefits would not constitute a detriment subject to two conditions. First, the individual contract must not prohibit union membership; and, secondly, the additional payments must be by contractual right (not being, that is, in the discretionary power of the employer) and 'reasonably relate' to the services provided by the worker.

The application of this latter element is unclear, although it might prevent some benefits being used as 'douceurs', or sweeteners, subject to a reasonableness test (on this see the latest developments in *Haddon* v *Van Den Burgh Foods Ltd* [1999] IRLR 672, *Foley* v *Post Office* (2000) IRLR 827 and *Midland Bank* v *Madden* [2000] IRLR 288, at 7.3.3 below). If it is interpreted as a condition that an employer must be able to show a reasonable performance-related reason for an additional benefit to a worker over and above the terms applicable under a collective agreement, it might prove to be an important restriction on widespread *Wilson* and *Palmer* type tactics. One might envisage an employer having to show why each individual worker was paid more to transfer to an individual contract relative to those remaining on collectively agreed terms. What added value can the employer show in terms of the 'services provided by the worker'? If the added value is minimal or disproportionate, the exception may not apply and a potentially unlawful detriment may be held to have taken place. No doubt flexibility will be the main return expected by an employer, as in the *Palmer* case. If all else failed, an employer could then presumably fall back onto the TULR(C)A 1992, s. 148(3) defence of purpose, though this too is subject to the reasonableness test.

Until the new regulations are introduced, the second limb of the House of Lords' decision in *Wilson* and *Palmer* will continue to have significant impact in all circumstances of differential treatment where the purpose of the employer is to change his relationship with his employees rather than punish or deter union membership. Also, having essentially the same effect, s. 148(3) remains in force (discussed at 7.3.3 below).

Even if the Government introduces new regulations under s. 17, the effect of s. 17(4) will provide an exception to the general principle that discrimination in wages and benefits between those covered by a collective agreement and those who accept personal contracts will be an unlawful detriment. The new regulations will also have to take into account the contents of s. 148(3), TULR(C)A 1992.

Having examined this legislative background, it is interesting to consider how the outcome of the *Wilson* and *Palmer* scenarios might now differ under the amended s. 146 of TULR(C)A, assuming that the new regulations are implemented as explained above. First, the failure to pay the extra financial benefits to those remaining within collective bargaining would now be a 'deliberate failure to act' within s. 146(1) of the 1992 Act. The fact that it is an omission is irrelevant. However, as the discrimination in both cases relates to pay, the new regulations would presumably prevent the employers' deliberate failure being a detriment subject to the reasonableness test in s. 17(4)(b) of the 1999 Act. If that was not enough, s. 148(3) of the 1992 Act would also favour the employers, again subject to the reasonableness test. It seems likely, therefore, that employers could continue to utilise the tactics employed in *Wilson* and *Palmer* even after the Government's proposed legislative changes are complete.

7.3.3   Section 148(3)

It bears repeating that the Government have left s. 148(3) of the 1992 Act intact (though amended to cover omissions) despite the many calls for its repeal made to Government during the consultation process following the publication of the White Paper. The Government's rationale for this is difficult to fathom. Regulations under s. 17 of the 1999 Act would seem, from the comments of Ministers, to be designed to cover at least some of the same ground — intended to make some employer behaviour an unlawful detriment apparently irrespective of s. 148(3). If this is not the intention, s. 148(3) of the 1992 Act will surely frustrate any attempted re-balancing of the equation. What better way to approach this problem than with a blank canvas rather than the impediment of an existing and strongly employer-orientated provision?

In moving an amendment to the Bill in the House of Lords to repeal s. 148(3), Lord Wedderburn stated his suspicion that the Government wanted to retain the provision because of its reference to 'reasonable employers'. As explained at 7.2.5 above, the section favours employers unless (as amended), '[the tribunal] considers that no reasonable employer would act or fail to act in the way concerned'.

Lord McIntosh replied to the amendment on behalf of the Government. He drew a clear distinction between the right to belong to a trade union and rights to collective bargaining. The contents of Schedule 2 of the new Act did not relate 'to any entitlement for an individual to have his or her terms determined by a collective agreement'. Such rights were provided elsewhere in the new legislation and s. 148(3) must now be seen in this context. He concluded:

> The Government have looked very carefully at section 148(3) and have concluded that it serves a useful purpose in this new context and ought to be retained ... Repeal would raise doubts as to the intended purpose and effect of changing the law. We wish to avoid any such confusion. (HL Debs, 7 June 1999, col. 1287)

Lastly, Lord McIntosh made clear that if employers attempted to put pressure on employees to accept individual contracts in place of collectively agreed terms, the situation would be adequately dealt with by regulation under s. 17 of the 1999 Act.

In attempting to persuade the Government to dispense with s. 148(3), Lord Wedderburn expressed great concern that the reasonable employer test was an inadequate countermeasure against the overall balance of the provision. This was particularly true in view of the 'reasonable response' formula (stemming from *Iceland Frozen Foods* v *Jones* [1982] IRLR 439, EAT) that had been shown 'to get rid of any substantive notion of reasonableness'.

Since Lord Wedderburn's comments, it is worth noting that the 'reasonable responses' test has been questioned by the decisions of the EAT in *Haddon* v *Van den Burgh Foods Ltd* and *Midland Bank* v *Madden*. In a distinct move away from the previous test, and in apparent full sympathy with the criticisms levelled at it by Lord Wedderburn, the then President of the EAT, Morison J, in *Haddon* moved the balance of fairness significantly back in favour of the employee, following his judgment '. . . that a combination of the judicial embellishment upon the statute has led tribunals to adopt a perversity test of reasonableness and to depress the chances of success for the applicant' (para. 28). However, the new President of the EAT, Lindsay J, in *Madden* did not fully support the approach taken by his predecessor. The *Madden* decision recently reached the Court of Appeal which firmly quashed the approach promoted by Morison J in *Haddon* and reinstated the original long-standing test (see *Foley* v *Post Office* and *HSBC Bank plc* v *Madden* [2000] IRLR 827).

If the Government intended to simplify the law and to make the activities of employers like Associated British Ports and Associated Newspapers unlawful as discriminatory against trade unionists, they have not yet succeeded. Even in light of the amendments in Schedule 2 of the 1999 Act and the anticipated regulations under s. 17, employers still seem more able than not to succeed in doing exactly what they did against the employees in the *Wilson* and *Palmer* cases if they tread carefully with an eye on the reasonableness of their actions.

7.4   ACTION SHORT OF DISMISSAL AND STATUTORY RECOGNITION

The likelihood that employers will still be able to discriminate against trade unionists will be a worry for trade unions with long-standing voluntary agreements or hoping to use the much-publicised statutory recognition procedures. An employer is likely to succeed in offering personal contracts with a financial inducement to employees to opt out of collectively agreed terms. The employer might even continue to recognise the unions for the remaining employees, much as happened in the *Palmer* case. If recognition is terminated, the unions might apply for statutory recognition utilising the Schedule 1 procedures. If vigorously contested by the employer, this could take some considerable time, leaving union membership to 'wither on the vine' in the meantime.

If the unions have 50 per cent or less in membership (or otherwise face a ballot at the discretion of the CAC: see Schedule 1, para. 22), they will face the arduous, if not impossible, task of seeking positive support in a ballot from at least 40 per cent of employees in the whole bargaining unit. Many of the employees will have recently agreed possibly more lucrative personal contracts and may be apathetic at best on the issue of recognition.

Neither would there seem any reason why an employer who recognises a trade union voluntarily following a formal application under Schedule 1, or who is forced to recognise by decision of the CAC, could not apply the same tactic to diminish the effectiveness of collective bargaining. Even though such an employer is ultimately unable to derecognise the union for a period of three years, he could still attempt to undermine union effectiveness and influence by removing employees from the collective arena in the hope, perhaps, that membership numbers might decline, leading eventually to derecognition.

The Government's failure to seize the opportunity and fully protect collective rights following the House of Lords' decision in *Wilson* and *Palmer* could yet prove to be a central weapon in the armoury of employers attempting to defeat, or at least circumvent, the intended effect of the flagship statutory recognition provisions.

Chapter 8
Blacklisting of Trade Union Members

8.1   INTRODUCTION

The blacklisting of trade union members and activists came to the fore in the 1980s and early 1990s. One organisation in particular, The Economic League, established a database of union and political activists which could be accessed (for a fee) by employers who wished to cross-check the list against new job applicants. The information was held on a manual paper filing system so as to avoid the Data Protection Act 1984 which applied only to data kept on computer files. Because the files could not be checked for accuracy by those whose names appeared, it was alleged that many individuals were identified erroneously (particularly those with common names), or were the subject of inaccurate recording of their union and political affiliations. Hundreds of workers are alleged to have suffered significant damage through lost employment prospects for many years as a result of the lists held by The Economic League and other similar organisations.

The Economic League ceased to exist in 1993, following a press campaign led by the *Guardian*. It would appear, however, that the files were simply transferred to another organisation that carried on the business, still avoiding the protections available to individuals under the Data Protection Act 1984 by utilising paper rather than computer files.

The Government gave a commitment in *Fairness at Work* to prohibit the formation and use of such lists used to discriminate against trade union members. In the Explanatory Notes to the 1999 Act, it was stated:

In the past, organisations have compiled and disseminated blacklists of supposed trade union activists. People on such lists could have difficulty finding work. Inclusion could be defamatory and unjustified but it would often be impossible in practice to obtain a remedy. Although there is no evidence that blacklisting is widespread, the practice of blacklisting in the UK has been repeatedly criticised by the International Labour Organisation and in *Fairness at Work* the Government propose to prohibit blacklisting of trade union members.

It is true to say that the Government could have waited for the full implementation of the Data Protection Act 1998, which originated from the EC Data Protection Directive 95/46/EC. The 1998 Act requires those holding data on individuals to be more pro-active in disclosing personal data and to allow access by those on whom the information is kept. Importantly, it includes within its coverage manual files. Despite the fact that trade union related blacklists would in practice almost certainly fall foul of the 1998 Act (see Schedule 1), the Act has one major flaw as far as the Government are concerned. It will not offer total protection until it is fully implemented in 2007. The Government therefore decided to push ahead and provide the means to introduce protective measures within the 1999 Act.

In its passage though the Parliamentary process, the provision had its share of critics from the opposition benches. It was criticised by Opposition Front Bench Spokesman Tim Boswell MP as, 'paying homage to an item of labour history, or even labour demonology, rather than something that could happen now'. His colleague John Bercow MP referred to it as 'abhorrent' that employers should be prevented from keeping lists of those who have caused 'damaging strikes' (Hansard HC Standing Committee E, 18 March 1999).

The Minister for Small Firms, Trade and Industry, Michael Wills MP, replied on behalf of the Government:

> In addressing the clause, it is important to remember why it is included in the Bill. It is designed to address a pernicious and iniquitous practice . . . We all know about the instances in the past where organisations compiled and distributed information to employers to encourage discrimination against trade unionists. Those blacklists were sometimes sold, for commercial reasons and sometimes circulated free of charge for ideological motives. It did not take much for workers to appear on just blacklists; they were often included for nothing more than being a shop steward or for having sought to recruit other workers. People who were placed on such lists experienced genuine difficulties and spent years out of work as a result of discrimination. (Hansard HC Standing Committee E, 18 March 1999)

8.2 THE BLACKLISTING PROVISIONS

Section 3 of the 1999 Act was introduced to address the concerns noted above. The full text reads as follows:

(1)   The Secretary of State may make regulations prohibiting the compilation of lists which—

(a)   contain details of members of trade unions or persons who have taken part in the activities of trade unions, and

(b)   are compiled with a view to being used by employers or employment agencies for the purposes of discrimination in relation to recruitment or in relation to the treatment of workers.

(2)   The Secretary of State may make regulations prohibiting—

(a)   the use of lists to which subsection (1) applies;

(b)   the sale or supply of lists to which subsection (1) applies.

(3)   Regulations under this section may, in particular—

(a)   confer jurisdiction (including exclusive jurisdiction) on employment tribunals and on the Employment Appeal Tribunal;

(b)   include provision for or about the grant and enforcement of specified remedies by courts and tribunals;

(c)   include provision for the making of awards of compensation calculated in accordance with the regulations;

(d)   include provision permitting proceedings to be brought by trade unions on behalf of members in specified circumstances;

(e)   include provision about cases where an employee is dismissed by his employer and the reason or principal reason for the dismissal, or why the employee was selected for dismissal, relates to a list to which subsection (1) applies;

(f)   create criminal offences;

(g)   in specified cases or circumstances, extend liability for a criminal offence created under paragraph (f) to a person who aids the commission of the offence or to a person who is an agent, principal, employee, employer or officer of a person who commits the offence;

(h)   provide for specified obligations or offences not to apply in specified circumstances;

(i)   include supplemental, incidental, consequential and transitional provision, including provision amending an enactment;

(j)   make different provision for different cases or circumstances.

(4)   Regulations under this section creating an offence may not provide for it to be punishable—

(a)   by imprisonment,

(b)   by a fine in excess of level 5 on the standard scale in the case of an offence triable only summarily, or

(c)   by a fine in excess of the statutory maximum in the case of summary conviction for an offence triable either way.

(5)   In this section—

'list' includes any index or other set of items whether recorded electronically or by any other means, and

'worker' has the meaning given by section 13.

(6)   Subject to subsection (5), expressions used in this section and in the Trade Union and Labour Relations (Consolidation) Act 1992 have the same meaning in this section as in that Act.

Clearly, s. 3 does not of itself prohibit blacklisting. It provides that the Secretary of State may introduce regulations to prohibit the use, sale or supply of such lists by affirmative resolution under s. 42. The Government have stated that they intend to consult widely on the text of draft regulations in 2001, and only then will the detailed information be available as to the scope and effect of the prohibition.

At present it would seem that such regulations will provide a general right for individuals (and/or their trade unions) to complain to an employment tribunal against both the users and compilers of blacklists if they are the victims of discrimination by blacklisting. The new regulations are also likely to introduce criminal sanctions against those compiling blacklists and, by association, against those who supply or use the lists thereafter. Punishment for such a conviction, however, will fall short of imprisonment, the maximum fine being £5,000.

While we wait for the regulations, it might be worth noting a significant omission from the section (and indeed the whole Act) that leaves a parallel area of trade union discrimination untouched — the informal process of discrimination against trade union members at the recruitment stage. Under s. 137 of the TULR(C)A 1992, individuals are protected from discrimination when seeking employment by reason of their trade union *membership*. The section is differently worded from ss. 146 and 152, which provide protection from action short of dismissal and dismissal respectively (on dismissal for previous trade union activities, see *Birmingham City District Council* v *Beyer* [1977] IRLR 211 and *Fitzpatrick* v *British Railways Board* [1991] IRLR 376). Both these sections specifically provide protection against discrimination for union activities for those dismissed when their previous trade union *activities* are discovered. Section 137 does not offer that same protection for those refused employment. Because of this weakness in s. 137, no clear protection is available for a worker if an employer refuses employment by reason of previous trade union activities while having no particular objection to union membership *per se*.

The only decision stating that such protection might be available within s. 137 is *Harrison* v *Kent County Council* [1995] ICR 434, EAT. At the same time as the EAT was making this decision, however, the House of Lords in *Associated Newspapers Ltd* v *Wilson*; *Associated British Ports* v *Palmer* [1995] IRLR 258 were casting doubt on the general approach taken in *Harrison* that issues of union membership were inseparable from the union activities stemming from that membership. For more on this distinction between union membership and activities, see Chapter 7 on discrimination against trade union members and, more specifically, the *obiter* comments of the House of Lords in *Wilson* and *Palmer* at 7.2.6.

Chapter 9
Industrial Action Ballots

9.1   INTRODUCTION

The law on industrial action ballots is governed by ss. 226 to 235 of the TULR(C)A 1992. The provisions are complex and it is beyond the scope of this book to cover them in detail. However, important changes have been made to the provisions by the 1999 Act and these will be considered in this chapter. They stem from the Government's consultation exercise in which responses and suggestions were requested to the proposals and ideas expressed in the White Paper *Fairness at Work*. A number of responses were received by the Department of Trade and Industry suggesting changes to the law on industrial action ballots, mostly from trade unions. Section 4 of the 1999 Act gives effect to Schedule 3, which introduces some significant amendments to the original balloting legislation. The amendments in Schedule 3 took effect from 18 September 2000.

It should also be noted that the 1995 Code of Practice on Industrial Action Ballots and Notice to Employers was revised and brought into effect also on 18 September 2000. The new Code takes into account all of the amendments made by the 1999 Act. It was introduced under the powers available to the Secretary of State in s. 203 of the 1992 Act to.

> ... issue Codes of Practice containing such practical guidance as he thinks fit for the purpose—
>
> (a)   of promoting the improvement of industrial relations, or
>
> (b)   of promoting what appear to him to be desirable practices in relation to the conduct by trade unions of ballots and elections.

9.2   ADVANCE NOTICE OF THE BALLOT AND INDUSTRIAL ACTION

Section 226A of TULR(C)A 1992 requires a trade union to take such steps as are 'reasonably necessary' to communicate certain information to each employer of union members to be balloted, in advance of the ballot taking place. Section 226A(1)(a) requires a notice to be sent by the union to each employer which must comply with s. 226A(2). The notice must be received not later than seven days before the ballot is due to commence, must specify the commencement date of the ballot and describe the employees who it is reasonable for the union to believe will be balloted so that the employer can readily identify them. This latter obligation on a union has now been much reduced as explored below.

After the ballot and before industrial action is commenced, Section 234A requires a trade union to give seven days' notice of the industrial action, and obliges the union to describe the members who are to be asked to take part in the action. This notice must also state whether the action is to be continuous (and if so when it is to start) or discontinuous (giving the intended dates of any action).

It is the requirement that unions identify their members in these provisions that has caused some concern and prompted amendments by the 1999 Act. The changes stem from the decision of the Court of Appeal in *Blackpool and Fylde College* v *NATFHE* [1994] IRLR 227, CA. In this case, the union sent the principal of the college a notice, on 14 January 1994, which the union believed to be in compliance with s. 226A. It advised the employer that the union was to 'hold a ballot of all our members in your institution'. Following the ballot, on 10 February, the union again wrote to the principal advising him that it had instructed 'all its members employed by your institution to take part in discontinuous industrial action. The first intended date of this industrial action, which will be on this occasion strike action, is 1 March 1994'. The second notice was sent to comply with s. 234A.

The college sought an injunction against the union arguing that neither notice complied with the relevant provisions. They did not enable the college sufficiently to identify its employees to be balloted or to be called to take action. The union argued that acceptance of the employer's arguments would require them to name their members. On 24 February 1994, Morison J in the High Court granted the injunction restraining the union from holding its first planned action on 1 March. The union appealed to the Court of Appeal.

The Court of Appeal held that the notices sent by the union did not satisfy the requirements in ss. 226A and 234A of the 1992 Act as they had not described the employees sufficiently so as to allow the employer to 'readily ascertain them'. As such, the action did not enjoy the immunity from civil action available to trade unions under s. 219. The union must be able to pinpoint an easily identifiable group of employees, perhaps by department, or it must name individuals. Alternatively, a combination of the two might be sufficient. It was a question of fact in each particular case as to whether a statutory notice provided the necessary information.

The Government received many representations in the consultation process from trade unions stating that they should not be required to provide members' details to the employer in any circumstances concerning industrial action. The Government agreed, and Schedule 3, para. 3 of the 1999 Act amends s. 226A of the 1992 Act, while para. 11 amends s. 234A. The amendments remove reference to the union's obligation to identify those to be balloted so that the employer might 'readily ascertain them'. Sections 226A(2)(c) and 234A(3)(a) are completely re-written. Section 226A(2)(c) now obliges a union to identify its members only to the extent of a notice:

(c)   containing such information in the union's possession as would help the employer to make plans and bring information to the attention of those of his employees who it is reasonable for the union to believe (at the time when the steps to comply with that paragraph are taken) will be entitled to vote in the ballot.

Moreover, for the further avoidance of doubt, new ss. 226A(3A) and 234A(5A) are included which are similarly worded. Section 226(3A) states:

(3A)   These rules apply for the purposes of paragraph (c) of subsection (2)—
(a)   if the union possesses information as to the number, category or work-place of the employees concerned, a notice must contain that information (at least);
(b)   if a notice does not name any employees, that fact shall not be a ground for holding that it does not comply with paragraph (c) of subsection (2)

The latter point in para. (b) removes the possibility of an employer arguing that members' names must be provided for the ballot to be conducted lawfully. The same amendment is made to s. 234A by the introduction of a new s. 234A(5A) by Schedule 3, para. 11 of the 1999 Act.

9.3   PROVIDING A SAMPLE VOTING PAPER TO EACH EMPLOYER

Prior to amendment by the 1999 Act, s. 226A(1) of TULR(C)A 1992 required a trade union to send a sample ballot paper to each employer of its members who it was reasonable for the union to believe would be entitled to vote in the ballot. The sample ballot paper must have been received by each employer no later than three days before the first ballot paper was sent out. Where several employers were involved, and there were different forms of ballot paper for each employer, s. 226A(3) required the union to send a sample of each of the ballot papers to all of the employers. If one sample ballot paper was omitted from this, the ballot would not have been carried out in accordance with the statute and immunity would be lost for the whole action.

The Government have amended section s. 226A to remove this effect. The 1999 Act, Schedule 3, para. 3(3) inserts a new s. 226A(3B) into TULR(C)A 1992. This provides that a sample ballot paper need only be sent to an employer in respect of that employer's own employees. The union need no longer send samples relating to the employees of other employers. If a union omits to send one employer from several a sample ballot paper relating to that employer's employees, any action against that employer will be unlawful (without a re-ballot). The action against the other employers, however, will now remain lawful.

9.4   ENTITLEMENT TO VOTE AND INDUCING MEMBERS TO TAKE ACTION

Section 227(1) of TULR(C)A 1992 requires a trade union to afford equal entitlement to vote to each of its members who it is reasonable for the union to believe at the time of the ballot is to be asked to take part in the action. No other members are entitled to vote. Before it was repealed by the 1999 Act, s. 227(2) provided that the support of the ballot was removed if any person who was a member of the union when the ballot was held was denied the entitlement to vote and was then later induced to take part in the action (for the difference between denying entitlement to vote and inadvertently failing to allow someone to vote, see *British Railways Board* v *National Union of Railwaymen* [1989] IRLR 349, CA, and reference to the new s. 232B below at 9.9).

The effect of the now repealed s. 227(2) was that unions could not ask members to take part in the action if they had not taken part in the ballot even though they were members at the time. This might happen, for example, where employees had changed jobs, being moved into the balloted group after the ballot had taken place. If the union involved them in the action, they risked losing immunity for the whole dispute. The unions were, however, free to ask new members to take part in the action where they joined the union after the ballot (see *London Underground Ltd* v *National Union of Rail Maritime and Transport Workers* [1995] IRLR 636, CA).

The Government seized the opportunity to introduce some logical order into this rather confusing legislative mire. Section 227(2) was repealed by Schedule 3, para. 4 to the 1999 Act, and its amended equivalent moved to s. 232A. This new section adds an extra limb to the effect of the old s. 227(2) by stating that it must have been reasonable at the time of the ballot for the union to believe that the member would have been asked to participate in the action, if the immunity is to be lost for inducing that member to take part. Its new position in the 1992 Act also places it more logically adjacent to another new section, s. 232B, which deals with minor and accidental failures in ballot procedure, which is dealt with at 9.9 below.

The new s. 232A, therefore, removes the protection of a ballot for industrial action if:

(a)   the individual concerned was a member at the time of the ballot;

(b)   it was reasonable at that time for the union to believe that the member would be induced to take part (or continue to take part) in the action;

(c)   the member was not accorded the entitlement to vote; and

(d)   the member was then induced to take part in the subsequent action.

9.5   SEPARATE WORKPLACE BALLOTS

Before its recent repeal and replacement by the 1999 Act, s. 228 of TULR(C)A 1992 defined the circumstances in which a trade union (or several unions) could hold an aggregate industrial action ballot in a dispute involving several workplaces. Section 228(1) began by laying down the general rule that a separate ballot must be held for each workplace. Lawful industrial action could then only take place in each workplace where a majority of that workplace had voted in favour of action. This was designed to prevent a majority of more militant workplaces outvoting those employees at smaller workplaces who might be opposed to the dispute in an aggregate ballot. The 'workplace' in this context meant the premises occupied by the employer at which the employees worked or their work had the closest connection (s. 228(4)). This definition caused considerable confusion, as shown in *InterCity West Coast Ltd v National Union of Rail Maritime and Transport Workers* [1996] IRLR 583, CA.

Two exceptions to the general rule were allowed under s. 228. The first was of limited relevance and applied if the union could show that it reasonably believed at the time of the ballot that the members balloted had the same workplace. The second exception was more important, though complex in application.

The second exception allowed aggregate ballots where the union had a reasonable belief at the time of the ballot that the conditions in s. 228(3) were satisfied. In short, these were that a common factor (or factors) existed between all those to be balloted, such as an occupational description or grade of employee, and that the factor was shared by the relevant groups of employees balloted. For instance, the ballot might have involved all skilled tradesmen working under the terms of a national agreement involving many workplaces and a variety of employers.

Where a union did not intend to ballot all the members sharing a common factor who worked for a particular employer, matters were made more complex by s. 228(3)(c). Within an aggregate ballot, a union was not entitled to ballot an artificial constituency of less than the total number of members with a central factor in common. In other words, if the common factor relied upon to hold an aggregate ballot was that it concerned electricians then *all* electricians employed by that employer had to be balloted. Otherwise, the ballots had to be held on a workplace by workplace basis.

Lastly, a union was not allowed to ballot members in a workplace (or, more likely, a number of workplaces) if the *only* common factor relied upon was the workplace itself. Just to add a little more spice to the difficulties facing trade unions attempting to negotiate this legal minefield, if members working overseas were involved, separate provisions applied as to whether they should be included in the ballot or not via s. 232(1).

It was perhaps not surprising that trade unions and other interested bodies lobbied Government heavily to add clarity to this confusing and potentially very costly situation. Despite this lobbying, the Government accepted the challenge only at the last minute in the passage of the Bill, introducing an amendment at the Third Reading in the House of Lords. Section 228 was replaced with new ss. 228 and 228A.

Schedule 3, para. 5 to the 1999 Act introduces the new s. 228. Section 228(3) requires that separate workplace ballots should be held unless certain conditions are satisfied, as outlined in s. 228A below. As before, the difficulties of this section are avoided if the union can show that it reasonably believes that all the members balloted have the same workplace (s. 228(2)). Section 228(4) changes the definition of the 'workplace'. It is now described as the premises from which the employee works or with which the employee has the closest connection. Whether the employer actually occupies the premises is now irrelevant. It is hoped that this will avoid some of the problems evident in *InterCity West Coast Ltd v National Union of Rail Maritime and Transport Workers* (above).

The first route by which a trade union may hold an aggregate ballot across two or more workplaces is provided by s. 228A(2). It states:

> (2)   This subsection is satisfied in relation to a ballot if the workplace of each member entitled to vote in the ballot is the workplace of at least one member of the union who is affected by the dispute.

Members of the union 'affected by the dispute' are described in s. 228A(5). If the dispute relates (wholly or partly) to a decision that the union believes the employer has made or will make concerning general terms and conditions of employment, the engagement or termination of employment of one or more workers or the allocation of work between workers, the members affected will be those whom the decision directly affects. If it concerns a matter of discipline, those affected will be those whom the matter directly affects. If the dispute relates to membership or non-membership of a trade union, those affected will be those whose membership or non-membership is in dispute. And lastly, if the dispute concerns facilities for trade union officials, the members affected will be those officials of the union who have used or would use the facilities. These dispute issues are drawn from s. 244(1)(a)–(f) of TULR(C)A 1992 which describe the various issues over which there can be a legitimate trade dispute.

The union is therefore free to hold an aggregate ballot of all its members employed in all workplaces in which there is at least one member affected as described above depending on the subject matter of the dispute. This allows a trade union to hold an aggregate ballot of members within a select few workplaces from many operated by a particular employer, provided at least one affected member works at each workplace where members are to be balloted.

This opens up the possibility that unions will be free to carry out aggregate ballots of selective groups of workplaces for tactical reasons that would not have been allowed previously. Suppose an employer has four plants in different parts of the country — A, B, C and D. A trade union enjoys recognition rights within the company as a whole and enters a dispute concerning national pay rates. Its officers know that its members at plant A are heavily in favour of strike action and its members at plant D are heavily against. Members' views in plants B and C are evenly balanced. The union believes that a strike at A, B and C would effectively close D too. It therefore decides to hold a strike ballot entitling its members only at plants A, B and C to vote in accordance with s. 227. The members at plant D can be omitted as the union has no intention of inducing them to take part and they are therefore not entitled to vote. This could provide a mandate for strike action which would not have been possible under the old s. 228. Section 228(3)(c)(i) would have prevented it, and the union would have had to carry out separate workplace ballots or ballot all four plants together.

The next new option available to a union, or group of unions, enabling an aggregate ballot to be held is governed by s. 228A(3). This allows a union to ballot all members in a particular occupational category (or categories) employed by one or more employer with whom the union is in dispute. This is determined by the reasonable belief of the union (or unions) that its members are in the same occupational group.

Lastly, s. 228A(4) allows a union (or unions) to hold an aggregate ballot if *all* members of the union (or unions) employed by all the employers with whom the union is in dispute are to be balloted.

9.6   OVERTIME AND CALL-OUT BANS

In accordance with s. 229(2) of TULR(C)A 1992, each industrial action ballot paper must contain one or both of two questions asking whether the union member is prepared to take part in a 'strike' or in 'industrial action short of a strike'. This might seem straightforward enough. However, in the case of *Connex South Eastern Ltd* v *National Union of Rail Maritime and Transport Workers* [1999] IRLR 249, CA, the issue became somewhat confused.

The RMT union decided to call a ban on overtime and rest-day working by its members as part of a dispute over booking-on allowances for rest-day working. The union balloted only on the question of strike action and the members voted in favour. The union informed the employer of its intention to implement a ban on overtime and rest-day working from 14 to 19 December 1998. The company applied for an injunction restraining the union from calling the action. They argued that the union's proposed action was action short of a strike and not the strike action on which the union had balloted. As the union had not balloted on action short of a strike, the company argued that the proposed action was unlawful.

The company's application was rejected. In the High Court, Popplewell J found that the proposed action was a 'concerted stoppage of work' and therefore fell within the definition of a strike in s. 246 of the 1992 Act that utilised that phrase. The company appealed to the Court of Appeal. Because of the urgency of the matter, the appeal was heard later that same day.

The Court of Appeal dismissed the employer's appeal. The ban on overtime and rest-day working meant that the employees did not work in the periods when they would otherwise have worked, and these were stoppages of work and strike action as defined in s. 246.

Despite the success for the union, the decision was something of a double-edged sword. It is usually much easier for a union to obtain a ballot mandate in response to the 'action short of strike' question. Now, in the *Connex* decision, the Court of Appeal had confirmed that a *strike* mandate had to be obtained before bans on overtime and rest-day working could be implemented. While the RMT union could hardly complain that its own arguments had been accepted, other unions did and the Government decided that the law required clarification. Schedule 3, para. 6(2) to the 1999 Act amended s. 229 of TULR(C)A 1992 by adding a new s. 229(2A). This states:

> (2A)   For the purposes of subsection (2) an overtime ban and call-out ban constitute industrial action short of a strike.

The amendment reverses the decision of the Court of Appeal on the subject of overtime and call-out bans. Rather surprisingly, however, no mention is made of bans on rest-day working in the new subsection. In line with the decision of the Court of Appeal, it would seem that bans on rest-day working remain strike action and require a strike ballot mandate. But this is likely to be confusing. In most industrial contexts, weekend working, for instance, is considered to be overtime but is also rest-day working.

One possible argument available to a union that wishes to include weekend rest-day working within a ban on overtime is to show that both the employer and the employees accept overtime as defined in this way in their normal working practices. Thus, it would be included as 'overtime' within s. 229(2A). By this argument, it might be possible to distinguish the *Connex* case in which there was an accepted and clear difference between overtime and rest-day working, the former applying only to the extension of the working day. On the other hand, following the Court of Appeal's clear decision and comments, the Government had an opportunity to include rest-day working within the new s. 229(2A) but chose not to do so.

9.7 STATEMENTS ON THE VOTING PAPER

Industrial relations and employment law practitioners will be familiar with the statutory content of industrial action ballot papers as dictated by s. 229 of TULR(C)A 1992. Before amendment, s. 229(4) required a standard statement to appear on every ballot paper. It provided:

> (4)   The following statement must (without being qualified or commented upon by anything else on the voting paper) appear on every voting paper—
> 'If you take part in a strike or other industrial action, you may be in breach of your contract of employment.'

The Conservative Government were accused at the time of attempting to influence voting union members by the inclusion of this statement. It was argued that the provision was designed to make them fear for their jobs if they voted for industrial action. It is indeed difficult to think of any other reason for its inclusion. After all, the statement merely described the legal position that had always existed when industrial action was taken.

The Labour Government decided not to repeal the provision, but rather to update it and, in so doing, inform voters of the new protections from dismissal available to those taking lawful industrial action under s. 16 of and Schedule 5 to the 1999 Act. Schedule 5 introduces a new s. 238A to TULR(C)A 1992. It is designed to declare automatically unfair any dismissal of an employee taking lawful industrial action in the first eight weeks of the action (or longer in certain circumstances) if the principal reason for the dismissal is the fact that the employee took that industrial action. The provision is dealt with in more detail in Chapter 2.

Schedule 3, para. 6(3) to the 1999 Act amends s. 229(4) of the 1992 Act to extend the statutory statement. It now reads:

If you take part in a strike or other industrial action, you may be in breach of your contract of employment. However, if you are dismissed for taking part in strike or other industrial action which is called officially and is otherwise lawful, the dismissal will be unfair if it takes place fewer than eight weeks after you started taking part in the action, and depending on the circumstances may be unfair if it takes place later.

It is worth stressing that this new protection from dismissal applies only to *lawful* industrial action. This emphasises the importance that trade unions abide closely with the statutory requirements on industrial action ballots. If a trade union inadvertently breaches the ballot requirements and commences action, it will not enjoy statutory immunity from civil action. But, importantly, the new protection available to its members from dismissal will also be lost. This opens up the prospect of union members suing their own union in negligence should they lose their jobs following a ballot mistake where they might otherwise have been protected.

9.8   BALLOTS INVOLVING MERCHANT SEAMEN

Section 230(2A), (2B) and (2C) of TULR(C)A 1992 refer to ballots concerning merchant seamen. Section 230(2C) defines a merchant seaman as 'a person whose employment, or the greater part of it, is carried out on board sea-going ships'. It is an obvious fact that merchant seamen are often away from home for long periods, making the conduct of an industrial action ballot difficult if large numbers are not to be excluded.

Section 230(2A) allowed a trade union to ballot seamen on board ship or at the port at which the ship is docked. However, s. (2B) allowed this only where the seamen to be balloted were at sea or at a port outside Great Britain, 'throughout the period during which votes may be cast'. This caused difficulties for unions where a ship was away for just part of the balloting period. Organising a ballot required detailed research into the itineraries of all merchant vessels carrying union members.

The Government have substituted new s. 230(2A) and (2B), allowing unions to ballot members who are on board ship or in a foreign port for just *part* of the period in which votes may be cast. A union can decide to do this where 'it will be convenient' for the member to receive a ballot paper and vote in this way.

9.9   ACCIDENTAL MINOR FAILURES IN BALLOTING PROCEDURE

It was recognised by the Court of Appeal, in *British Railways Board* v *National Union of Railwaymen* [1989] IRLR 349, CA, that an industrial action ballot can be a complex affair with many thousands of members in all parts of the country and even abroad. In that case, Lord Donaldson MR noted that it would be impossible to ensure that every single member had the opportunity to vote. He went on:

Indeed, if the situation had been that the NUR claimed to produce evidence that every one of the entitled members had received a ballot paper and returned it, I think that the Court would have been justified in looking very carefully at that evidence to see whether something had not been fiddled. (para. 25)

The Court of Appeal in that case had taken careful note of the wording of s. 11(6) of the then Trade Union Act 1984 (now s. 230(2) of TULR(C)A 1992), which obliged a union to do only what was 'reasonably practicable' to ensure that every member received a ballot paper. The Court of Appeal held that immunity would not be lost should one member, or a small number of members, be accidentally omitted from a ballot.

This commonsense approach has now been confirmed in statute by a new s. 232B of the 1992 Act via Schedule 3, para. 9 to the 1999 Act. The new section provides a clear test to be adopted should the validity of a ballot be contested because a union member or several members have been omitted from the ballot in error. Section 232B provides:

(1)   If—
    (a)   in relation to a ballot there is a failure (or there are failures) to comply with a provision mentioned in subsection (2) or with more than one of those provisions, and
    (b)   the failure is accidental and on a scale which is unlikely to affect the result of the ballot or, as the case may be, the failures are accidental and taken together are on a scale which is unlikely to affect the result of the ballot, the failure (or failures) shall be disregarded.

Section 232B(2) refers to s. 227(1) (equal entitlement to vote), s. 230(2) (the right of every member to receive a ballot paper) and s. 230(2A) (voting right applicable to merchant seamen).

9.10   INFORMING THE EMPLOYER OF THE BALLOT RESULT

Section 231A of TULR(C)A 1992 requires trade unions to inform 'every relevant employer' of union members who have participated in the ballot, of the result. This should be done as soon as reasonably practicable and must include the same information as must be provided to members balloted under s. 231. This consists of the total numbers of votes cast, numbers voting 'yes', numbers voting 'no' and the numbers of spoilt papers. Section 226(2) removes the protection of the immunities if a trade union does not comply with this requirement.

Section 231A(2) defines a 'relevant employer' as anyone who it is reasonable for the union to believe at the time of the ballot was the employer of those entitled to vote. Prior to amendment by the 1999 Act, if a trade union was involved in a multi-employer ballot and failed to supply this information to just one of the employers, the union would lose its immunity from civil action in respect of all the employers and would have had to re-ballot to retrieve the situation. If the union had commenced action before realising its mistake, it would be vulnerable to costly legal action pursued by all the employers damaged. This is remedied by the addition of a new s. 226(3A) by Schedule 3, para. 2(3) to the 1999 Act. The new subsection has the effect of restricting the damage caused by the failure to the employer affected only. In other words, the protection of the ballot will be lost only in respect of the employer (or employers) who have not been informed of the result. Action against the other employers, who have been correctly informed, can continue and remain lawful.

9.11   THE BALLOT'S PERIOD OF EFFECTIVENESS

Until the provisions of the 1999 Act were implemented, s. 234(1) of TULR(C)A 1992 provided that industrial action must be commenced within four weeks of the 'date of the ballot'. Section 246 defines this as the last date on which votes may be cast. If action was not taken within this period, the protection of the ballot would lapse, as happened in *RJB Mining (UK) Ltd* v *National Union of Mineworkers* [1995] IRLR 556, CA, causing an injunction to be granted preventing the proposed action.

This restriction has led to situations where trade unions have felt compelled to take industrial action towards the end of the four-week period even though talks were continuing with the employer aimed at resolving the dispute. Provided action is started in the period, it can be recommenced (within reason) after the period has expired (see *Monsanto plc* v *Transport and General Workers Union* [1986] IRLR 406, CA). Too much of a delay, however, between the initial and subsequent actions can leave the union open to the accusation that the original ballot mandate has expired, as happened in *Post Office* v *Union of Communication Workers* [1990] IRLR 143, CA.

The Government have addressed the issue by introducing a degree of flexibility into s. 234(1) of the 1992 Act, which now reads:

(1)   Subject to the following provisions, a ballot ceases to be effective for the purposes of section 233(3)(b) in relation to industrial action by members of a trade union at the end of a period, beginning with the date of the ballot—

(a)   of four weeks, or

(b)   of such longer duration not exceeding eight weeks as is agreed between the union and the members' employer.

Section 234(1)(b) is obviously the operative change to the effect of the subsection. While it clearly reduces the need for the union to take action as a precautionary measure within the previously inflexible four-week period, it also makes clear that agreement must be reached separately with each employer within a multi-employer dispute. If one employer agrees to extend and another does not, the extension will apply only in respect of the former employer.

9.12   SUSPENSION OF INDUSTRIAL ACTION

As was seen at 9.2 above, s. 234A of TULR(C)A 1992 obliges a trade union to send to the employer a formal notice of the union's intention to call upon some or all of its members to take industrial action following a ballot. The notice must be received by the employer at least seven days before the action starts, and must also state whether the action is to be continuous or discontinuous.

Before the implementation of the 1999 Act, s. 234A(7) provided that a new notice had to be provided where the union suspended industrial action (perhaps to discuss possible settlement terms) and then later re-commenced action. The Government noted that this had the effect of deterring unions from suspending action, pending the outcome of talks with the employer, for fear that the impetus of the dispute might be lost in the period, requiring another notice to be served. The Government have therefore introduced a new s. 234A(7B) by way of para. 11(5) of Schedule 3 to the new Act. This provides for the union and the employer to agree, before action is suspended, for action to cease and re-commence at a later date without a new notice being issued by the union.

A further deficiency of s. 234A(7) involved its effect on industrial action suspended in order for a union to comply with a court order, which was later re-commenced when the order was lifted. If the industrial action was interrupted by legal action, such as an injunction obtained by the employer, s. 234A(7) hinted that a new notice need not be provided if the injunction was lifted and action re-commenced. The Government decided that a greater degree of certainty was required and introduced a new s. 234A(7A). This now states quite clearly that a new notice need not be provided to the employer on the re-commencement of industrial action temporarily suspended in order to comply with a court order.

Chapter 10
Trade Union Recognition I

10.1   INTRODUCTION

Statutory union recognition in the UK has had a brief and colourful history, and it is not unlikely that further industrial *causes célèbres* will be forged around this issue in the early years of this century. What is certain is that the 172 paragraphs of Schedule 1 to the Employment Relations Act 1999 (inserted into TULR(C)A 1992 as Schedule A1 and enforceable from 6 June 2000) will prove fertile ground for legal battles in the coming years.

The following two chapters will examine the provisions of Schedule A1 in detail, explaining how the procedure is intended to operate and analysing the problems of interpretation and application that may be encountered. The analysis will follow a chronological approach, with this chapter dealing with the context and claims for recognition, and Chapter 11 proceeding from the conduct of recognition ballots to issues concerning changes to the bargaining unit, derecognition, and protection against detriment and dismissal for those participating in the recognition process.

Before beginning the analysis of the provisions themselves, it is necessary briefly to set the legislation in its historical and industrial context.

10.2   HISTORICAL CONTEXT

Schedule A1 was drafted in such great detail and length precisely in order to avoid the pitfalls of the previous experiment on compulsory recognition contained in the Employment Protection Act 1975. The Government's thinking in this respect was explained by Mr Michael Wills, Minister for Small Firms, Trade and Industry, during the Committee Stage of the Bill:

> I recognise that Schedule 1 is complex, but we were governed by our experience of previous employment relations legislation. The provisions of the Employment Protection Act 1975 were pithy ... Unfortunately, that Bill [*sic*] was problematic for several reasons, not least because of its very pithiness. A major shortcoming

was its lack of detailed criteria and procedures for making decisions. (Hansard HC Standing Committee E, 16 March 1999, col. 345)

As the Minister further noted, the lack of any clear statutory guidance to the Advisory, Conciliation and Arbitration Service (ACAS) as to how it should exercise its various discretions under the Act of 1975 led to several applications for judicial review of decisions taken by ACAS. Mr Wills continued:

We are determined not to let that happen again. Our proposals ... are more comprehensive, because we want the law to be precise and complete. We want to give clear guidance to employers, trade unions, workers and the CAC on every aspect of what the law requires and allows ...

That is a lofty ambition, and it is open to question whether Schedule 1 of the 1999 Act does indeed provide such 'clear and comprehensive guidance' in all respects.

10.2.1 Recognition procedure under the 1975 Act

The basic procedure of the 1975 Act, set out in s. 11, was that any independent trade union could refer a recognition issue to ACAS. Once a recognition issue had been referred, ACAS was required, under s. 12, to 'examine the issue, consult all parties who it considers will be affected by the outcome of the reference, and make such inquiries as it thinks fit'.

The width of that discretion — coupled with the lack of transparent guidance as to how it was to be exercised — caused substantial legal difficulties. It also caused practical problems, because the respective employer and union representatives on the ACAS Council had difficulty agreeing on the appropriate criteria for determining matters central to recognition claims, particularly the scope of the relevant bargaining unit. This issue is once again likely to be one of the main areas of dispute in the procedure established by the 1999 Act.

ACAS was required at all times to attempt to encourage the parties to reach a settlement by conciliated means, and managed to settle 80 per cent of the references by conciliation. Failing a conciliated settlement, ACAS was required to prepare a report on its inquiries and make any recommendation for recognition.

Once a recommendation had been made, employers covered by it were required by s. 15(2) to 'take such steps to carry on negotiations as might reasonably be expected to be taken by an employer ready and willing to carry out the recommendation'. Unions who believed that employers were not complying with the recommendation could apply to the CAC to enforce the recommendation, ultimately by the making of an award improving the substantive terms and conditions of the relevant workers' contracts. (ACAS recommended recognition in 158 cases, but in its 1981 Report on the Act estimated that employers complied in only 55 of those cases.)

The first difficulty was the protracted consultation and inquiry procedure that ACAS was obliged to carry out. The procedure took too long — references took a year, on average, to reach the final report stage, and more than a fifth took 18 months. In the 1999 Act the Government have been careful to prescribe time limits for every stage of the process, with scope for extension where necessary. Even so, the new legislative timetable allows for a period of up to 80 working days — excluding extensions by agreement or as set by the CAC — from the initial trade union request for recognition to the holding of a ballot on the issue. This could cause difficulties for the trade unions involved, not least on a purely practical level of maintaining the employees' interest in the issue. Experience of operating recognition legislation in the United States shows that the longer the delay before a ballot is held, the less likely the union is to win. (See Labour Research Department, *Will Fairness Work?* (June 1998), at p. 12.)

Secondly, there were problems with inter-union disputes, where more than one union sought recognition over the same group of workers. The TUC was effective in resolving some of these disputes in accordance with the Bridlington procedure, but the most serious difficulties occurred when non-TUC unions or staff associations were competing with TUC affiliates.

Thirdly, some employers were completely opposed to any attempt by a union to secure recognition and would take whatever measures were necessary to make sure that their workplaces remained 'union-free'. The most famous example of this was the Grunwick dispute, where management sacked union members who were seeking recognition and then denied access to ACAS to gauge opinion on the recognition question among the remaining workers. Litigation commenced which eventually reached the House of Lords. Their Lordships held that since ACAS had not produced a satisfactory survey of employee opinion, it had failed in its statutory duty under s. 14 to ascertain the opinions of the relevant workers. ACAS had no power to force the employer to grant it access, and the fact that it was the employer's actions which had prevented ACAS from fulfilling its duty was, according to the Law Lords, irrelevant (*Grunwick Ltd* v *ACAS* [1978] IRLR 38).

The question of outright employer opposition to the idea of compulsory trade union recognition remains one of the most problematic areas for legislation in this field. Many employers will have never had any experience of collective bargaining, and others will have become accustomed over the last two decades to dealing directly with their staff in the absence of what they perceive to be the unnecessary and unwanted interference of trade union 'third parties'. Coupled with creative legal advice and legislation which is extremely complex, determined opposition to attempts to secure recognition may well find a fruitful outlet in litigation.

The recognition procedure established by the 1975 Act fell into disrepute largely due to high-profile court cases such as that involving Grunwick. There are already fears that the same fate could befall the new procedure. During the Committee Stage of the 1999 Act, Mr David Chidgey, Liberal Democrat MP for Eastleigh, referred to:

... disturbing reports about American firms that market themselves as specialists in union-busting and advertise the fact that they have great expertise in disrupting bargaining arrangements ... we understand that they are gearing up to marketing their services in the United Kingdom ...' (Hansard HC Standing Committee E, 16 March 1999, col. 431)

Responding to these concerns on behalf of the Government, Mr Wills stated that the United Kingdom:

> ... has no tradition of union-busting consultants, and I believe that any company that adopted union-busting tactics would risk paying a high price ... People in this country would not welcome such activities, and companies that carried them out would be likely to find themselves in difficulty...' (Hansard HC Standing Committee E, 16 March 1999, col. 432)

Nevertheless, reports persist of well-attended seminars conducted by union-busting American law firms (e.g., *File on Four*, Radio 4, 30 November 1999).

A final difficulty with the operation of the 1975 Act concerned the attitudes of judges towards it. Some were clearly hostile to the idea of employers being forced to negotiate with trade unions. Accordingly, they adopted a deliberate policy of construing the provisions in a narrow, legalistic manner. Perhaps the best example of this approach is to be found in the judgment of Browne-Wilkinson J in *Powley* v *ACAS* [1978] ICR 123, where he used the concept of freedom of contract as justification for a restrictive interpretation of the 1975 Act:

> It is therefore clear that as a result of the statutory machinery an individual can have a substantial measure of control over his own working life compulsorily delegated to an agent, or trade union, which he has not selected and may even have his contract of service varied without his consent. These are very large powers, every bit as large as powers of compulsory acquisition of property; and, in my judgment, the court should seek to ensure that, as in the case of compulsory purchase powers, the conditions for the exercise of the powers conferred by the Act of 1975 are strictly observed. Parliament has decreed, in the interests of industrial relations as a whole, that these procedures for the compulsory acquisition of an individual's right to regulate his working life shall exist, but it is the court's duty to ensure that the rights of the individual are not to be lost to him except in strict accordance with the statutory procedure laid down. (at p. 135)

It will be interesting to see whether any members of the judiciary take a similar attitude towards the 1999 recognition procedure, and view it as a Draconian incursion into the right of an individual to regulate his or her own working life, or for that matter, the right of an employer to run its business as it sees fit.

10.2.2   Industrial impact of the 1975 Act

Despite the problems with the procedure as outlined above, ACAS figures show that recognition had been accorded on behalf of 65,000 workers as the direct outcome of references for recognition made under s. 11 of the Act of 1975. A further 77,500 workers were covered by some form of recognition as a direct result of cases completed under ACAS's voluntary conciliation machinery. ACAS concluded that 'recognition stemming from s. 11 references had no more than a marginal impact except in one or two sectors of industry' and that 'the ... provisions clearly failed to achieve the expected major breakthrough' (ACAS, Annual Report, 1981). In any event, on the election of a Conservative Government in 1979, the statutory procedure was repealed by the passage of the Employment Act 1980.

What is less clear is what indirect impact the statutory procedures had. The TUC claimed that the membership of its affiliated unions increased by over 1 million during the period in which the recognition procedure was in force. A 1986 report suggested that the 1975 Act contributed to unions securing recognition agreements on a voluntary basis, 'not only by making employees more aware of the feasibility of collective representation, but also by encouraging employers to recognise unions voluntarily in order to obtain orderly bargaining structures and to avoid the public scrutiny which would result from a reference under the statutory procedures'.

There is evidence that prior to the introduction of the new recognition procedure unions are having some success in persuading previously reluctant employers to conclude recognition agreements, particularly where more than 50 per cent of the workforce are union members. For example, Noons, which had opposed the GMB union request for recognition for some time, concluded an agreement in early 1999. Mr Noon stated that 'Once we became aware that the majority of our workforce were GMB members we decided there should be recognition. That is democracy' (*Daily Mail*, 4 March 1999). At the beginning of 2000, the TUC reported the results of a survey which showed that unions achieved 74 new recognition agreements, covering over 21,000 workers, in the first 10 months of 1999 (*Financial Times*, 7 January 2000). ACAS has also reported that in the year to August 2000 it has been asked to assist in 263 voluntary recognition cases — double the number on average during the 1990s.

10.3   RECOGNITION AND THE EMPLOYMENT RELATIONS ACT 1999: OVERVIEW OF PROCEDURE

The procedure is commenced by the union seeking recognition making a request for recognition to the employer. 'Recognition' in this context means recognition for the purposes of conducting collective bargaining, as distinct from recognition for some other purpose such as information and consultation over workplace change. The meaning of 'collective bargaining' will be considered separately (see 10.4, below).

The union's request must state the group of workers — the 'bargaining unit' — over which the union seeks recognition (note that two or more unions acting jointly are entitled to request recognition over the same bargaining unit). The first step is for the parties to try to agree a bargaining unit. If the employer rejects the unit proposed by the union, the union may apply to the CAC to decide the appropriate bargaining unit. If the union has the support of a majority of workers within that unit, in the sense that more than 50 per cent of the unit are members of the union, it is expected that there will usually be an automatic declaration of recognition (i.e., without the need for a ballot). If the union does not have majority support within the bargaining unit in terms of membership, the CAC must satisfy itself that the union enjoys a reasonable level of support before proceeding with the application. This means that at least 10 per cent of the bargaining unit must be union members, and the union must be able to show that a majority of the workers in the bargaining unit would be likely to favour recognition.

If this level of support can be demonstrated, the CAC will then move on to conduct a secret ballot of the workers in the bargaining unit. During the balloting process the employer must give the union reasonable access to the workers to canvass support. An award of recognition will not be made unless the result of the ballot shows that there is a majority in favour of recognition amongst those voting and at least 40 per cent of those eligible to vote also support recognition.

Following the declaration of recognition, the employer and the union are expected to agree upon a method to conduct collective bargaining. If they cannot do this, either party can request the CAC to establish such a method.

A declaration of recognition lasts for three years, after which the employer or a group of workers may apply to the CAC for the union to be derecognised. The derecognition procedure mirrors the recognition process in several respects. Special protection against detriment and dismissal is given to all workers involved in the recognition process. In a significant and related development, the new legislation will require employers to consult and inform recognised trade unions on matters to do with training of workers in the relevant bargaining unit.

During the Parliamentary stages of the Act, a new Part III was introduced to Schedule A1 entitled 'Changes affecting bargaining unit'. This allows for parties to apply to the CAC to determine a new bargaining unit (failing agreement between themselves) where either believes that the original unit is no longer appropriate or has ceased to exist as a result of changes to the employer's business. Detailed provision is also made to deal with the consequences of the new unit overlapping with another, established bargaining unit.

Mention should also be made that at any time before the ballot (after initiation of the statutory procedure) the parties may voluntarily agree on recognition and the appropriate bargaining unit. If they manage to conclude what is termed in the legislation an 'agreement for recognition' then no further steps need to be taken under the statutory procedure. ('Agreements for recognition', which are dealt with in Part II of the Schedule ('Voluntary Recognition'), should not be confused with recognition agreements that employers and unions have concluded without any reference whatsoever to the statutory procedure.) A union party to an 'agreement for recognition' will have the right to apply to the CAC to impose a method for collective bargaining — and seek any associated remedies — if this issue cannot be agreed with the employer.

10.4   KEY CONCEPTS AND ADMINISTRATIVE BODIES

The two central concepts underpinning Schedule A1 are 'collective bargaining' and the 'bargaining unit'. These are considered below at 10.4.2 and 10.4.3 respectively. Reference is also made on several occasions to requirements concerning the 'validity' and 'admissibility' of applications under the statutory procedure (i.e., for recognition, derecognition and changes to the bargaining unit). Since the requirements vary in the context of the different types of application, the details are explained at the appropriate points below.

In the text that follows, paragraph references are to Schedule A1 of the 1992 Act, unless stated otherwise.

10.4.1   The administrative bodies

The body with primary responsibility for overseeing the new procedures is the CAC. The CAC is discussed in detail in Chapter 12. For present purposes it is important to note that in exercising any of its functions under Schedule A1, the CAC must 'have regard to the object of encouraging and promoting fair and efficient practices and arrangements in the workplace' (para. 171). Unlike ACAS under the 1975 Act, there is no duty on the CAC to promote or encourage collective bargaining, or for that matter recognition (the Government stated in the House of Lords that the CAC will be expected to remain 'strictly neutral' as regards the merits of collective bargaining (Lord McIntosh, Hansard HL 7 June 1999, col. 1196)). It is also important to note that in exercising its discretion and making decisions, the CAC is in many instances required to consider any evidence submitted to it by the union and employer (for example, when deciding whether the request for recognition is valid and the application for recognition is admissible, the CAC must consider evidence given by the union and employer — para. 15(3)).

ACAS will be involved in the operation of the procedures, particularly in the context of offering its conciliation services to parties attempting to negotiate matters concerning recognition. ACAS is also empowered to issue a Code of Practice on the scope of the employer's duty to provide reasonable access to the relevant workers for the union during a recognition ballot, a matter likely to be of considerable significance. For further details on access and the Code of Practice, see 11.2.4.

10.4.2   Collective bargaining

Where the CAC makes an award of recognition to a trade union for the purpose of conducting 'collective bargaining', this will only encompass negotiations on 'pay, hours and holidays' (para. 3(3)). The parties may voluntarily broaden the coverage of an agreement for recognition (para. 3(4)).

In other contexts, 'collective bargaining' has the wider definition, contained in s. 178 of the TULR(C)A 1992 (this definition includes negotiations on terms and conditions of employment, termination of employment, and disciplinary matters). In determining whether to refuse an application for recognition on the grounds that it might disrupt existing collective bargaining arrangements, the wider definition will apply (see paras 35 and 44 which concern, respectively, admissibility and validity of an application for recognition). This will mean that where existing collective bargaining in respect of a bargaining unit does not, for example, cover pay, a union making an application for recognition to bargain over pay in relation to that same unit must be refused by the CAC. Similarly, the s. 178 definition will apply in relation to an existing 'outside bargaining unit' in the context of applications under Part III concerning changes to the bargaining unit (para. 94(2); see Chapter 11, at 11.5).

10.4.3   Bargaining unit

The bargaining unit is defined as the 'group of workers' in respect of whom the union seeks to be recognised to conduct collective bargaining (para. 2(2)). In the event of the parties failing to agree an appropriate bargaining unit, the CAC must determine the 'appropriate' unit, having regard to a variety of factors but giving priority to the need for the unit to be compatible with 'effective management' (para. 19(3) and (4)). The determination of the bargaining unit will often be decisive of the outcome of the application for recognition, particularly if a union is well organised amongst a particular group of workers or at a particular site, but is much weaker across the whole organisation. If the appropriate bargaining unit in that instance is the whole workforce, the union's chances of succeeding with its application will be greatly reduced.

10.5   INVALIDITY OF THE REQUEST FOR RECOGNITION

The request for recognition may fail because it is invalid (note that the request for recognition must be distinguished from the application to the CAC, which may be either invalid or inadmissible; this is considered at 10.9). The request will be invalid either if the employer to whom it is made is below the small employer threshold (see 10.5.1), or if the union making the request does not hold a certificate of independence (see 10.5.2). It will also be invalid if it does not comply with four formal requirements, namely that it:

(a)   is in writing;
(b)   identifies the union and the proposed bargaining unit over which recognition is sought;
(c)   states that it is made under Schedule A1 of the 1992 Act; and
(d)   is received by the employer (paras 8(a)–(c), and 5).

10.5.1   Small employer exclusion

One of the controversial aspects of the recognition procedure is that it excludes workers who work for small employers. Small employers are defined as those having fewer than 21 workers on the date the employer received the request for recognition, or, if the employer had more than 21 workers on that date, where its average workforce over the 13 weeks preceding that date was less than 21 (para. 7(1)(a) and (b)). The average is calculated by taking the number of workers employed in each of the 13 weeks, aggregating those numbers and dividing the total by 13 (para. 7(2)).

The workforce of the employer must include any workers employed by an associated employer or employers (para. 7(1)). 'Associated employer' bears the same meaning as in s. 297 of TULR(C)A 1992, namely that one employer is a company of which the other has control, or that both are companies of which a third person has control. 'Control' in this sense can be direct or indirect. This narrow definition of 'associated employer' has raised some fears that medium-sized employers might thwart union attempts at recognition by, for example, breaking their business down into smaller units through the mechanism of franchising.

The small employer threshold may be revised upwards or downwards by the Secretary of State for Trade and Industry if its operation proves to be unsatisfactory (para. 7(6)(b)). Similarly, the Secretary of State may disapply or vary the threshold in particular circumstances (para. 7(6)(a)).

10.5.2   Independent trade unions

The request for recognition will similarly be invalid if the union making it does not hold a certificate of independence (para. 6). Certificates of independence are issued by the Certification Officer and can be obtained only provided the union satisfies a number of statutory conditions, relating to the extent of control that an employer has over the activities of a trade union.

10.6   STARTING THE PROCEDURE FOR STATUTORY RECOGNITION

Once a valid request has been made, the parties then have an initial 'first period' of ten working days in which to conduct negotiations and possibly agree a bargaining unit and recognition (para. 10(1) and (6)).

The employer has three choices during the first period, namely:

(a)   accept the request and agree recognition, in which case no further steps are to be taken under Part I of Schedule A1 (para. 10(1));
(b)   not to accept the request for recognition but inform the union that it is willing to negotiate (para. 10(2)); or
(c)   to reject the request, either expressly or by ignoring it (para. 11).

If the employer opts for negotiations, the parties then have a 'second period' of 20 working days, or such longer period as agreed (para. 10(7)), in which to agree the bargaining unit and possibly the question of recognition. If they reach agreement on both issues then no further steps are to be taken (para. 10(4)).

ACAS may be asked by either party to help in conducting the negotiations during the second period (para. 10(5)). If the employer proposes that ACAS assists, and the union either rejects the proposal, or fails to accept it within ten working days starting with the day after the proposal was made, the union cannot take the procedure any further (para. 12(5)).

10.7   APPLICATION TO THE CAC

If no agreement has been reached during either the first or the second periods, or the employer has rejected the request or failed to respond to it before the end of the first period, the union may then apply to the CAC (paras 11(1)(a) and (b), 12(1)(a) and (b)). This application will ask the CAC to decide two questions, namely:

(a)   whether the bargaining unit proposed by the union is appropriate, and if not, whether some other unit is appropriate; and
(b)   whether the union has the support of a majority of workers within the appropriate bargaining unit (paras 11(2) and 12(2)).

If negotiations have taken place and agreement has been reached within the second period on the question of the bargaining unit, but no agreement has been reached on the question of recognition, the union may then apply to the CAC asking it to determine whether the union has the support of the majority of workers within the agreed bargaining unit (para. 12(3) and (4); this refers to the automatic recognition procedure — see 10.13).

10.8   ACCEPTANCE OF THE APPLICATION BY THE CAC

Once an application has been received by the CAC, it must give notice of this fact to the parties (para. 13). Assuming there have been no competing applications (see 10.9.2.4 below), the CAC must then decide whether the request is valid and whether the application is admissible (para. 15(2)). (See 10.5 above on validity of requests for recognition and 10.9 below on admissibility of applications.) This decision must be taken within ten working days of the receipt of the application or such longer period as the CAC specifies (para. 15(6)). If the CAC decides either that the request is not valid or that the application is not admissible, the application cannot be accepted and no further steps will be taken (para. 15(4)). If both those conditions (of validity and admissibility) are satisfied, the application must be accepted and the parties notified accordingly (para. 15(5)).

10.9   'ADMISSIBILITY' REQUIREMENTS FOR APPLICATIONS

In order for recognition applications to be capable of acceptance by the CAC, they must first satisfy a number of conditions concerning 'admissibility'. These require-ments are contained in paras 33–42 of Schedule A1 and are explained below.

10.9.1   Formal admissibility requirements

The application must be in such form as the CAC specifies and be supported by such documents as the CAC specifies (para. 33). The union must give the employer notice of the application, together with a copy of it and any supporting documents (para. 34).

10.9.2   Substantive admissibility requirements

These requirements can be divided into five categories:

(a)   those aimed at preventing frivolous applications that stand no chance of success;

(b)   those aimed at preventing new applications disrupting pre-existing bargaining arrangements;

(c)   those aimed at removing any possibility of competing applications between unions;

(d)   those aimed at prohibiting applications concerning overlapping bargaining units; and

(e)   those aimed at preventing repeat applications within three years.

10.9.2.1   *Deterring frivolous applications*

Perhaps the most important of the admissibility criteria is that the CAC must decide whether the union has *reasonable support* within the proposed bargaining unit. The Government have defined 'reasonable support' for this purpose as meaning that at least 10 per cent of the proposed unit must be members of the relevant union, and also that a majority of the workers in the unit 'would be likely to favour recognition of the union' (para. 36). In the context of a joint application, the 10 per cent membership threshold refers to an aggregation of all the members of all the unions involved. In theory this will mean that in a company employing 22 staff, where the whole workforce is to be viewed as the bargaining unit, three union members — one from each of three unions, for example — would be enough for those unions to trigger the statutory machinery by making a joint application. It should also be remembered that the unions would need to satisfy the CAC that a majority (i.e., more than 50 per cent) of the bargaining unit would be likely to favour recognition.

While the legislation does not make it clear how the CAC will arrive at its decision, it is expected that survey or other evidence produced by the union will be crucial — the White Paper suggested a 'petition signed by a sufficient number of employees' (or, as was the case in the *New Millenium Experience Co. Ltd and British Actors Equity* (Case No. TUR 1/6/00, 8.9.2000), a 'straw poll' conducted by the union was sufficient evidence of support for recognition). There is, however, a potential practical difficulty here. As will be seen later, the legislation requires employers to cooperate with unions — and in particular to give them reasonable access to the workers within the relevant bargaining unit — but only in the context of an actual ballot on recognition. The duty of reasonable access does not require the employer to allow the union access to the relevant workers before the ballot process begins. If faced with a non-cooperative employer, unions will only be able to produce the relevant evidence of likely majority support by organising their existing members to carry out petitions and/or obtain survey evidence.

10.9.2.2 Pre-existing bargaining arrangements

In order to ensure that pre-existing bargaining arrangements are not disrupted, a recognition application *will not be admissible* if the CAC is satisfied that any workers within the relevant bargaining unit (as proposed by the union or agreed with the employer) are already covered by a collective agreement between the employer and any other recognised union (para. 35(1)). (Note that 'collective bargaining' in this context bears the wider definition contained in s. 178.) However, there are two exceptions to this general rule.

First, para. 35(1) will not apply (i.e., a recognition application will be admissible) where the matters in respect of which the union is recognised in relation to the collective agreement do not cover pay, hours or holidays, *and* that union is also the union making the recognition application (i.e., where an existing union with a limited collective agreement makes an application to obtain negotiating rights on pay, holidays and hours which it hitherto did not have).

Secondly, the CAC must ignore any pre-existing recognition agreement if it was made by a non-independent union, and there has been, in the three years prior to the date of that recognition agreement, another recognition agreement in force allowing the non-independent union to conduct collective bargaining on behalf of 'the same or substantially the same' bargaining unit as covered by the existing agreement (para. 35). The CAC has the authority here to decide whether one group of workers (the bargaining unit) is 'the same or substantially the same' as another. In making its decision, the CAC 'may take account of the views of any person it believes has an interest in the matter' (para. 35(5)).

In other words, if the employer has previously dealt with a non-independent union and has agreed a new recognition deal with that union to avert a statutory application by an independent union, such a tactic will not generally succeed. This issue of what happens when an employer who has never previously dealt with a union concludes a deal with a non-independent union in order to avoid the statutory process is dealt with by Part VI of Schedule A1 which concerns derecognition applications. A special 'fast-track' procedure is provided for derecognition of non-independent unions by workers employed by the relevant employer (see 11.6.5).

10.9.2.3 Joint applications

As was noted above, one of the difficulties with the 1975 Act concerned demarcation disputes and competing claims by different unions over the same groups of workers. The Government have attempted to remove any likelihood of a repetition of these problems by effectively stating that if more than one union wishes to make an application for recognition over the same group of workers, they must do so together and cooperatively.

Where a number of unions do make a joint application, that application will not be admissible unless the unions show that:

(a)   they will cooperate with each other in a manner likely to secure and maintain stable and effective collective bargaining arrangements; and

(b)   if the employer wishes, they will enter into single-table bargaining arrangements (para. 37(2)).

There may be difficulties with this provision, particularly as to the meaning of 'stable and effective collective bargaining arrangements' and the evidence the unions must provide to the CAC to demonstrate their ability to deliver the same. It may be that a union will need to show a history of successfully operating single-table bargaining arrangements, although the CAC would need to make fine judgments if another employer produced evidence of disruptive tactics by that same union in the course of collective bargaining.

10.9.2.4   Overlapping competing applications
These provisions apply where the CAC has accepted an application from a union in relation to a bargaining unit and the application is pending (para. 38(1)). Acceptance of the application means that the CAC has already decided that the application is valid and admissible. In those circumstances another application in relation to another bargaining unit (a competing application) would not be admissible if there was any overlap between the two units — even to the extent of a single employee — and the two applications are made by different unions (para. 38(2)). However, if a competing application also satisfied the 10 per cent 'reasonable support' test (see 10.9.2.1. above) then the original application must also be cancelled and treated as though it had never been admissible (para. 51).

Similarly, if the CAC has received an application but not yet accepted it, and another application is then made, the CAC must decide whether the 10 per cent membership test is satisfied in relation to any or all of the applications before proceeding (para. 14). If that test is met by more than one of the applications, or none of them, the CAC must not accept any of the applications (para. 14(7)). Alternatively, if the 10 per cent test is satisfied only in relation to one application, the CAC must proceed with that application only (para. 14(8)). This decision must be made within ten days or such longer period as the CAC specifies (para. 14(6)).

10.9.2.5   Preventing repeat applications within three years
Once the CAC has accepted an application made under paras 11 or 12, or proceeds with an application under para. 20 (which applies where the agreed or decided bargaining unit differs from that originally proposed), then another application must not be made in relation to the same or substantially the same bargaining unit by the same union, within a period of three years from the date after the day on which the CAC gave notice of acceptance (para. 39). Similarly, a new application by the same

union may not be made in relation to the same or substantially the same bargaining unit where the CAC has issued a declaration under para. 29(4) that the union is not entitled to be recognised (para. 40). Lastly, the same three-year embargo applies where the CAC has issued a declaration under para. 121(3) following a ballot on derecognition that bargaining arrangements are to cease to have effect (para. 41).

The net effect of these provisions is that unions need to ponder the matter carefully before making applications, and be reasonably confident that success is within their grasp in the short term rather than the medium term. Three years is a long time to wait between what are likely to be hard-fought recognition campaigns. Applications that are not accepted because they are found to be inadmissible are outside the scope of these provisions.

10.10   WITHDRAWAL AND NOTICE TO CEASE CONSIDERATION OF THE APPLICATION

Once an application has been accepted by the CAC, the union can still withdraw it (if new evidence comes to light which suggests, for example, that a ballot would not succeed) prior to a declaration of recognition being made or notification being given by the CAC of its intention to hold a secret ballot of the relevant workers (para. 16). (However, withdrawal of the application after it has been accepted would still prevent the union from making another application in relation to the same or substantially the same bargaining unit for three years. For this reason it may be that this provision will be something of a dead letter.) Similarly, the parties may jointly give notice to the CAC that they want no further steps to be taken in relation to the application, provided they do so either before an automatic declaration of recognition is made under para. 22(2), or within a period of ten working days after they have received notification of the CAC's intention to hold a secret ballot (para. 17).

10.11   DETERMINATION OF THE APPROPRIATE BARGAINING UNIT

Once the CAC has accepted an application, it must then, within a period of 20 working days or such longer period as it may notify, try to assist the parties to agree on the appropriate bargaining unit (para. 18).

If the union has at least 50 per cent membership within the proposed unit, the union will also ask the CAC to make a declaration of automatic recognition on the basis that there is majority support (see 10.13 below). This request will be made once the parties have agreed *an* appropriate bargaining unit, or the CAC has determined *the* appropriate bargaining unit (emphasis added).

The use of the indefinite and definite articles may be of some significance in the operation of this part of the legislation. The distinction that appears to have been drawn is that the parties can agree between themselves any unit that they consider to be appropriate, whereas the CAC must decide upon the single appropriate bargaining unit. If there are two units that might appear to be equally appropriate, the CAC must determine which unit is *the* appropriate unit. This formulation may result in applications for judicial review in finely balanced cases where the CAC's determination of the bargaining unit has effectively decided the recognition issue.

If the parties have not agreed an appropriate unit within the 20 working-day period, the CAC must then decide what is the appropriate bargaining unit within ten working days or such longer period as it may decide (para. 19(2)).

In deciding the appropriate unit the overriding duty of the CAC is to take account of the need for the unit to be compatible with effective management (para. 19(3)). Five other matters are also to be taken into account, provided they do not conflict with this need:

(a)   the views of the employer and of the union or unions;

(b)   existing national and local bargaining arrangements;

(c)   the desirability of avoiding small fragmented bargaining units within an undertaking;

(d)   the characteristics of workers falling within the proposed unit and of any other employees of the employer whom the CAC considers relevant; and

(e)   the location of the workers (para. 19(4)).

10.11.1   Need for unit to be compatible with effective management

In explaining why the Government had decided to impose 'effective management' as the overriding criterion in the determination of the appropriate bargaining unit, Michael Wills stated that:

That is the modern definition of recognition: it is tailored for single status, single-table bargaining workplaces, if that is what the employer wants. There will be no return to fragmentation and the damaging demarcation disputes of the past. (Hansard HC Standing Committee E, 16 March 1999, col. 347)

There is an obvious question as to how the CAC will determine which unit is compatible with effective management. Clearly the CAC has to take into account the five matters listed in 10.11 above; but it is implicit in the passage quoted above that really what is intended is that the employer's views on 'effective management' will be accorded the most weight, and the other factors will be considered to resolve any remaining doubts that the CAC might have about the issue.

Having regard to the CAC's duty to promote efficiency as well as fairness, and the absence of any duty to encourage or promote collective bargaining or trade union recognition, a concern is that it will only be relatively rarely that the CAC would take a different view from the employer as to whether a particular unit was or was not 'compatible with effective management'.

An example of such a rare case could be where the employer was demonstrably misrepresenting to the CAC the true picture on the ground; such as where the employer, in a multi-site organisation, stated that pay was set centrally whereas in fact local management had substantial autonomy in setting terms and conditions.

Most recent CAC decisions, however, indicate that union apprehension on this issue may prove to be unfounded. In *Benteler Automotive UK and ISTC* (17.10.2000, Case No. TUR 1/4/00) an employer's assertions as to the inappropriateness of the union's proposed bargaining unit was subject to detailed scrutiny. The ISTC had proposed that the bargaining unit should consist only of shop floor weekly paid production operatives and material handlers and not include monthly paid technical, supervisory or administrative staff who it alleged had no common interest with shop floor production staff and who were in practice treated differently by management in a number of ways. Management contended that the union had formulated its proposal without understanding the management desire to project a 'whole company' philosophy. A split of this nature would damage the culture of partnership and the operation of team-working between the production operatives and manufacturing support staff and thus undermine 'effective management'. In rejecting the employer's submissions the CAC was of the opinion that '. . . the current position at the company does not yet accord with the whole-company, one team culture and approach to which Benteler aspires . . .' and thus as the bargaining unit actually reflected existing management organisation and practice it was clearly compatible with effective management. In *GMPU and Red Letter Bradford Ltd* (18.12.2000, Case No. TUR 1/15/00) the dispute arose over the union proposal to include shop floor workers in Despatch, Production and IT (who made up the vast majority of employees) in the bargaining unit and exclude management staff who enjoyed significantly different terms and conditions of employment. The employer argued that the exclusion of management was divisive and damaged team spirit — given the company ethos of partnership between all grades. The CAC rejected the employer's arguments and found that as there were patently significant distinctions between these two different types of employee the union's proposed bargaining unit was 'compatible with effective management'.

10.11.2   Small fragmented bargaining units

One of the major problems for unions will arise in multi-site organisations. As noted above, the Government have clearly stated that if an employer wants single-status single-table bargaining then that is what it should have. In a multi-site organisation a union may have strong organisation at one site only, and it will want that site to be the bargaining unit. From there it will try to organise across the remainder of the organisation, gradually increasing numbers. However, if employment relations are centralised the union will stand very little chance of persuading the CAC, in the face of an employer opposed to recognition, that a single site is the appropriate bargaining unit. On the other hand, if employment relations are handled by local management on a site-by-site basis the union will probably fair better, notwithstanding the exhortation to avoid small fragmented bargaining units.

10.12   VALIDITY OF APPLICATION

If the CAC has determined the appropriate bargaining unit which differs from that originally proposed by the union, or the parties have agreed an appropriate unit different from the one proposed, the CAC must then decide whether or not the application is valid (para. 20(1) and (2)). This decision must be taken within ten working days, or such longer period as the CAC may decide (para. 20(6)).

'Validity' in this context refers to the same matters as were considered by the CAC in determining whether the application was 'admissible' (see 10.9 above; however, the provisions concerning validity are set out separately in Schedule A1, at paras 43–51). If the CAC decides that the application is invalid, it must notify the parties of this decision and take no further steps in relation to the application (para. 20(4)). Alternatively, if the CAC decides that the application is not invalid it must proceed with it and notify the parties of this decision (para. 20(5)).

If the bargaining unit agreed by the parties or the unit determined by the CAC is the same as the unit originally proposed by the union, the CAC must also proceed with the application (para. 21).

10.13   AUTOMATIC RECOGNITION

If there is 50 per cent membership in the appropriate unit, the CAC must normally make a declaration that the union is to be recognised as entitled to conduct collective bargaining on behalf of the relevant workers (a declaration of automatic recognition (para. 22(1) and (2)). Such a declaration will normally be made without the need for any ballot of the relevant workers. However, the CAC must arrange for a ballot to be held if one of three qualifying conditions is found to exist, namely:

(a)   the CAC is satisfied that a ballot should be held in the interests of good industrial relations;

(b)   a significant number of the union members within the unit inform the CAC that they do not want the union to conduct collective bargaining on their behalf; or

(c)   membership evidence is produced which leads the CAC to conclude that there are doubts as to whether a significant number of the union members within the unit want the union to conduct collective bargaining (para. 22(4)(a)–(c)).

'Membership evidence' is defined as evidence about the circumstances in which the union members became members, or evidence about the length of time for which those members have been members, where the CAC is satisfied that such evidence should be taken into account (para. 22(5)).

10.13.1 'Good industrial relations'

'Good industrial relations' is one of those phrases that can mean different things to different people and can vary according to the industrial and historical context. What might have passed for 'good industrial relations' in 1977 might not necessarily be regarded as such in 2001. Employers' groups and government agencies will, for example, be far less tolerant of industrial action — even to a relatively limited extent — than they would have been 20 years ago.

In particular, the parties involved in the recognition issue under consideration are likely to have different ideas as to how 'good industrial relations' is defined and whether a ballot is necessary to preserve or foster those relations. Although the legislation does not make this requirement express, the CAC would be well advised to take into account the respective views of the employer and the union on this issue. A declaration of recognition and the process of collective bargaining (where it has not existed before) will obviously involve substantial changes to the way that an employer deals with and communicates with its staff, but of itself this could not be regarded as a threat to 'good industrial relations'.

The CAC may be faced with difficulties when confronted by an employer who declares that unless a ballot is held it would not regard any declaration of recognition as legitimate and would refuse to bargain in good faith with the union. In other words, the employer may state that there will not be any good industrial relations unless a ballot is held. It is to be hoped that the CAC would resist ultimatums of this kind and would only order ballots under this ground sparingly — where, for example, there was evidence of serious disputation and good reason to believe that a ballot would soften attitudes and promote negotiations.

10.13.2 'Significant number of union members'

The second condition is where a significant number of the union members inform the CAC that they do not want the union to conduct collective bargaining on their behalf. What would constitute a 'significant number of union members'? The answer will depend on the size of the bargaining unit, and 'significant' is likely to mean a number that is large enough to affect the outcome of the ballot. (Michael Wills stated as much during the Committee proceedings — Hansard HC, Standing Committee E, 16 March 1999, at col. 390.)

Having regard to the 40 per cent threshold that the union must win to obtain a declaration of recognition, 'significant' could be a very small number indeed. Five members in a unit of 100 would be enough to affect the outcome, for example. This will potentially give employers the opportunity to offer small groups of union members incentives or inducements to tell the CAC that they do not want the union recognised. (As will be seen in Chapter 11, there is nothing in the legislation that prohibits the offering of inducements in the form of enhanced personal contracts or otherwise to encourage union members or other workers to take action that would help prevent the union from gaining recognition.) It is suggested that the CAC should be alert to this possibility and should investigate the reasons why the union members are saying that they do not want their union recognised.

10.13.3 'Membership evidence leading to doubts'

The third condition is where membership evidence is produced which suggests that there are doubts as to whether a significant number of the union members within the bargaining unit want the union to conduct collective bargaining on their behalf. Membership evidence can either relate to the circumstances in which members joined, or to the length of their membership.

Evidence concerning circumstances of joining may include suggestions that members did not join voluntarily and felt pressured into doing so by more militant colleagues. In order to regard such evidence as producing the requisite 'doubts', the CAC will need to take into account all the circumstances in which those members joined, including any statements given by those who recruited them and how that was done. As noted above in 10.13.2, the CAC will need to bear in mind the possibility of employer inducements to members to make certain statements, and an inquiry to establish whether any inducements have been made should be undertaken where appropriate.

In relation to this part of the Schedule, Mr Wills made the following statement:

> ... in their enthusiasm to recruit new members and gain recognition, unions might ... market themselves to people who do not wish a union to bargain on their behalf ... If ... the employer can show that a significant number of union members have recently cancelled their check-off authorisations and appear to be leaving the union, that might prompt the CAC to hold a ballot. (Hansard HC Standing Committee E, 16 March 1999, col. 388)

Presumably the first sentence refers to the recruitment of workers who are on personal contracts and wish to remain employed on that basis. However, if the union can clearly show — whether by producing its recruitment material or otherwise — that members were recruited expressly in the context of a recognition campaign in order to achieve collective bargaining on behalf of all the relevant workers, the CAC may be suspicious of the motivations of individual members coming forward with information that they are not interested in union representation for the purposes of collective bargaining. Evidence of cancellation of check-off by a 'significant' number of members might indeed suggest that a ballot is necessary, although this may be evidence of employer inteference.

As regards the length of membership, it is submitted that it cannot be right that the fact that several union members have only recently joined should be a decisive factor in pointing to the need for a ballot. In the context of a recognition campaign, new members will be recruited expressly on the basis that if they do so in sufficient numbers, a declaration of automatic recognition will follow soon afterwards. This is clearly legitimate, and is indeed part of the purpose of the recognition legislation.

Accordingly, it is difficult to envisage many circumstances in which evidence as to the length of membership should properly be taken into account.

10.13.4   Power to amend

The Secretary of State has the power to amend the provisions concerning automatic recognition 'in any way he thinks fit' if the CAC expresses the view that the provisions are having 'an unsatisfactory effect' (para. 166). This may become necessary if the provisions prove susceptible to employer manipulation in the ways illustrated above.

Chapter 11
Trade Union Recognition II

11.1 INTRODUCTION

Chapter 10 analysed the process of recognition requests and recognition applications, specifically focusing on the determination of the appropriate bargaining unit and the award of automatic recognition. This chapter will complete the examination of the procedure, from the balloting process, through to the award of recognition and enforcement. It will also additionally consider recognition applications where there has been a change to the bargaining unit, derecognition issues, and protection for workers involved in the recognition process against detriment and dismissal.

In this chapter, paragraph references are to Schedule A1 of the 1992 Act, unless stated otherwise.

11.2 BALLOTS

Provision is made for ballots at various stages throughout the statutory recognition procedure. Ballots are to be held to determine whether the union should be recognised, to secure changes to the bargaining unit where a new unit has been determined by the CAC, and in derecognition applications. In all cases the process for the conduct of ballots is virtually identical (it is expected that the system for conducting recognition ballots will be similar to that presently in operation for the conduct of industrial action ballots) and is described below in the context of the determination of the union's application for recognition. Where differences arise at other points of the procedure they will be discussed at the appropriate stage in the text.

11.2.1 Appointment of the qualified independent person

The ballot must be conducted by a qualified independent person (QIP) appointed by the CAC, in accordance with conditions that may be specified by the Secretary of State (para. 25(7)(a)). The ballot must be conducted within a period of 20 working days (or such longer period as the CAC may specify) starting with the day after the QIP was appointed (para. 25(3)).

A person can only be a QIP if 'there are no grounds for believing either that he will carry out any functions conferred on him in relation to the ballot otherwise than competently or that his independence in relation to the ballot might reasonably be called into question' (para. 25(7)(b)). The QIP has general responsibility for conducting the ballot, and in particular must carry out the following tasks:

(a) receive details from the CAC of the names and home addresses of the workers within the bargaining unit (para. 26(5));

(b) send those workers any information supplied to the QIP by the union (para. 26(6));

(c) forward the bill for the gross costs of the ballot to the employer and the union (para. 28(4)); and

(d) inform the CAC of the ballot result (para. 29(1)).

11.2.2   The balloting timetable

There is likely to be an immediate practical problem with the timetable for conducting ballots. Once the CAC has decided to arrange the ballot, it must ('as soon as reasonably practicable') inform the employer and the union of that decision, the name of the QIP, the period within which the ballot must be conducted, whether the ballot is postal, and (if the ballot is not postal) details of the workplace or places where the ballot is to be conducted (para. 25(9)(a)–(e)).

The employer then has ten working days — from the date when it was informed that a ballot is to be held — in which to forward the names and addresses of the workers to the CAC (see 11.2.4 below). The CAC in turn must forward those details to the QIP 'as soon as is reasonably practicable' (para. 26(5)). Allowing for postal delays, it is possible that the QIP will not receive details of the relevant workers until a few days before the ballot is to be held — if the ballot is to be conducted within 20 days of the QIP's appointment as the statute intends.

This time frame will make it practically impossible in most cases for the union to be able to distribute any relevant literature to the workers concerned, since it cannot do so directly itself but only through the QIP. The union will not have the names and addresses of the workers constituting the bargaining unit. The *Fairness at Work* White Paper stated that the union would be provided with these details (at p. 41). However, the Government were later persuaded that, just as some union members might want to keep the fact of their membership secret from their employer, 'employees could have an equally valid wish not to be identified to the union or unions seeking recognition' (Lord McIntosh, Hansard HL, 7 June 1999, at col. 1206).

Having regard to these matters, as a matter of practice it is unlikely that ballots will be conducted within the intended 20-day timetable, at least in cases where the union indicates that it wishes to distribute literature to the relevant workers, and the CAC will often have to exercise its discretion to extend this period.

11.2.3   Workplace or postal ballots

The ballot must be conducted by the QIP either at a workplace or workplaces decided by the CAC, or by post or by a combination of both methods, depending on the CAC's preference (para. 25(4)). In deciding how the ballot is to be conducted, the CAC must have regard to:

(a)   the likelihood of the ballot being affected by unfairness or malpractice if it were conducted at a workplace;
(b)   costs and practicality; and
(c)   such other matters as the CAC considers appropriate (para. 25(5)).

The CAC must not opt for a combination of the two methods unless there are 'special factors' that make such a decision appropriate (para. 25(6)). Such 'special factors' might arise from the location of the workers or the nature of their employment, or other matters put to the CAC by the union or employer (para. 25(6)(a) and (b)). An example of such a ballot — which in practice will probably be rare — was said by the Government to be oil-rig workers. Those workers on-duty would be balloted on the rig, while workers on shore would be balloted by post (Lord McIntosh, Hansard HL, 7 June 1999, col. 1196).

Unions would probably prefer secret ballots to be conducted in the workplace where possible, as this would tend to maximise voter turnout. (In the United States, workplace polling by the Labour Relations Boards — the US equivalent of the CAC — has resulted in turnouts of 80–95 per cent — see *Wood and Goddard*, (1999) 37 BJIR 216.) In practice it is probable that most ballots will be conducted by post, since this would remove the possibility of any argument about whether or not the ballot was fair, particularly in the context of a recognition campaign that had proved highly emotive. This point was made by Michael Wills during Committee in response to a proposed Conservative amendment that would have removed the possibility of workplace ballots:

... a postal ballot is relatively difficult to interfere with and is less obtrusive than a workplace ballot. It may ... be more appropriate in the case of a highly emotive dispute over recognition ... (Hansard HC, Standing Committee E, 16 March 1999, at col. 392)

However, the Minister recognised that holding workplace ballots may be appropriate in certain cases, particularly where the CAC formed the view that by doing so a higher turnout would be obtained. A low turnout, he argued, would 'tend to foster feelings of dissatisfaction' and would not encourage 'good industrial relations ... A union might believe that it could have won in a workplace ballot'. Bearing these factors in mind, the CAC will be need to consider carefully all the circumstances of the particular case before deciding whether to specify which form of ballot is to be conducted.

11.2.4 The employer's duties in the balloting process

11.2.4.1 Introduction

The legislation states that the employer has three main duties in relation to the conduct of the ballot:

(a) The employer must cooperate generally in connection with the ballot, with the union and the QIP (para. 26(2)).

(b) The employer must give the union 'such access to the workers constituting the bargaining unit as is reasonable to enable the union to inform the workers of the object of the ballot and to seek their support and their opinions on the issues involved' (para. 26(3)).

(c) The final duty concerns the provision of information to the CAC and is split into three parts:

(i) within ten working days starting with the day the employer was informed about the ballot, the employer must give the CAC the names and home addresses of the relevant workers (para. 26(4)(a));

(ii) as soon as reasonably practicable the employer must inform the CAC of the name of any worker who subsequently joins the bargaining unit; and

(iii) the employer must inform the CAC of any worker who has subsequently left the bargaining unit (para. 26(4)(b) and (c)).

Both ACAS and the Secretary of State for Trade and Industry may issue Codes of Practice about the scope of the duty to provide reasonable access for the purposes of ballots (para. 26(8)(a) and (b)). The DTI published a draft Code in February 2000, and after a period of consultation the final code *Access to Workers During Recognition and Derecognition Ballots* was published May 2000 and laid before Parliament under s. 204(2) of TULR(C)A 1992. Reference is made to its provisions as appropriate and the Code is reproduced in Appendix 6.

If the employer fails to comply with any of the three statutory duties, the CAC may order the employer to take such steps as it considers reasonable to remedy the failure, within such time as the CAC specifies (para. 27(1)(a) and (b)). If the employer then fails to comply with that order, the CAC may make a declaration of recognition and dispense with the need to conduct a ballot (para. 27(2)). However, para. 27(2) is not mandatory, so even if the employer completely denies access to the union for the purposes of the ballot, the CAC is not bound to take any steps against the employer; and if it does not do so then the ballot will have to be held regardless (see also below).

11.2.4.2 Duty to grant reasonable access — the Code on Access

The introduction to the Code on Access states that its purpose is to ensure that 'the union can reach the workers involved', but the point is made that account will need to be taken of local circumstances in order to determine what form and what amount of access is appropriate. The introduction also states that the Code aims 'to encourage reasoned and responsible behaviour ... and to ensure that acrimony is avoided'. The point is made that the fact that a ballot is taking place at all means that an award of recognition is likely and 'a working relationship between the parties will have to be sustained' after the balloting process has been completed. This longer-term perspective should encourage both the employer and the union to behave responsibly and in a cooperative spirit during the balloting period. In order to encourage this, the Code provides that parties should avoid, *inter alia*, the use of defamatory material, provocative propaganda, personal attacks and personalised negative campaigning (para. 43).

The Code deals with preparations for access, access in operation, general responsibilities of employers and trade unions, and the consequences of non-compliance with the access provisions. The main aspects under each heading will be briefly considered.

Preparations for access (paras 14–22)   The Code exhorts parties to begin preparations as soon as the CAC notifies its intention to conduct a ballot, and in particular encourages parties to establish an access agreement covering the union's programme for where and when it will contact the workers, and a mechanism for resolving any disputes that may arise during the operation of the agreement. In terms of formulating access proposals, the Code states that it 'is reasonable for the union to request information from the employer ... about [the employer's] typical methods of communicating with his workforce and provide such other practical information as may be needed about, say, workplace premises or patterns of work'.

Access in operation (paras 23–41)   This covers matters such as: who is to be granted access; where and when access is to take place; the frequency and duration of union activities; written communications; and atypical workers. The 'access period' is the period from when the CAC informs the parties of the name of the QIP to the actual date on which the ballot is conducted.

The Code states that employers should grant access to such of their employees who are nominated lead union representatives, whether at the particular workplace or (in the case of a multi-site organisation) at another workplace. In the latter case the union would need to show that it was reasonable for those individuals to travel to the particular workplace and be prepared to pay travelling costs. Full-time union officials are also to be granted access.

Access is to be granted to the workers at their workplace, unless this is not practicable in the circumstances. If (for example) particular health and safety considerations mean that this is not possible then the union might need to consider access at an alternative, off-site facility. The method of access will generally be determined according to the employer's usual method of communicating with the workers; if mass meetings are held by the employer in a meeting room then the union should have the same facilities.

In order to avoid disruption to the business, access should normally be arranged during less busy periods of working time, particularly where a large meeting is to be held (e.g., a lunch hour or at the end of a shift). In terms of frequency and duration, the Code recommends the following as a minimum:

- One mass meeting of 30 minutes' duration for every ten days of the access period. If the employer hold similar meetings more often then equality of access should be conferred on the union.
- At least one day in the access period for union 'surgeries', whereby a union representative or official would be able to see individual workers (or small groups of two or three workers) for short periods of time (15 minutes) in order to discuss the issues in that setting. This is subject to the employer's ability to arrange adequate cover for any particular worker or workers. The employer should allow workers time off with pay for this purpose, unless the surgery takes place outside normal working hours. The Code suggests that with large bargaining units, or where more than one workplace is involved, more than one day for surgeries should be permitted. Any accredited union representative who conducts such a surgery, and who is also an employee of the employer, should be given time off with pay to do so. That worker should give as much notice as possible to the employer of the surgery, and it will only be in exceptional cases that time off can be refused.

As regards distribution of written material, the Code states that the employer should put a prominent notice board at the union's disposal and should not interfere with any material so displayed. The union should also be allowed to place additional material, such as leaflets, near the notice board. Electronic forms of communication, such as internal e-mail, intranets, and access to the union website, should be permitted within the parameters expressly or impliedly allowed by the employer in other contexts.

Access to atypical workers should take account of the particular working arrangements and patterns of these workers with a view to ensuring equivalent access to them. This may mean that union surgeries will have to be arranged on a more flexible basis.

General responsibilities of employers and unions (paras 42–46)   The exhortation to avoid acrimony and the concomitant requirement to avoid personal attacks and related matters was mentioned previously in the introduction to the Code. The parties are also specifically encouraged to adhere to any access agreement they have concluded, and more generally to behave responsibly and with consideration to the needs of the other during the access period. Neither party should seek to disrupt a meeting being held by the other, for example. The employer should provide the union with reasonable facilities, and in return the union should avoid undue disruption to the employer's business.

Non-compliance with access provisions (paras 12–13, 21-22 and 47–54)   Breach of the Code will not result in any legal sanction as such, but by virtue of s. 207 of

TULR(C)A 1992, its provisions are admissible in evidence and may be taken into account in any proceedings before any tribunal, court or the CAC. In considering whether to make orders and/or an award of recognition, the CAC will therefore have regard to the compliance by employers and unions with the provisions of the Code. The CAC has the power to order the employer to make good any failure to comply with its duties to allow reasonable access, and in the event of further failure (after the issuing of an order by the CAC) to grant a declaration of recognition.

The Code also makes the point that in the event of minor disputes the parties should attempt to resolve the differences themselves — utilising the conciliation facilities of ACAS if necessary or the good offices of the QIP, without going to the CAC in the first instance.

Comment on the Code and duty to grant reasonable access   It is important to note that the general duty of cooperation would in no way inhibit the employer from campaigning vigorously itself against recognition, if it was so minded. During Committee in the Lords, Lord McCarthy noted that during a 'recognition campaign … all the controls in this situation' would be in the employer's hands (Hansard HL, 7 June 1999, at col. 1203). He relied on this as justification for a proposed amendment guaranteeing certain facilities to the union during the campaign. The amendment was rejected by the Government in favour of allowing this, and other matters, to be dealt with in the Code on Access.

An important issue that arises will be whether the employer would be in breach of its duty of cooperation by, *inter alia*, distributing what might be regarded as anti-union propaganda, such as warnings that jobs would be lost in the event of recognition (see further at 11.8). Although the bare words of the statute envisaged that the employer's duties would be largely of a procedural nature, the Code on Access has introduced substantive elements, particularly under Section D concerning the general obligations of the parties to avoid acrimonious situations. The exhortation to avoid 'provocative propaganda', 'personalised negative campaigning' and 'behaviour likely to cause unnecessary offence' ought to restrict the scope for hard-hitting negative campaigns that some union-busting firms may have had in mind. In that sense it should help prevent the occurrence of intractable disputes. However, the Code is limited in that it only applies during the 'period of access', and since recognition campaigns will in reality begin several weeks or even months before that, employers will still have scope for negative campaigns if they so wish.

11.2.5   Notification of the result of the ballot

As soon as reasonably practicable after the result of the ballot is notified by the QIP, the CAC must inform the union and the employer of the result (para. 29(1)). If a majority of those voting, and at least 40 per cent of the workers constituting the bargaining unit, vote in favour of recognition, a declaration of recognition will be made (para. 29(2)). The 40 per cent threshold may be amended subsequently by the Secretary of State if its operation proves to be problematic (para. 29(5)). This threshold was one of the main objections raised by trade unions to the 1999 procedure. Paragraph 29(5) (and the equivalent provisions in other balloting contexts) also allows the Secretary of State to make 'different provision for different circumstances', so in theory the 40 per cent threshold might be varied in a particular situation. However, given the precedent that would thereby be set, it is unlikely that this power would be exercised other than in highly exceptional circumstances.

11.2.6   Costs of the ballot

The gross costs of the ballot are to borne equally by the union and the employer (para. 28(2)). If more than one union is involved then those unions shall bear their half of the costs in equal shares, or in such other proportion as they may indicate to the QIP (para. 28(3)). The costs of the ballot mean the reasonable charges of the QIP, and such other costs 'wholly, exclusively and necessarily incurred' by the QIP in connection with the ballot (para. 28(7)). This would include, for example, postage incurred by the QIP distributing union literature to the relevant workers, but not any material sent out directly by the union itself to its own members in the bargaining unit. It may also include such other costs as the employer and union agree (para. 28(7)(c)).

Once the QIP has sent to the union and the employer a demand for payment of their share of the costs of the ballot, they must pay the amount stated to the QIP within 15 working days (para. 28(5)).

11.3   CONSEQUENCES OF RECOGNITION

Gaining recognition is the first hurdle for the union. The next is actually to establish a viable procedure for conducting collective bargaining. The parties must agree (with or without the help of ACAS) a method by which they will conduct collective bargaining or the CAC will specify one.

11.3.1   Negotiations to establish a procedure for collective bargaining

Once a declaration of recognition has been made, the parties will be expected to conduct negotiations — within what is known as the 'negotiation period' — with a view to agreeing a method by which they will conduct collective bargaining. They are given 30 working days in which to do this (para. 30(4)). This period can be extended by agreement.

If no agreement on the method to conduct collective bargaining is made during the negotiation period, either party may apply to the CAC for assistance (para. 30(3)). Although the legislation does not make such an application mandatory, if no application is made the CAC will not have the power to specify a method for collective bargaining (see 11.3.2 below).

If such an application for assistance is made, the CAC must then try to help the parties agree a method for conducting collective bargaining. Such efforts by the CAC must be carried out within the 'agreement period', which is 20 working days from the date the CAC receives the application for assistance (para. 31(8)). This period can be extended by the CAC with the consent of all the parties.

11.3.2   Imposition of method for collective bargaining by CAC

If at the end of the agreement period (20 working days) the parties have still not agreed the method by which they will conduct collective bargaining, the CAC then has the responsibility to specify the relevant method to the parties (para. 31(3)). Any method (see the model method at 11.3.2.1 below) so specified is deemed to have effect as though it were contained in a legally enforceable contract made by the parties (para. 31(4)). The parties may agree that either the whole or parts of the method specified by the CAC should not have legally binding effect, or they may vary or replace the method specified by the CAC (para. 31(5)). If they do then that agreement itself shall be enforceable as a legally binding contract. The remedy available for breach of such contracts will be specific performance (para. 31(6)).

If the parties have agreed a specific method to conduct collective bargaining, and one or more of them then fails to carry out that method, 'the parties' together may apply to the CAC for assistance (para. 32). The CAC will again try to help the parties agree the method for collective bargaining within the 20-day agreement period, failing which it will impose a method on them. This aspect of the procedure reveals a certain risk for unions, because if an agreement as to a method has been reached but the employer has not carried it out, on the present wording of para. 32(2), the union will effectively be left without a remedy unless the employer consents to an application to the CAC for assistance. It is also unclear whether this paragraph applies where the agreement in question must have been reached during the negotiation period, or whether it could have also been reached during the agreement period or at some later stage.

11.3.2.1   *The model method on collective bargaining*
In February 2000, a draft model method of collective bargaining was published by the DTI under para. 168 for consultation. The Trade Union Recognition (Method of Collective Bargaining) Order 2000 (SI 2000 No. 1300) was laid before Parliament on 12 May and came into force on 6 June 2000. This model is reproduced in Appendix 7.

The model makes provision for the establishment of a joint negotiating body (JNB), whose members are to comprise equal numbers of union and employer representatives (with at least three on each side). The employer's representatives must have authority to take final decisions, or make recommendations on final decisions, about pay, hours and holidays. A six-stage bargaining process is set out, starting with the submission by the union side of its claim, followed by a meeting of the JNB to consider the claim, submission of a response by the employer, a further meeting of the JNB to consider the employer's response, another meeting in the event of a failure to agree, and finally the involvement of ACAS. Strict time frames are set for each stage. Agreements on pay, hours and holidays are to be set in writing as a

legally enforceable collective agreement (by way of an order for specific performance). Information must be disclosed by the employer in accordance with the ACAS
Code of Practice on disclosure of information for collective bargaining purposes.
Union representatives who are employees of the employer are to be given paid time
off to prepare the claim and attend meetings, and to hold meetings with the bargaining
unit to discuss the claim. The employer must also make certain facilities available to
the union side of the JNB.

11.3.3   Enforcement issues

The notion of procedure agreements for collective bargaining being legally
enforceable is a new departure for British law, which has always traditionally
regarded such agreements and collective agreements themselves as being binding in
honour only. (This is reflected in TULR(C)A 1992 itself — s. 179 provides that
collective agreements are presumed not to have legal force unless the agreement is
in writing and states clearly that is intended to be legally binding.) The reason the
Government felt it necessary to give agreements contractually binding status was in
order to create an enforcement framework in the event that one of the parties failed
to observe the method stipulated. However, it should be noted that any agreement
reached by the parties during the negotiation or agreement periods (not the CAC
imposed method) will not be legally binding unless otherwise stated.

As stated at 11.3.2 above, the enforcement mechanism specified for a failure to
observe the terms of a method imposed by the CAC is an application to a court for
an order for specific performance (para. 31(6)). Failure to comply with an order for
specific performance will be a contempt of court punishable by a fine and, in rare
cases, imprisonment. This procedural remedy is not accompanied by a substantive
sanction, such as in the form of a claim for improved terms and conditions, as was
the case under the Employment Protection Act 1975. It has been argued that this
reliance on a procedural model for enforcement may well allow a recalcitrant
employer to delay and prevaricate, accepting the form of recognition but denying the
substance.

The Government's rationale regarding this limited means of enforcement was
explained as follows:

> . . . we wanted as far as possible to promote dialogue and avoid confrontation. That
> is why the ultimate sanction is for the parties to be forced to talk to each other. We
> cannot force them to agree and it would be wrong to impose some third party as
> arbitrator. There [*sic*] might be a way of dealing with short-term disputes but that
> does nothing to promote long-term partnership and dialogue. (Lord McIntosh,
> Hansard HL, 7 June 1999, col. 1276)

Whether the remedy of specific performance will prove adequate remains to be seen.
Other members of the House of Lords were not convinced. Lord McCarthy, for
example, wanted the Government to introduce a method by which the CAC could

nominate an arbitrator to resolve any outstanding issues of substantive disagreement. This was rejected by Lord McIntosh, who said that the 'the Bill is aimed more at promoting partnership than resolving disputes' (*ibid*, at col. 1279). However, it must be remembered that specific performance is an equitable remedy and the courts retain discretion over whether to make such an order in any particular case. Matters to be taken into account in making an order for specific performance include whether the party seeking the order has 'clean hands'. This may mean that unions that have resorted to industrial action, prior to issuing court proceedings, will struggle to obtain orders for specific performance.

Courts have also generally been reluctant to grant specific performance to force parties to maintain and observe private contractual relationships. For example, it has been held that the courts are particularly reluctant to make an order for specific performance where the nature of the contract was such that it entailed 'daily impact of person upon person' (*C. H. Giles & Co. Ltd* v *Morris and Others* [1972] 1 WLR 307). It could be argued that a legally enforceable recognition agreement is just such a contract. Thus, if the courts maintain their traditional caution regarding orders for specific performance in the new context of the 1999 Act, there is a danger that the recognition provisions will be largely emasculated. In addition, doubts have been raised as to whether, should an order be flouted by an employer, the judiciary will, in practice, always be willing to countenance union actions for contempt of court against employers with, for example, pressing 'business reasons' for non-compliance.

11.4   SEMI-VOLUNTARY RECOGNITION

Part II of Schedule A1 to the TULR(C)A 1992 makes special provision for 'agreements for recognition'. Broadly speaking, this covers agreements reached at any stage after the statutory procedure has been commenced but before the CAC has conducted a ballot or made an award of automatic recognition. The scheme of Part II is to enable the parties to such an agreement (or one of them) to apply to the CAC with a request to specify a method by which collective bargaining is to be conducted. It also provides that agreements for recognition are to last for a period of three years, after which time they may be terminated by either party.

Originally Part II was intended to bring purely voluntary recognition agreements within the statutory framework, but it was conceded that this would introduce unnecessary complexity and legalism into areas where voluntary recognition had been operating quite successfully.

11.4.1   'Agreements for recognition'

Agreements for recognition are defined in para. 52(2) as:

(a)   agreements made between the employer and the union, during the 'permitted period', following a valid request for recognition made by the union under para. 4; and

(b)   where under the agreement, the employer recognises the union as entitled to conduct collective bargaining on behalf of a group of workers.

The 'permitted period' is defined in para. 52(3) as the period beginning with the date on which the employer receives the union's request and ending when the first of nine matters occurs. Without enumerating those nine matters, the effect is that the union has withdrawn from the statutory procedure before the CAC proceeds to hold a ballot of the workers in the relevant bargaining unit to determine the issue because the employer has agreed to recognise the union. Where the union has made an application to the CAC under paras 11 or 12 and the CAC has not decided the issue of admissibility, or alternatively has decided that the application is admissible, the agreement for recognition must be reached either before a declaration of automatic recognition has been made or before the CAC's notice of its intention to hold a ballot on the issue expires (para. 52(4) and (5)).

If a union withdraws from the statutory procedure without so far having reached any agreement for recognition, and subsequently enters into a recognition agreement, that agreement will be outside the scope of Part II.

11.4.2   Applications to determine whether agreement for recognition exists

There may be cases where there is a dispute between the parties as to whether a particular agreement is an 'agreement for recognition' within the meaning of Part II. In this situation, para. 55 permits either party to apply to the CAC to decide this issue. The CAC must notify the parties to the agreement of receipt of such an application and make its decision within ten working days after receipt of the application (para. 55(3) and (5)) (the ten working-day period can be extended by the CAC).

11.4.3   Terminating an agreement for recognition

Unless the agreement provides otherwise, the employer cannot unilaterally terminate an agreement for recognition before the period of three years has expired, beginning with the day after the date of the agreement (para. 56(1), (4) and (5)). It can do so earlier with the consent of the union, and the union can unilaterally terminate the agreement at any time (para. 56(3)).

11.4.4   Application to CAC to specify a method of collective bargaining

The parties to an agreement for recognition may not be able to reach agreement on a method by which to conduct collective bargaining. In this situation, para. 58(3) provides that either party may apply to the CAC for assistance. This is subject to the proviso that the parties have attempted to reach agreement on a method by which to conduct collective bargaining within a negotiation period of 30 working days, beginning with the day after which the agreement for recognition was made (para. 58(2), (4) and (5)). Similarly, application may be made (by either party) to the CAC if the parties have agreed a method for collective bargaining but one of them is failing to carry it out (para. 59).

Prior to acting on an application under paras 58 or 59, the CAC must decide within ten working days (or such longer period as it may specify) if the application is 'admissible' within the provisions of paras 60 and 61 (paras 62(2) and (6)). In this context admissibility means:

(a)   the small employer threshold is satisfied (para. 60(3));
(b)   the union has a certificate of independence (para. 60(4));
(c)   the application is in the form specified by the CAC and accompanied by such documents as the CAC specifies (para. 61); and
(d)   a copy of the application and supporting documents have been given to the employer (or union as the case may be) (para. 61(2) and (3)).

Once the CAC has accepted the application then the procedure is the same as that which applies under Part I (see 11.3), i.e. the CAC must try to help the parties agree a method for collective bargaining, failing which it must specify a method, which is legally enforceable by means of an order for specific performance (para. 63).

11.5   CHANGES TO BARGAINING UNIT AFTER DECLARATION OF RECOGNITION ISSUED

During the Committee Stage of the Bill, a new Part III was inserted into Schedule A1 to deal with the situation where either party believes that there have been material changes to the bargaining unit after the CAC has declared recognition and the specification of the bargaining method has been made. Part III allows either the employer or the union to apply to the CAC for a determination as to what is the appropriate bargaining unit, or whether such a unit still exists, because they believe that the original bargaining unit is no longer appropriate by reason of a change in industrial reality.

11.5.1   Application where either party believes the original unit is no longer appropriate

The CAC must not accept such an application by the employer or union for decision unless it is satisfied that there is *prima facie* evidence that the original unit is no longer appropriate by reason of one of the following matters:

(a)   a change in the organisation or structure of the business carried on by the employer;
(b)   a change in the business activities pursued by the employer; or
(c)   a substantial change in the number of workers employed in the original unit (para. 67(2)(a)–(c)).

The difficulty is likely to be that employers and trade unions will not agree on whether a certain change means that the existing bargaining unit is no longer 'appropriate', and it is not clear how the CAC will resolve such disputes.

These matters will be complicated by the apparent width of para. 67(2). A surprising example was suggested by Mr Wills during the Committee stage in the Commons (16 March 1999) in relation to what constitutes 'a change in the (business) activities pursued by the employer'. It was said that if the employer changed his business from chicken production to egg production, that might justify an application to the CAC under these provisions. This example is difficult to follow, since the concerns of the workers regarding their terms and conditions would presumably remain much the same, whether they were producing chickens or eggs.

The same problem would seem to apply in relation to 'a change in the organisation or structure of the employer's business' — on a strict reading, any change in structure would seem to suffice. A change in ownership, or management changes, or the introduction of a performance-related pay scheme, all would appear to fall within this phrase. As for a 'substantial change in the numbers of workers in the bargaining unit', this is likely to mean a number large enough to affect the outcome of a recognition ballot. Depending on the size of the bargaining unit in question, this may not have to be very large at all. The key issue will be whether such changes mean that the original unit is no longer 'appropriate' for collective bargaining purposes, and the CAC's industrial judgment and common sense will have a crucial role to play here.

The CAC must decide whether or not to accept an application for decision within ten working days after the date it was received, or such longer period as it considers appropriate (para. 68(2) and (6)(a) and (b)). If it does not accept the application, then no further steps are to be taken under Part III.

If the CAC does accept the application for decision, the parties then have an initial ten working-day period (or such longer period as they might agree) in which to agree a new bargaining unit or units which differ from the original bargaining unit (para. 69(1)(b) and (4)(a) and (b)). The option of splitting up an original unit into several units was introduced during the Committee Stage in the Lords (7 June 1999) to deal with (for example) the case of decentralised wage setting in a multi-site organisation.

If the parties manage to agree a new unit or units, the CAC must then issue a new declaration of recognition which replaces the original declaration, with modifications as to the method of collective bargaining if required (para. 69(1)(b) and (3)(a)–(c)). If there is one or more workers within the original unit who are not now within the new agreed unit (or any of the new units) then the CAC must declare that bargaining arrangements as regards these workers are to end by a specified date (para. 73).

However, if the new agreed unit (or any of the new units) contains at least one worker falling within a defined 'outside bargaining unit' (see 11.5.1.1 below), the CAC must take no further steps under Part III and the statutory procedure is terminated (para. 69(2)). The effect of this is to leave the existing bargaining arrangements intact — for the time being. An option for the employer would be simply to start the Part III procedure again, but this time to refuse to reach an agreement with the union.

11.5.1.1   The 'outside bargaining unit' and the new agreed unit
An 'outside bargaining unit' is defined as a unit that meets the following criteria:

(a)   it is not the original unit;
(b)   a union is recognised as entitled to conduct collective bargaining on behalf of the workers within the unit; and
(c)   that union is not a party to the declaration of recognition covering the original unit (para. 69(5)(a)–(c)).

Although para. 69 does not say so expressly, it must be assumed that an 'outside unit' includes units covered by either statutory or non-statutory bargaining arrangements. A distinction between the two is made later in Part III in the provisions dealing with the consequences of the CAC deciding the new unit.

11.5.1.2   Procedure where the CAC decides new unit(s)
If the parties cannot agree on a new unit or units within the first period, the CAC must then decide in the second period whether the original unit continues to be appropriate; if not, whether another unit is (or units are) appropriate or whether there is no other appropriate unit. The second period is the period of ten working days after the first period ends, or such longer period as the CAC may specify (paras 70(2) and (7)(a) and (b)).

In deciding whether the original bargaining unit is no longer appropriate, the CAC must take into account only those matters specified in para. 67(2)(a)–(c) (para. 70(3): see 11.5.1). In deciding whether another bargaining unit is (or units are) appropriate, the CAC must follow the same process as it carried out when determining the appropriateness of the original bargaining unit (para. 70(4) and (5)). If the CAC decides that two or more units are appropriate then it must ensure that no worker falls within more than one of them (para. 70(6)).

If the CAC decides that the original bargaining unit is still appropriate, no further steps are to be taken (para. 71). If the CAC decides that the original unit is no longer appropriate, and that another unit is (or units are) appropriate and there is no overlap with other units (see below) then, depending on the level of support within the new unit, a new declaration of recognition will be made.

If there is any overlap (i.e., one or more workers) between the new unit or units and any 'statutory outside bargaining unit', the CAC must declare that the bargaining arrangements for the workers in the new unit or units, and for each overlapping statutory outside unit to the extent of the overlap, shall cease to have effect (para. 83). The arrangements end within 65 days or — if the CAC believes that continuing the arrangements would be contrary to the interests of good industrial relations — immediately (para. 83(8)).

Similarly, if there is any overlap between the new unit or units and a 'voluntary outside bargaining unit' (but not with a statutory outside unit), the CAC must declare that the bargaining arrangements for the workers within the new unit shall cease to have effect (para. 84(2)). The definition of 'voluntary outside unit' appears to include workers covered either by a purely voluntary recognition agreement, or by an agreement for recognition made under Part II. Again, the arrangements end within the 65 working-day period or sooner if the CAC so decides.

The effect of paras 83 and 84 is that there will be no bargaining arrangements for any new unit or units in the event of any overlap with 'outside' units. If the parties cannot agree any new arrangements and the original arrangements have lasted for less than three years, this will mean an end to collective bargaining at least until the three-year period has expired.

If there is no overlap between the new bargaining unit and any other bargaining unit, the CAC must then decide whether the difference between the original unit and the new unit or units is such that the level of support for the union in the new unit or units needs to be assessed (para. 85). If the CAC concludes that the level of support does not need to be assessed, a new declaration of recognition must be made, replacing the original declaration with modifications as appropriate (para. 85(2)).

If the CAC decides that the level of support does need to be assessed, the inquiry process concerning the level of support for recognition that was carried out in relation to the original unit must be repeated again as regards every new unit, up to and including a new ballot if necessary (paras 86–89).

11.5.2   Employer believes that the original unit has ceased to exist

Employers can serve a statutory notice on a recognised union stating that the recognised bargaining unit has ceased to exist. The notice must identify the unit and bargaining arrangements, state the date on which it is given, state that the unit has ceased to exist, and state that the bargaining arrangements will likewise end after 35 working days after the date of the notice (para. 74(2)(a)–(d)).

The affected union may apply to the CAC for a determination as to whether the unit has indeed ceased to exist (para. 75(2)(a)). It can also ask the CAC to determine whether the original unit is no longer appropriate by reason of any of the matters specified in para. 67(2)(a)–(c), and if so, whether some other unit is appropriate.

If the CAC concludes that the original unit no longer exists then it must issue a declaration that the bargaining arrangements will likewise end (para. 77(2)). If it decides that the original unit has not ceased to exist and that it is still appropriate, the employer's notice must be treated as not having been given (para. 77(3)). Lastly, if the CAC decides that the original unit has not ceased to exist but that it is no longer appropriate, the same procedure as described at 11.5.1.2 must be undertaken.

11.5.3   Residual workers

If the CAC decides that a new unit or units are appropriate and makes a declaration of recognition accordingly, some workers who fell within the original unit may fall outside the new unit or units. In such a case, the CAC must declare that the bargaining arrangements concerning any such workers must cease to have effect on a specified date (para. 90(2)).

As noted at 11.5.1.2 above, where some workers within the new unit or units also fall within a statutory outside bargaining unit, the CAC must declare that the bargaining arrangements as regards those workers must end on a specified date (para. 83(2)). In every such case, the CAC must identify all relevant statutory outside units, and each such unit is to be regarded as a 'parent unit' (para. 91(2)). Those workers within the parent unit who do not fall within the new unit or units are regarded as a 'residual unit' (para. 91(3)) and the CAC must declare that the union originally recognised in respect of the parent unit shall be recognised in respect of the residual unit, with modifications to the method of collective bargaining if necessary (para. 91(4)). This is subject to any applications concerning the inappropriateness or non-existence of the parent unit (para. 91(5)). Any such declaration replaces the declaration regarding the parent unit (para. 91(7)).

11.5.4   Comment on Part III

An important point to note about Part III is that there is no limitation on either party's ability to challenge the appropriateness of the existing bargaining unit, in the sense that such an application could theoretically be made within one month after the original declaration of recognition was made. Similarly, there does not appear to be any limitation on the number of times such applications could be made, unlike the applications for recognition and derecognition, which can be made only once every three years.

Since a statutory declaration of recognition will be made only after a lengthy process of investigation, negotiation, determinations by the CAC and balloting of the relevant workers, it could be argued that it is in the interests of stability that these matters should not be revisited shortly after the declaration of recognition has been made. Exceptional cases aside, it is difficult to see why a different approach should have been taken in relation to changes to the bargaining unit. These provisions may encourage employers to restructure their businesses so as to engineer changes to the bargaining unit, thus enabling them to invoke the complex procedure set out in Part III, and it is suggested that the CAC will need to monitor the operations of these provisions closely if they are not to be vulnerable to abuse.

11.6   DERECOGNITION

The statutory derecognition procedure applies (with the exception of the voluntary recognition of non-independent 'sweetheart' unions) only where the CAC has issued a declaration of recognition and the parties have agreed (with or without the assistance of the CAC) a method by which they will conduct collective bargaining. Employers who are party to voluntary recognition agreements can still end them, as presently, by simply giving notice.

The statutory procedure, which is set out in Parts IV, V and VI of Schedule A1, allows for derecognition applications to be made in the following cases:

(a)   where the employer contends that the size of its workforce has fallen below 21 workers (paras 96–103 (Part IV));

(b)   where the employer or workers believe that there is less than majority support for the collective bargaining arrangements (paras 104–121 (Part IV));

(c)   where the original declaration of recognition was made automatically on the basis of majority union membership and the employer believes that membership within the bargaining unit is now less than 50 per cent (paras 122–133 (Part V)); and

(d)   where the workers want to end voluntary recognition of a non-independent union (paras 134–148 (Part VI)).

Before considering each of these situations in detail, it should be borne in mind that, derecognition of non-independent unions apart, the statutory derecognition procedure cannot be invoked until three years have passed following the date of the CAC's declaration of recognition (paras 97 and 125)). The end of this three-year period is known as the 'relevant date'. Similarly, as with unions seeking recognition, employers and workers seeking derecognition only get 'one bite at the cherry' every three years, i.e. a derecognition application will not be admissible if the CAC has already accepted such an application within the previous three years (paras 101(4), 109(1), 113(1) and 130(1)). This restriction does not apply to applications made by workers to derecognise non-independent unions.

It should also be noted that the provisions of Part IV can be invoked by the employer or the workers, whether the CAC has made the declaration of recognition following a ballot or not, or following a change to the bargaining unit (para. 96(1) and (3)).

11.6.1   Derecognition where employer believes that workforce is less than 21 workers

An employer can serve what amounts to a derecognition notice on a union if the employer believes that its workforce has fallen to an average of less than 21 workers. As with the equivalent provisions concerning admissibility of union applications for recognition of bargaining units within small employers (see 10.5.1), the average is to be calculated over a 13-week period, ending after the declaration of recognition has lasted for three years (para. 99(1)).

The procedure is commenced by the service of a notice by the employer of its intention to end the bargaining arrangements (para. 99(2)). The notice must be served on the union and the CAC. The CAC has ten working days following receipt of the notice — or such longer period as it may specify — in which to determine whether the notice is valid in the sense that it complies with the formal requirements of para. 99(3) (para. 100(1) and (5)). If the CAC decides that the notice is invalid, the parties will be notified accordingly and the notice is to be treated as though it had not been given (para. 100(2)). If the CAC decides that the notice is valid, the parties must be notified and the bargaining arrangements will end on the date specified by the employer, unless the union applies to the CAC challenging the accuracy of the employer's assessment of the size of its workforce and/or that the 13-week period did not end after the relevant date (para. 100(3) and (4)).

The formal requirements specified in para. 99(3) are that the notice must:

(a)   identify the relevant bargaining arrangements;
(b)   specify the 13-week period by which the average workforce size has been calculated;
(c)   state the date on which the notice is given;
(d)   be given within five working days of the day after the last day of the relevant 13-week period;
(e)   state that the employer and any associated employer employed an average of less than 21 workers within the relevant 13-week period; and
(f)   state that the bargaining arrangements are to end on a specified date, which is within 35 working days after the date on which the notice was given.

A union application to the CAC must be made within ten working days starting with the day after the date on which the employer's notice was given, and it must be made in such form and with such documents as the CAC specifies (para. 101(1)(b) and (2)). The union must serve a copy of the notice and any supporting documents on the employer (para. 101(3)). A union application cannot be made if a 'relevant application' in relation to the same bargaining unit was made and accepted by the CAC within three years of the date of the application (para. 101(4)). A 'relevant application' for these purposes is a previous application by the same union under para. 101, an application for derecognition by the employer under paras 106, 107 or 128, or by the workers under para. 112 (para. 101(5)). If these formal requirements are not met (i.e., the application is 'inadmissible'), the union's application must be rejected and the bargaining arrangements will end on the date specified in the employer's notice (para. 102(4)).

If the CAC decides that the union's application is 'admissible', it must notify the parties of this decision within ten working days of receipt of the application or such longer period as it may specify (paras 102(5) and (6)). It must then allow the employer and the union to put forward their views on the issues in question, and provide its decision on these matters within ten working days after notifying acceptance of the application or such longer period as it may specify ('the decision period') (paras 103(1)(b) and (6)). If the CAC decides in favour of the union on either matter, the bargaining arrangements continue and the employer's notice is to be treated as not having been given (para. 103(3)). Otherwise, the bargaining arrangements shall cease on the date specified by the employer in the notice or the day after the end of the decision period, which ever is later (para. 103(2) and (5)).

11.6.2   Derecognition where employer believes there is no longer majority support for bargaining in the bargaining unit

Under these provisions an employer can serve a written request to end bargaining arrangements on the relevant union. As will be seen, this process effectively mirrors that to be undertaken once a recognition request has been served by a union on an employer under Part I of Schedule A1. The employer's request will not be valid unless it is in writing, identifies the bargaining arrangements, states that it has been made under Schedule A1, and is received by the union (para. 104(2)(a)–(d)).

The parties then have two periods in which to conduct negotiations with a view to ending the bargaining arrangements. The first period is ten working days following the day on which the union received the request, or (if there is more than one union) the day on which the last of the unions received the request (para. 105(6)). The union can agree in the first period to end the bargaining arrangements, in which case no further steps are to be taken (para. 105(1)). Alternatively, it can state that it does not accept the request but is willing to negotiate, in which case the parties have a period of 20 working days or such longer period as they may from time to time agree in which to conduct negotiations (para. 105(2) and (7)). ACAS can be requested by either party to assist with negotiations (para. 105(5)), and if the employer fails to respond to a union proposal for the assistance of ACAS within ten working days of the proposal being made, or the employer rejects such a proposal, then the employer cannot take the procedure any further (para. 107(3)).

If the union rejects or fails to respond to the employer's request within the first period, or no agreement is reached within the second period, the employer can then apply to the CAC for a secret ballot to be held on whether the bargaining arrangements should end (paras 106 and 107). Such an application has to be in such form and accompanied by such documents as the CAC specifies (para. 108(1)). Similarly, the application will be inadmissible unless the union is given notice of the application and receives a copy of it together with any supporting documents (para. 108(2)).

The CAC must not proceed with a derecognition application made under paras 106 or 107 unless it is satisfied that at least 10 per cent of the relevant workers want an end to the bargaining arrangements and there is *prima facie* evidence that a majority of those workers would support a derecognition proposal. Just as will be the case with unions seeking to gain recognition, employers desiring derecognition will need to canvass the relevant workers in order to satisfy these requirements.

The CAC must notify the parties that it has received an application made under paras 106 or 107 (para. 111(1)). Within ten working days of the receipt of the application, or such longer period as it may specify, the CAC must decide whether the formal validity and admissibility requirements set out above are satisfied (para. 111(2) and (6)). In making its decision the CAC must have regard to any evidence submitted by the employer or the union (para. 111(3)). If the CAC decides that these requirements are met, it must accept the application, notify the parties of the acceptance and proceed to conduct a secret ballot on the derecognition question (paras 111(5) and 117(1) and (3)). On the other hand, if any of the validity or admissibility requirements are not met, the CAC must not accept the application, must notify the parties accordingly and no further steps are to be taken (para. 111(4)).

The balloting process, set out in paras 117–121, is the same as that undertaken when a union makes an application for recognition under Part I (see 11.2). The employer is under the same three statutory duties. A failure to comply with those duties may result in the CAC making an order for compliance under para. 119(1), and a failure to comply with such an order may result in the CAC refusing the application (para. 119(2)). If the CAC refuses the application on that basis the ballot shall be cancelled or, if it has already been held, shall be of no effect (para. 119(4)). The same 40 per cent threshold applies for employer success. If the result of the ballot is that a majority of workers voting and at least 40 per cent of workers in the bargaining unit favour derecognition, the CAC will declare that the bargaining arrangements are to end on a specified date (para. 121(3)). Otherwise, the application must be refused (para. 121(4)).

11.6.3 Derecognition where the workers believe that there is no longer majority support for bargaining in the bargaining unit

A worker or workers disaffected with the recognised union may also seek to press for a derecognition ballot under Part IV. Similar admissibility requirements apply to the equivalent application made by the employer (paras 112–114). The CAC must give notice to the worker or workers making the application, the union and the employer of receipt of an application made under para. 112(1)). The CAC has ten working days, or such longer period as it may specify, to decide whether the application is admissible, having regard to evidence submitted by the workers, the union and the employer (para. 115(2), (3) and (6)). If the CAC decides that the application is admissible, it must accept the application and proceed to assist negotiations with a view to ending the bargaining arrangements or the workers withdrawing their application, pending the conduct of a secret ballot (paras 115(5) and 116); if the application is not admissible, no further steps are to be taken (para. 115(4)).

As previously, these negotiations are to be conducted with 20 working days following the acceptance of the application by the CAC, or such longer period as it may decide with the consent of all the parties (para. 116(2)). If there is no agreement or withdrawal, the CAC must conduct a secret ballot under paras 117–121. The process is the same as applies for employer applications for derecognition, except as regards the consequences of an employer failing to comply with an order made by the CAC under para. 119(1)). Here, where the employer has failed to fulfil the three duties imposed by para. 118, provided that a secret ballot has not been held, the CAC order may be recorded in the county court and be enforced in the same way as an order of that court (para. 119(3)). The reason why provision has been made for this manner of enforcement in this instance as opposed to other cases is not at all clear.

11.6.4 Derecognition where recognition was automatic

A simplified derecognition procedure will apply in cases where recognition has been automatic (i.e. without a ballot) by virtue of the levels of union membership (para. 122). An employer's request to the union in these circumstances must comply with the following requirements in order to be valid:

(a)   it must be in writing;
(b)   it must be received by the union;
(c)   it must identify the bargaining arrangements;
(d)   it must state that it is made under Schedule A1; and
(e)   it must state that fewer than half of the members of the bargaining unit are
members of the union (para. 127(2)(a)–(e)).

After the union receives the request the parties have ten working days, or such
longer period as they may from time to time agree, in which to conduct negotiations
with a view to ending the bargaining arrangements (para. 128(1) and (3)). If they so
agree then no further steps are to be taken; otherwise, the employer may apply to the
CAC for the holding of a secret ballot on the derecognition question (para. 128(2)).
The admissibility requirements are the same as under Part IV (see 11.6.2), with the
exception that the CAC must be satisfied that less than half of the workers in the
bargaining unit are union members (para. 131(1)).

The CAC must give notice of receipt of an employer application and, within a
period of ten working days or such longer period as it may specify, decide whether
the application is valid and admissible (para. 132(1), (2) and (6)). If the application
is either invalid or inadmissible, it must not be accepted and no further steps are to
be taken (para. 132(4)); otherwise, the CAC must accept the application, notify the
parties of the acceptance and proceed to conduct a secret ballot on derecognition
(para. 132(5)). The provisions on balloting as set out in paras 117–121 then apply as
previously explained (see 11.2 and 11.6.2).

11.6.5   Derecognition of non-independent union by workers

This application enables a union to eliminate employer bargaining arrangements with
house staff associations so as to allow the union to apply for recognition formally.
Where an employer has a voluntary recognition agreement with a non-independent
union, a worker or workers within the bargaining unit covered by the agreement may
apply to the CAC for a derecognition ballot (it will be remembered that only
independent unions can apply for an award of statutory recognition: para. 6). The
beginning of the process is otherwise similar to that where an employer seeks a
derecognition ballot in a case where recognition has not been automatic. The request
by the workers to the employers must comply with the same admissibility
requirements (the time limit issue apart), including the requirement that at least 10
per cent of the workers in the bargaining unit desire an end to the bargaining
arrangements and a majority of the unit would similarly favour a cessation of the
present arrangements (paras 137 and 139).

Additionally, the application will not be admissible if the union faced with
derecognition can demonstrate that it does have a certificate of independence
(para. 138). The application will also be inadmissible if the CAC is satisfied that the
union has applied to the Certification Officer (CO) for a certificate of independence
(para. 140).

After receiving the application, the CAC must give notification of receipt to all the parties (para. 141(1)), and then decide within ten working days or such longer period as it may specify whether the application is admissible, having regard to any evidence submitted by the employer, the union and the workers (para. 141(2), (3) and (6)). As before, if the application is not admissible no further steps are to be taken (para. 141(4)). If the application is admissible, the CAC must accept it and give notification of the acceptance to all the parties (para. 141(5)).

Once the application is accepted, there then follows a 20-day negotiation period (or such longer period as the CAC may decide with the consent of all the parties) during which the CAC must try to assist the parties to negotiate with a view to agreeing either the end of the bargaining arrangements or the workers withdrawing their application (para. 142). Although it is not expressly stated, if there is agreement or the workers withdraw their application no further steps need to be taken (it must be assumed that the failure to include an express provision to this effect is an error in the drafting process).

The procedure then becomes more complicated, with a series of provisions (paras 143–146) aimed at dealing with the various circumstances that might arise as a result of a non-independent union making an application for a certificate of independence to the CO.

The first scenario (as provided by para. 143) is where the CAC accepts a derecognition application by the workers and then becomes aware that a union has, before the derecognition application was made, made an application for a certificate of independence to the CO and that latter application is still pending. Assuming there has been no agreement to end the bargaining arrangements and the workers have not withdrawn their application, the negotiation period is suspended while the CO makes his decision. If the CO's decision is that the union is independent, the CAC must give notice accordingly to all the parties and the workers' application under para. 137 is to be treated as not having been made. If, however, the CO decides that the union is not independent, the CAC must give notice to the parties accordingly and a new 20 working-day negotiation period (which can be extended as previously) will begin (para. 145(1)–(4)).

The second scenario concerns the (probably) rare situation in which there is more than one non-independent union recognised, and two (or more) of them have made applications to the CO for certificates of independence which pre-date the workers' application for derecognition, but the CAC only becomes aware of the fact of the applications at different times during its consideration of the workers' application. Paragraph 143(1) read with para. 145 provides that in the event that the CAC becomes aware, during the second negotiation period, that another of the unions has made an application for a certificate of independence to the CO which is pending, and that application pre-dates the workers' application for derecognition, the provisions of para. 143 operate as previously explained above.

The third scenario is where the CAC does not learn of an application for a certificate of independence during the 20-day negotiation period but is informed that a certificate of independence has been issued during a so-called 'relevant period' (see below), and the CAC is satisfied that a certificate of independence has been issued to the union, or any of the unions if more than one (para. 146(1)(a)–(c)). The 'relevant period' here means the period starting with the first day of the first negotiation period and ending with the first of any of the following events to occur:

(a)   any agreement between the parties to end the bargaining arrangements;
(b)   any withdrawal of the application by the workers; or
(c)   the CAC being informed of the result of a ballot held under Part VI (para. 146(2)).

The provisions of para. 146 also apply if the CAC gives notice under para. 145(2) that the CO has decided that a union which made an application for a certificate of independence is not independent, but then during the 'relevant period' the CAC is satisfied that a certificate of independence has been issued to another of the (formerly) non-independent unions. The 'relevant period' here means the period beginning with the first day of the second negotiation period and ending with the first of the three events set out above (i.e. agreement, withdrawal, notification of ballot result) (para. 146(4)).

Should para. 146 apply then the CAC must notify the parties that it is satisfied about the issue of a certificate of independence to the union (or any of them, if more than one) and the workers' application under para. 137 is to be treated as not having been made.

These provisions appear to be a rather good example of the unnecessary use of a legislative sledgehammer to crack a smallish walnut. During the Report Stage in the Lords, Lord MacIntosh explained the rationale behind these provisions as follows:

> ... we believe it is right that a union which may be independent of control of the employer and which has applied for a certificate of independence should not be subject to derecognition under Part VI unless it fails to obtain that certificate ... we [also] believe it is important to prevent unscrupulous employers using an application for a certificate of independence by a sweetheart union which they control to delay a perfectly fair application under Part VI. We have therefore provided that the union's application must be made before the application for derecognition, to prevent applications made simply to delay matters. An application for derecognition will be stalled only until the certification officer reaches a verdict on the union's application for a certificate of independence. If the certification officer refuses the certificate, the application will then be allowed to proceed, even if the union appeals against the certification officer's decision. Of course, if an appeal is made and succeeds at any time during the course of an application for derecognition, the application will lapse. (Hansard (HL) Report, 8 July 1999, coll. 1069–1070).

From this explanation it seems that para. 146 is intended to cover the situation where a union that has appealed against a refusal by the CO to grant a certificate of independence succeeds in that appeal. It is unfortunate that para. 146 does not make this plain expressly. Unlike the provisions of para. 143 (see above), there is no requirement in para. 146 that the union that subsequently obtains the certificate of independence must have made its original application prior to the workers' application for derecognition under para. 137. In attempting to cover all possible scenarios, it appears that the Government may have created unnecessary complexity and given unscrupulous employers and non-independent 'sweetheart' unions the very opportunity for delaying tactics which the Government so assiduously sought to prevent. It is to be hoped that the Government revisit these provisions at an early stage in order to remove this anomaly and introduce some much-needed clarity and simplicity. Given that para. 140 already provides that the existence of an application for a certificate of independence which pre-dates the workers' derecognition application will make the latter inadmissible, it is doubtful whether much of what is contained in paras 143–146 adds anything other than detail and complexity to an already lengthy and complex Schedule. The main practical effect appears to be that it will be more difficult for workers to succeed in derecognition applications under Part VI.

Lastly, if an application under para. 137 has been accepted (the workers' application to end arrangements) and there is no agreement on derecognition or withdrawal of the application and paras 143–146 do not apply, the balloting provisions in paras 117–121 apply as previously explained (see 11.2 and 11.6.2).

11.6.6   Derecognition where there are overlapping bargaining units

If as a result of a previous declaration of statutory recognition there is an overlap of at least one employee between the statutory bargaining unit and the unit where the non-independent union is recognised, the CAC must declare that the bargaining arrangements between the employer and the non-independent union are to end on a specified date.

11.7   LOSS OF CERTIFICATE OF INDEPENDENCE

Part VII of Schedule A1 to the 1992 Act applies to a union that has a statutory declaration of recognition or an agreement for recognition with an employer and the CAC has specified a collective bargaining method that the parties have not replaced (paras 149 and 150). If such a union loses its certificate of independence, the statutory bargaining arrangements cease to have effect and the parties will be deemed to be in a relationship of voluntary recognition (para. 152). If the union succeeds in an appeal against the loss of its certificate of independence then from the date of reissue of the certificate by the CO the statutory bargaining arrangements shall be revived (para. 153). During the period when the statutory bargaining arrangements do not have effect, the provisions of Parts III to VI inclusive do not apply (para. 154). This appears to have the curious — and surely unintended — effect of removing from the workers the right to make an application for derecognition of a non-independent union under Part VI.

11.8   PROTECTION AGAINST DETRIMENT AND DISMISSAL

Part VIII of Schedule A1 confers special protection against detriment, dismissal and selection for redundancy for workers involved with the statutory recognition process. Workers subjected to a detriment because of their involvement with a purely voluntary recognition process do not have this special protection, but they are likely to be protected under the existing law preventing victimisation of trade union members on the grounds of trade union membership and activities (see s. 152(1)(a), (b) and s. 146(1)(a), (b), TULR(C)A 1992).

As regards the protection conferred by Part VIII, there is the question whether it extends to acts of detriment or dismissal taking place before the commencement of any statutory process. The wording of the grounds on which detrimental action and dismissal are prohibited (set out below) suggests that in most cases protection will be afforded. For example, workers dismissed because they took part in a recruitment campaign as a prelude to an application by a union for automatic recognition are likely to be protected as they have been dismissed because they 'acted with a view to obtaining . . . recognition of a union . . . under [Schedule A1]' (para. 161(2)(a)).

11.8.1   Protection against detriment

Workers have the right not to be subjected to any detriment by their employer by an act or a deliberate failure to act on any one of eight grounds (para. 156(1)). The eight grounds are that the worker:

(a)   acted with a view to obtaining or preventing recognition of a union by the employer under Schedule A1;

(b)   indicated that he or she supported or did not support recognition of a union by the employer under Schedule A1;

(c)   acted with a view to securing or preventing the ending of bargaining arrangements under Schedule A1;

(d)   indicated that he or she supported or did not support the ending of bargaining arrangements under Schedule A1;

(e)   influenced or sought to influence the way in which votes were to be cast by other workers in a ballot arranged under Schedule A1;

(f)   influenced or sought to influence other workers to vote or abstaining from voting in such a ballot;

(g)   voted in such a ballot; or

(h)   proposed to do, failed to do, or proposed to decline to do, any of the matters referred to above (para. 156(2)(a)–(h)).

At first glance this appears to be a fairly comprehensive list offering substantial protection to workers involved in any way in the statutory recognition or derecognition process. There are, however, significant limitations.

First, a worker will not be protected if the detriment took place because the worker's act constituted an 'unreasonable act or omission' by him or her (para. 156(3)). As originally drafted the Act would have deprived workers of protection simply if the act constituted a breach of contract, but this provision was removed when the Government realised that an employer could simply insert a provision into all the workers' contracts requiring them not to support any proposals for union recognition. However, during the debate on this provision in the Report Stage in the Lords, Lord McIntosh opined that most breaches of contract would still be viewed as 'unreasonable' acts (Hansard HL, 8 July 1999, col. 1072).

This provision is likely to involve tribunals in making fine judgments on the merits of particular cases. For example, if a union meeting during a ballot to inform the workers of the issues lasts ten minutes longer than originally agreed with the employer, and the employer views the conduct of his workers as a breach of contract and subjects the workers to a detriment by making minor deductions of wages accordingly, will the conduct of the workers be held to be 'unreasonable'? Similarly, if two or three workers are found to be discussing the recognition question at work at a time when the employer has expressly forbidden such discussion, would that conduct be 'unreasonable'? This example may also give rise to arguments about the scope of the right to freedom of expression as contained in the Human Rights Act 1998, which came into force in October 2000.

Where the detriment consists of the dismissal of an employee, such a dismissal will be caught by the specific prohibition on dismissal (see 11.8.2 below). However, in the case of the termination of the contract of a worker who is not an employee, these provisions on detriment do still apply. The same cap on compensation that applies to employees making claims for ordinary unfair dismissal under the Employment Rights Act 1996 will apply (para. 160). Currently this is £6,900 for the basic award and £50,000 for the compensatory award.

A further issue concerns the scope of actions that might be said to be a 'detriment'. This might be important in the context of information being distributed by an employer in the course of a hotly-contested recognition ballot. For example, would the distribution of letters to employees saying that jobs will be lost if the union is recognised and other similar negative campaigning tactics, be a 'detriment'? Employers might argue that they were merely providing information to the workers about the issues involved. Having regard to the way in which the prohibition of action short of dismissal on grounds of trade union activities contained in s. 146 of TULR(C)A 1992 has been interpreted, to require that action be taken against a particular individual, it is quite possible that such action will not be regarded as a 'detriment'. But such conduct is arguably a threat, and one that the employer could repeat — in varying forms — for as long as the recognition procedure operated.

Another problem concerns the offering of personal contracts as incentives not to campaign or vote for recognition. Provided nothing is said about union membership, this sort of activity would be legitimate. The reason for this is that s. 148(3) of TULR(C)A 1992 provides that where the employer acted with at least one purpose being to 'further a change in their relationship with all or any class of their employees' such an act (or omission) is not to be regarded as a detriment. The offering of personal contracts or other financial incentives could prove to be a very effective strategic tactic, and seriously undermine recognition campaigns. With the law as presently framed, there will not be much that a union can do about it (see further the discussion in Chapter 7).

Actions for alleged infringements of the right not to be subjected to a detriment are to be brought to an employment tribunal, within three months of the act (or, if the act is part of a series, the last of the acts) taking place (para. 157). A deliberate failure to act (which causes the detriment) is to be treated as having happened when it was decided upon (para. 157(2)(b)). In the absence of any contrary evidence, an employer will be deemed to have decided upon the failure to act either when he does an act inconsistent with doing the failed act, or when the period expires within which the employer may reasonably have been expected to do the failed act (para. 157(3)).

The burden of proof is on the employer to establish the ground on which he acted or failed to act (para. 158). Compensation is to be awarded on a just and equitable basis, having regard to the infringement complained of and any loss sustained by the complainant that is attributable to the act complained of (para. 159(2)). The loss will include any expenses reasonably incurred as a consequence of the act or failure in question, together with the loss of any benefit that the worker might otherwise have expected to receive (para. 159(3)).

Compensation can be reduced on a just and equitable basis where the worker contributed to the loss (para. 159(5)). Workers must take reasonable steps to mitigate their loss (para. 159(4)).

11.8.2 Protection against dismissal

Much of the preceding discussion concerning protection against detriment also applies to protection against dismissal. The effect of para. 161 is that if the reason for the dismissal was for one of those set out in para. 161(2)(a)–(h), or if more than one reason the main reason was one of those reasons, the dismissal will be automatically unfair. The reasons set out in para. 161(2)(a)–(h) are the same as set out in para. 156(2)(a)–(h) (see 11.8.1). Similarly, the employer can argue that the reason for dismissal was not a prohibited one because the employee's (not worker's) conduct constituted an 'unreasonable act or omission' (para. 161(3)). There is no upper age limit on the right to claim unfair dismissal under para. 161(1).

Employees can also make applications for interim relief in cases of alleged automatically unfair dismissal, provided that any such application is lodged within seven days of the effective date of termination.

Lastly, selection for redundancy will be automatically unfair if the reason or principal reason for dismissal is that the employee was redundant but the circumstances constituting the redundancy applied equally to other employees holding similar positions who were not dismissed, and the reason for the employee's selection (or principal reason) was one of the grounds set out in para. 161(2) (para. 162).

Chapter 12
Institutional Changes

12.1 ABOLITION OF THE TRADE UNION COMMISSIONERS

The Offices of Commissioner for the Rights of Trade Union Members (CROTUM) and Commissioner for Protection against Unlawful Industrial Action (CPUIA) were created by the Conservative Government in 1988 and 1993 respectively. They were established on account of the Government's concern that there was no guarantee that the new statutory obligations developed in the 1980s, to control trade union internal and external affairs, would be enforced unless agencies were founded to help individuals pursue their remedies under the relevant legislation.

The CROTUM was empowered under the Employment Act 1988 to provide assistance (by paying legal costs or by obtaining legal advice) to trade union members who wished to take legal action in the courts against their own union for union breaches of certain statutory rights (relating to a failure of administration and governance). In 1990 the remit of the office was extended to include assistance to pursue legal action for alleged breaches of union rules, including rules relating to appointment and election to union office, balloting of members, disciplinary proceedings and the application of union funds or property.

The role of the CPUIA was to provide assistance (modelled on the powers of the CROTUM) to an individual member of the public who wished to exercise the statutory right (created by the Trade Union Reform and Employment Rights Act 1993; now s. 235A of TULR(C)A 1992) to bring legal action against a trade union for organising or threatening to organise unlawful industrial action where he or she was, or was likely to be, deprived of goods or services.

The creation of these bodies was heavily criticised at the time of their inception as an unwarranted interference in the private affairs of trade unions. There was a fear that dissident union members or disgruntled members of the public would take advantage of this legal assistance to cause severe inconvenience to unions and hinder their legitimate activities. However, the worst fears of the trade unions were unfounded. The statistics derived from the Commissioners' annual reports show that the offices have had very little formal impact, with the number of applicants given material assistance being in single figures year on year.

Subsequently, in the White Paper *Fairness at Work*, it was recognised that these agencies had very limited effect and were 'inefficient and unnecessary'. Section 28 of the 1999 Act repeals ss. 109–114 and 235B–235C of TULR(C)A 1992 which established the two Commissioners and outlined their functions and procedure. Although both agencies have been abolished, it is not the case, however, that the substance of the trade union obligations that the Commissioners were empowered to assist have been extinguished. With regard to matters of internal trade union law (where the CROTUM previously advised and assisted with an application to the court) the Certification Officer (CO) has now been given the responsibility to adjudicate on most (but not all) alleged trade union breaches of the rules and statute (see 12.2 below).

12.2   THE CERTIFICATION OFFICER

The office of the CO has a lengthy historical pedigree. The original forerunner to the CO was the Registrar of Friendly Societies, who administered the registration of unions under the Trade Union Act 1871. Registration under this Act was a voluntary matter with little detriment to a union that declined to register. This was abolished by the Industrial Relations Act 1971 and replaced by a system of registration administered by a Registrar of Trade Unions. Unlike the previous system in operation, registration was necessary to gain the benefits of trade union status and without it unions were subject to substantial liabilities.

After the repeal of the Industrial Relations Act 1971, the Registrar of Trade Unions was replaced by the office of the CO created by the Employment Protection Act 1975. The CO is appointed by the Secretary of State for Trade and Industry and is financed and staffed by ACAS, although formally independent of both ACAS and the Government.

Under the Employment Protection Act 1975, the duties of the CO were limited to supervising trade union compliance with the statutory requirements outlined in the Trade Union and Labour Relations Act 1974 and with administering the list of trade unions and certifying their independence. As the statutory regulation of trade unions increased during the 1980s and early 1990s, the CO's administrative, supervisory and judicial functions expanded.

The main responsibilities of the CO are contained in TULR(C)A 1992 and include:

(a)   maintaining a list of trade unions and employers' associations and certifying the independence of trade unions who are on this list and who apply for a certificate of independence;

(b)   seeing that unions keep appropriate accounts and comply with the statutory provisions governing union accounting and superannuation matters;

(c)   ensuring compliance with statutory procedures relating to the setting up and operation of union political funds and approving political fund ballot rules;

(d)   ensuring the observance of the statutory rules concerning union mergers and transfer of engagements;

(e)   hearing complaints over the handling of secret ballots for union elections, over the conduct of merger ballots and for breaches of the political fund rules;

(f)   hearing complaints over the failure of a union to compile and maintain a register of members' names and addresses;

(g)   hearing and investigating complaints about alleged financial malpractice.

The 1999 Act extends the CO's powers to enable him to hear complaints about most aspects of the law where the CROTUM previously provided assistance. The rationale for this (set out in *Fairness at Work*) was that by giving the responsibility to the CO, trade union members and others will be able to secure their rights more easily and effectively without the cost and confrontation of court proceedings. These points were re-stated by Mr Michael Wills, Minister for Small Firms, Trade and Industry, during the Committee Stage of the Bill:

> We propose to extend and redefine the role of the Certification Officer to empower him to adjudicate disputes between individual trade unionists and their unions in relation to many of those areas where the CROTUM can currently provide assistance. The Certification Officer is well respected and already provides an accessible alternative to the courts to resolve disputes involving trade unions. The extension of the Certification Officer's powers is in line with the Government's wish to encourage potential litigants — in any branch of the civil law — to use practical alternatives to court proceedings to resolve their disputes. That saves court time and often produces quicker, cheaper and more effective remedies for the parties concerned. (Hansard HC Standing Committee E, 4 March 1999, col. 276)

Schedule 6 to the 1999 Act (amending the TULR(C)A 1992) provides for an extension of the CO's jurisdiction relating to breaches of statutory rights and rule book infractions, and introduces a new enforcement procedure for the CO's existing jurisdiction.

12.2.1   Extended jurisdiction for breach of statutory rights

Schedule 6, para. 6 amends s. 31, TULR(C)A 1992 (on the remedy available to a trade union member where a union member's right to access to inspect union accounts (in s. 30, TULR(C)A 1992) is violated). The amendment provides that the CO now has jurisdiction (in conjunction with the court) to adjudicate on breaches of this right. However, an applicant cannot apply to both the court and the CO (s. 31(6), (7)). The CO should determine the application within six months, is entitled to make 'enquiries as he thinks fit' and give both parties the opportunity to be heard (s. 31(2A) and (2C)). Where the CO finds the claim well-founded he may make an order (enforceable in the same way as a court order) to ensure enforcement of the right (to inspect the accounts, to be accompanied by an accountant and to be supplied with extracts or copies of the accounts: s. 31(2B).

Schedule 6, para. 13 inserts a new s. 72A into the TULR(C)A 1992, giving the CO jurisdiction (as an alternative, not as an addition to court proceedings) over complaints of a breach of the statutory rules on the use of general funds for political objects (s. 71, TULR(C)A 1992). Similar procedural requirements as outlined above apply, although here the application is for a declaration and reasons for the decision must be given (s. 72A(2)). Where the union intends to remedy the breach the declaration must specify the steps the union needs to take to do so (s. 72A(4)). The CO also has the authority to issue any necessary orders (s. 72A(5)). Both declarations and orders are enforceable as if made by the court (s. 72A(7) and (9)).

12.2.2 Jurisdiction over breaches of union rules

Schedule 6, para. 19 to the 1999 Act (creating ss. 108A–108C of TULR(C)A 1992) introduces new powers for the CO to investigate certain breaches of union rules; previously the only remedy was a common law action in the civil courts. Now, a member of a trade union has the right to apply to the CO if there has been a breach or threatened breach of a trade union's rules (including the rules of any branch or section) relating to any of the matters set out in s. 108A(2) of TULR(C)A 1992. The matters are:

(a) the appointment or election of a person to, or the removal of a person from, any office;

(b) disciplinary proceedings by the union (including expulsion);

(c) the balloting of members on any issue other than industrial action;

(d) the constitution or proceedings of any executive committee or of any decision-making meeting:

(e) such other matters as may be specified in an order made by the Secretary of State.

'Industrial action' is defined as a strike or other industrial action by persons employed under contracts of employment (s. 108A(9)). An 'executive committee' is defined as a body that has the power to make executive decisions on behalf of the union or a constituent body of the union; 'any decision-making meeting' is a meeting of union members or members of a major constituent body (or representatives of members) that, under the rules, has the power to make final decisions (s. 108A(10)–(12)).

The applicant must be a member of the union, or have been a member at the time of the alleged or threatened breach, and the application must be made within a six-month time limit from the date of the breach or the conclusion of the internal complaint procedure, or one year from the invoking of that procedure (s. 108A(3), (6), (7)). Once an application has been made to the CO the applicant may not complain to the court on the same matter; and the CO may not entertain an application if, alternatively, an application has been made to the court (s. 108A(14), (15)). No application may be made by an employee of the union who alleges breaches of the rules regarding disciplinary action or dismissal (s. 108A(5)).

The CO may refuse to accept an application unless satisfied that the applicant has taken all reasonable steps to resolve the claim by the use of any existing union internal complaints procedure (s. 108B(1)). If the application has been accepted by the CO he must determine it within six months of its being made. He has powers to initiate enquiries regarding the claim, must provide the applicant and the trade union with an opportunity to be heard, and must give reasons for his decision to make or refuse the declaration asked for (s. 108B(2)).

Where a declaration is made the CO may also make an enforcement order unless 'to do so would be inappropriate'. This order imposes on the union one or more of the following requirements:

(a)   to take such steps to remedy the breach, or withdraw the threat of a breach, as may be specified in the order;
(b)   to abstain from such acts as may be so specified with a view to securing that a breach or threat of the same or a similar kind does not occur in the future. (s. 108B(3)).

Where an order imposes a requirement on the union as in (a) above, the order must specify the period within which the union must comply with the requirement of the order (s. 108B(4)). A declaration or an enforcement order made by the CO is to be treated as if made by the court (s. 108B(6) and (8)). Any union member is entitled to enforce an enforcement order, not just the original applicant (s. 108B(7)).

The commencement date for these provisions is 25 October 1999 and the CO's power to consider such applications is restricted to alleged breaches occurring on or after 27 July 1999. The CO's Annual Report for 1999–2000 reported that no decisions were issued in the period 25 October 1999 to 31 March 2000, although ten applications are still outstanding.

12.2.3   Enforcement procedure for existing jurisdiction

The 1999 Act provides for a new enforcement mechanism in areas where previously the CO only had the power to issue decisions and declarations. Binding orders (enforceable as an order of the court) may be granted where:

(a)   union has failed to maintain the register of members (Schedule 6, paras 2–5; amending ss. 24, 24A, 25 and 26 of TULR(C)A 1992);
(b)   a union permits an officer (having offended against certain provisions of the 1992 Act) to hold union office contrary to the statute (Schedule 6, para. 7; amending s. 45C of TULR(C)A 1992);
(c)   a union has failed to comply with the statutory requirements to hold a balloted election for union office (Schedule 6, paras 9–11; amending ss. 54, 55 and 56 of TULR(C)A 1992);

(d)   a union has failed to comply with the statutory requirements to hold ballots on political resolutions or failed to comply with ballot rules (Schedule 6, paras 14–16; amending ss. 79, 80 and 81 of TULR(C)A 1992).

Where there is an application to the CO for an order to force the union to comply with the relevant provision, that individual cannot then apply to the court (and *vice versa* should the application be first made to the court). However, a different person is not barred from applying to the CO or court on the same issue; although when considering the new application the CO or court should have regard to any previous decisions or deliberations on the matter.

The procedure to obtain and enforce an order under this jurisdiction is complex and detailed. In brief, on an application the CO should make such enquiries as he thinks necessary and must give the applicant and trade union the opportunity to be heard. A declaration may then be made, specifying the trade union's failure, giving reasons for the decision. Unless the CO deems it inappropriate, an enforcement order (enforceable by any member of the union) may now be made, ordering the union to remedy the failure (such as to hold a ballot in accordance with political ballot rules or an election ballot in accordance with the statutory requirements) or to abstain from future acts so that the failure is not repeated. A declaration or enforcement order is to be treated as if granted by a court.

In addition, the powers of the CO to investigate trade union affairs are strengthened where complaints are made relating to breach of political fund rules (Schedule 6, para. 17; amending s. 82 of TULR(C)A 1992) and where there is a failure to comply with the statutory rules on union amalgamations and transfers (Schedule 6, para. 18; amending s. 103 of TULR(C)A 1992). The relevant paragraphs state that the CO is entitled to make 'such enquiries as he thinks fit' and that where information is to be furnished to him in connection with such enquiries he may still proceed with a determination of the complaint where the requested information has not been provided by a specified due date.

12.2.4   Appeal procedure

The 1999 Act introduces new rights of appeal to the Employment Appeal Tribunal (on points of law) from the CO's decisions. Paragraph 8 of Schedule 6, inserting a new s. 45D into the TULR(C)A 1992, introduces the right to appeal for an application regarding the duty to maintain a register of members, the request for access to accounts and the duty to ensure that offenders do not hold union office. A new s. 56A of TULR(C)A 1992 (inserted by Schedule 6, para. 12) provides for an appeal to the Employment Appeal Tribunal for those applications relating to complaints about union balloting arrangements for elections under s. 55 of the 1992 Act. Section 108C of TULR(C)A 1992 provides that an appeal on any question of law arising from a determination by the CO in rule book proceedings also lies to the Employment Appeal Tribunal.

12.2.5   Miscellaneous provisions

The TULR(C)A 1992 was further amended by Schedule 6, para. 22 to the 1999 Act, requiring the CO to make provisions about the disclosure and restriction of disclosure of the identity of a complainant. Prior to this amendment, the 1992 Act provided that the identity of a complainant would be revealed only with the consent of the individual concerned. Under a new s. 256(2) and (2A), the CO is required to disclose a complainant's identity to the union unless the circumstances are such that the CO thinks it should not be disclosed. Thus, to ensure openness, the presumption will be that a complainant's identity will be revealed.

Paragraph 23 of Schedule 6 introduces a new provision (s. 256A) permitting the CO, on giving reasons, to refuse to entertain applications by a 'vexatious litigant'. This is an individual who is subject to an order in force under s. 33(1) of the Employment Tribunals Act 1996, or s. 42(1) of the Supreme Court Act 1981, s. 1 of the Vexatious Actions (Scotland) Act 1898 or s. 32 of the Judicature (Northern Ireland) Act 1978.

The Employment Relations Act 1999 has also amended the 1992 Act to change the period covered by the CO's report from the calendar year basis to a financial year (Schedule 6, para. 24: the reporting arrangements of the CAC and ACAS have also been similarly altered).

12.3   THE ADVISORY, CONCILIATION AND ARBITRATION SERVICE

ACAS was established by the Employment Protection Act 1975 as a single unifying agency to take over the responsibilities of conciliation and aspects of arbitration previously held by the Department of Employment and the Commission on Industrial Relations. ACAS was also charged under the Employment Protection Act with the broader remit of 'promoting the improvement of industrial relations, and in particular of encouraging the extension of collective bargaining and the development and, where necessary, reform of collective bargaining machinery'.

This requirement to promote and encourage the extension of collective bargaining was repealed by the Trade Union Reform and Employment Rights Act 1993 and substituted by a re-affirmation of ACAS's conciliation and arbitration duties. The new s. 209 of TULR(C)A 1992 stated that the duty of ACAS was 'to promote the improvement of industrial relations, in particular, by exercising its functions in relation to the settlement of trade disputes (by conciliation and arbitration)'. In carrying out this duty ACAS engages in several activities, in both collective and individual conciliation (where ACAS assists in the settlement of trade disputes and employment tribunal proceedings), collective arbitration (where ACAS will appoint an arbitrator who will consider submissions and make a binding award) and dispute mediation (where a mediator is appointed whose recommendations may form the basis of a settlement of the dispute).

ACAS also has authority to act in a general advisory role on matters of industrial relations and employment policies. Of particular importance has been the develop-ment of advisory mediation. This it sees as a means of 'addressing underlying difficulties affecting the employment relationship'. So, for example, where concili-ation has been requested over a particular issue, it may be the case that ACAS identifies a broader problem that requires longer-term solutions. ACAS may facilitate the setting up of a joint working party, with staff from ACAS chairing, to consider these broader issues. This role has expanded over the last decade, in part due to economic and industrial change. Industrial reorganisation caused by the privatisation of public sector organisations, mergers and the development of new sectors of the economy have all contributed to the restructuring and decentralisation of collective bargaining. ACAS, through the setting up of advisory joint councils, has advised and encouraged consultation, both before the changes in collective bargaining are formalised and during the implementation of any changes.

In the White Paper *Fairness at Work*, ACAS's advisory function (with ACAS operating jointly with both workers and employers to secure harmonious industrial relations) was identified as being of particular importance. ACAS was seen as a proponent and facilitator of the 'partnership at work' principle that is the main focus of Government employment policy. In order to enhance this role, s. 26 of the 1999 Act repeals the wording that was introduced in 1993, leaving the statutory function of ACAS to be 'to promote the improvement of industrial relations'. This change was explained by Michael Wills, the Minister for Small Firms, Trade and Industry, in the following terms:

The amended wording is in line with our wish to enhance the standing of ACAS's work on dispute resolution. The current wording requires ACAS to give priority to fire-fighting rather than fire prevention. That does not make sense, especially in the context of our overall approach to industrial relations. It is obviously important to settle disputes quickly and effectively. However, surely it is as important to ensure that disputes do not arise in the first place.

ACAS provides a range of services to employers, workers and unions that can help settle disputes ... for example, ACAS is able to provide in-depth advice to organisations with a history of poor labour relations or with a major problem in managing change in the workplace. Such work is undertaken by joint working parties in a non-adversarial atmosphere.

Under ACAS's guidance, such organisations can identify and resolve their deep-seated problems, thereby establishing a new culture at work. The Bill is intended to assist with that. Such activity can represent very good value for public expenditure. It is far better to prevent disputes than to suffer the dislocations to an industrial sector or public service that strikes may create.

Section 26 makes a small yet important change to ACAS's statutory terms of reference. It has been welcomed by the ACAS council and signals an appreciation of ACAS's work in dispute prevention.' (Hansard HC Standing Committee E, 4 March 1999, col. 268)

On the basis of this affirmation of ACAS's work in this field, it may be the case that in the near future ACAS will benefit from the 'partnership' funding provided under s. 30 of the Employment Relations Act 1999 (see 12.5).

12.4   THE CENTRAL ARBITRATION COMMITTEE

The CAC was established as a separate body within ACAS by the Employment Protection Act 1975, inheriting many of the duties formerly exercised by the Industrial Arbitration Board. The CAC's original jurisdiction was extensive. It had the responsibility to adjudicate on recognition disputes (under the Employment Protection Act) where the employer had refused to comply with a decision of ACAS to recommend recognition. If the CAC subsequently ordered recognition, and the employer refused to comply, the CAC could award the workers involved in the dispute improved terms and conditions of employment. The recognition provisions of the Employment Protection Act 1975 were repealed by the Employment Act 1980.

Another major function of the CAC was to consider applications by unions under Schedule 11 of the Employment Protection Act. Under Schedule 11, if, in the absence of any agreement, a particular employer was failing to observe terms and conditions that were generally applicable in that trade or industry, the CAC had the authority to make an award to such workers to enhance their terms and conditions to that comparable level. Schedule 11 operated in a similar manner to the Fair Wages Resolution, whereby government contractors had to pay wages at a similar level to that generally accepted in the relevant industry. The Schedule 11 formula was repealed in 1980 and the Fair Wages Resolution was rescinded in 1983.

The focus of the CAC's remaining work has been on voluntary arbitration and on the adjudication of complaints where employers have failed to disclose information to recognised unions as required by ss. 181–185 of TULR(C)A 1992. Where, with the consent of the parties, disputes are referred by ACAS to the CAC for arbitration, a chair sits with two 'wing-persons' to consider written submissions, often amplified by oral representations. On making an award the Committee is not obliged to give reasons but usually does so in the form of 'general considerations'. The CAC annual reports show that with the repeal of most of the CAC's duties the workload of the CAC has declined drastically. In 1977 there were over 1,000 references to the CAC. By 1997 this had fallen to 22.

With the creation of the new statutory recognition procedure the CAC's role is set to expand. As described in chapters 10 and 11, the CAC has the primary responsibility to oversee, administer and determine a recognition application — to decide the appropriate bargaining unit and whether the union enjoys an appropriate level of support, to arrange the secret ballot, through to the award of recognition. In order better to administer the complex recognition procedure, the CAC decision-making powers have been streamlined and the appointment system has been restructured.

The amendments now provide that in the decision-making process the chairman will not be as dominant as has been the case previously. Section 25 of the 1999 Act amends s. 263 of TULR(C)A 1992 (which deals with proceedings before the CAC) and inserts a new s. 263A. This section states that when discharging its functions under the recognition (and derecognition) scheme, the CAC shall consist of a panel of three appointed by the chairman of the CAC. This must include the chairman or deputy chairman and one representative of each side of industry (s. 263A(1), (2)). If the panel cannot reach a unanimous decision but a majority of the panel agree (i.e. two out of three), it is their opinion that decides the case. Otherwise, if there is no majority at all (i.e. all three have different opinions) then the chairman of the panel has the authority to decide the issue 'with the full powers of an umpire or, in Scotland, an oversman'.

The 1999 Act also introduces minor alterations to the appointment process to the CAC. Section 24 amends s. 260 of TULR(C)A 1992 by substituting two new subsections. Previously ACAS had an input into appointments to the CAC, with members appointed from a list submitted by ACAS. The new provisions leave the choice of appointments (of chairman, deputy chairman and members) solely to the Secretary of State, after consultation with ACAS. The only proviso is that all must be experienced in industrial relations as an employer or employee representative. The reasoning behind this change was to ensure that the Secretary of State had a wider group of members to choose from than had previously been the case (as ACAS nominations tended to be from its own panel of arbitrators).

12.5   PARTNERSHIPS AT WORK

The *Fairness at Work* White Paper stressed the Government's desire to encourage a 'partnership' culture in contemporary industrial relations. Thus, s. 30 of the 1999 Act provides that the Secretary of State is authorised to make funding available for 'the purpose of encouraging and helping employers (or their representatives) and employees (or their representatives) to improve the way they work together'. The Explanatory Notes to the Act suggest that under this section funding will be available for training and any other activities to help develop partnerships at work and the dissemination of good practice. It is assumed that organisations will be able to apply for training budgets from this 'partnership fund'.

Appendix 1
Employment Relations Act 1999

CHAPTER 26
ARRANGEMENT OF SECTIONS

Trade unions

Section

EMPLOYMENT RELATIONS ACT 1999

1999 CHAPTER 26

An Act to amend the law relating to employment, to trade unions and to employment agencies and businesses. [27th July 1999]

BE IT ENACTED by the Queen's most Excellent Majesty, by and with the advice and consent of the Lords Spiritual and Temporal, and Commons, in this present Parliament assembled, and by the authority of the same, as follows:—

Trade unions

1. Collective bargaining: recognition

(1) The Trade Union and Labour Relations (Consolidation) Act 1992 shall be amended as follows.

(2) After Chapter V of Part I (rights of trade union members) there shall be inserted—

'CHAPTER VA

COLLECTIVE BARGAINING: RECOGNITION

70A. Recognition of trade unions

Schedule A1 shall have effect.'

(3) Immediately before Schedule 1 there shall be inserted the Schedule set out in Schedule 1 to this Act.

2. Detriment related to trade union membership

Schedule 2 shall have effect.

3. Blacklists

(1) The Secretary of State may make regulations prohibiting the compilation of lists which—

(a) contain details of members of trade unions or persons who have taken part in the activities of trade unions, and

(b) are compiled with a view to being used by employers or employment agencies for the purposes of discrimination in relation to recruitment or in relation to the treatment of workers.

(2) The Secretary of State may make regulations prohibiting—

(a) the use of lists to which subsection (1) applies;

(b) the sale or supply of lists to which subsection (1) applies.

(3) Regulations under this section may, in particular—

(a) confer jurisdiction (including exclusive jurisdiction) on employment tribunals and on the Employment Appeal Tribunal;

(b) include provision for or about the grant and enforcement of specified remedies by courts and tribunals;

(c) include provision for the making of awards of compensation calculated in accordance with the regulations;

(d) include provision permitting proceedings to be brought by trade unions on behalf of members in specified circumstances;

(e) include provision about cases where an employee is dismissed by his employer and the reason or principal reason for the dismissal, or why the employee was selected for dismissal, relates to a list to which subsection (1) applies;

(f) create criminal offences;

(g) in specified cases or circumstances, extend liability for a criminal offence created under paragraph (f) to a person who aids the commission of the offence or to a person who is an agent, principal, employee, employer or officer of a person who commits the offence;

(h) provide for specified obligations or ofrences not to apply in specified circumstances;

(i) include supplemental, incidental, consequential and transitional provision, including provision amending an enactment;

(j) make different provision for different cases or circumstances.

(4) Regulations under this section creating an offence may not provide for it to be punishable—

(a) by imprisonment,

(b) by a fine in excess of level 5 on the standard scale in the case of an offence triable only summarily, or

(c) by a fine in excess of the statutory maximum in the case of summary conviction for an offence triable either way.

(5) In this section—

'list' includes any index or other set of items whether recorded electronically or by any other means, and

'worker' has the meaning given by section 13.

(6) Subject to subsection (5), expressions used in this section and in the Trade Union and Labour Relations (Consolidation) Act 1992 have the same meaning in this section as in that Act.

4. Ballots and notices

Schedule 3 shall have effect.

5. Training

In Chapter VA of Part I of the Trade Union and Labour Relations (Consolidation) Act 1992 (collective bargaining: recognition) as inserted by section 1 above, there shall be inserted after section 70A—

'70B Training

(1) This section applies where—

(a) a trade union is recognised, in accordance with Schedule A1, as entitled to conduct collective bargaining on behalf of a bargaining unit (within the meaning of Part I of that Schedule), and

(b) a method for the conduct of collective bargaining is specified by the Central Arbitration Committee under paragraph 31(3) of that Schedule (and is not the subject of an agreement under paragraph 31(5)(a) or (b)).

(2) The employer must from time to time invite the trade union to send representatives to a meeting for the purpose of—

(a) consulting about the employer's policy on training for workers within the bargaining unit,

(b) consulting about his plans for training for those workers during the period of six months starting with the day of the meeting, and

(c) reporting about training provided for those workers since the previous meeting.

(3) The date set for a meeting under subsection (2) must not be later than—

(a) in the case of a first meeting, the end of the period of six months starting with the day on which this section first applies in relation to a bargaining unit, and

(b) in the case of each subsequent meeting, the end of the period of six months starting with the day of the previous meeting.

(4) The employer shall, before the period of two weeks ending with the date of a meeting, provide to the trade union any information—

(a) without which the union's representatives would be to a material extent impeded in participating in the meeting, and

(b) which it would be in accordance with good industrial relations practice to disclose for the purposes of the meeting.

(5) Section 182(1) shall apply in relation to the provision of information under subsection (4) as it applies in relation to the disclosure of information under section 181.

(6) The employer shall take account of any written representations about matters raised at a meeting which he receives from the trade union within the period of four weeks starting with the date of the meeting.

(7) Where more than one trade union is recognised as entitled to conduct collective bargaining on behalf of a bargaining unit, a reference in this section to 'the trade union' is a reference to each trade union.

(8) Where at a meeting under this section (Meeting 1) an employer indicates his intention to convene a subsequent meeting (Meeting 2) before the expiry of the period of six months beginning with the date of Meeting 1, for the reference to a period of six months in subsection (2)(b) there shall be substituted a reference to the expected period between Meeting 1 and Meeting 2.

(9) The Secretary of State may by order made by statutory instrument amend any of subsections (2) to (6).

(10) No order shall be made under subsection (9) unless a draft has been laid before, and approved by resolution of, each House of Parliament.

70C. Section 70B: complaint to employment tribunal

(1) A trade union may present a complaint to an employment tribunal that an employer has failed to comply with his obligations under section 70B in relation to a bargaining unit.

(2) An employment tribunal shall not consider a complaint under this section unless it is presented—

(a) before the end of the period of three months beginning with the date of the alleged failure, or

(b) within such further period as the tribunal considers reasonable in a case where it is satisfied that it was not reasonably practicable for the complaint to be presented before the end of that period of three months.

(3) Where an employment tribunal finds a complaint under this section well-founded it—

(a) shall make a declaration to that effect, and

(b)   may make an award of compensation to be paid by the employer to each person who was, at the time when the failure occurred, a member of the bargaining unit.

(4)   The amount of the award shall not, in relation to each person, exceed two weeks' pay.

(5)   For the purpose of subsection (4) a week's pay—

(a)   shall be calculated in accordance with Chapter II of Part XIV of the Employment Rights Act 1996 (taking the date of the employer's failure as the calculation date), and

(b)   shall be subject to the limit in section 227(1) of that Act.

(6)   Proceedings for enforcement of an award of compensation under this section—

(a)   may, in relation to each person to whom compensation is payable, be commenced by that person, and

(b)   may not be commenced by a trade union.'

6.   Unfair dismissal connected with recognition: interim relief

In sections 128(1)(b) and 129(1) of the Employment Rights Act 1996 (interim relief) after '103' there shall be inserted 'or in paragraph 161(2) of Schedule A1 to the Trade Union and Labour Relations (Consolidation) Act 1992'.

Leave for family and domestic reasons

7.   Maternity and patental leave

The provisions set out in Part I of Schedule 4 shall be substituted for Part VIII of the Employment Rights Act 1996.

8.   Time off for domestic incidents

The provisions set out in Part II of Schedule 4 shall be inserted after section 57 of that Act.

9.   Consequential amendments

Part III of Schedule 4 (which makes amendments consequential on sections 7 and 8) shall have effect.

Disciplinary and grievance hearings

10.   Right to be accompanied

(1)   This section applies where a worker—

(a)   is required or invited by his employer to attend a disciplinary or grievance hearing, and

(b)   reasonably requests to be accompanied at the hearing.

(2)   Where this section applies the employer must permit the worker to be accompanied at the hearing by a single companion who—

(a)   is chosen by the worker and is within subsection (3),

(b)   is to be permitted to address the hearing (but not to answer questions on behalf of the worker), and

(c)   is to be permitted to confer with the worker during the hearing.

(3)   A person is within this subsection if he is—

(a)   employed by a trade union of which he is an official within the meaning of sections 1 and 119 of the Trade Union and Labour Relations (Consolidation) Act 1992,

(b) an official of a trade union (within that meaning) whom the union has reasonably certified in writing as having experience of, or as having received training in, acting as a worker's companion at disciplinary or grievance hearings, or

(c) another of the employer's workers.

(4) If—

(a) a worker has a right under this section to be accompanied at a hearing,

(b) his chosen companion will not be available at the time proposed for the hearing by the employer, and

(c) the worker proposes an alternative time which satisfies subsection (5), the employer must postpone the hearing to the time proposed by the worker.

(5) An alternative time must—

(a) be reasonable, and

(b) fall before the end of the period of five working days beginning with the first working day after the day proposed by the employer.

(6) An employer shall permit a worker to take time off during working hours for the purpose of accompanying another of the employer's workers in accordance with a request under subsection (1)(b).

(7) Sections 168(3) and (4), 169 and 171 to 173 of the Trade Union and Labour Relations (Consolidation) Act 1992 (time off for carrying out trade union duties) shall apply in relation to subsection (6) above as they apply in relation to section 168(1) of that Act.

11. Complaint to employment tribunal

(1) A worker may present a complaint to an employment tribunal that his employer has failed, or threatened to fail, to comply with section 10(2) or (4).

(2) A tribunal shall not consider a complaint under this section in relation to a failure or threat unless the complaint is presented—

(a) before the end of the period of three months beginning with the date of the failure or threat, or

(b) within such further period as the tribunal considers reasonable in a case where it is satisfied that it was not reasonably practicable for the complaint to be presented before the end of that period of three months.

(3) Where a tribunal finds that a complaint under this section is well-founded it shall order the employer to pay compensation to the worker of an amount not exceeding two weeks' pay.

(4) Chapter II of Part XIV of the Employment Rights Act 1996 (calculation of a week's pay) shall apply for the purposes of subsection (3); and in applying that Chapter the calculation date shall be taken to be—

(a) in the case of a claim which is made in the course of a claim for unfair dismissal, the date on which the employer's notice of dismissal was given or, if there was no notice, the effective date of termination, and

(b) in any other case, the date on which the relevant hearing took place (or was to have taken place).

(5) The limit in section 227(1) of the Employment Rights Act 1996 (maximum amount of week's pay) shall apply for the purposes of subsection (3) above.

(6) No award shall be made under subsection (3) in respect of a claim which is made in the course of a claim for unfair dismissal if the tribunal makes a supplementary award under section 127A(2) of the Employment Rights Act 1996 (internal appeal procedures).

12. Detriment and dismissal

(1)   A worker has the right not to be subjected to any detriment by any act, or any deliberate failure to act, by his employer done on the ground that he—

(a)   exercised or sought to exercise the right under section 10(2) or (4), or

(b)   accompanied or sought to accompany another worker (whether of the same employer or not) pursuant to a request under that section.

(2)   Section 48 of the Employment Rights Act 1996 shall apply in relation to contraventions of subsection (1) above as it applies in relation to contraventions of certain sections of that Act.

(3)   A worker who is dismissed shall be regarded for the purposes of Part X of the Employment Rights Act 1996 as unfairly dismissed if the reason (or, if more than one, the principal reason) for the dismissal is that he—

(a)   exercised or sought to exercise the right under section 10(2) or (4), or

(b)   accompanied or sought to accompany another worker (whether of the same employer or not) pursuant to a request under that section.

(4)   Sections 108 and 109 of that Act (qualifying period of employment and upper age limit) shall not apply in relation to subsection (3) above.

(5)   Sections 128 to 132 of that Act (interim relief) shall apply in relation to dismissal for the reason specified in subsection (3)(a) or (b) above as they apply in relation to dismissal for a reason specified in section 128(1)(b) of that Act.

(6)   In the application of Chapter II of Part X of that Act in relation to subsection (3) above, a reference to an employee shall be taken as a reference to a worker.

13. Interpretation

(1)   In sections 10 to 12 and this section 'worker' means an individual who is—

(a)   a worker within the meaning of section 230(3) of the Employment Rights Act 1996,

(b)   an agency worker,

(c)   a home worker,

(d)   a person in Crown employment within the meaning of section 191 of that Act, other than a member of the naval, military, air or reserve forces of the Crown, or

(e)   employed as a relevant member of the House of Lords staff or the House of Commons staff within the meaning of section 194(6) or 195(5) of that Act.

(2)   In subsection (1) 'agency worker' means an individual who—

(a)   is supplied by a person ('the agent') to do work for another ('the principal') by arrangement between the agent and the principal,

(b)   is not a party to a worker's contract, within the meaning of section 230(3) of that Act, relating to that work, and

(c)   is not a party to a contract relating to that work under which he undertakes to do the work for another party to the contract whose status is, by virtue of the contract, that of a client or customer of any professional or business undertaking carried on by the individual;

and, for the purposes of sections 10 to 12, both the agent and the principal are employers of an agency worker.

(3)   In subsection (1) 'home worker' means an individual who—

(a)   contracts with a person, for the purposes of the person's business, for the execution of work to be done in a place not under the person's control or management, and

(b)   is not a party to a contract relating to that work under which the work is to be executed for another party to the contract whose status is, by virtue of the contract, that of a client or customer of any professional or business undertaking carried on by the individual;

and, for the purposes of sections 10 to 12, the person mentioned in paragraph (a) is the home worker's employer.

(4)   For the purposes of section 10 a disciplinary hearing is a hearing which could result in—

(a)   the administration of a formal warning to a worker by his employer,

(b)   the taking of some other action in respect of a worker by his employer, or

(c)   the confirmation of a warning issued or some other action taken.

(5)   For the purposes of section 10 a grievance hearing is a hearing which concerns the performance of a duty by an employer in relation to a worker.

(6)   For the purposes of section 10(5)(b) in its application to a part of Great Britain a working day is a day other than—

(a)   a Saturday or a Sunday,

(b)   Christmas Day or Good Friday, or

(c)   a day which is a bank holiday under the Banking and Financial Dealings Act 1971 in that part of Great Britain.

14.   Contracting out and conciliation

Sections 10 to 13 of this Act shall be treated as provisions of Part V of the Employment Rights Act 1996 for the purposes of—

(a)   section 203(1), (2)(e) and (f), (3) and (4) of that Act (restrictions on contracting out), and

(b)   section 18(1)(d) of the Employment Tribunals Act 1996 (conciliation).

15.   National security employees

Sections 10 to 13 of this Act shall not apply in relation to a person employed for the purposes of—

(a)   the Security Service,

(b)   the Secret Intelligence Service, or

(c)   the Government Communications Headquarters.

Other rights of individuals

16.   Unfair Dismissal of striking workers

Schedule 5 shall have effect.

17.   Collective agreements: detriment and dismissal

(1)   The Secretary of State may make regulations about cases where a worker—

(a)   is subjected to detriment by his employer, or

(b)   is dismissed,

on the grounds that he refuses to enter into a contract which includes terms which differ from the terms of a collective agreement which applies to him.

(2)   The regulations may—

(a)   make provision which applies only in specified classes of case;

(b)   make different provision for different circumstances;

(c)   include supplementary, incidental and transitional provision.

(3)   In this section—

'collective agreement' has the meaning given by section 178(1) of the Trade Union and Labour Relations (Consolidation) Act 1992; and

'employer' and 'worker' have the same meaning as in section 296 of that Act.

(4)   The payment of higher wages or higher rates of pay or overtime or the payment of any signing on or other bonuses or the provision of other benefits having a monetary value to other workers employed by the same employer shall not constitute a detriment to any worker not receiving the same or similar payments or benefits within the meaning of subsection (1)(a) of this section so long as—

(a)   there is no inhibition in the contract of employment of the worker receiving the same from being the member of any trade union, and

(b)   the said payments of higher wages or rates of pay or overtime or bonuses or the provision of other benefits are in accordance with the terms of a contract of employment and reasonably relate to services provided by the worker under that contract.

18.   Agreement to exclude dismissal rights

(1)   In section 197 of the Employment Rights Act 1996 (fixed-term contracts) subsections (1) and (2) (agreement to exclude unfair dismissal provisions) shall be omitted; and subsections (2) to (5) below shall have effect in consequence.

(2)   In sections 44(4), 46(2), 47(2), 47A(2) and 47B(2) of that Act—

(a)   the words from the beginning to 'the dismissal,' shall be omitted, and

(b)   for 'that Part' there shall be substituted 'Part X'.

(3)   In section 45A(4) of that Act the words from ', unless' to the end shall be omitted.

(4)   In section 23 of the National Minimum Wage Act 1998, for subsection (4) there shall be substituted—

'(4)   This section does not apply where the detriment in question amounts to dismissal within the meaning of—

(a)   Part X of the Employment Rights Act 1996 (unfair dismissal), or

(b)   Part XI of the Employment Rights (Northern Ireland) Order 1996 (corresponding provision for Northern Ireland),

except where in relation to Northern Ireland the person in question is dismissed in circumstances in which, by virtue of Article 240 of that Order (fixed term contracts), Part XI does not apply to the dismissal.'

(5)   In paragraph 1 of Schedule 3 to the Tax Credits Act 1999, for sub-paragraph (3) there shall be substituted—

'(3)   This paragraph does not apply where the detriment in question amounts to dismissal within the meaning of—

(a)   Part X of the Employment Rights Act 1996 (unfair dismissal), or

(b)   Part XI of the Employment Rights (Northern Ireland) Order 1996 (corresponding provision for Northern Ireland),

except where in relation to Northern Ireland the employee is dismissed in circumstances in which, by virtue of Article 240 of that Order (fixed term contracts), Part XI does not apply to the dismissal.'

(6)   Section 197(1) of the Employment Rights Act 1996 does not prevent Part X of that Act from applying to a dismissal which is regarded as unfair by virtue of section 99 or 104 of that Act (pregnancy and childbirth, and assertion of statutory right).

19. Part-time work: discrimination

(1) The Secretary of State shall make regulations for the purpose of securing that persons in part-time employment are treated, for such purposes and to such extent as the regulations may specify, no less favourably than persons in full-time employment.

(2) The regulations may—

(a) specify classes of person who are to be taken to be, or not to be, in part-time employment;

(b) specify classes of person who are to be taken to be, or not to be, in full-time employment;

(c) specify circumstances in which persons in part-time employment are to be taken to be, or not to be, treated less favourably than persons in full-time employment;

(d) make provision which has effect in relation to persons in part-time employment generally or provision which has effect only in relation to specified classes of persons in part-time employment.

(3) The regulations may—

(a) confer jurisdiction (including exclusive jurisdiction) on employment tribunals and on the Employment Appeal Tribunal;

(b) create criminal offences in relation to specified acts or omissions by an employer, by an organisation of employers, by an organisation of workers or by an organisation existing for the purposes of a profession or trade carried on by the organisation's members;

(c) in specified cases or circumstances, extend liability for a criminal offence created under paragraph (b) to a person who aids the commission of the offence or to a person who is an agent, principal, employee, employer or officer of a person who commits the offence;

(d) provide for specified obligations or offences not to apply in specified circumstances;

(e) make provision about notices or information to be given, evidence to be produced and other procedures to be followed;

(f) amend, apply with or without modifications, or make provision similar to any provision of the Employment Rights Act 1996 (including, in particular, Parts V, X and XIII) or the Trade Union and Labour Relations (Consolidation) Act 1992;

(g) provide for the provisions of specified agreements to have effect in place of provisions of the regulations to such extent and in such circumstances as may be specified;

(h) include supplemental, incidental, consequential and transitional provision, including provision amending an enactment;

(i) make different provision for different cases or circumstances.

(4) Without prejudice to the generality of this section the regulations may make any provision which appears to the Secretary of State to be necessary or expedient—

(a) for the purpose of implementing Council Directive 97/81/EC on the framework agreement on part-time work in its application to terms and conditions of employment;

(b) for the purpose of dealing with any matter arising out of or related to the United Kingdom's obligations under that Directive;

(c) for the purpose of any matter dealt with by the framework agreement or for the purpose of applying the provisions of the framework agreement to any matter relating to part-time workers.

(5)   Regulations under this section which create an offence—

(a)   shall provide for it to be triable summarily only, and

(b)   may not provide for it to be punishable by imprisonment or by a fine in excess of level 5 on the standard scale.

20.   Part-time work: code of practice

(1)   The Secretary of State may issue codes of practice containing guidance for the purpose of—

(a)   eliminating discrimination in the field of employment against part-time workers;

(b)   facilitating the development of opportunities for part-time work;

(c)   facilitating the flexible organisation of working time taking into account the needs of workers and employers;

(d)   any matter dealt with in the framework agreement on part-time work annexed to Council Directive 97/81/EC.

(2)   The Secretary of State may revise a code and issue the whole or part of the revised code.

(3)   A person's failure to observe a provision of a code does not make him liable to any proceedings.

(4)   A code—

(a)   is admissible in evidence in proceedings before an employment tribunal, and

(b)   shall be taken into account by an employment tribunal in any case in which it appears to the tribunal to be relevant.

21.   Code of practice: supplemental

(1)   Before issuing or revising a code of practice under section 20 the Secretary of State shall consult such persons as he considers appropriate.

(2)   Before issuing a code the Secretary of State shall—

(a)   publish a draft code,

(b)   consider any representations made to him about the draft,

(c)   if he thinks it appropriate, modify the draft in the light of any representations made to him.

(3)   If, having followed the procedure under subsection (2), the Secretary of State decides to issue a code, he shall lay a draft code before each House of Parliament.

(4)   If the draft code is approved by resolution of each House of Parliament, the Secretary of State shall issue the code in the form of the draft.

(5)   In this section and section 20(3) and (4)—

(a)   a reference to a code includes a reference to a revised code,

(b)   a reference to a draft code includes a reference to a draft revision, and

(c)   a reference to issuing a code includes a reference to issuing part of a revised code.

22.   National minimum wage: communities

The following shall be inserted after section 44 of the National Minimum Wage Act 1998 (exclusions: voluntary workers)—

'44A.   Religious and other communities: resident workers

(1)   A residential member of a community to which this section applies does not qualify for the national minimum wage in respect of employment by the community.

(2)   Subject to subsection (3), this section applies to a community if—

(a)   it is a charity or is established by a charity,

(b)   a purpose of the community is to practise or advance a belief of a religious or similar nature, and

(c)   all or some of its members live together for that purpose.

(3)   This section does not apply to a community which—

(a)   is an independent school, or

(b)   provides a course of further or higher education.

(4)   The residential members of a community are those who live together as mentioned in subsection (2)(c).

(5)   In this section—

(a)   'charity' has the same meaning as in section 44, and

(b)   'independent school' has the same meaning as in section 463 of the Education Act 1996 (in England and Wales), section 135 of the Education (Scotland) Act 1980 (in Scotland) and Article 2 of the Education and Libraries (Northern Ireland) Order 1986 (in Northern Ireland).

(6)   In this section 'course of further or higher education' means—

(a)   in England and Wales, a course of a description referred to in Schedule 6 to the Education Reform Act 1988 or Schedule 2 to the Further and Higher Education Act 1992;

(b)   in Scotland, a course or programme of a description mentioned in or falling within section 6(1) or 38 of the Further and Higher Education (Scotland) Act 1992;

(c)   in Northern Ireland, a course of a description referred to in Schedule 1 to the Further Education (Northern Ireland) Order 1997 or a course providing further education within the meaning of Article 3 of that Order.'

23.   Power to confer rights on individuals

(1)   This section applies to any right conferred on an individual against an employer (however defined) under or by virtue of any of the following—

(a)   the Trade Union and Labour Relations (Consolidation) Act 1992;

(b)   the Employment Rights Act 1996;

(c)   this Act;

(d)   any instrument made under section 2(2) of the European Communities Act 1972.

(2)   The Secretary of State may by order make provision which has the effect of conferring any such right on individuals who are of a specified description.

(3)   The reference in subsection (2) to individuals includes a reference to individuals expressly excluded from exercising the right.

(4)   An order under this section may—

(a)   provide that individuals are to be treated as parties to workers' contracts or contracts of employment;

(b)   make provision as to who are to be regarded as the employers of individuals;

(c)   make provision which has the effect of modifying the operation of any right as conferred on individuals by the order;

(d)   include such consequential, incidental or supplementary provisions as the Secretary of State thinks fit.

(5)   An order under this section may make provision in such way as the Secretary of State thinks fit, whether by amending Acts or instruments or otherwise.

(6)   Section 209(7) of the Employment Rights Act 1996 (which is superseded by this section) shall be omitted.

(7)   Any order made or having effect as if made under section 209(7), so far as effective immediately before the commencement of this section, shall have efrect as if made under this section.

CAC, ACAS, Commissioners and Certification Officer

24.   CAC: members

In section 260 of the Trade Union and Labour Relations (Consolidation) Act 1992 (members of the Committee) these subsections shall be substituted for subsections (1) to (3)—

'(1)   The Central Arbitration Committee shall consist of members appointed by the Secretary of State.

(2)   The Secretary of State shall appoint a member as chairman, and may appoint a member as deputy chairman or members as deputy chairmen.

(3)   The Secretary of State may appoint as members only persons experienced in industrial relations, and they shall include some persons whose experience is as representatives of employers and some whose experience is as representatives of workers.

(3A)   Before making an appointment under subsection (1) or (2) the Secretary of State shall consult ACAS and may consult other persons.'

25.   CAC: proceedings

(1)   The Trade Union and Labour Relations (Consolidation) Act 1992 shall be amended as follows.

(2)   In section 263 (proceedings of the Committee) this subsection shall be inserted after subsection (6)—

'(7)   In relation to the discharge of the Committee's functions under Schedule A1—

(a)   section 263A and subsection (6) above shall apply, and

(b)   subsections (1) to (5) above shall not apply.'

(3)   This section shall be inserted after section 263—

'263A.   Proceedings of the Committee under Schedule A1

(1)   For the purpose of discharging its functions under Schedule Al in any particular case, the Central Arbitration Committee shall consist of a panel established under this section.

(2) The chairman of the Committee shall establish a panel or panels, and a panel shall consist of these three persons appointed by him—

(a)   the chairman or a deputy chairman of the Committee, who shall be chairman of the panel;

(b)   a member of the Committee whose experience is as a representative of employers;

(c)   a member of the Committee whose experience is as a representative of workers.

(3)   The chairman of the Committee shall decide which panel is to deal with a particular case.

(4) A panel may at the discretion of its chairman sit in private where it appears expedient to do so.

(5) If—

(a) a panel cannot reach a unanimous decision on a question arising before it, and

(b) a majority of the panel have the same opinion,

the question shall be decided according to that opinion.

(6) If—

(a) a panel cannot reach a unanimous decision on a question arising before it, and

(b) a majority of the panel do not have the same opinion,

the chairman of the panel shall decide the question acting with the full powers of an umpire or, in Scotland, an oversman.

(7) Subject to the above provisions, a panel shall determine its own procedure.'

(4) In section 264 (awards of the Committee)—

(a) in subsection (1) after 'award' there shall be inserted ', or in any decision or declaration of the Committee under Schedule A1,';

(b) in subsection (2) after 'of the Committee,' there shall be inserted 'or of a decision or declaration of the Committee under Schedule A1,'.

26. ACAS: general duty

In section 209 of the Trade Union and Labour Relations (Consolidation) Act 1992 (ACAS' general duty) the words from ', in particular' to the end shall be omitted.

27. ACAS: reports

(1) In section 253(1) of the Trade Union and Labour Relations (Consolidation) Act 1992 (ACAS: annual report) for 'calendar year' there shall be substituted 'financial year'.

(2) In section 265(1) of that Act (ACAS: report about CAC) for 'calendar year' there shall be substituted 'financial year'.

28. Abolition of Commissioners

(1) These offices shall cease to exist—

(a) the office of Commissioner for the Rights of Trade Union Members;

(b) the office of Commissioner for Protection Against Unlawful Industrial Action.

(2) In the Trade Union and Labour Relations (Consolidation) Act 1992 these provisions shall cease to have effect—

(a) Chapter VIII of Part I (provision by Commissioner for the Rights of Trade Union Members of assistance in relation to certain proceedings);

(b) sections 235B and 235C (provision of assistance by Commissioner for Protection Against Unlawful Industrial Action of assistance in relation to certain proceedings);

(c) section 266 (and the heading immediately preceding it) and sections 267 to 271 (Commissioners' appointment, remuneration, staff, reports, accounts, etc.).

(3) In section 32A of that Act (statement to members of union following annual return) in the third paragraph of subsection (6)(a) (application for assistance from Commissioner for the Rights of Trade Union Members) for the words from 'may' to 'case,' there shall be substituted 'should'.

29. The Certification Officer
Schedule 6 shall have effect.

Miscellaneous

30. Partnership at work
(1)   The Secretary of State may spend money or provide money to other persons for the purpose of encouraging and helping employers (or their representatives) and employees (or their representatives) to improve the way they work together.

(2)   Money may be provided in such way as the Secretary of State thinks fit (whether as grants or otherwise) and on such terms as he thinks fit (whether as to repayment or otherwise).

31. Employment agencies
Schedule 7 shall have effect.

32. Employment rights: employment outside Great Britain
(1)   In section 285(1) of the Trade Union and Labour Relations (Consolidation) Act 1992 (employment outside Great Britain) for 'Chapter II (procedure for handling redundancies)' there shall be substituted 'sections 193 and 194 (duty to notify Secretary of State of certain redundancies)'.

(2)   After section 287(3) of that Act (offshore employment) there shall be inserted—

'(3A)   An Order in Council under this section shall be subject to annulment in pursuance of a resolution of either House of Parliament.'.

(3)   Section 196 of the Employment Rights Act 1996 (employment outside Great Britain) shall cease to have effect; and in section 5(1) for 'sections 196 and' there shall be substituted 'section'.

(4)   After section 199(6) of that Act (mariners) there shall be inserted—

'(7)   The provisions mentioned in subsection (8) apply to employment on board a ship registered in the register maintained under section 8 of the Merchant Shipping Act 1995 if and only if—

(a)   the ship's entry in the register specifies a port in Great Britain as the port to which the vessel is to be treated as belonging,

(b)   under his contract of employment the person employed does not work wholly outside Great Britain, and

(c)   the person employed is ordinarily resident in Great Britain.

(8)   The provisions are—

(a)   sections 8 to 10,

(b)   Parts II, III and V,

(c)   Part VI, apart from sections 58 to 60,

(d)   Parts VII and VIII,

(e)   sections 92 and 93, and

(f)   Part X.'

33. Unfair dismissal: special and additional awards
(1)   The following provisions (which require, or relate to, the making of special awards by employment tribunals in unfair dismissal cases) shall cease to have effect—

(a)   sections 117(4)(b), 118(2) and (3) and 125 of the Employment Rights Act 1996 (and the word 'or' before section 117(4)(b));

(b) sections 157 and 158 of the Trade Union and Labour Relations (Consolidation) Act 1992.

(2) In section 117(3)(b) of the Employment Rights Act 1996 (amount of additional award) for 'the appropriate amount' there shall be substituted 'an amount not less than twenty-six nor more than fifty-two weeks' pay'; and subsections (5) and (6) of section 117 shall cease to have effect.

(3) In section 14 of the Employment Rights (Dispute Resolution) Act 1998—

(a) subsection (1) shall cease to have effect, and

(b) in subsection (2) for 'that Act' substitute 'the Employment Rights Act 1996'.

34. Indexation of amounts, etc.

(1) This section applies to the sums specified in the following provisions—

(a) section 31(1) of the Employment Rights Act 1996 (guarantee payments: limits);

(b) section 120(1) of that Act (unfair dismissal: minimum amount of basic award);

(c) section 124(1) of that Act (unfair dismissal: limit of compensatory award);

(d) section 186(1)(a) and (b) of that Act (employee's rights on insolvency of employer: maximum amount payable);

(e) section 227(1) of that Act (maximum amount of a week's pay for purposes of certain calculations);

(f) section 156(1) of the Trade Union and Labour Relations (Consolidation) Act 1992 (unfair dismissal: minimum basic award);

(g) section 176(6) of that Act (right to membership of trade union: remedies).

(2) If the retail prices index for September of a year is higher or lower than the index for the previous September, the Secretary of State shall as soon as practicable make an order in relation to each sum mentioned in subsection (1)—

(a) increasing each sum, if the new index is higher, or

(b) decreasing each sum, if the new index is lower,

by the same percentage as the amount of the increase or decrease of the index.

(3) In making the calculation required by subsection (2) the Secretary of State shall—

(a) in the case of the sum mentioned in subsection (1)(a), round the result up to the nearest 10 pence,

(b) in the case of the sums mentioned in subsection (1)(b), (c), (f) and (g), round the result up to the nearest £100, and

(c) in the case of the sums mentioned in subsection (1)(d) and (e), round the result up to the nearest £10.

(4) For the sum specified in section 124(1) of the Employment Rights Act 1996 (unfair dismissal: limit of compensatory award) there shall be substituted the sum of £50,000 (subject to subsection (2) above).

(5) In this section 'the retail prices index' means—

(a) the general index of retail prices (for all items) published by the Office for National Statistics, or

(b) where that index is not published for a month, any substituted index or figures published by that Office.

(6) An order under this section—

    (a)   shall be made by statutory instrument,
    (b)   may include transitional provision, and
    (c)   shall be laid before Parliament after being made.

35.   Guarantee payments

For section 31(7) of the Employment Rights Act 1996 (guarantee payments: limits) there shall be substituted—

'(7) The Secretary of State may by order vary—
    (a)   the length of the period specified in subsection (2);
    (b)   a limit specified in subsection (3) or (4).'

36.   Sections 33 to 35: consequential

(1)   The following provisions (which confer power to increase sums) shall cease to have effect—
    (a)   sections 120(2), 124(2), 186(2) and 227(2) to (4) of the Employment Rights Act 1996;
    (b)   sections 159 and 176(7) and (8) of the Trade Union and Labour Relations (Consolidation) Act 1992.

(2)   Section 208 of the Employment Rights Act 1996 (review of limits) shall cease to have effect.

(3)   An increase effected, before section 34 comes into force, by virtue of a provision repealed by this section shall continue to have effect notwithstanding this section (but subject to section 34(2) and (4)).

37.   Compensatory award etc.: removal of limit in certain cases

(1)   After section 124(1) of the Employment Rights Act 1996 (limit of compensatory award etc) there shall be inserted—

'(1A)   Subsection (1) shall not apply to compensation awarded, or a compensatory award made, to a person in a case where he is regarded as unfairly dismissed by virtue of section 100, 103A, 105(3) or 105(6A).'

(2)   Section 127B of that Act (power to specify method of calculation of compensation where dismissal a result of protected disclosure) shall cease to have effect.

38.   Transfer of undertakings

(1)   This section applies where regulations under section 2(2) of the European Communities Act 1972 (general implementation of Treaties) make provision for the purpose of implementing, or for a purpose concerning, a Community obligation of the United Kingdom which relates to the treatment of employees on the transfer of an undertaking or business or part of an undertaking or business.

(2)   The Secretary of State may by regulations make the same or similar provision in relation to the treatment of employees in circumstances other than those to which the Community obligation applies (including circumstances in which there is no transfer, or no transfer to which the Community obligation applies).

(3)   Regulations under this section shall be subject to annulment in pursuance of a resolution of either House of Parliament.

39.   Minimum wage: information

(1)   Information obtained by a revenue official in the course of carrying out a function of the Commissioners of Inland Revenue may be—

(a)   supplied by the Commissioners of Inland Revenue to the Secretary of State for any purpose relating to the National Minimum Wage Act 1998;

(b)   supplied by the Secretary of State with the authority of the Commissioners of Inland Revenue to any person acting under section 13(1)(b) of that Act;

(c)   supplied by the Secretary of State with the authority of the Commissioners of Inland Revenue to an officer acting for the purposes of any of the agricultural wages legislation.

(2)   In this section—

'revenue official' means an officer of the Commissioners of Inland Revenue appointed under section 4 of the Inland Revenue Regulation Act 1890 (appointment of collectors, officers and other persons), and

'the agricultural wages legislation' has the same meaning as in section 16 of the National Minimum Wage Act 1998 (agricultural wages officers).

40.   Dismissal of school staff

(1)   In paragraph 27(3)(b) of Schedule 16 to the School Standards and Framework Act 1998 (dismissal of staff: representations and appeal) for 'for a period of two years or more (within the meaning of the Employment Rights Act 1996)' there shall be substituted ', within the meaning of the Employment Rights Act 1996, for a period at least as long as the period for the time being specified in section 108(1) of that Act (unfair dismissal: qualifying period)'.

(2)   In paragraph 24(4)(b) of Schedule 17 to the School Standards and Framework Act 1998 (dismissal of staff. representations and appeal) for 'for a period of two years or more (within the meaning of the Employment Rights Act 1996)' there shall be substituted ', within the meaning of the Employment Rights Act 1996, for a period at least as long as the period for the time being specified in section 108(1) of that Act (unfair dismissal: qualifying period)'.

41.   National security

Schedule 8 shall have effect.

General

42.   Orders and regulations

(1)   Any power to make an order or regulations under this Act shall be exercised by statutory instrument.

(2)   No order or regulations shall be made under section 3, 17, 19 or 23 unless a draft has been laid before, and approved by resolution of, each House of Parliament.

43.   Finance

There shall be paid out of money provided by Parliament—

(a)   any increase attributable to this Act in the sums so payable under any other enactment;

(b)   any other expenditure of the Secretary of State under this Act.

44.   Repeals

The provisions mentioned in Schedule 9 are repealed (or revoked) to the extent specified in column 3.

45. Commencement

(1)   The preceding provisions of this Act shall come into force in accordance with provision made by the Secretary of State by order made by statutory instrument.

(2)   An order under this section—

   (a)   may make different provision for different purposes;

   (b)   may include supplementary, incidental, saving or transitional provisions.

46. Extent

(1)   Any amendment or repeal in this Act has the same extent as the provision amended or repealed.

(2)   An Order in Council under paragraph 1(1)(b) of Schedule 1 to the Northern Ireland Act 1974 (legislation for Northern Ireland in the interim period) which contains a statement that it is made only for purposes corresponding to any of the purposes of this Act—

   (a)   shall not be subject to paragraph 1(4) and (5) of that Schedule (affirmative resolution of both Houses of Parliament), but

   (b)   shall be subject to annulment in pursuance of a resolution of either House of Parliament.

(3)   Apart from sections 39 and 45 and subject to subsection (1), the preceding sections of this Act shall not extend to Northern Ireland.

47. Citation

This Act may be cited as the Employment Relations Act 1999.

SCHEDULES

Section 1   SCHEDULE 1
COLLECTIVE BARGAINING: RECOGNITION

The Schedule to be inserted immediately before Schedule 1 to the Trade Union and Labour Relations (Consolidation) Act 1992 is as follows—

'SCHEDULE A1
COLLECTIVE BARGAINING: RECOGNITION

PART I
RECOGNITION

Introduction

1.   A trade union (or trade unions) seeking recognition to be entitled to conduct collective bargaining on behalf of a group or groups of workers may make a request in accordance with this Part of this Schedule.

2.—(1)   This paragraph applies for the purposes of this Part of this Schedule.

(2)   References to the bargaining unit are to the group of workers concerned (or the groups taken together).

(3)   References to the proposed bargaining unit are to the bargaining unit proposed in the request for recognition.

(4)   References to the employer are to the employer of the workers constituting the bargaining unit concerned.

(5)   References to the parties are to the union (or unions) and the employer.

3.—(1)   This paragraph applies for the purposes of this Part of this Schedule.

(2)   The meaning of collective bargaining given by section 178(1) shall not apply.

(3)   References to collective bargaining are to negotiations relating to pay, hours and holidays; but this has effect subject to sub-paragraph (4).

(4)   If the parties agree matters as the subject of collective bargaining, references to collective bargaining are to negotiations relating to the agreed matters; and this is the case whether the agreement is made before or after the time when the CAC issues a declaration, or the parties agree, that the union is (or unions are) entitled to conduct collective bargaining on behalf of a bargaining unit.

(5)   Sub-paragraph (4) does not apply in construing paragraph 31(3).

(6)   Sub-paragraphs (2) to (5) do not apply in construing paragraph 35 or 44.

Request for recognition

4.—(1)   The union or unions seeking recognition must make a request for recognition to the employer.

(2)   Paragraphs 5 to 9 apply to the request.

5.   The request is not valid unless it is received by the employer.

6.   The request is not valid unless the union (or each of the unions) has a certificate under section 6 that it is independent.

7.—(1)   The request is not valid unless the employer, taken with any associated employer or employers, employs—

(a)   at least 21 workers on the day the employer receives the request, or

(b)   an average of at least 21 workers in the 13 weeks ending with that day.

(2)   To find the average under sub-paragraph (1)(b)—

(a)   take the number of workers employed in each of the 13 weeks (including workers not employed for the whole of the week);

(b)   aggregate the 13 numbers;

(c)   divide the aggregate by 13.

(3)   For the purposes of sub-paragraph (1)(a) any worker employed by an associated company incorporated outside Great Britain must be ignored unless the day the request was made fell within a period during which he ordinarily worked in Great Britain.

(4)   For the purposes of sub-paragraph (1)(b) any worker employed by an associated company incorporated outside Great Britain must be ignored in relation to a week unless the whole or any part of that week fell within a period during which he ordinarily worked in Great Britain.

(5) For the purposes of sub-paragraphs (3) and (4) a worker who is employed on board a ship registered in the register maintained under section 8 of the Merchant Shipping Act 1995 shall be treated as ordinarily working in Great Britain unless—

(a)   the ship's entry in the register specifies a port outside Great Britain as the port to which the vessel is to be treated as belonging,

(b)   the employment is wholly outside Great Britain, or

(c)   the worker is not ordinarily resident in Great Britain.

(6)   The Secretary of State may by order—

(a)   provide that sub-paragraphs (1) to (5) are not to apply, or are not to apply in specified circumstances, or

(b)   vary the number of workers for the time being specified in sub-paragraph (1);

and different provision may be made for different circumstances.

(7)   An order under sub-paragraph (6)—

(a)   shall be made by statutory instrument, and

(b)   may include supplementary, incidental, saving or transitional provisions.

(8)   No such order shall be made unless a draft of it has been laid before Parliament and approved by a resolution of each House of Parliament.

8.   The request is not valid unless it—

(a)   is in writing,

(b)   identifies the union or unions and the bargaining unit, and

(c)   states that it is made under this Schedule.

9.   The Secretary of State may by order made by statutory instrument prescribe the form of requests and the procedure for making them; and if he does so the request is not valid unless it complies with the order.

Parties agree

10.—(1)   If before the end of the first period the parties agree a bargaining unit and that the union is (or unions are) to be recognised as entitled to conduct collective bargaining on behalf of the unit, no further steps are to be taken under this Part of this Schedule.

(2)   If before the end of the first period the employer informs the union (or unions) that the employer does not accept the request but is willing to negotiate, sub-paragraph (3) applies.

(3)   The parties may conduct negotiations with a view to agreeing a bargaining unit and that the union is (or unions are) to be recognised as entitled to conduct collective bargaining on behalf of the unit.

(4)   If such an agreement is made before the end of the second period no further steps are to be taken under this Part of this Schedule.

(5)   The employer and the union (or unions) may request ACAS to assist in conducting the negotiations.

(6)   The first period is the period of 10 working days starting with the day after that on which the employer receives the request for recognition.

(7)   The second period is—

(a)   the period of 20 working days starting with the day after that on which the first period ends, or

(b)   such longer period (so starting) as the parties may from time to time agree.

Employer rejects request

11.—(1)   This paragraph applies if—

(a)   before the end of the first period the employer fails to respond to the request, or

(b)   before the end of the first period the employer informs the union (or unions) that the employer does not accept the request (without indicating a willingness to negotiate).

(2)   The union (or unions) may apply to the CAC to decide both these questions—

(a)   whether the proposed bargaining unit is appropriate or some other bargaining unit is appropriate;

(b)   whether the union has (or unions have) the support of a majority of the workers constituting the appropriate bargaining unit.

Negotiations fail

12.—(1) Sub-paragraph (2) applies if—

(a) the employer informs the union (or unions) under paragraph 10(2), and

(b) no agreement is made before the end of the second period.

(2) The union (or unions) may apply to the CAC to decide both these questions—

(a) whether the proposed bargaining unit is appropriate or some other bargaining unit is appropriate;

(b) whether the union has (or unions have) the support of a majority of the workers constituting the appropriate bargaining unit.

(3) Sub-paragraph (4) applies if—

(a) the employer informs the union (or unions) under paragraph 10(2), and

(b) before the end of the second period the parties agree a bargaining unit but not that the union is (or unions are) to be recognised as entitled to conduct collective bargaining on behalf of the unit.

(4) The union (or unions) may apply to the CAC to decide the question whether the union has (or unions have) the support of a majority of the workers constituting the bargaining unit.

(5) But no application may be made under this paragraph if within the period of 10 working days starting with the day after that on which the employer informs the union (or unions) under paragraph 10(2) the employer proposes that ACAS be requested to assist in conducting the negotiations and—

(a) the union rejects (or unions reject) the proposal, or

(b) the union fails (or unions fail) to accept the proposal within the period of 10 working days starting with the day after that on which the employer makes the proposal.

Acceptance of applications

13. The CAC must give notice to the parties of receipt of an application under paragraph 11 or 12.

14.—(1) This paragraph applies if—

(a) two or more relevant applications are made,

(b) at least one worker falling within one of the relevant bargaining units also falls within the other relevant bargaining unit (or units), and

(c) the CAC has not accepted any of the applications.

(2) A relevant application is an application under paragraph 11 or 12.

(3) In relation to a relevant application, the relevant bargaining unit is—

(a) the proposed bargaining unit, where the application is under paragraph 11(2) or 12(2);

(b) the agreed bargaining unit, where the application is under paragraph 12(4).

(4) Within the acceptance period the CAC must decide, with regard to each relevant application, whether the 10 per cent test is satisfied.

(5) The 10 per cent test is satisfied if members of the union (or unions) constitute at least 10 per cent of the workers constituting the relevant bargaining unit.

(6) The acceptance period is—

(a) the period of 10 working days starting with the day after that on which the CAC receives the last relevant application, or

(b) such longer period (so starting) as the CAC may specify to the parties by notice containing reasons for the extension.

(7) If the CAC decides that—

(a) the 10 per cent test is satisfied with regard to more than one of the relevant applications, or

(b) the 10 per cent test is satisfied with regard to none of the relevant applications,

the CAC must not accept any of the relevant applications.

(8) If the CAC decides that the 10 per cent test is satisfied with regard to one only of the relevant applications the CAC—

(a) must proceed under paragraph 15 with regard to that application, and

(b) must not accept any of the other relevant applications.

(9) The CAC must give notice of its decision to the parties.

(10) If by virtue of this paragraph the CAC does not accept an application, no further steps are to be taken under this Part of this Schedule in relation to that application.

15.—(1) This paragraph applies to these applications—

(a) any application with regard to which no decision has to be made under paragraph 14;

(b) any application with regard to which the CAC must proceed under this paragraph by virtue of paragraph 14.

(2) Within the acceptance period the CAC must decide whether—

(a) the request for recognition to which the application relates is valid within the terms of paragraphs 5 to 9, and

(b) the application is made in accordance with paragraph 11 or 12 and admissible within the terms of paragraphs 33 to 42.

(3) In deciding those questions the CAC must consider any evidence which it has been given by the employer or the union (or unions).

(4) If the CAC decides that the request is not valid or the application is not made in accordance with paragraph 11 or 12 or is not admissible—

(a) the CAC must give notice of its decision to the parties,

(b) the CAC must not accept the application, and

(c) no further steps are to be taken under this Part of this Schedule.

(5) If the CAC decides that the request is valid and the application is made in accordance with paragraph 11 or 12 and is admissible it must—

(a) accept the application, and

(b) give notice of the acceptance to the parties.

(6) The acceptance period is—

(a) the period of 10 working days starting with the day after that on which the CAC receives the application, or

(b) such longer period (so starting) as the CAC may specify to the parties by notice containing reasons for the extension.

Withdrawal of application

16.—(1) If an application under paragraph 11 or 12 is accepted by the CAC, the union (or unions) may not withdraw the application—

(a) after the CAC issues a declaration under paragraph 22(2), or

(b) after the union (or the last of the unions) receives notice under paragraph 22(3) or 23(2).

(2) If an application is withdrawn by the union (or unions)—

(a)   the CAC must give notice of the withdrawal to the employer, and

(b)   no further steps are to be taken under this Part of this Schedule.

Notice to cease consideration of application

17.—(1)   This paragraph applies if the CAC has received an application under paragraph 11 or 12 and—

(a)   it has not decided whether the application is admissible, or

(b)   it has decided that the application is admissible.

(2)   No further steps are to be taken under this Part of this Schedule if, before the final event occurs, the parties give notice to the CAC that they want no further steps to be taken.

(3)   The final event occurs when the first of the following occurs—

(a)   the CAC issues a declaration under paragraph 22(2) in consequence of the application;

(b)   the last day of the notification period ends;

and the notification period is that defined by paragraph 24(5) and arising from the application.

Appropriate bargaining unit

18.—(1)   If the CAC accepts an application under paragraph 11(2) or 12(2) it must try to help the parties to reach within the appropriate period an agreement as to what the appropriate bargaining unit is.

(2)   The appropriate period is—

(a)   the period of 20 working days starting with the day after that on which the CAC gives notice of acceptance of the application, or

(b)   such longer period (so starting) as the CAC may specify to the parties by notice containing reasons for the extension.

19.—(1)   This paragraph applies if—

(a)   the CAC accepts an application under paragraph 11(2) or 12(2), and

(b)   the parties have not agreed an appropriate bargaining unit at the end of the appropriate period.

(2)   The CAC must decide the appropriate bargaining unit within—

(a)   the period of 10 working days starting with the day after that on which the appropriate period ends, or

(b)   such longer period (so starting) as the CAC may specify to the parties by notice containing reasons for the extension.

(3)   In deciding the appropriate bargaining unit the CAC must take these matters into account—

(a)   the need for the unit to be compatible with effective management;

(b)   the matters listed in sub-paragraph (4), so far as they do not conflict with that need.

(4)   The matters are—

(a)   the views of the employer and of the union (or unions);

(b)   existing national and local bargaining arrangements;

(c)   the desirability of avoiding small fragmented bargaining units within an undertaking;

(d)   the characteristics of workers falling within the proposed bargaining unit and of any other employees of the employer whom the CAC considers relevant;

(e)   the location of workers.

(5)   The CAC must give notice of its decision to the parties.

Union recognition

20.—(1)   This paragraph applies if—

(a)   the CAC accepts an application under paragraph 11(2) or 12(2),

(b)   the parties have agreed an appropriate bargaining unit at the end of the appropriate period, or the CAC has decided an appropriate bargaining unit, and

(c)   that bargaining unit differs from the proposed bargaining unit.

(2)   Within the decision period the CAC must decide whether the application is invalid within the terms of paragraphs 43 to 50.

(3)   In deciding whether the application is invalid, the CAC must consider any evidence which it has been given by the employer or the union (or unions).

(4)   If the CAC decides that the application is invalid—

(a)   the CAC must give notice of its decision to the parties,

(b)   the CAC must not proceed with the application, and

(c)   no further steps are to be taken under this Part of this Schedule.

(5)   If the CAC decides that the application is not invalid it must—

(a)   proceed with the application, and

(b)   give notice to the parties that it is so proceeding.

(6)   The decision period is—

(a)   the period of 10 working days starting with the day after that on which the parties agree an appropriate bargaining unit or the CAC decides an appropriate bargaining unit, or

(b)   such longer period (so starting) as the CAC may specify to the parties by notice containing reasons for the extension.

21.—(1)   This paragraph applies if—

(a)   the CAC accepts an application under paragraph 11(2) or 12(2),

(b)   the parties have agreed an appropriate bargaining unit at the end of the appropriate period, or the CAC has decided an appropriate bargaining unit, and

(c)   that bargaining unit is the same as the proposed bargaining unit.

(2)   This paragraph also applies if the CAC accepts an application under paragraph 12(4).

(3)   The CAC must proceed with the application.

22.—(1)   This paragraph applies if—

(a)   the CAC proceeds with an application in accordance with paragraph 20 or 21, and

(b)   the CAC is satisfied that a majority of the workers constituting the bargaining unit are members of the union (or unions).

(2)   The CAC must issue a declaration that the union is (or unions are) recognised as entitled to conduct collective bargaining on behalf of the workers constituting the bargaining unit.

(3)   But if any of the three qualifying conditions is fulfilled, instead of issuing a declaration under sub-paragraph (2) the CAC must give notice to the parties that it intends to arrange for the holding of a secret ballot in which the workers constituting the bargaining unit are asked whether they want the union (or unions) to conduct collective bargaining on their behalf.

(4)   These are the three qualifying conditions—

(a) the CAC is satisfied that a ballot should be held in the interests of good industrial relations;

(b) a significant number of the union members within the bargaining unit inform the CAC that they do not want the union (or unions) to conduct collective bargaining on their behalf;

(c) membership evidence is produced which leads the CAC to conclude that there are doubts whether a significant number of the union members within the bargaining unit want the union (or unions) to conduct collective bargaining on their behalf.

(5) For the purposes of sub-paragraph (4)(c) membership evidence is—

(a) evidence about the circumstances in which union members became members;

(b) evidence about the length of time for which union members have been members, in a case where the CAC is satisfied that such evidence should be taken into account.

23.—(1) This paragraph applies if—

(a) the CAC proceeds with an application in accordance with paragraph 20 or 21, and

(b) the CAC is not satisfied that a majority of the workers constituting the bargaining unit are members of the union (or unions).

(2) The CAC must give notice to the parties that it intends to arrange for the holding of a secret ballot in which the workers constituting the bargaining unit are asked whether they want the union (or unions) to conduct collective bargaining on their behalf.

24.—(1) This paragraph applies if the CAC gives notice under paragraph 22(3) or 23(2).

(2) Within the notification period—

(a) the union (or unions), or

(b) the union (or unions) and the employer,

may notify the CAC that the party making the notification does not (or the parties making the notification do not) want the CAC to arrange for the holding of the ballot.

(3) If the CAC is so notified—

(a) it must not arrange for the holding of the ballot,

(b) it must inform the parties that it will not arrange for the holding of the ballot, and why, and

(c) no further steps are to be taken under this Part of this Schedule.

(4) If the CAC is not so notified it must arrange for the holding of the ballot.

(5) The notification period is the period of 10 working days starting—

(a) for the purposes of sub-paragraph (2)(a), with the day on which the union (or last of the unions) receives the CAC's notice under paragraph 22(3) or 23(2), or

(b) for the purposes of sub-paragraph (2)(b), with that day or (if later) the day on which the employer receives the CAC's notice under paragraph 22(3) or 23(2).

25.—(1) This paragraph applies if the CAC arranges under paragraph 24 for the holding of a ballot.

(2) The ballot must be conducted by a qualified independent person appointed by the CAC.

(3) The ballot must be conducted within—

(a) the period of 20 working days starting with the day after that on which the qualified independent person is appointed, or

(b)   such longer period (so starting) as the CAC may decide.

(4)   The ballot must be conducted—

(a)   at a workplace or workplaces decided by the CAC,

(b)   by post, or

(c)   by a combination of the methods described in sub-paragraphs (a) and (b),

depending on the CAC's preference.

(5)   In deciding how the ballot is to be conducted the CAC must take into account—

(a)   the likelihood of the ballot being affected by unfairness or malpractice if it were conducted at a workplace or workplaces;

(b)   costs and practicality;

(c)   such other matters as the CAC considers appropriate.

(6)   The CAC may not decide that the ballot is to be conducted as mentioned in sub-paragraph (4)(c) unless there are special factors making such a decision appropriate; and special factors include—

(a)   factors arising from the location of workers or the nature of their employment;

(b)   factors put to the CAC by the employer or the union (or unions).

(7)   A person is a qualified independent person if—

(a)   he satisfies such conditions as may be specified for the purposes of this paragraph by order of the Secretary of State or is himself so specified, and

(b)   there are no grounds for believing either that he will carry out any functions conferred on him in relation to the ballot otherwise than competently or that his independence in relation to the ballot might reasonably be called into question.

(8)   An order under sub-paragraph (7)(a) shall be made by statutory instrument subject to annulment in pursuance of a resolution of either House of Parliament.

(9)   As soon as is reasonably practicable after the CAC is required under paragraph 24 to arrange for the holding of a ballot it must inform the parties—

(a)   that it is so required;

(b)   of the name of the person appointed to conduct the ballot and the date of his appointment;

(c)   of the period within which the ballot must be conducted;

(d)   whether the ballot is to be conducted by post or at a workplace or workplaces;

(e)   of the workplace or workplaces concerned (if the ballot is to be conducted at a workplace or workplaces).

26.—(1)   An employer who is informed by the CAC under paragraph 25(9) must comply with the following three duties.

(2)   The first duty is to co-operate generally, in connection with the ballot, with the union (or unions) and the person appointed to conduct the ballot; and the second and third duties are not to prejudice the generality of this.

(3)   The second duty is to give to the union (or unions) such access to the workers constituting the bargaining unit as is reasonable to enable the union (or unions) to inform the workers of the object of the ballot and to seek their support and their opinions on the issues involved.

(4)   The third duty is to do the following (so far as it is reasonable to expect the employer to do so)—

(a)   to give to the CAC, within the period of 10 working days starting with the day after that on which the employer is informed under paragraph 25(9), the names and home addresses of the workers constituting the bargaining unit;

(b)   to give to the CAC, as soon as is reasonably practicable, the name and home address of any worker who joins the unit after the employer has complied with paragraph (a);

(c)   to inform the CAC, as soon as is reasonably practicable, of any worker whose name has been given to the CAC under paragraph (a) or (b) but who ceases to be within the unit.

(5)   As soon as is reasonably practicable after the CAC receives any information under sub-paragraph (4) it must pass it on to the person appointed to conduct the ballot.

(6)   If asked to do so by the union (or unions) the person appointed to conduct the ballot must send to any worker—

(a)   whose name and home address have been given under sub-paragraph (5), and

(b)   who is still within the unit (so far as the person so appointed is aware), any information supplied by the union (or unions) to the person so appointed.

(7)   The duty under sub-paragraph (6) does not apply unless the union bears (or unions bear) the cost of sending the information.

(8)   Each of the following powers shall be taken to include power to issue Codes of Practice about reasonable access for the purposes of sub-paragraph (3)—

(a)   the power of ACAS under section 199(1);

(b)   the power of the Secretary of State under section 203(1)(a).

27.—(1)   If the CAC is satisfied that the employer has failed to fulfil any of the three duties imposed by paragraph 26, and the ballot has not been held, the CAC may order the employer—

(a)   to take such steps to remedy the failure as the CAC considers reasonable and specifies in the order, and

(b)   to do so within such period as the CAC considers reasonable and specifies in the order.

(2)   If the CAC is satisfied that the employer has failed to comply with an order under sub-paragraph (1), and the ballot has not been held, the CAC may issue a declaration that the union is (or unions are) recognised as entitled to conduct collective bargaining on behalf of the bargaining unit.

(3)   If the CAC issues a declaration under sub-paragraph (2) it shall take steps to cancel the holding of the ballot; and if the ballot is held it shall have no effect.

28.—(1)   This paragraph applies if the holding of a ballot has been arranged under paragraph 24 whether or not it has been cancelled.

(2)   The gross costs of the ballot shall be borne—

(a)   as to half, by the employer, and

(b)   as to half, by the union (or unions).

(3)   If there is more than one union they shall bear their half of the gross costs—

(a)   in such proportions as they jointly indicate to the person appointed to conduct the ballot, or

(b)   in the absence of such an indication, in equal shares.

(4)   The person appointed to conduct the ballot may send to the employer and the union (or each of the unions) a demand stating—

(a) the gross costs of the ballot, and

(b) the amount of the gross costs to be borne by the recipient.

(5) In such a case the recipient must pay the amount stated to the person sending the demand, and must do so within the period of 15 working days starting with the day after that on which the demand is received.

(6) In England and Wales, if the amount stated is not paid in accordance with sub-paragraph (5) it shall, if a county court so orders, be recoverable by execution issued from that court or otherwise as if it were payable under an order of that court.

(7) References to the costs of the ballot are to—

(a) the costs wholly, exclusively and necessarily incurred in connection with the ballot by the person appointed to conduct it,

(b) such reasonable amount as the person appointed to conduct the ballot charges for his services, and

(c) such other costs as the employer and the union (or unions) agree.

29.—(1) As soon as is reasonably practicable after the CAC is informed of the result of a ballot by the person conducting it, the CAC must act under this paragraph.

(2) The CAC must inform the employer and the union (or unions) of the result of the ballot.

(3) If the result is that the union is (or unions are) supported by—

(a) a majority of the workers voting, and

(b) at least 40 per cent of the workers constituting the bargaining unit,

the CAC must issue a declaration that the union is (or unions are) recognised as entitled to conduct collective bargaining on behalf of the bargaining unit.

(4) If the result is otherwise the CAC must issue a declaration that the union is (or unions are) not entitled to be so recognised.

(5) The Secretary of State may by order amend sub-paragraph (3) so as to specify a different degree of support; and different provision may be made for different circumstances.

(6) An order under sub-paragraph (5) shall be made by statutory instrument.

(7) No such order shall be made unless a draft of it has been laid before Parliament and approved by a resolution of each House of Parliament.

Consequences of recognition

30.—(1) This paragraph applies if the CAC issues a declaration under this Part of this Schedule that the union is (or unions are) recognised as entitled to conduct collective bargaining on behalf of a bargaining unit.

(2) The parties may in the negotiation period conduct negotiations with a view to agreeing a method by which they will conduct collective bargaining.

(3) If no agreement is made in the negotiation period the employer or the union (or unions) may apply to the CAC for assistance.

(4) The negotiation period is—

(a) the period of 30 working days starting with the start day, or

(b) such longer period (so starting) as the parties may from time to time agree.

(5) The start day is the day after that on which the parties are notified of the declaration.

31.—(1) This paragraph applies if an application for assistance is made to the CAC under paragraph 30.

(2)   The CAC must try to help the parties to reach in the agreement period an agreement on a method by which they will conduct collective bargaining.

(3)   If at the end of the agreement period the parties have not made such an agreement the CAC must specify to the parties the method by which they are to conduct collective bargaining.

(4)   Any method specified under sub-paragraph (3) is to have effect as if it were contained in a legally enforceable contract made by the parties.

(5)   But if the parties agree in writing—

(a)   that sub-paragraph (4) shall not apply, or shall not apply to particular parts of the method specified by the CAC, or

(b)   to vary or replace the method specified by the CAC,

the written agreement shall have effect as a legally enforceable contract made by the parties.

(6)   Specific performance shall be the only remedy available for breach of anything which is a legally enforceable contract by virtue of this paragraph.

(7)   If at any time before a specification is made under sub-paragraph (3) the parties jointly apply to the CAC requesting it to stop taking steps under this paragraph, the CAC must comply with the request.

(8)   The agreement period is—

(a)   the period of 20 working days starting with the day after that on which the CAC receives the application under paragraph 30, or

(b)   such longer period (so starting) as the CAC may decide with the consent of the parties.

Method not carried out

32.—(1)   This paragraph applies if—

(a)   the CAC issues a declaration under this Part of this Schedule that the union is (or unions are) recognised as entitled to conduct collective bargaining on behalf of a bargaining unit,

(b)   the parties agree a method by which they will conduct collective bargaining, and

(c)   one or more of the parties fails to carry out the agreement.

(2)   The parties may apply to the CAC for assistance.

(3)   Paragraph 31 applies as if 'paragraph 30' (in each place) read 'paragraph 30 or paragraph 32'.

General provisions about admissibility

33.   An application under paragraph 11 or 12 is not admissible unless—

(a)   it is made in such form as the CAC specifies, and

(b)   it is supported by such documents as the CAC specifies.

34.   An application under paragraph 11 or 12 is not admissible unless the union gives (or unions give) to the employer—

(a)   notice of the application, and

(b)   a copy of the application and any documents supporting it.

35.—(1)   An application under paragraph 11 or 12 is not admissible if the CAC is satisfied that there is already in force a collective agreement under which a union is (or unions are) recognised as entitled to conduct collective bargaining on behalf of any workers falling within the relevant bargaining unit.

(2)   But sub-paragraph (1) does not apply to an application under paragraph 11 or 12 if—

(a)   the union (or unions) recognised under the collective agreement and the union (or unions) making the application under paragraph 11 or 12 are the same, and

(b)   the matters in respect of which the union is (or unions are) entitled to conduct collective bargaining do not include pay, hours or holidays.

(3)   A declaration of recognition which is the subject of a declaration under paragraph 83(2) must for the purposes of sub-paragraph (1) be treated as ceasing to have effect to the extent specified in paragraph 83(2) on the making of the declaration under paragraph 83(2).

(4)   In applying sub-paragraph (1) an agreement for recognition (the agreement in question) must be ignored if—

(a)   the union does not have (or none of the unions has) a certificate under section 6 that it is independent,

(b)   at some time there was an agreement (the old agreement) between the employer and the union under which the union (whether alone or with other unions) was recognised as entitled to conduct collective bargaining on behalf of a group of workers which was the same or substantially the same as the group covered by the agreement in question, and

(c)   the old agreement ceased to have effect in the period of three years ending with the date of the agreement in question.

(5)   It is for the CAC to decide whether one group of workers is the same or substantially the same as another, but in deciding the CAC may take account of the views of any person it believes has an interest in the matter.

(6)   The relevant bargaining unit is—

(a)   the proposed bargaining unit, where the application is under paragraph 11(2) or 12(2);

(b)   the agreed bargaining unit, where the application is under paragraph 12(4).

36.—(1)   An application under paragraph 11 or 12 is not admissible unless the CAC decides that—

(a)   members of the union (or unions) constitute at least 10 per cent of the workers constituting the relevant bargaining unit, and

(b)   a majority of the workers constituting the relevant bargaining unit would be likely to favour recognition of the union (or unions) as entitled to conduct collective bargaining on behalf of the bargaining unit.

(2)   The relevant bargaining unit is—

(a)   the proposed bargaining unit, where the application is under paragraph 11(2) or 12(2);

(b)   the agreed bargaining unit, where the application is under paragraph 12(4).

(3)   The CAC must give reasons for the decision.

37.—(1)   This paragraph applies to an application made by more than one union under paragraph 11 or 12.

(2)   The application is not admissible unless—

(a)   the unions show that they will co-operate with each other in a manner likely to secure and maintain stable and effective collective bargaining arrangements, and

(b)   the unions show that, if the employer wishes, they will enter into arrangements under which collective bargaining is conducted by the unions acting together on behalf of the workers constituting the relevant bargaining unit.

(3) The relevant bargaining unit is—

(a) the proposed bargaining unit, where the application is under paragraph 11(2) or 12(2);

(b) the agreed bargaining unit, where the application is under paragraph 11(4).

38.—(1) This paragraph applies if—

(a) the CAC accepts a relevant application relating to a bargaining unit or proceeds under paragraph 20 with an application relating to a bargaining unit,

(b) the application has not been withdrawn,

(c) no notice has been given under paragraph 17(2),

(d) the CAC has not issued a declaration under paragraph 22(2), 27(2), 29(3) or 29(4) in relation to that bargaining unit, and

(e) no notification has been made under paragraph 24(2).

(2) Another relevant application is not admissible if—

(a) at least one worker falling within the relevant bargaining unit also falls within the bargaining unit referred to in sub-paragraph (1), and

(b) the application is made by a union (or unions) other than the union (or unions) which made the application referred to in sub-paragraph (1).

(3) A relevant application is an application under paragraph 11 or 12.

(4) The relevant bargaining unit is—

(a) the proposed bargaining unit, where the application is under paragraph 11(2) or 12(2);

(b) the agreed bargaining unit, where the application is under paragraph 12(4).

39.—(1) This paragraph applies if the CAC accepts a relevant application relating to a bargaining unit or proceeds under paragraph 20 with an application relating to a bargaining unit.

(2) Another relevant application is not admissible if—

(a) the application is made within the period of 3 years starting with the day after that on which the CAC gave notice of acceptance of the application mentioned in sub-paragraph (1),

(b) the relevant bargaining unit is the same or substantially the same as the bargaining unit mentioned in sub-paragraph (1), and

(c) the application is made by the union (or unions) which made the application mentioned in sub-paragraph (1).

(3) A relevant application is an application under paragraph 11 or 12.

(4) The relevant bargaining unit is—

(a) the proposed bargaining unit, where the application is under paragraph 11(2) or 12(2);

(b) the agreed bargaining unit, where the application is under paragraph 12(4).

(5) This paragraph does not apply if paragraph 40 or 41 applies.

40.—(1) This paragraph applies if the CAC issues a declaration under paragraph 29(4) that a union is (or unions are) not entitled to be recognised as entitled to conduct collective bargaining on behalf of a bargaining unit; and this is so whether the ballot concerned is held under this Part or Part III of this Schedule.

(2) An application under paragraph 11 or 12 is not admissible if—

(a) the application is made within the period of 3 years starting with the day after that on which the declaration was issued,

(b) the relevant bargaining unit is the same or substantially the same as the bargaining unit mentioned in sub-paragraph (1), and

(c) the application is made by the union (or unions) which made the application leading to the declaration.

(3) The relevant bargaining unit is—

(a) the proposed bargaining unit, where the application is under paragraph 11(2) or 12(2);

(b) the agreed bargaining unit, where the application is under paragraph 12(4).

41.—(1) This paragraph applies if the CAC issues a declaration under paragraph 121(3) that bargaining arrangements are to cease to have effect; and this is so whether the ballot concerned is held under Part IV or Part V of this Schedule.

(2) An application under paragraph 11 or 12 is not admissible if—

(a) the application is made within the period of 3 years starting with the day after that on which the declaration was issued,

(b) the relevant bargaining unit is the same or substantially the same as the bargaining unit to which the bargaining arrangements mentioned in sub-paragraph (1) relate, and

(c) the application is made by the union which was a party (or unions which were parties) to the proceedings leading to the declaration.

(3) The relevant bargaining unit is—

(a) the proposed bargaining unit, where the application is under paragraph 11(2) or 12(2);

(b) the agreed bargaining unit, where the application is under paragraph 12(4).

42.—(1) This paragraph applies for the purposes of paragraphs 39 to 41.

(2) It is for the CAC to decide whether one bargaining unit is the same or substantially the same as another, but in deciding the CAC may take account of the views of any person it believes has an interest in the matter.

General provisions about validity

43.—(1) Paragraphs 44 to 50 apply if the CAC has to decide under paragraph 20 whether an application is valid.

(2) In those paragraphs—

(a) references to the application in question are to that application, and

(b) references to the relevant bargaining unit are to the bargaining unit agreed by the parties or decided by the CAC.

44.—(1) The application in question is invalid if the CAC is satisfied that there is already in force a collective agreement under which a union is (or unions are) recognised as entitled to conduct collective bargaining on behalf of any workers falling within the relevant bargaining unit.

(2) But sub-paragraph (1) does not apply to the application in question if—

(a) the union (or unions) recognised under the collective agreement and the union (or unions) making the application in question are the same, and

(b) the matters in respect of which the union is (or unions are) entitled to conduct collective bargaining do not include pay, hours or holidays.

(3) A declaration of recognition which is the subject of a declaration under paragraph 83(2) must for the purposes of sub-paragraph (1) be treated as ceasing to have efrect to the extent specified in paragraph 83(2) on the making of the declaration under paragraph 83(2).

(4) In applying sub-paragraph (1) an agreement for recognition (the agreement in question) must be ignored if—

(a)   the union does not have (or none of the unions has) a certificate under section 6 that it is independent,

(b)   at some time there was an agreement (the old agreement) between the employer and the union under which the union (whether alone or with other unions) was recognised as entitled to conduct collective bargaining on behalf of a group of workers which was the same or substantially the same as the group covered by the agreement in question, and

(c)   the old agreement ceased to have effect in the period of three years ending with the date of the agreement in question.

(5)   It is for the CAC to decide whether one group of workers is the same or substantially the same an another, but in deciding the CAC may take account of the views of any person it believes has an interest in the matter.

45.   The application in question is invalid unless the CAC decides that—

(a)   members of the union (or unions) constitute at least 10 per cent of the workers constituting the relevant bargaining unit, and

(b)   a majority of the workers constituting the relevant bargaining unit would be likely to favour recognition of the union (or unions) as entitled to conduct collective bargaining on behalf of the bargaining unit.

46.—(1)   This paragraph applies if—

(a)   the CAC accepts an application under paragraph 11 or 12 relating to a bargaining unit or proceeds under paragraph 20 with an application relating to bargaining unit,

(b)   the application has not been withdrawn,

(c)   no notice has been given under paragraph 17(2),

(d)   the CAC has not issued a declaration under paragraph 22(2), 27(2), 29(3) or 29(4) in relation to that bargaining unit, and

(e)   no notification has been made under paragraph 24(2).

(2)   The application in question is invalid if—

(a)   at least one worker falling within the relevant bargaining unit also falls within the bargaining unit referred to in sub-paragraph (1), and

(b)   the application in question is made by a union (or unions) other than the union (or unions) which made the application referred to in sub-paragraph (1).

47.—(1)   This paragraph applies if the CAC accepts an application under paragraph 11 or 12 relating to a bargaining unit or proceeds under paragraph 20 with an application relating to a bargaining unit.

(2)   The application in question is invalid if—

(a)   the application is made within the period of 3 years starting with the day after that on which the CAC gave notice of acceptance of the application mentioned in sub-paragraph (1),

(b)   the relevant bargaining unit is the same or substantially the same as the bargaining unit mentioned in sub-paragraph (1), and

(c)   the application is made by the union (or unions) which made the application mentioned in sub-paragraph (1).

(3)   This paragraph does not apply if paragraph 48 or 49 applies.

48.—(1)   This paragraph applies if the CAC issues a declaration under paragraph 29(4) that a union is (or unions are) not entitled to be recognised as entitled to conduct collective bargaining on behalf of a bargaining unit; and this is so whether the ballot concerned is held under this Part or Part III of this Schedule.

(2)   The application in question is invalid if—

(a)   the application is made within the period of 3 years starting with the date of the declaration,

(b)   the relevant bargaining unit is the same or substantially the same as the bargaining unit mentioned in sub-paragraph (1), and

(c)   the application is made by the union (or unions) which made the application leading to the declaration.

49.—(1)   This paragraph applies if the CAC issues a declaration under paragraph 121(3) that bargaining arrangements are to cease to have effect; and this is so whether the ballot concerned is held under Part IV or Part V of this Schedule.

(2)   The application in question is invalid if—

(a)   the application is made within the period of 3 years starting with the day after that on which the declaration was issued,

(b)   the relevant bargaining unit is the same or substantially the same as the bargaining unit to which the bargaining arrangements mentioned in sub-paragraph (1) relate, and

(c)   the application is made by the union which was a party (or unions which were parties) to the proceedings leading to the declaration.

50.—(1)   This paragraph applies for the purposes of paragraphs 47 to 49.

(2)   It is for the CAC to decide whether one bargaining unit is the same or substantially the same as another, but in deciding the CAC may take account of the views of any person it believes has an interest in the matter.

Competing applications

51.—(1)   For the purposes of this paragraph—

(a)   the original application is the application referred to in paragraph 38(1) or 46(1), and

(b)   the competing application is the other application referred to in paragraph 38(2) or the application in question referred to in paragraph 46(2);
but an application cannot be an original application unless it was made under paragraph 11(2) or 12(2).

(2)   This paragraph applies if—

(a)   the CAC decides that the competing application is not admissible by reason of paragraph 38 or is invalid by reason of paragraph 46,

(b)   at the time the decision is made the parties to the original application have not agreed the appropriate bargaining unit under paragraph 18, and the CAC has not decided the appropriate bargaining unit under paragraph 19, in relation to the application, and

(c)   the 10 per cent test (within the meaning given by paragraph 14) is satisfied with regard to the competing application.

(3)   In such a case—

(a)   the CAC must cancel the original application,

(b)   the CAC must give notice to the parties to the application that it has been cancelled,

(c)   no further steps are to be taken under this Part of this Schedule in relation to the application, and

(d)   the application shall be treated as if it had never been admissible.

PART II
VOLUNTARY RECOGNITION

Agreements for recognition

52.—(1)　This paragraph applies for the purposes of this Part of this Schedule.

(2)　An agreement is an agreement for recognition if the following conditions are fulfilled in relation to it—

　　(a)　the agreement is made in the permitted period between a union (or unions) and an employer in consequence of a request made under paragraph 4 and valid within the terms of paragraphs 5 to 9;

　　(b)　under the agreement the union is (or unions are) recognised as entitled to conduct collective bargaining on behalf of a group or groups of workers employed by the employer;

　　(c)　if sub-paragraph (5) applies to the agreement, it is satisfied.

(3)　The permitted period is the period which begins with the day on which the employer receives the request and ends when the first of the following occurs—

　　(a)　the union withdraws (or unions withdraw) the request;

　　(b)　the union withdraws (or unions withdraw) any application under paragraph 11 or 12 made in consequence of the request;

　　(c)　the CAC gives notice of a decision under paragraph 14(7) which precludes it from accepting such an application under paragraph 11 or 12;

　　(d)　the CAC gives notice under paragraph 15(4)(a) or 20(4)(a) in relation to such an application under paragraph 11 or 12;

　　(e)　the parties give notice to the CAC under paragraph 17(2) in relation to such an application under paragraph 11 or 12;

　　(f)　the CAC issues a declaration under paragraph 22(2) in consequence of such an application under paragraph 11 or 12;

　　(g)　the CAC is notified under paragraph 24(2) in relation to such an application under paragraph 11 or 12;

　　(h)　the last day of the notification period ends (the notification period being that defined by paragraph 24(5) and arising from such an application under paragraph 11 or 12);

　　(i)　the CAC is required under paragraph 51(3) to cancel such an application under paragraph 11 or 12.

(4)　Sub-paragraph (5) applies to an agreement if—

　　(a)　at the time it is made the CAC has received an application under paragraph 11 or 12 in consequence of the request mentioned in sub-paragraph (2), and

　　(b)　the CAC has not decided whether the application is admissible or it has decided that it is admissible.

(5)　This sub-paragraph is satisfied if, in relation to the application under paragraph 11 or 12, the parties give notice to the CAC under paragraph 17 before the final event (as defined in paragraph 17) occurs.

Other interpretation

53.—(1)　This paragraph applies for the purposes of this Part of this Schedule.

(2)　In relation to an agreement for recognition, references to the bargaining unit are to the group of workers (or the groups taken together) to which the agreement for recognition relates.

(3)　In relation to an agreement for recognition, references to the parties are to the union (or unions) and the employer who are parties to the agreement.

54—(1)　This paragraph applies for the purposes of this Part of this Schedule.

(2)　The meaning of collective bargaining given by section 178(1) shall not apply.

(3)　Except in paragraph 63(2), in relation to an agreement for recognition references to collective bargaining are to negotiations relating to the matters in respect of which the union is (or unions are) recognised as entitled to conduct negotiations under the agreement for recognition.

(4)　In paragraph 63(2) the reference to collective bargaining is to negotiations relating to pay, hours and holidays.

Determination of type of agreement

55.—(1)　This paragraph applies if one or more of the parties to an agreement applies to the CAC for a decision whether or not the agreement is an agreement for recognition.

(2)　The CAC must give notice of receipt of an application under sub-paragraph (1) to any parties to the agreement who are not parties to the application.

(3)　The CAC must within the decision period decide whether the agreement is an agreement for recognition.

(4)　If the CAC decides that the agreement is an agreement for recognition it must issue a declaration to that effect.

(5)　If the CAC decides that the agreement is not an agreement for recognition it must issue a declaration to that effect.

(6)　The decision period is—

(a)　the period of 10 working days starting with the day after that on which the CAC receives the application under sub-paragraph (1), or

(b)　such longer period (so starting) as the CAC may specify to the parties to the agreement by notice containing reasons for the extension.

Termination of agreement for recognition

56.—(1)　The employer may not terminate an agreement for recognition before the relevant period ends.

(2)　After that period ends the employer may terminate the agreement, with or without the consent of the union (or unions).

(3)　The union (or unions) may terminate an agreement for recognition at any time, with or without the consent of the employer.

(4)　Sub-paragraphs (1) to (3) have effect subject to the terms of the agreement or any other agreement of the parties.

(5)　The relevant period is the period of three years starting with the day after the date of the agreement.

57.—(1)　If an agreement for recognition is terminated, as from the termination the agreement and any provisions relating to the collective bargaining method shall cease to have effect.

(2) For this purpose provisions relating to the collective bargaining method are—

(a)　any agreement between the parties as to the method by which collective bargaining is to be conducted with regard to the bargaining unit, or

(b)　anything effective as, or as if contained in, a legally enforceable contract and relating to the method by which collective bargaining is to be conducted with regard to the bargaining unit.

Application to CAC to specify method

58.—(1) This paragraph applies if the parties make an agreement for recognition.

(2) The parties may in the negotiation period conduct negotiations with a view to agreeing a method by which they will conduct collective bargaining.

(3) If no agreement is made in the negotiation period the employer or the union (or unions) may apply to the CAC for assistance.

(4) The negotiation period is—

    (a)   the period of 30 working days starting with the start day, or

    (b)   such longer period (so starting) as the parties may from time to time agree.

(5) The start day is the day after that on which the agreement is made.

59.—(1) This paragraph applies if—

    (a)   the parties to an agreement for recognition agree a method by which they will conduct collective bargaining, and

    (b)   one or more of the parties fails to carry out the agreement as to a method.

(2) The employer or the union (or unions) may apply to the CAC for assistance.

60.—(1) This paragraph applies if an application for assistance is made to the CAC under paragraph 58 or 59.

(2) The application is not admissible unless the conditions in sub-paragraphs (3) and (4) are satisfied.

(3) The condition is that the employer, taken with any associated employer or employers, must—

    (a)   employ at least 21 workers on the day the application is made, or

    (b)   employ an average of at least 21 workers in the 13 weeks ending with that day.

(4) The condition is that the union (or every union) has a certificate under section 6 that it is independent.

(5) To find the average under sub-paragraph (3)(b)—

    (a)   take the number of workers employed in each of the 13 weeks (including workers not employed for the whole of the week);

    (b)   aggregate the 13 numbers;

    (c)   divide the aggregate by 13.

(6) For the purposes of sub-paragraph (3)(a) any worker employed by an associated company incorporated outside Great Britain must be ignored unless the day the application was made fell within a period during which he ordinarily worked in Great Britain.

(7) For the purposes of sub-paragraph (3)(b) any worker employed by an associated company incorporated outside Great Britain must be ignored in relation to a week unless the whole or any part of that week fell within a period during which he ordinarily worked in Great Britain.

(8) For the purposes of sub-paragraphs (6) and (7) a worker who is employed on board a ship registered in the register maintained under section 8 of the Merchant Shipping Act 1995 shall be treated as ordinarily working in Great Britain unless—

    (a)   the ship's entry in the register specifies a port outside Great Britain as the port to which the vessel is to be treated as belonging,

    (b)   the employment is wholly outside Great Britain, or

    (c)   the worker is not ordinarily resident in Great Britain.

(9) An order made under paragraph 7(6) may also—

(a) provide that sub-paragraphs (2), (3) and (5) to (8) of this paragraph are not to apply, or are not to apply in specified circumstances, or

(b) vary the number of workers for the tiine being specified in sub-paragraph (3).

61.—(1) An application to the CAC is not admissible unless—

(a) it is made in such form as the CAC specifies, and

(b) it is supported by such documents as the CAC specifies.

(2) An application which is made by a union (or unions) to the CAC is not admissible unless the union gives (or unions give) to the employer—

(a) notice of the application, and

(b) a copy of the application and any documents supporting it.

(3) An application which is made by an employer to the CAC is not admissible unless the employer gives to the union (or each of the unions)—

(a) notice of the application, and

(b) a copy of the application and any documents supporting it.

CAC's response to application

62.—(1) The CAC must give notice to the parties of receipt of an application under paragraph 58 or 59.

(2) Within the acceptance period the CAC must decide whether the application is admissible within the terms of paragraphs 60 and 61.

(3) In deciding whether an application is admissible the CAC must consider any evidence which it has been given by the employer or the union (or unions).

(4) If the CAC decides that the application is not admissible—

(a) the CAC must give notice of its decision to the parties,

(b) the CAC must not accept the application, and

(c) no further steps are to be taken under this Part of this Schedule.

(5) If the CAC decides that the application is admissible it must—

(a) accept the application, and

(b) give notice of the acceptance to the parties.

(6) The acceptance period is—

(a) the period of 10 working days starting with the day after that on which the CAC receives the application, or

(b) such longer period (so starting) as the CAC may specify to the parties by notice containing reasons for the extension.

63.—(1) If the CAC accepts an application it must try to help the parties to reach in the agreement period an agreement on a method by which they will conduct collective bargaining.

(2) If at the end of the agreement period the parties have not made such an agreement the CAC must specify to the parties the method by which they are to conduct collective bargaining.

(3) Any method specified under sub-paragraph (2) is to have effect as if it were contained in a legally enforceable contract made by the parties.

(4) But if the parties agree in writing—

(a) that sub-paragraph (3) shall not apply, or shall not apply to particular parts of the method specified by the CAC, or

(b) to vary or replace the method specified by the CAC,

the written agreement shall have effect as a legally enforceable contract made by the parties.

(5)   Specific performance shall be the only remedy available for breach of anything which is a legally enforceable contract by virtue of this paragraph.

(6)   If the CAC accepts an application, the applicant may not withdraw it after the end of the agreement period.

(7)   If at any time before a specification is made under sub-paragraph (2) the parties jointly apply to the CAC requesting it to stop taking steps under this paragraph, the CAC must comply with the request.

(8)   The agreement period is—

(a)   the period of 20 working days starting with the day after that on which the CAC gives notice of acceptance of the application, or

(b)   such longer period (so starting) as the parties may from time to time agree.

PART III
CHANGES AFFECTING BARGAINING UNIT

Introduction

64—(1)   This Part of this Schedule applies if—

(a)   the CAC has issued a declaration that a union is (or unions are) recognised as entitled to conduct collective bargaining on behalf of a bargaining unit, and

(b)   provisions relating to the collective bargaining method apply in relation to the unit.

(2)   In such a case, in this Part of this Schedule—

(a)   references to the original unit are to the bargaining unit on whose behalf the union is (or unions are) recognised as entitled to conduct collective bargaining, and

(b)   references to the bargaining arrangements are to the declaration and to the provisions relating to the collective bargaining method which apply in relation to the original unit.

(3) For this purpose provisions relating to the collective bargaining method are—

(a)   the parties' agreement as to the method by which collective bargaining is to be conducted with regard to the original unit,

(b)   anything effective as, or as if contained in, a legally enforceable contract and relating to the method by which collective bargaining is to be conducted with regard to the original unit, or

(c)   any provision of this Part of this Schedule that a method of collective bargaining is to have effect with regard to the original unit.

65. References in this Part of this Schedule to the parties are to the employer and the union (or unions) concerned.

Either party believes unit no longer appropriate

66.—(1)   This paragraph applies if the employer believes or the union believes (or unions believe) that the original unit is no longer an appropriate bargaining unit.

(2)   The employer or union (or unions) may apply to the CAC to make a decision as to what is an appropriate bargaining unit.

67.—(1)   An application under paragraph 66 is not admissible unless the CAC decides that it is likely that the original unit is no longer appropriate by reason of any of the matters specified in sub-paragraph (2).

(2)   The matters are—

(a)   a change in the organisation or structure of the business carried on by the employer;

(b)   a change in the activities pursued by the employer in the course of the business carried on by him;

(c)   a substantial change in the number of workers employed in the original unit.

68.—(1)   The CAC must give notice to the parties of receipt of an application under paragraph 66.

(2)   Within the acceptance period the CAC must decide whether the application is admissible within the terms of paragraphs 67 and 92.

(3)   In deciding whether the application is admissible the CAC must consider any evidence which it has been given by the employer or the union (or unions).

(4)   If the CAC decides that the application is not admissible —

(a)   the CAC must give notice of its decision to the parties,

(b)   the CAC must not accept the application, and

(c)   no further steps are to be taken under this Part of this Schedule.

(5)   If the CAC decides that the application is admissible it must—

(a)   accept the application, and

(b)   give notice of the acceptance to the parties.

(6)   The acceptance period is—

(a)   the period of 10 working days starting with the day after that on which the CAC receives the application, or

(b)   such longer period (so starting) as the CAC may specify to the parties by notice containing reasons for the extension.

69.—(1)   This paragraph applies if—

(a)   the CAC gives notice of acceptance of the application, and

(b)   before the end of the first period the parties agree a bargaining unit or units (the new unit or units) differing from the original unit and inform the CAC of their agreement.

(2)   If in the CAC's opinion the new unit (or any of the new units) contains at least one worker falling within an outside bargaining unit no further steps are to be taken under this Part of this Schedule.

(3)   If sub-paragraph (2) does not apply—

(a)   the CAC must issue a declaration that the union is (or unions are) recognised as entitled to conduct collective bargaining on behalf of the new unit or units;

(b)   so far as it affects workers in the new unit (or units) who fall within the original unit, the declaration shall have effect in place of any declaration that the union is (or unions are) recognised as entitled to conduct collective bargaining on behalf of the original unit;

(c)   the method of collective bargaining relating to the original unit shall have effect in relation to the new unit or units, with any modifications which the CAC considers necessary to take account of the change of bargaining unit and specifies in the declaration.

(4)   The first period is—

(a)   the period of 10 working days starting with the day after that on which the CAC gives notice of acceptance of the application, or

(b)   such longer period (so starting) as the parties may from time to time agree and notify to the CAC.

(5)   An outside bargaining unit is a bargaining unit which fulfils these conditions—

(a)   it is not the original unit;

(b)   a union is (or unions are) recognised as entitled to conduct collective bargaining on its behalf,

(c)   the union (or at least one of the unions) is not a party referred to in paragraph 64.

70.—(1)   This paragraph applies if—

(a)   the CAC gives notice of acceptance of the application, and

(b)   the parties do not inform the CAC before the end of the first period that they have agreed a bargaining unit or units differing from the original unit.

(2)   During the second period—

(a)   the CAC must decide whether or not the original unit continues to be an appropriate bargaining unit;

(b)   if the CAC decides that the original unit does not so continue, it must decide what other bargaining unit is or units are appropriate;

(c)   the CAC must give notice to the parties of its decision or decisions under paragraphs (a) and (b).

(3)   In deciding whether or not the original unit continues to be an appropriate bargaining unit the CAC must take into account only these matters—

(a)   any change in the organisation or structure of the business carried on by the employer;

(b)   any change in the activities pursued by the employer in the course of the business carried on by him;

(c)   any substantial change in the number of workers employed in the original unit.

(4)   In deciding what other bargaining unit is or units are appropriate the CAC must take these matters into account—

(a)   the need for the unit or units to be compatible with effective management;

(b)   the matters listed in sub-paragraph (5), so far as they do not conflict with that need.

(5)   The matters are—

(a)   the views of the employer and of the union (or unions);

(b)   existing national and local bargaining arrangements;

(c)   the desirability of avoiding small fragmented bargaining units within an undertaking;

(d)   the characteristics of workers falling within the original unit and of any other employees of the employer whom the CAC considers relevant;

(e)   the location of workers.

(6)   If the CAC decides that two or more bargaining units are appropriate its decision must be such that no worker falls within more than one of them.

(7)   The second period is—

(a)   the period of 10 working days starting with the day after that on which the first period ends, or

(b)   such longer period (so starting) as the CAC may specify to the parties by notice containing reasons for the extension.

71.   If the CAC gives notice under paragraph 70 of a decision that the original unit continues to be an appropriate bargaining unit no further steps are to be taken under this Part of this Schedule.

72.   Paragraph 82 applies if the CAC gives notice under paragraph 70 of—

(a)   a decision that the original unit is no longer an appropriate bargaining unit, and

(b)   a decision as to the bargaining unit which is (or units which are) appropriate.

73.—(1)   This paragraph applies if—

(a)   the parties agree under paragraph 69 a bargaining unit or units differing from the original unit,

(b)   paragraph 69(2) does not apply, and

(c)   at least one worker falling within the original unit does not fall within the new unit (or any of the new units).

(2)   In such a case—

(a)   the CAC must issue a declaration that the bargaining arrangements, so far as relating to the worker or workers mentioned in sub-paragraph (1)(c), are to cease to have effect on a date specified by the CAC in the declaration, and

(b)   the bargaining arrangements shall cease to have effect accordingly.

Employer believes unit has ceased to exist

74.—(1)   If the employer—

(a)   believes that the original unit has ceased to exist, and

(b)   wishes the bargaining arrangements to cease to have effect,

he must give the union (or each of the unions) a notice complying with sub-paragraph (2) and must give a copy of the notice to the CAC.

(2)   A notice complies with this sub-paragraph if it—

(a)   identifies the unit and the bargaining arrangements,

(b)   states the date on which the notice is given,

(c)   states that the unit has ceased to exist, and

(d)   states that the bargaining arrangements are to cease to have effect on a date which is specified in the notice and which falls after the end of the period of 35 working days starting with the day after that on which the notice is given.

(3)   Within the validation period the CAC must decide whether the notice complies with sub-paragraph (2).

(4)   If the CAC decides that the notice does not comply with sub-paragraph (2)—

(a)   the CAC must give the parties notice of its decision, and

(b)   the employer's notice shall be treated as not having been given.

(5)   If the CAC decides that the notice complies with sub-paragraph (2) it must give the parties notice of the decision.

(6)   The bargaining arrangements shall cease to have effect on the date specified under sub-paragraph (2)(d) if—

(a)   the CAC gives notice under sub-paragraph (5), and

(b)   the union does not (or unions do not) apply to the CAC under paragraph 75.

(7)   The validation period is—

(a)   the period of 10 working days starting with the day after that on which the CAC receives the copy of the notice, or

(b)　such longer period (so starting) as the CAC may specify to the parties by notice containing reasons for the extension.

75.—(1)　Paragraph 76 applies if—

(a)　the CAC gives notice under paragraph 74(5), and

(b)　within the period of 10 working days starting with the day after that on which the notice is given the union makes (or unions make) an application to the CAC for a decision on the questions specified in sub-paragraph (2).

(2)　The questions are—

(a)　whether the original unit has ceased to exist;

(b)　whether the original unit is no longer appropriate by reason of any of the matters specified in sub-paragraph (3).

(3)　The matters are—

(a)　a change in the organisation or structure of the business carried on by the employer;

(b)　a change in the activities pursued by the employer in the course of the business carried on by him;

(c)　a substantial change in the number of workers employed in the original unit.

76.—(1)　The CAC must give notice to the parties of receipt of an application under paragraph 75.

(2)　Within the acceptance period the CAC must decide whether the application is admissible within the terms of paragraph 92.

(3)　In deciding whether the application is admissible the CAC must consider any evidence which it has been given by the employer or the union (or unions).

(4)　If the CAC decides that the application is not admissible—

(a)　the CAC must give notice of its decision to the parties,

(b)　the CAC must not accept the application, and

(c)　no further steps are to be taken under this Part of this Schedule.

(5)　If the CAC decides that the application is admissible it must—

(a)　accept the application, and

(b)　give notice of the acceptance to the parties.

(6)　The acceptance period is—

(a)　the period of 10 working days starting with the day after that on which the CAC receives the application, or

(b)　such longer period (so starting) as the CAC may specify to the parties by notice containing reasons for the extension.

77.—(1)　If the CAC accepts an application it—

(a)　must give the employer and the union (or unions) an opportunity to put their views on the questions in relation to which the application was made;

(b)　must decide the questions before the end of the decision period.

(2)　If the CAC decides that the original unit has ceased to exist—

(a)　the CAC must give the parties notice of its decision, and

(b)　the bargaining arrangements shall cease to have effect on the termination date.

(3)　If the CAC decides that the original unit has not ceased to exist, and that it is not the case that the original unit is no longer appropriate by reason of any of the matters specified in paragraph 75(3)—

(a)　the CAC must give the parties notice of its decision, and

(b) the employer's notice shall be treated as not having been given.

(4) If the CAC decides that the original unit has not ceased to exist, and that the original unit is no longer appropriate by reason of any of the matters specified in paragraph 75(3), the CAC must give the parties notice of its decision.

(5) The decision period is—

(a) the period of 10 working days starting with the day after that on which the CAC gives notice of acceptance of the application, or

(b) such longer period (so starting) as the CAC may specify to the parties by notice containing reasons for the extension.

(6) The termination date is the later of—

(a) the date specified under paragraph 74(2)(d), and

(b) the day after the last day of the decision period.

78.—(1) This paragraph applies if—

(a) the CAC gives notice under paragraph 77(4), and

(b) before the end of the first period the parties agree a bargaining unit or units (the new unit or units) differing from the original unit and inform the CAC of their agreement.

(2) If in the CAC's opinion the new unit (or any of the new units) contains at least one worker falling within an outside bargaining unit no further steps are to be taken under this Part of this Schedule.

(3) If sub-paragraph (2) does not apply—

(a) the CAC must issue a declaration that the union is (or unions are) recognised as entitled to conduct collective bargaining on behalf of the new unit or units;

(b) so far as it affects workers in the new unit (or units) who fall within the original unit, the declaration shall have effect in place of any declaration that the union is (or unions are) recognised as entitled to conduct collective bargaining on behalf of the original unit;

(c) the method of collective bargaining relating to the original unit shall have effect in relation to the new unit or units, with any modifications which the CAC considers necessary to take account of the change of bargaining unit and specifies in the declaration.

(4) The first period is—

(a) the period of 10 working days starting with the day after that on which the CAC gives notice under paragraph 77(4), or

(b) such longer period (so starting) as the parties may from time to time agree and notify to the CAC.

(5) An outside bargaining unit is a bargaining unit which fulfils these conditions—

(a) it is not the original unit;

(b) a union is (or unions are) recognised as entitled to conduct collective bargaining on its behalf,

(c) the union (or at least one of the unions) is not a party referred to in paragraph 64.

79.—(1) This paragraph applies if—

(a) the CAC gives notice under paragraph 77(4), and

(b) the parties do not inform the CAC before the end of the first period that they have agreed a bargaining unit or units differing from the original unit.

(2) During the second period the CAC—

(a)   must decide what other bargaining unit is or units are appropriate;

(b)   must give notice of its decision to the parties.

(3) In deciding what other bargaining unit is or units are appropriate, the CAC must take these matters into account—

(a)   the need for the unit or units to be compatible with effective management;

(b)   the matters listed in sub-paragraph (4), so far as they do not conflict with that need.

(4)   The matters are—

(a)   the views of the employer and of the union (or unions);

(b)   existing national and local bargaining arrangements;

(c)   the desirability of avoiding small fragmented bargaining units within an undertaking;

(d)   the characteristics of workers falling within the original unit and of any other employees of the employer whom the CAC considers relevant;

(e)   the location of workers.

(5)   If the CAC decides that two or more bargaining units are appropriate its decision must be such that no worker falls within more than one of them.

(6)   The second period is—

(a)   the period of 10 working days starting with the day after that on which the first period ends, or

(b)   such longer period (so starting) as the CAC may specify to the parties by notice containing reasons for the extension.

80.   Paragraph 82 applies if the CAC gives notice under paragraph 79 of a decision as to the bargaining unit which is (or units which are) appropriate.

81.—(1)   This paragraph applies if—

(a)   the parties agree under paragraph 78 a bargaining unit or units differing from the original unit,

(b)   paragraph 78(2) does not apply, and

(c)   at least one worker falling within the original unit does not fall within the new unit (or any of the new units).

(2)   In such a case —

(a)   the CAC must issue a declaration that the bargaining arrangements, so far as relating to the worker or workers mentioned in sub-paragraph (1)(c), are to cease to have effect on a date specified by the CAC in the declaration, and

(b)   the bargaining arrangements shall cease to have effect accordingly.

Position where CAC decides new unit

82.—(1)   This paragraph applies if the CAC gives notice under paragraph 70 of—

(a)   a decision that the original unit is no longer an appropriate bargaining unit, and

(b)   a decision as to the bargaining unit which is (or units which are) appropriate.

(2)   This paragraph also applies if the CAC gives notice under paragraph 79 of a decision as to the bargaining unit which is (or units which are) appropriate.

(3) The CAC—

(a)   must proceed as stated in paragraphs 83 to 89 with regard to the appropriate unit (if there is one only), or

(b) must proceed as stated in paragraphs 83 to 89 with regard to each appropriate unit separately (if there are two or more).

(4) References in those paragraphs to the new unit are to the appropriate unit under consideration.

83.—(1) This paragraph applies if in the CAC's opinion the new unit contains at least one worker falling within a statutory outside bargaining unit.

(2) In such a case—

(a) the CAC must issue a declaration that the relevant bargaining arrangements, so far as relating to workers falling within the new unit, are to cease to have effect on a date specified by the CAC in the declaration, and

(b) the relevant bargaining arrangements shall cease to have effect accordingly.

(3) The relevant bargaining arrangements are—

(a) the bargaining arrangements relating to the original unit, and

(b) the bargaining arrangements relating to each statutory outside bargaining unit containing workers who fall within the new unit.

(4) The bargaining arrangements relating to the original unit are the bargaining arrangements as defined in paragraph 64.

(5) The bargaining arrangements relating to an outside unit are—

(a) the declaration recognising a union (or unions) as entitled to conduct collective bargaining on behalf of the workers constituting the outside unit, and .

(b) the provisions relating to the collective bargaining method.

(6) For this purpose the provisions relating to the collective bargaining method are—

(a) any agreement by the employer and the union (or unions) as to the method by which collective bargaining is to be conducted with regard to the outside unit,

(b) anything effective as, or as if contained in, a legally enforceable contract and relating to the method by which collective bargaining is to be conducted with regard to the outside unit, or

(c) any provision of this Part of this Schedule that a method of collective bargaining is to have effect with regard to the outside unit.

(7) A statutory outside bargaining unit is a bargaining unit which fulfils these conditions—

(a) it is not the original unit;

(b) a union is (or unions are) recognised as entitled to conduct collective bargaining on its behalf by virtue of a declaration of the CAC;

(c) the union (or at least one of the unions) is not a party referred to in paragraph 64.

(8) The date specified under sub-paragraph (1)(a) must be—

(a) the date on which the relevant period expires, or

(b) if the CAC believes that to maintain the relevant bargaining arrangements would be impracticable or contrary to the interests of good industrial relations, the date after the date on which the declaration is issued;

and the relevant period is the period of 65 working days starting with the day after that on which the declaration is issued.

84.—(1) This paragraph applies if in the CAC's opinion the new unit contains—

(a) at least one worker falling within a voluntary outside bargaining unit, but

(b) no worker falling within a statutory outside bargaining unit.

(2)   In such a case—

(a)   the CAC must issue a declaration that the original bargaining arrangements, so far as relating to workers falling within the new unit, are to cease to have effect on a date specified by the CAC in the declaration, and

(b)   the original bargaining arrangements shall cease to have effect accordingly.

(3)   The original bargaining arrangements are the bargaining arrangements as defined in paragraph 64.

(4)   A voluntary outside bargaining unit is a bargaining unit which fulfils these conditions—

(a)   it is not the original unit;

(b)   a union is (or unions are) recognised as entitled to conduct collective bargaining on its behalf by virtue of an agreement with the employer;

(c)   the union (or at least one of the unions) is not a party referred to in paragraph 64.

(5)   The date specified under sub-paragraph (2)(a) must be—

(a)   the date on which the relevant period expires, or

(b)   if the CAC believes that to maintain the original bargaining arrangements would be impracticable or contrary to the interests of good industrial relations, the date after the date on which the declaration is issued;

and the relevant period is the period of 65 working days starting with the day after that on which the declaration is issued.

85.—(1)   If the CAC's opinion is not that mentioned in paragraph 83(1) or 84(1) it must—

(a)   decide whether the difference between the original unit and the new unit is such that the support of the union (or unions) within the new unit needs to be assessed, and

(b)   inform the parties of its decision.

(2)   If the CAC's decision is that such support does not need to be assessed—

(a)   the CAC must issue a declaration that the union is (or unions are) recognised as entitled to conduct collective bargaining on behalf of the new unit;

(b)   so far as it affects workers in the new unit who fall within the original unit, the declaration shall have effect in place of any declaration that the union is (or unions are) recognised as entitled to conduct collective bargaining on behalf of the original unit;

(c)   the method of collective bargaining relating to the original unit shall have effect in relation to the new unit, with any modifications which the CAC considers necessary to take account of the change of bargaining unit and specifies in the declaration.

86.—(1)   This paragraph applies if the CAC decides under paragraph 85(1) that the support of the union (or unions) within the new unit needs to be assessed.

(2)   The CAC must decide these questions—

(a)   whether members of the union (or unions) constitute at least 10 per cent of the workers constituting the new unit;

(b)   whether a majority of the workers constituting the new unit would be likely to favour recognition of the union (or unions) as entitled to conduct collective bargaining on behalf of the new unit.

(3)   If the CAC decides one or both of the questions in the negative—

(a)   the CAC must issue a declaration that the bargaining arrangements, so far as relating to workers falling within the new unit, are to cease to have efrect on a date specified by the CAC in the declaration, and

(b)   the bargaining arrangements shall cease to have effect accordingly.

87.—(1)   This paragraph applies if—

(a)   the CAC decides both the questions in paragraph 86(2) in the affirmative, and

(b)   the CAC is satisfied that a majority of the workers constituting the new unit are members of the union (or unions).

(2)   The CAC must issue a declaration that the union is (or unions are) recognised as entitled to conduct collective bargaining on behalf of the workers constituting the new unit.

(3)   But if any of the three qualifying conditions is fulfilled, instead of issuing a declaration under sub-paragraph (2) the CAC must give notice to the parties that it intends to arrange for the holding of a secret ballot in which the workers constituting the new unit are asked whether they want the union (or unions) to conduct collective bargaining on their behalf.

(4)   These are the three qualifying conditions—

(a)   the CAC is satisfied that a ballot should be held in the interests of good industrial relations;

(b)   a significant number of the union members within the new unit inform the CAC that they do not want the union (or unions) to conduct collective bargaining on their behalf;

(c)   membership evidence is produced which leads the CAC to conclude that there are doubts whether a significant number of the union members within the new unit want the union (or unions) to conduct collective bargaining on their behalf.

(5)   For the purposes of sub-paragraph (4)(c) membership evidence is—

(a)   evidence about the circumstances in which union members became members;

(b)   evidence about the length of time for which union members have been members, in a case where the CAC is satisfied that such evidence should be taken into account.

(6)   If the CAC issues a declaration under sub-paragraph (2)—

(a)   so far as it affects workers in the new unit who fall within the original unit, the declaration shall have effect in place of any declaration that the union is (or unions are) recognised as entitled to conduct collective bargaining on behalf of the original unit;

(b)   the method of collective bargaining relating to the original unit shall have effect in relation to the new unit, with any modifications which the CAC considers necessary to take account of the change of bargaining unit and specifies in the declaration.

88.—(1)   This paragraph applies if—

(a)   the CAC decides both the questions in paragraph 86(2) in the affirmative, and

(b)   the CAC is not satisfied that a majority of the workers constituting the new unit are members of the union (or unions).

(2)   The CAC must give notice to the parties that it intends to arrange for the holding of a secret ballot in which the workers constituting the new unit are asked

whether they want the union (or unions) to conduct collective bargaining on their behalf.

89.—(1) If the CAC gives notice under paragraph 87(3) or 88(2) the union (or unions) may within the notification period notify the CAC that the union does not (or unions do not) want the CAC to arrange for the holding of the ballot; and the notification period is the period of 10 working days starting with the day after that on which the union (or last of the unions) receives the CAC's notice.

(2)   If the CAC is so notified—

(a)   it must not arrange for the holding of the ballot,

(b)   it must inform the parties that it will not arrange for the holding of the ballot, and why,

(c)   it must issue a declaration that the bargaining arrangements, so far as relating to workers falling within the new unit, are to cease to have effect on a date specified by it in the declaration, and

(d)   the bargaining arrangements shall cease to have effect accordingly.

(3)   If the CAC is not so notified it must arrange for the holding of the ballot.

(4)   Paragraph 25 applies if the CAC arranges under this paragraph for the holding of a ballot (as well as if the CAC arranges under paragraph 24 for the holding of a ballot).

(5)   Paragraphs 26 to 29 apply accordingly, but as if references to the bargaining unit were references to the new unit.

(6)   If as a result of the ballot the CAC issues a declaration that the union is (or unions are) recognised as entitled to conduct collective bargaining on behalf of the new unit—

(a)   so far as it affects workers in the new unit who fall within the original unit, the declaration shall have effect in place of any declaration that the union is (or unions are) recognised as entitled to conduct collective bargaining on behalf of the original unit;

(b)   the method of collective bargaining relating to the original unit shall have effect in relation to the new unit, with any modifications which the CAC considers necessary to take account of the change of bargaining unit and specifies in the declaration.

(7)   If as a result of the ballot the CAC issues a declaration that the union is (or unions are) not entitled to be recognised as entitled to conduct collective bargaining on behalf of the new unit—

(a)   the CAC must state in the declaration the date on which the bargaining arrangements, so far as relating to workers falling within the new unit, are to cease to have effect, and

(b)   the bargaining arrangements shall cease to have efrect accordingly.

(8) Paragraphs (a) and (b) of sub-paragraph (6) also apply if the CAC issues declaration under paragraph 27(2).

Residual workers

90.—(1)   This paragraph applies if—

(a)   the CAC decides an appropriate bargaining unit or units under paragraph 70 or 79, and

(b)   at least one worker falling within the original unit does not fall within the new unit (or any of the new units).

(2) In such a case —

(a) the CAC must issue a declaration that the bargaining arrangements, so far as relating to the worker or workers mentioned in sub-paragraph (1)(b), are to cease to have effect on a date specified by the CAC in the declaration, and

(b) the bargaining arrangements shall cease to have effect accordingly.

91.—(1) This paragraph applies if—

(a) the CAC has proceeded as stated in paragraphs 83 to 89 with regard to the new unit (if there is one only) or with regard to each new unit (if there are two or more), and

(b) in so doing the CAC has issued one or more declarations under paragraph 83.

(2) The CAC must—

(a) consider each declaration issued under paragraph 83, and

(b) in relation to each declaration, identify each statutory outside bargaining unit which contains at least one worker who also falls within the new unit to which the declaration relates;

and in this paragraph each statutory outside bargaining unit so identified is referred to as a parent unit.

(3) The CAC must then—

(a) consider each parent unit, and

(b) in relation to each parent unit, identify any workers who fall within the parent unit but who do not fall within the new unit (or any of the new units);

and in this paragraph the workers so identified in relation to a parent unit are referred to as a residual unit.

(4) In relation to each residual unit, the CAC must issue a declaration that the outside union is (or outside unions are) recognised as entitled to conduct collective bargaining on its behalf.

(5) But no such declaration shall be issued in relation to a residual unit if the CAC has received an application under paragraph 66 or 75 in relation to its parent unit.

(6) In this paragraph references to the outside union (or to outside unions) in relation to a residual unit are to the union which is (or unions which are) recognised as entitled to conduct collective bargaining on behalf of its parent unit.

(7) If the CAC issues a declaration under sub-paragraph (4)—

(a) the declaration shall have effect in place of the existing declaration that the outside union is (or outside unions are) recognised as entitled to conduct collective bargaining on behalf of the parent unit, so far as the existing declaration relates to the residual unit;

(b) if there is a method of collective bargaining relating to the parent unit, it shall have effect in relation to the residual unit with any modifications which the CAC considers necessary to take account of the change of bargaining unit and specifies in the declaration.

Applications under this Part

92.—(1) An application to the CAC under this Part of this Schedule is not admissible unless—

(a) it is made in such form as the CAC specifies, and

(b) it is supported by such documents as the CAC specifies.

(2)   An application which is made by a union (or unions) to the CAC under this Part of this Schedule is not admissible unless the union gives (or unions give) to the employer—

(a)   notice of the application, and

(b)   a copy of the application and any documents supporting it.

(3)   An application which is made by an employer to the CAC under this Part of this Schedule is not admissible unless the employer gives to the union (or each of the unions)—

(a)   notice of the application, and

(b)   a copy of the application and any documents supporting it.

Withdrawal of application

93.—(1)   If an application under paragraph 66 or 75 is accepted by the CAC, the applicant (or applicants) may not withdraw the application—

(a)   after the CAC issues a declaration under paragraph 69(3) or 78(3),

(b)   after the CAC decides under paragraph 77(2) or 77(3),

(c)   after the CAC issues a declaration under paragraph 83(1), 85(2), 86(3) or 87(2) in relation to the new unit (where there is only one) or a declaration under any of those paragraphs in relation to any of the new units (where there is more than one),

(d)   after the union has (or unions have) notified the CAC under paragraph 89(1) in relation to the new unit (where there is only one) or any of the new units (where there is more than one), or

(e)   after the end of the notification period referred to in paragraph 89(1) and relating to the new unit (where there is only one) or any of the new units (where there is more than one).

(2)   If an application is withdrawn by the applicant (or applicants)—

(a)   the CAC must give notice of the withdrawal to the other party (or parties), and

(b)   no further steps are to be taken under this Part of this Schedule.

Meaning of collective bargaining

94.—(1)   This paragraph applies for the purposes of this Part of this Schedule.

(2)   Except in relation to paragraphs 69(5), 78(5) and 83(6), the meaning of collective bargaining given by section 178(1) shall not apply.

(3)   In relation to a new unit references to collective bargaining are to negotiations relating to the matters which were the subject of collective bargaining in relation to the corresponding original unit; and the corresponding original unit is the unit which was the subject of an application under paragraph 66 or 75 in consequence of which the new unit was agreed by the parties or decided by the CAC.

(4)   But if the parties agree matters as the subject of collective bargaining in relation to the new unit, references to collective bargaining in relation to that unit are to negotiations relating to the agreed matters; and this is the case whether the agreement is made before or after the time when the CAC issues a declaration that the union is (or unions are) recognised as entitled to conduct collective bargaining on behalf of the new unit.

(5)   In relation to a residual unit in relation to which a declaration is issued under paragraph 9 1, references to collective bargaining are to negotiations relating to the matters which were the subject of collective bargaining in relation to the corresponding parent unit.

(6) In construing paragraphs 69(3)(c), 78(3)(c), 85(2)(c), 87(6)(b) and 89(6)(b)—

(a) sub-paragraphs (3) and (4) do not apply, and

(b) references to collective bargaining are to negotiations relating to pay, hours and holidays.

Method of collective bargaining

95.—(1) This paragraph applies for the purposes of this Part of this Schedule.

(2) Where a method of collective bargaining has efrect in relation to a new unit, that method shall have effect as if it were contained in a legally enforceable contract made by the parties.

(3) But if the parties agree in writing—

(a) that sub-paragraph (2) shall not apply, or shall not apply to particular parts of the method, or

(b) to vary or replace the method,

the written agreement shall have efrect as a legally enforceable contract made by the parties.

(4) Specific performance shall be the only remedy available for breach of anything which is a legally enforceable contract by virtue of this paragraph.

PART IV
DERECOGNITION: GENERAL

Introduction

96.—(1) This Part of this Schedule applies if the CAC has issued a declaration that a union is (or unions are) recognised as entitled to conduct collective bargaining on behalf of a bargaining unit.

(2) In such a case references in this Part of this Schedule to the bargaining arrangements are to the declaration and to the provisions relating to the collective bargaining method.

(3) For this purpose the provisions relating to the collective bargaining method are—

(a) the parties' agreement as to the method by which collective bargaining is to be conducted,

(b) anything effective as, or as if contained in, a legally enforceable contract and relating to the method by which collective bargaining is to be conducted, or

(c) any provision of Part III of this Schedule that a method of collective bargaining is to have effect.

97. For the purposes of this Part of this Schedule the relevant date is the date of the expiry of the period of 3 years starting with the date of the CAC's declaration.

98. References in this Part of this Schedule to the parties are to the employer and the union (or unions) concerned.

Employer employs fewer than 21 workers

99.—(1) This paragraph applies if—

(a) the employer believes that he, taken with any associated employer or employers, employed an average of fewer than 21 workers in any period of 13 weeks, and

(b) that period ends on or after the relevant date.

(2) If the employer wishes the bargaining arrangements to cease to have effect, he must give the union (or each of the unions) a notice complying with sub-paragraph (3) and must give a copy of the notice to the CAC.

(3) A notice complies with this sub-paragraph if it—

(a) identifies the bargaining arrangements,

(b) specifies the period of 13 weeks in question,

(c) states the date on which the notice is given,

(d) is given within the period of 5 working days starting with the day after the last day of the specified period of 13 weeks,

(e) states that the employer, taken with any associated employer or employers, employed an average of fewer than 21 workers in the specified period of 13 weeks, and

(f) states that the bargaining arrangements are to cease to have effect on a date which is specified in the notice and which falls after the end of the period of 35 working days starting with the day after that on which the notice is given.

(4) To find the average number of workers employed by the employer, taken with any associated employer or employers, in the specified period of 13 weeks—

(a) take the number of workers employed in each of the 13 weeks (including workers not employed for the whole of the week);

(b) aggregate the 13 numbers;

(c) divide the aggregate by 13.

(5) For the purposes of sub-paragraph (1)(a) any worker employed by an associated company incorporated outside Great Britain must be ignored in relation to a week unless the whole or any part of that week fell within a period during which he ordinarily worked in Great Britain.

(6) For the purposes of sub-paragraph (5) a worker who is employed on board a ship registered in the register maintained under section 8 of the Merchant Shipping Act 1995 shall be treated as ordinarily working in Great Britain unless—

(a) the ship's entry in the register specifies a port outside Great Britain as the port to which the vessel is to be treated as belonging,

(b) the employment is wholly outside Great Britain, or

(c) the worker is not ordinarily resident in Great Britain.

(7) An order made under paragraph 7(6) may also—

(a) provide that sub-paragraphs (1) to (6) of this paragraph and paragraphs 100 to 103 are not to apply, or are not to apply in specified circumstances, or

(b) vary the number of workers for the time being specified in sub-paragraphs (1)(a) and (3)(e).

100.—(1) Within the validation period the CAC must decide whether the notice complies with paragraph 99(3).

(2) If the CAC decides that the notice does not comply with para-graph 99(3)—

(a) the CAC must give the parties notice of its decision, and

(b) the employer's notice shall be treated as not having been given.

(3) If the CAC decides that the notice complies with paragraph 99(3) it must give the parties notice of the decision.

(4) The bargaining arrangements shall cease to have effect on the date specified under paragraph 99(3)(f) if—

(a)   the CAC gives notice under sub-paragraph (3), and

(b)   the union does not (or unions do not) apply to the CAC under paragraph 101.

(5)   The validation period is—

(a)   the period of 10 working days starting with the day after that on which the CAC receives the copy of the notice, or

(b)   such longer period (so starting) as the CAC may specify to the parties by notice containing reasons for the extension.

101.—(1)   This paragraph applies if—

(a)   the CAC gives notice under paragraph 100(3), and

(b)   within the period of 10 working days starting with the day after that on which the notice is given, the union makes (or unions make) an application to the CAC for a decision whether the period of 13 weeks specified under paragraph 99(3)(b) ends on or after the relevant date and whether the statement made under paragraph 99(3)(e) is correct.

(2)   An application is not admissible unless—

(a)   it is made in such form as the CAC specifies, and

(b)   it is supported by such documents as the CAC specifies.

(3)   An application is not admissible unless the union gives (or unions give) to the employer—

(a)   notice of the application, and

(b)   a copy of the application and any documents supporting it.

(4)   An application is not admissible if—

(a)   a relevant application was made within the period of 3 years prior to the date of the application,

(b)   the relevant application and the application relate to the same bargaining unit, and

(c)   the CAC accepted the relevant application.

(5)   A relevant application is an application made to the CAC—

(a)   by the union (or the unions) under this paragraph,

(b)   by the employer under paragraph 106, 107 or 128, or

(c)   by a worker (or workers) under paragraph 112.

102.—(1)   The CAC must give notice to the parties of receipt of an application under paragraph 101.

(2)   Within the acceptance period the CAC must decide whether the application is admissible within the terms of paragraph 101.

(3)   In deciding whether an application is admissible the CAC must consider any evidence which it has been given by the employer or the union (or unions).

(4)   If the CAC decides that the application is not admissible—

(a)   the CAC must give notice of its decision to the parties,

(b)   the CAC must not accept the application,

(c)   no further steps are to be taken under this Part of this Schedule, and

(d)   the bargaining arrangements shall cease to have effect on the date specified under paragraph 99(3)(f).

(5)   If the CAC decides that the application is admissible it must—

(a)   accept the application, and

(b)   give notice of the acceptance to the parties.

(6)   The acceptance period is—

(a)   the period of 10 working days starting with the day after that on which the CAC receives the application, or

(b)   such longer period (so starting) as the CAC may specify to the parties by notice containing reasons for the extension.

103.—(1)   If the CAC accepts an application it—

(a)   must give the employer and the union (or unions) an opportunity to put their views on the questions whether the period of 13 weeks specified under paragraph 99(3)(b) ends on or after the relevant date and whether the statement made under paragraph 99(3)(e) is correct;

(b)   must decide the questions within the decision period and must give reasons for the decision.

(2)   If the CAC decides that the period of 13 weeks specified under paragraph 99(3)(b) ends on or after the relevant date and that the statement made under paragraph 99(3)(e) is correct the bargaining arrangements shall cease to have effect on the termination date.

(3)   If the CAC decides that the period of 13 weeks specified under paragraph 99(3)(b) does not end on or after the relevant date or that the statement made under paragraph 99(3)(e) is not correct, the notice under paragraph 99 shall be treated as not having been given.

(4)   The decision period is—

(a)   the period of 10 working days starting with the day after that on which the CAC gives notice of acceptance of the application, or

(b)   such longer period (so starting) as the CAC may specify to the parties by notice containing reasons for the extension.

(5)   The termination date is the later of—

(a)   the date specified under paragraph 99(3)(f), and

(b)   the day after the last day of the decision period.

Employer's request to end arrangements

104.—(1)   This paragraph and paragraphs 105 to 111 apply if after the relevant date the employer requests the union (or each of the unions) to agree to end the bargaining arrangements.

(2)   The request is not valid unless it—

(a)   is in writing,

(b)   is received by the union (or each of the unions),

(c)   identifies the bargaining arrangements, and

(d)   states that it is made under this Schedule.

105.—(1)   If before the end of the first period the parties agree to end the bargaining arrangements no further steps are to be taken under this Part of this Schedule.

(2)   Sub-paragraph (3) applies if before the end of the first period—

(a)   the union informs the employer that the union does not accept the request but is willing to negotiate, or

(b)   the unions inform the employer that the unions do not accept the request but are willing to negotiate.

(3)   The parties may conduct negotiations with a view to agreeing to end the bargaining arrangements.

(4)   If such an agreement is made before, the end of the second period no further steps are to be taken under this Part of this Schedule.

(5)   The employer and the union (or unions) may request ACAS to assist in conducting the negotiations.

(6)   The first period is the period of 10 working days starting with the day after—

(a)   the day on which the union receives the request, or

(b)   the last day on which any of the unions receives the request.

(7)   The second period is—

(a)   the period of 20 working days starting with the day after that on which the first period ends, or

(b)   such longer period (so starting) as the parties may from time to time agree.

106.—(1)   This paragraph applies if—

(a)   before the end of the first period the union fails (or unions fail) to respond to the request, or

(b)   before the end of the first period the union informs the employer that it does not (or unions inform the employer that they do not) accept the request (without indicating a willingness to negotiate).

(2)   The employer may apply to the CAC for the holding of a secret ballot to decide whether the bargaining arrangements should be ended.

107.—(1)   This paragraph applies if —

(a)   the union informs (or unions inform) the employer under paragraph 105(2), and

(b)   no agreement is made before the end of the second period.

(2)   The employer may apply to the CAC for the holding of a secret ballot to decide whether the bargaining arrangements should be ended.

(3)   But no application may be made if within the period of 10 working days starting with the day after that on which the union informs (or unions inform) the employer under paragraph 105(2) the union proposes (or unions propose) that ACAS be requested to assist in conducting the negotiations and—

(a)   the employer rejects the proposal, or

(b)   the employer fails to accept the proposal within the period of 10 working days starting with the day after that on which the union makes (or unions make) the proposal.

108.—(1)   An application under paragraph 106 or 107 is not admissible unless—

(a)   it is made in such form as the CAC specifies, and

(b)   it is supported by such documents as the CAC specifies.

(2)   An application under paragraph 106 or 107 is not admissible unless the employer gives to the union (or each of the unions)—

(a)   notice of the application, and

(b)   a copy of the application and any documents supporting it.

109.—(1)   An application under paragraph 106 or 107 is not admissible if—

(a)   a relevant application was made within the period of 3 years prior to the date of the application under paragraph 106 or 107,

(b)   the relevant application and the application under paragraph 106 or 107 relate to the same bargaining unit, and

(c)   the CAC accepted the relevant application.

(2)   A relevant application is an application made to the CAC—

(a)   by the union (or the unions) under paragraph 101,

(b) by the employer under paragraph 106, 107 or 128, or

(c) by a worker (or workers) under paragraph 112.

110.—(1) An application under paragraph 106 or 107 is not admissible unless the CAC decides that—

(a) at least 10 per cent of the workers constituting the bargaining unit favour an end of the bargaining arrangements, and

(b) a majority of the workers constituting the bargaining unit would be likely to favour an end of the bargaining arrangements.

(2) The CAC must give reasons for the decision.

111.—(1) The CAC must give notice to the parties of receipt of an application under paragraph 106 or 107.

(2) Within the acceptance period the CAC must decide whether—

(a) the request is valid within the terms of paragraph 104, and

(b) the application is made in accordance with paragraph 106 or 107 and admissible within the terms of paragraphs 108 to 110.

(3) In deciding those questions the CAC must consider any evidence which it has been given by the employer or the union (or unions).

(4) If the CAC decides that the request is not valid or the application is not made in accordance with paragraph 106 or 107 or is not admissible—

(a) the CAC must give notice of its decision to the parties,

(b) the CAC must not accept the application, and

(c) no further steps are to be taken under this Part of this Schedule.

(5) If the CAC decides that the request is valid and the application is made in accordance with paragraph 106 or 107 and is admissible it must—

(a) accept the application, and

(b) give notice of the acceptance to the parties.

(6) The acceptance period is—

(a) the period of 10 working days starting with the day after that on which the CAC receives the application, or

(b) such longer period (so starting) as the CAC may specify to the parties by notice containing reasons for the extension.

Workers' application to end arrangements

112.—(1) A worker or workers falling within the bargaining unit may after the relevant date apply to the CAC to have the bargaining arrangements ended.

(2) An application is not admissible unless—

(a) it is made in such form as the CAC specifies, and

(b) it is supported by such documents as the CAC specifies.

(3) An application is not admissible unless the worker gives (or workers give) to the employer and to the union (or each of the unions)—

(a) notice of the application, and

(b) a copy of the application and any documents supporting it.

113.—(1) An application under paragraph 112 is not admissible if—

(a) a relevant application was made within the period of 3 years prior to the date of the application under paragraph 112,

(b) the relevant application and the application under paragraph 112 relate to the same bargaining unit, and

(c) the CAC accepted the relevant application.

(2)   A relevant application is an application made to the CAC—

(a)   by the union (or the unions) under paragraph 101,

(b)   by the employer under paragraph 106, 107 or 128, or

(c)   by a worker (or workers) under paragraph 112.

114.—(1)   An application under paragraph 112 is not admissible unless the CAC decides that—

(a)   at least 10 per cent of the workers constituting the bargaining unit favour an end of the bargaining arrangements, and

(b)   a majority of the workers constituting the bargaining unit would be likely to favour an end of the bargaining arrangements.

(2) The CAC must give reasons for the decision.

115.—(1)   The CAC must give notice to the worker (or workers), the employer and the union (or unions) of receipt of an application under paragraph 112.

(2)   Within the acceptance period the CAC must decide whether the application is admissible within the terms of paragraphs 112 to 114.

(3)   In deciding whether the application is admissible the CAC must consider any evidence which it has been given by the employer, the union (or unions) or any of the workers falling within the bargaining unit.

(4)   If the CAC decides that the application is not admissible—

(a)   the CAC must give notice of its decision to the worker (or workers), the employer and the union (or unions),

(b)   the CAC must not accept the application, and

(c)   no further steps are to be taken under this Part of this Schedule.

(5)   If the CAC decides that the application is admissible it must—

(a)   accept the application, and

(b)   give notice of the acceptance to the worker (or workers), the employer and the union (or unions).

(6)   The acceptance period is—

(a)   the period of 10 working days starting with the day after that on which the CAC receives the application, or

(b)   such longer period (so starting) as the CAC may specify to the worker (or workers), the employer and the union (or unions) by notice containing reasons for the extension.

116.—(1)   If the CAC accepts the application, in the negotiation period the CAC must help the employer, the union (or unions) and the worker (or workers) with a view to—

(a)   the employer and the union (or unions) agreeing to end the bargaining arrangements, or

(b)   the worker (or workers) withdrawing the application.

(2)   The negotiation period is—

(a)   the period of 20 working days starting with the day after that on which the CAC gives notice of acceptance of the application, or

(b)   such longer period (so starting) as the CAC may decide with the consent of the worker (or workers), the employer and the union (or unions).

Ballot on derecognition

117.—(1)   This paragraph applies if the CAC accepts an application under paragraph 106 or 107.

(2)   This paragraph also applies if—

(a)   the CAC accepts an application under paragraph 112, and

(b)   in the period mentioned in paragraph 116(1) there is no agreement or withdrawal as there described.

(3)   The CAC must arrange for the holding of a secret ballot in which the workers constituting the bargaining unit are asked whether the bargaining arrangements should be ended.

(4)   The ballot must be conducted by a qualified independent person appointed by the CAC.

(5)   The ballot must be conducted within—

(a)   the period of 20 working days starting with the day after that on which the qualified independent person is appointed, or

(b)   such longer period (so starting) as the CAC may decide.

(6)   The ballot must be conducted—

(a)   at a workplace or workplaces decided by the CAC,

(b)   by post, or

(c)   by a combination of the methods described in sub-paragraphs (a) and (b), depending on the CAC's preference.

(7)   In deciding how the ballot is to be conducted the CAC must take into account—

(a)   the likelihood of the ballot being affected by unfairness or malpractice if it were conducted at a workplace or workplaces;

(b)   costs and practicality;

(c)   such other matters as the CAC considers appropriate.

(8)   The CAC may not decide that the ballot is to be conducted as mentioned in sub-paragraph (6)(c) unless there are special factors making such a decision appropriate; and special factors include—

(a)   factors arising from the location of workers or the nature of their employment;

(b)   factors put to the CAC by the employer or the union (or unions).

(9)   A person is a qualified independent person if—

(a)   he satisfies such conditions as may be specified for the purposes of this paragraph by order of the Secretary of State or is himself so specified, and

(b)   there are no grounds for believing either that he will carry out any functions conferred on him in relation to the ballot otherwise than competently or that his independence in relation to the ballot might reasonably be called into question.

(10)   An order under sub-paragraph (9)(a) shall be made by statutory instrument subject to annulment in pursuance of a resolution of either House of Parliament.

(11) As soon as is reasonably practicable after the CAC is required under sub-paragraph (3) to arrange for the holding of a ballot it must inform the employer and the union (or unions)—

(a)   that it is so required;

(b)   of the name of the person appointed to conduct the ballot and the date of his appointment;

(c)   of the period within which the ballot must be conducted;

(d)   whether the ballot is to be conducted by post or at a workplace or workplaces;

(e)   of the workplace or workplaces concerned (if the ballot is to be conducted at a workplace or workplaces).

118.—(1)   An employer who is informed by the CAC under paragraph 117(11) must comply with the following three duties.

(2)   The first duty is to co-operate generally, in connection with the ballot, with the union (or unions) and the person appointed to conduct the ballot; and the second and third duties are not to prejudice the generality of this.

(3)   The second duty is to give to the union (or unions) such access to the workers constituting the bargaining unit as is reasonable to enable the union (or unions) to inform the workers of the object of the ballot and to seek their support and their opinions on the issues involved.

(4)   The third duty is to do the following (so far as it is reasonable to expect the employer to do so—

(a)   to give to the CAC, within the period of 10 working days starting with the day after that on which the employer is informed under paragraph 117(11), the names and home addresses of the workers constituting the bargaining unit;

(b)   to give to the CAC, as soon as is reasonably practicable, the name and home address of any worker who joins the unit after the employer has complied with paragraph (a);

(c)   to inform the CAC, as soon as is reasonably practicable, of any worker whose name has been given to the CAC under paragraph (a) or (b) but who ceases to be within the unit.

(5)   As soon as is reasonably practicable after the CAC receives any information under sub-paragraph (4) it must pass it on to the person appointed to conduct the ballot.

(6)   If asked to do so by the union (or unions) the person appointed to conduct the ballot must send to any worker—

(a)   whose name and home address have been given under sub-paragraph (5), and

(b)   who is still within the unit (so far as the person so appointed is aware), any information supplied by the union (or unions) to the person so appointed.

(7)   The duty under sub-paragraph (6) does not apply unless the union bears (or unions bear) the cost of sending the information.

(8)   Each of the following powers shall be taken to include power to issue Codes of Practice about reasonable access for the purposes of sub-paragraph (3)—

(a)   the power of ACAS under section 199(1);

(b)   the power of the Secretary of State under section 203(1)(a).

119.—(1)   If the CAC is satisfied that the employer has failed to fulfil any of the three duties imposed by paragraph 118, and the ballot has not been held, the CAC may order the employer—

(a)   to take such steps to remedy the failure as the CAC considers reasonable and specifies in the order, and

(b)   to do so within such period as the CAC considers reasonable and specifies in the order.

(2)   If—

(a)   the ballot has been arranged in consequence of an application under paragraph 106 or 107,

(b)   the CAC is satisfied that the employer has failed to comply with an order under sub-paragraph (1), and

(c)   the ballot has not been held,

the CAC may refuse the application.

(3)   If—

    (a)   the ballot has been arranged in consequence of an application under paragraph 112, and

    (b)   the ballot has not been held,

an order under sub-paragraph (1), on being recorded in the county court, may be enforced in the same way as an order of that court.

(4)   If the CAC refuses an application under sub-paragraph (2) it shall take steps to cancel the holding of the ballot; and if the ballot is held it shall have no effect.

120.—(1)   This paragraph applies if the holding of a ballot has been arranged under paragraph 117(3), whether or not it has been cancelled.

(2)   The gross costs of the ballot shall be borne—

    (a)   as to half, by the employer, and

    (b)   as to half, by the union (or unions).

(3)   If there is more than one union they shall bear their half of the gross costs—

    (a)   in such proportions as they jointly indicate to the person appointed to conduct the ballot, or

    (b)   in the absence of such an indication, in equal shares.

(4)   The person appointed to conduct the ballot may send to the employer and the union (or each of the unions) a demand stating—

    (a)   the gross costs of the ballot, and

    (b)   the amount of the gross costs to be borne by the recipient.

(5)   In such a case the recipient must pay the amount stated to the person sending the demand, and must do so within the period of 15 working days starting with the day after that on which the demand is received.

(6)   In England and Wales, if the amount stated is not paid in accordance with sub-paragraph (5) it shall, if a county court so orders, be recoverable by execution issued from that court or otherwise as if it were payable under an order of that court.

(7)   References to the costs of the ballot are to—

    (a)   the costs wholly, exclusively and necessarily incurred in connection with the ballot by the person appointed to conduct it,

    (b)   such reasonable amount as the person appointed to conduct the ballot charges for his services, and

    (c)   such other costs as the employer and the union (or unions) agree.

121.—(1)   As soon as is reasonably practicable after the CAC is informed of the result of a ballot by the person conducting it, the CAC must act under this paragraph.

(2)   The CAC must inform the employer and the union (or unions) of the result of the ballot.

(3)   If the result is that the proposition that the bargaining arrangements should be ended is supported by—

    (a)   a majority of the workers voting, and

    (b)   at least 40 per cent of the workers constituting the bargaining unit,

the CAC must issue a declaration that the bargaining arrangements are to cease to have effect on a date specified by the CAC in the declaration.

(4)   If the result is otherwise the CAC must refuse the application under paragraph 106, 107 or 112.

(5)   If a declaration is issued under sub-paragraph (3) the bargaining arrangements shall cease to have effect accordingly.

(6)   The Secretary of State may by order amend sub-paragraph (3) so as to specify a different degree of support; and different provision may be made for different circumstances.

(7)   An order under sub-paragraph (6) shall be made by statutory instrument.

(8)   No such order shall be made unless a draft of it has been laid before Parliament and approved by a resolution of each House of Parliament.

PART V
DERECOGNITION WHERE RECOGNITION AUTOMATIC

Introduction

122.—(1)   This Part of this Schedule applies if—

(a)   the CAC has issued a declaration under paragraph 22(2) that a union is (or unions are) recognised as entitled to conduct collective bargaining on behalf of a bargaining unit, and

(b)   the parties have agreed under paragraph 30 or 31 a method by which they will conduct collective bargaining.

(2)   In such a case references in this Part of this Schedule to the bargaining arrangements are to—

(a)   the declaration, and

(b)   the parties' agreement.

123.—(1)   This Part of this Schedule also applies if—

(a)   the CAC has issued a declaration under paragraph 22(2) that a union is (or unions are) recognised as entitled to conduct collective bargaining on behalf of a bargaining unit, and

(b)   the CAC has specified to the parties under paragraph 31(3) the method by which they are to conduct collective bargaining.

(2)   In such a case references in this Part of this Schedule to the bargaining arrangements are to—

(a)   the declaration, and

(b)   anything effective as, or as if contained in, a legally enforceable contract by virtue of paragraph 31.

124.—(1)   This Part of this Schedule also applies if the CAC has issued a declaration under paragraph 87(2) that a union is (or unions are) recognised as entitled to conduct collective bargaining on behalf of a bargaining unit.

(2)   In such a case references in this Part of this Schedule to the bargaining arrangements are to —

(a)   the declaration, and

(b)   paragraph 87(6)(b).

125.   For the purposes of this Part of this Schedule the relevant date is the date of the expiry of the period of 3 years starting with the date of the CAC's declaration.

126.   References in this Part of this Schedule to the parties are to the employer and the union (or unions) concerned.

Employer's request to end arrangements

127.—(1)   The employer may after the relevant date request the union (or each of the unions) to agree to end the bargaining arrangements.

(2)   The request is not valid unless it—

     (a)   is in writing,

     (b)   is received by the union (or each of the unions),

     (c)   identifies the bargaining arrangements,

     (d)   states that it is made under this Schedule, and

     (e)   states that fewer than half of the workers constituting the bargaining unit are members of the union (or unions).

128.—(1)   If before the end of the negotiation period the parties agree to end the bargaining arrangements no further steps are to be taken under this Part of this Schedule.

(2)   If no such agreement is made before the end of the negotiation period, the employer may apply to the CAC for the holding of a secret ballot to decide whether the bargaining arrangements should be ended.

(3)   The negotiation period is the period of 10 working days starting with the day after—

     (a)   the day on which the union receives the request, or

     (b)   the last day on which any of the unions receives the request;

or such longer period (so starting) as the parties may from time to time agree.

129.—(1)   An application under paragraph 128 is not admissible unless—

     (a)   it is made in such form as the CAC specifies, and

     (b)   it is supported by such documents as the CAC specifies.

(2)   An application under paragraph 128 is not admissible unless the employer gives to the union (or each of the unions)—

     (a)   notice of the application, and

     (b)   a copy of the application and any documents supporting it.

130.—(1)   An application under paragraph 128 is not admissible if—

     (a)   a relevant application was made within the period of 3 years prior to the date of the application under paragraph 128,

     (b)   the relevant application and the application under paragraph 128 relate to the same bargaining unit, and

     (c)   the CAC accepted the relevant application.

(2)   A relevant application is an application made to the CAC—

     (a)   by the union (or the unions) under paragraph 101,

     (b)   by the employer under paragraph 106, 107 or 128, or

     (c)   by a worker (or workers) under paragraph 112.

131.—(1)   An application under paragraph 128 is not admissible unless the CAC is satisfied that fewer than half of the workers constituting the bargaining unit are members of the union (or unions).

(2)   The CAC must give reasons for the decision.

132.—(1)   The CAC must give notice to the parties of receipt of an application under paragraph 128.

(2)   Within the acceptance period the CAC must decide whether—

     (a)   the request is valid within the terms of paragraph 127, and

     (b)   the application is admissible within the terms of paragraphs 129 to 131.

(3)   In deciding those questions the CAC must consider any evidence which it has been given by the parties.

(4)   If the CAC decides that the request is not valid or the application is not admissible—

(a)   the CAC must give notice of its decision to the parties,

(b)   the CAC must not accept the application, and

(c)   no further steps are to be taken under this Part of this Schedule.

(5)   If the CAC decides that the request is valid and the application is admissible it must—

(a)   accept the application, and

(b)   give notice of the acceptance to the parties.

(6)   The acceptance period is—

(a)   the period of 10 working days starting with the day after that on which the CAC receives the application, or

(b)   such longer period (so starting) as the CAC may specify to the parties by notice containing reasons for the extension.

Ballot on derecognition

133.—(1)   Paragraph 117 applies if the CAC accepts an application under paragraph 128 (as well as in the cases mentioned in paragraph 117(1) and (2)).

(2)   Paragraphs 118 to 121 apply accordingly, but as if—

(a)   the reference in paragraph 119(2)(a) to paragraph 106 or 107 were to paragraph 106, 107 or 128;

(b)   the reference in paragraph 121(4) to paragraph 106, 107 or 112 were to paragraph 106, 107, 112 or 128.

PART VI
DERECOGNITION WHERE UNION NOT INDEPENDENT

Introduction

134.—(1)   This Part of this Schedule applies if—

(a)   an employer and a union (or unions) have agreed that the union is (or unions are) recognised as entitled to conduct collective bargaining on behalf of a group or groups of workers, and

(b)   the union does not have (or none of the unions has) a certificate under section 6 that it is independent.

(2)   In such a case references in this Part of this Schedule to the bargaining arrangements are to—

(a)   the parties' agreement mentioned in sub-paragraph (1)(a), and

(b)   any agreement between the parties as to the method by which they will conduct collective bargaining.

135.   In this Part of this Schedule—

(a)   references to the parties are to the employer and the union (or unions);

(b)   references to the bargaining unit are to the group of workers referred to in paragraph 134(1)(a) (or the groups taken together).

136.   The meaning of collective bargaining given by section 178(1) shall not apply in relation to this Part of this Schedule.

Workers' application to end arrangements

137.—(1)   A worker or workers falling within the bargaining unit may apply to the CAC to have the bargaining arrangements ended.

(2)   An application is not admissible unless—

(a)　it is made in such form as the CAC specifies, and

(b)　it is supported by such documents as the CAC specifies.

(3)　An application is not admissible unless the worker gives (or workers give) to the employer and to the union (or each of the unions)—

(a)　notice of the application, and

(b)　a copy of the application and any documents supporting it.

138.　An application under paragraph 137 is not admissible if the CAC is satisfied that any of the unions has a certificate under section 6 that it is independent.

139.—(1)　An application under paragraph 137 is not admissible unless the CAC decides that—

(a)　at least 10 per cent of the workers constituting the bargaining unit favour an end of the bargaining arrangements, and

(b)　a majority of the workers constituting the bargaining unit would be likely to favour an end of the bargaining arrangements.

(2)　The CAC must give reasons for the decision.

140.　An application under paragraph 137 is not admissible if the CAC is satisfied that—

(a)　the union (or any of the unions) has made an application to the Certification Officer under section 6 for a certificate that it is independent,and

(b)　the Certification Officer has not come to a decision on the application (or each of the applications).

141.—(1)　The CAC must give notice to the worker (or workers), the employer and the union (or unions) of receipt of an application under paragraph 137.

(2)　Within the acceptance period the CAC must decide whether the application is admissible within the terms of paragraphs 137 to 140.

(3)　In deciding whether the application is admissible the CAC must consider any evidence which it has been given by the employer, the union (or unions) or any of the workers falling within the bargaining unit.

(4)　If the CAC decides that the application is not admissible—

(a)　the CAC must give notice of its decision to the worker (or workers), the employer and the union (or unions),

(b)　the CAC must not accept the application, and

(c)　no further steps are to be taken under this Part of this Schedule.

(5)　If the CAC decides that the application is admissible it must—

(a)　accept the application, and

(b)　give notice of the acceptance to the worker (or workers), the employer and the union (or unions).

(6)　The acceptance period is—

(a)　the period of 10 working days starting with the day after that on which the CAC receives the application, or

(b)　such longer period (so starting) as the CAC may specify to the worker (or workers), the employer and the union (or unions) by notice containing reasons for the extension.

142.—(1)　If the CAC accepts the application, in the negotiation period the CAC must help the employer, the union (or unions) and the worker (or workers) with a view to—

(a)　the employer and the union (or unions) agreeing to end the bargaining arrangements, or

(b)   the worker (or workers) withdrawing the application.

(2)   The negotiation period is—

(a)   the period of 20 working days starting with the day after that on which the CAC gives notice of acceptance of the application, or

(b)   such longer period (so starting) as the CAC may decide with the consent of the worker (or workers), the employer and the union (or unions).

143.—(1)   This paragraph applies if—

(a)   the CAC accepts an application under paragraph 137,

(b)   during the period mentioned in paragraph 142(1) or 145(3) the CAC is satisfied that the union (or each of the unions) has made an application to the Certification Officer under section 6 for a certificate that it is independent, that the application (or each of the applications) to the Certification Officer was made before the application under paragraph 137 and that the Certification Officer has not come to a decision on the application (or each of the applications), and

(c)   at the time the CAC is so satisfied there has been no agreement or withdrawal as described in paragraph 142(1) or 145(3).

(2)   In such a case paragraph 142(1) or 145(3) shall cease to apply from the time when the CAC is satisfied as mentioned in sub-paragraph (1)(b).

144.—(1)   This paragraph applies if the CAC is subsequently satisfied that—

(a)   the Certification Officer has come to a decision on the application (or each of the applications) mentioned in paragraph 143(1)(b), and

(b)   his decision is that the union (or any of the unions) which made an application under section 6 is independent.

(2)   In such a case—

(a)   the CAC must give the worker (or workers), the employer and the union (or unions) notice that it is so satisfied, and

(b)   the application under paragraph 137 shall be treated as not having been made.

145.—(1)   This paragraph applies if the CAC is subsequently satisfied that—

(a)   the Certification Officer has come to a decision on the application (or each of the applications) mentioned in paragraph 143(1)(b), and

(b)   his decision is that the union (or each of the unions) which made an application under section 6 is not independent.

(2)   The CAC must give the worker (or workers), the employer and the union (or unions) notice that it is so satisfied.

(3)   In the new negotiation period the CAC must help the employer, the union (or unions) and the worker (or workers) with a view to—

(a)   the employer and the union (or unions) agreeing to end the bargaining arrangements, or

(b)   the worker (or workers) withdrawing the application.

(4)   The new negotiation period is—

(a)   the period of 20 working days starting with the day after that on which the CAC gives notice under sub-paragraph (2), or

(b)   such longer period (so starting) as the CAC may decide with the consent of the worker (or workers), the employer and the union (or unions).

146.—(1)   This paragraph applies if—

(a)   the CAC accepts an application under paragraph 137,

(b)   paragraph 143 does not apply, and

(c)   during the relevant period the CAC is satisfied that a certificate of independence has been issued to the union (or any of the unions) under section 6.

(2)   In such a case the relevant period is the period starting with the first day of the negotiation period (as defined in paragraph 142(2)) and ending with the first of the following to occur—

(a)   any agreement by the employer and the union (or unions) to end the bargaining arrangements;

(b)   any withdrawal of the application by the worker (or workers);

(c)   the CAC being informed of the result of a relevant ballot by the person conducting it;

and a relevant ballot is a ballot held by virtue of this Part of this Schedule.

(3)   This paragraph also applies if—

(a)   the CAC gives notice under paragraph 145(2), and

(b)   during the relevant period the CAC is satisfied that a certificate of independence has been issued to the union (or any of the unions) under section 6.

(4)   In such a case, the relevant period is the period starting with the first day of the new negotiation period (as defined in paragraph 145(4)) and ending with the first of the following to occur—

(a)   any agreement by the employer and the union (or unions) to end the bargaining arrangements;

(b)   any withdrawal of the application by the worker (or workers);

(c)   the CAC being informed of the result of a relevant ballot by the person conducting it;

and a relevant ballot is a ballot held by virtue of this Part of this Schedule.

(5)   If this paragraph applies—

(a)   the CAC must give the worker (or workers), the employer and the union (or unions) notice that it is satisfied as mentioned in sub-paragraph (1)(c) or (3)(b), and

(b)   the application under paragraph 137 shall be treated as not having been made.

Ballot on derecognition

147.—(1)   Paragraph 117 applies if—

(a)   the CAC accepts an application under paragraph 137, and

(b)   in the period mentioned in paragraph 142(1) or 145(3) there is no agreement or withdrawal as there described,

(as well as in the cases mentioned in paragraph 117(1) and (2)).

(2)   Paragraphs 118 to 121 apply accordingly, but as if—

(a)   the reference in paragraph 119(3)(a) to paragraph 112 were to paragraph 112 or 137;

(b)   the reference in paragraph 121(4) to paragraph 106, 107 or 112 were to paragraph 106, 107, 112 or 137.

(c)   the reference in paragraph 119(4) to the CAC refusing an application under paragraph 119(2) included a reference to it being required to give notice under paragraph 146(5).

Derecognition: other cases

148.—(1)   This paragraph applies if as a result of a declaration by the CAC another union is (or other unions are) recognised as entitled to conduct collective bargaining on behalf of a group of workers at least one of whom falls within the bargaining unit.

(2)   The CAC must issue a declaration that the bargaining arrangements are to cease to have effect on a date specified by the CAC in the declaration.

(3)   If a declaration is issued under sub-paragraph (2) the bargaining arrangements shall cease to have effect accordingly.

(4)   It is for the CAC to decide whether sub-paragraph (1) is fulfilled, but in deciding the CAC may take account of the views of any person it believes has an interest in the matter.

PART VII
LOSS OF INDEPENDENCE

Introduction

149.—(1)   This Part of this Schedule applies if the CAC has issued a declaration that a union is (or unions are) recognised as entitled to conduct collective bargaining on behalf of a bargaining unit.

(2)   In such a case references in this Part of this Schedule to the bargaining arrangements are to the declaration and to the provisions relating to the collective bargaining method.

(3)   For this purpose the provisions relating to the collective bargaining method are—

(a)   the parties' agreement as to the method by which collective bargaining is to be conducted,

(b)   anything effective as, or as if contained in, a legally enforceable contract and relating to the method by which collective bargaining is to be conducted, or

(c)   any provision of Part III of this Schedule that a method of collective bargaining is to have effect.

150.—(1)   This Part of this Schedule also applies if—

(a)   the parties have agreed that a union is (or unions are) recognised as entitled to conduct collective bargaining on behalf of a bargaining unit,

(b)   the CAC has specified to the parties under paragraph 63(2) the method by which they are to conduct collective bargaining, and

(c)   the parties have not agreed in writing to replace the method or that paragraph 63(3) shall not apply.

(2)   In such a case references in this Part of this Schedule to the bargaining arrangements are to—

(a)   the parties' agreement mentioned in sub-paragraph (1)(a), and

(b)   anything effective as, or as if contained in, a legally enforceable contract by virtue of paragraph 63.

151.   References in this Part of this Schedule to the parties are to the employer and the union (or unions) concerned.

Loss of certificate

152.—(1)   This paragraph applies if—

(a)   only one union is a party, and

(b)   under section 7 the Certification Officer withdraws the union's certificate of independence.

(2)   This paragraph also applies if—

(a)   more than one union is a party, and

(b)   under section 7 the Certification Officer withdraws the certificate of independence of each union (whether different certificates are withdrawn on the same or on different days).

(3)   Sub-paragraph (4) shall apply on the day after—

(a)   the day on which the Certification Officer informs the union (or unions) of the withdrawal (or withdrawals), or

(b)   if there is more than one union, and he informs them on different days, the last of those days.

(4)   The bargaining arrangements shall cease to have effect; and the parties shall be taken to agree that the union is (or unions are) recognised as entitled to conduct collective bargaining on behalf of the bargaining unit concerned.

Certificate re-issued

153.—(1)   This paragraph applies if—

(a)   only one union is a party,

(b)   paragraph 152 applies, and

(c)   as a result of an appeal under section 9 against the decision to withdraw the certificate, the Certification Officer issues a certfficate that the union is independent.

(2)   This paragraph also applies if—

(a)   more than one union is a party,

(b)   paragraph 152 applies, and

(c)   as a result of an appeal under section 9 against a decision to withdraw a certificate, the Certification Officer issues a certificate that any of the unions concerned is independent.

(3)   Sub-paragraph (4) shall apply, beginning with the day after—

(a)   the day on which the Certification Officer issues the certificate, or

(b)   if there is more than one union, the day on which he issues the first or only certificate.

(4)   The bargaining arrangements shall have effect again; and paragraph 152 shall cease to apply.

Miscellaneous

154.   Parts III to VI of this Schedule shall not apply in the case of the parties at any time when, by virtue of this Part of this Schedule, the bargaining arrangements do not have effect.

155.   If—

(a)   by virtue of paragraph 153 the bargaining arrangements have effect again beginning with a particular day, and

(b)   in consequence section 70B applies in relation to the bargaining unit concerned,

for the purposes of section 70B(3) that day shall be taken to be the day on which section 70B first applies in relation to the unit.

PART VIII
DETRIMENT

Detriment

156.—(1) A worker has a right not to be subjected to any detriment by any act, or any deliberate failure to act, by his employer if the act or failure takes place on any of the grounds set out in sub-paragraph (2).

(2) The grounds are that—

(a) the worker acted with a view to obtaining or preventing recognition of a union (or unions) by the employer under this Schedule;

(b) the worker indicated that he supported or did not support recognition of a union (or unions) by the employer under this Schedule;

(c) the worker acted with a view to securing or preventing the ending under this Schedule of bargaining arrangements;

(d) the worker indicated that he supported or did not support the ending under this Schedule of bargaining arrangements;

(e) the worker influenced or sought to influence the way in which votes were to be cast by other workers in a ballot arranged under this Schedule;

(f) the worker influenced or sought to influence other workers to vote or to abstain from voting in such a ballot;

(g) the worker voted in such a ballot;

(h) the worker proposed to do, failed to do, or proposed to decline to do, any of the things referred to in paragraphs (a) to (g).

(3) A ground does not fall within sub-paragraph (2) if it constitutes an unreasonable act or omission by the worker.

(4) This paragraph does not apply if the worker is an employee and the detriment amounts to dismissal within the meaning of the Employment Rights Act 1996.

(5) A worker may present a complaint to an employment tribunal on the ground that he has been subjected to a detriment in contravention of this paragraph.

(6) Apart from the remedy by way of complaint as mentioned in sub-paragraph (5), a worker has no remedy for infringement of the right conferred on him by this paragraph.

157.—(1) An employment tribunal shall not consider a complaint under paragraph 156 unless it is presented—

(a) before the end of the period of 3 months starting with the date of the act or failure to which the complaint relates or, if that act or failure is part of a series of similar acts or failures (or both), the last of them, or

(b) where the tribunal is satisfied that it was not reasonably practicable for the complaint to be presented before the end of that period, within such further period as it considers reasonable.

(2) For the purposes of sub-paragraph (1)—

(a) where an act extends over a period, the reference to the date of the act is a reference to the last day of that period;

(b) a failure to act shall be treated as done when it was decided on.

(3) For the purposes of sub-paragraph (2), in the absence of evidence establishing the contrary an employer must be taken to decide on a failure to act—

(a) when he does an act inconsistent with doing the failed act, or

(b)   if he has done no such inconsistent act, when the period expires within which he might reasonably have been expected to do the failed act if it was to be done.

158.   On a complaint under paragraph 156 it shall be for the employer to show the ground on which he acted or failed to act.

159.—(1)   If the employment tribunal finds that a complaint under paragraph 156 is well-founded it shall make a declaration to that effect and may make an award of compensation to be paid by the employer to the complainant in respect of the act or failure complained of.

(2)   The amount of the compensation awarded shall be such as the tribunal considers just and equitable in all the circumstances having regard to the infringement complained of and to any loss sustained by the complainant which is attributable to the act or failure which infringed his right.

(3)   The loss shall be taken to include—

(a)   any expenses reasonably incurred by the complainant in consequence of the act or failure complained of, and

(b)   loss of any benefit which he might reasonably be expected to have had but for that act or failure.

(4)   In ascertaining the loss, the tribunal shall apply the same rule concerning the duty of a person to mitigate his loss as applies to damages recoverable under the common law of England and Wales or Scotland.

(5)   If the tribunal finds that the act or failure complained of was to any extent caused or contributed to by action of the complainant, it shall reduce the amount of the compensation by such proportion as it considers just and equitable having regard to that finding.

160.—(1)   If the employment tribunal finds that a complaint under paragraph 156 is well-founded and—

(a)   the detriment of which the worker has complained is the termination of his worker's contract, but

(b)   that contract was not a contract of employment,
any compensation awarded under paragraph 159 must not exceed the limit specified in sub-paragraph (2).

(2)   The limit is the total of—

(a)   the sum which would be the basic award for unfair dismissal, calculated in accordance with section 119 of the Employment Rights Act 1996, if the worker had been an employee and the contract terminated had been a contract of employment, and

(b)   the sum for the time being specified in section 124(1) of that Act which is the limit for a compensatory award to a person calculated in accordance with section 123 of that Act.

Dismissal

161.—(1)   For the purposes of Part X of the Employment Rights Act 1996 (unfair dismissal) the dismissal of an employee shall be regarded as unfair if the dismissal was made—

(a)   for a reason set out in sub-paragraph (2), or

(b)   for reasons the main one of which is one of those set out in sub-paragraph (2).

(2)   The reasons are that—

(a)   the employee acted with a view to obtaining or preventing recognition of a union (or unions) by the employer under this Schedule;

(b)   the employee indicated that he supported or did not support recognition of a union (or unions) by the employer under this Schedule;

(c)   the employee acted with a view to securing or preventing the ending under this Schedule of bargaining arrangements;

(d)   the employee indicated that he supported or did not support the ending under this Schedule of bargaining arrangements;

(e)   the employee influenced or sought to influence the way in which votes were to be cast by other workers in a ballot arranged under this Schedule;

(f)   the employee influenced or sought to influence other workers to vote or to abstain from voting in such a ballot;

(g)   the employee voted in such a ballot;

(h)   the employee proposed to do, failed to do, or proposed to decline to do, any of the things referred to in paragraphs (a) to (g).

(3)   A reason does not fall within sub-paragraph (2) if it constitutes an unreasonable act or omission by the employee.

Selection for redundancy

162.   For the purposes of Part X of the Employment Rights Act 1996 (unfair dismissal) the dismissal of an employee shall be regarded as unfair if the reason or principal reason for the dismissal was that he was redundant but it is shown—

(a)   that the circumstances constituting the redundancy applied equally to one or more other employees in the same undertaking who held positions similar to that held by him and who have not been dismissed by the employer, and

(b)   that the reason (or, if more than one, the principal reason) why he was selected for dismissal was one falling within paragraph 161(2).

Employees with fixed-term contracts

163.   Section 197(1) of the Employment Rights Act 1996 (fixed-term contracts) does not prevent Part X of that Act from applying to a dismissal which is regarded as unfair by virtue of paragraph 161 or 162.

Exclusion of requirement as to qualifying period

164.   Sections 108 and 109 of the Employment Rights Act 1996 (qualifying period and upper age limit for unfair dismissal protection) do not apply to a dismissal which by virtue of paragraph 161 or 162 is regarded as unfair for the purposes of Part X of that Act.

Meaning of worker's contract

165.   References in this Part of this Schedule to a worker's contract are to the contract mentioned in paragraph (a) or (b) of section 296(1) or the arrangements for the employment mentioned in paragraph (c) of section 296(1).

PART IX
GENERAL

Power to amend

166.—(1)　If the CAC represents to the Secretary of State that paragraph 22 or 87 has an unsatisfactory effect and should be amended, he may by order amend it with a view to rectifying that effect.

(2)　He may amend it in such way as he thinks fit, and not necessarily in a way proposed by the CAC (if it proposes one).

(3)　An order under this paragraph shall be made by statutory instrument.

(4)　No such order shall be made unless a draft of it has been laid before Parliament and approved by a resolution of each House of Parliament.

Guidance

167.—(1)　The Secretary of State may issue guidance to the CAC on the way in which it is to exercise its functions under paragraph 22 or 87.

(2)　The CAC must take into account any such guidance in exercising those functions.

(3)　However, no guidance is to apply with regard to an application made to the CAC before the guidance in question was issued.

(4)　The Secretary of State must—

(a)　lay before each House of Parliament any guidance issued under this paragraph, and

(b)　arrange for any such guidance to be published by such means as appear to him to be most appropriate for drawing it to the attention of persons likely to be afrected by it.

Method of conducting collective bargaining

168.—(1)　After consulting ACAS the Secretary of State may by order specify for the purposes of paragraphs 31(3) and 63(2) a method by which collective bargaining might be conducted.

(2)　If such an order is made the CAC—

(a)　must take it into account under paragraphs 31(3) and 63(2), but

(b)　may depart from the method specified by the order to such extent as the CAC thinks it is appropriate to do so in the circumstances.

(3)　An order under this paragraph shall be made by statutory instrument subject to annulment in pursuance of a resolution of either House of Parliament.

Directions about certain applications

169.—(1)　The Secretary of State may make to the CAC directions as described in sub-paragraph (2) in relation to any case where—

(a)　two or more applications are made to the CAC,

(b)　each application is a relevant application,

(c)　each application relates to the same bargaining unit, and

(d)　the CAC has not accepted any of the applications.

(2)　The directions are directions as to the order in which the CAC must consider the admissibility of the applications.

(3)　The directions may include—

(a)   provision to deal with a case where a relevant application is made while the CAC is still considering the admissibility of another one relating to the same bargaining unit;

(b)   other incidental provisions.

(4)   A relevant application is an application under paragraph 101, 106, 107, 112 or 128.

Notice of declarations

170.—(1)   If the CAC issues a declaration under this Schedule it must notify the parties of the declaration and its contents.

(2)   The reference here to the parties is to—

(a)   the union (or unions) concerned and the employer concerned, and

(b)   if the declaration is issued in consequence of an application by a worker or workers, the worker or workers making it.

CAC's general duty

171.   In exercising functions under this Schedule in any particular case the CAC must have regard to the object of encouraging and promoting fair and efficient practices and arrangements in the workplace, so far as having regard to that object is consistent with applying other provisions of this Schedule in the case concerned.

General interpretation

172.—(1)   References in this Schedule to the CAC are to the Central Arbitration Committee.

(2)   For the purposes of this Schedule in its application to a part of Great Britain a working day is a day other than—

(a)   a Saturday or a Sunday,

(b)   Christmas day or Good Friday, or

(c)   a day which is a bank holiday under the Banking and Financial Dealings Act 1971 in that part of Great Britain.'

Section 2   SCHEDULE 2
                        UNION MEMBERSHIP: DETRIMENT

Introduction

1.   The Trade Union and Labour Relations (Consolidation) Act 1992 shall be amended as provided in this Schedule.

Detriment

2.—(1)   Section 146 (action short of dismissal on grounds related to union membership or activities) shall be amended as follows.

(2)   In subsection (1) for 'have action short of dismissal taken against him as an individual by his employer' substitute 'be subjected to any detriment as an individual by any act, or any deliberate failure to act, by his employer if the act or failure takes place'.

(3)   In subsection (3) for 'have action short of dismissal taken against him' substitute 'be subjected to any detriment as an individual by any act, or any deliberate failure to act, by his employer if the act or failure takes place'.

(4)   In subsection (4) for 'action short of dismissal taken against him' substitute 'a detriment to which he has been subjected as an individual by an act of his employer taking place'.

(5)   In subsection (5) for 'action has been taken against him' substitute 'he has been subjected to a detriment'.

(6)   After subsection (5) insert—

'(6)   For the purposes of this section detriment is detriment short of dismissal.'

Time limit for proceedings

3.—(1)   Section 147 shall be amended as follows.

(2)   Before 'An' insert '(1)'.

(3)   In paragraph (a) of subsection (1) (as created by sub-paragraph (2) above) for the words from 'action to which' to 'those actions' substitute 'act or failure to which the complaint relates or, where that act or failure is part of a series of similar acts or failures (or both) the last of them'.

(4)   After subsection (1) (as created by sub-paragraph (2) above) insert—

'(2) For the purposes of subsection (1)—

    (a)   where an act extends over a period, the reference to the date of the act is a reference to the last day of that period;

    (b)   a failure to act shall be treated as done when it was decided on.

(3)   For the purposes of subsection (2), in the absence of evidence establishing the contrary an employer shall be taken to decide on a failure to act—

    (a)   when he does an act inconsistent with doing the failed act, or

    (b)   if he has done no such inconsistent act, when the period expires within which he might reasonably have been expected to do the failed act if it was to be done.'

Consideration of complaint

4.—(1)   Section 148 shall be amended as follows.

(2)   In subsection (1) for 'action was taken against the complainant' substitute 'he acted or failed to act'.

(3)   In subsection (2) for 'action was taken by the employer or the purpose for which it was taken' substitute 'the employer acted or failed to act, or the purpose for which he did so'.

(4)   In subsection (3)—

    (a)   for 'action was taken by the employer against the complainant' substitute 'the employer acted or failed to act';

    (b)   for the words from 'took the action' to 'would take' substitute 'acted or failed to act, unless it considers that no reasonable employer would act or fail to act in the way concerned'.

(5)   For subsection (4) substitute—

'(4) Where the tribunal determines that—

    (a)   the complainant has been subjected to a detriment by an act or deliberate failure to act by his employer, and

    (b)   the act or failure took place in consequence of a previous act or deliberate failure to act by the employer,

paragraph (a) of subsection (3) is satisfied if the purpose mentioned in that paragraph was the purpose of the previous act or failure.'

(a)   if the union possesses information as to the number, category or work-place of the employees concerned, a notice must contain that information (at least);

(b)   if a notice does not name any employees, that fact shall not be a ground for holding that it does not comply with paragraph (a) of subsection (3).'

(4)   In subsection (7)—

(a)   insert at the beginning the words 'Subject to subsections (7A) and (7B),', and

(b)   in paragraph (a) the words 'otherwise than to enable the union to comply with a court order or an undertaking given to a court' shall cease to have effect.

(5)   After subsection (7) insert—

'(7A)   Subsection (7) shall not apply where industrial action ceases to be authorised or endorsed in order to enable the union to comply with a court order or an undertaking given to a court.

(7B) Subsection (7) shall not apply where—

(a)   a union agrees with an employer, before industrial action ceases to be authorised or endorsed, that it will cease to be authorised or endorsed with effect from a date specified in the agreement ('the suspension date') and that it may again be authorised or endorsed with effect from a date not earlier than a date specified in the agreement ('the resumption date'),

(b)   the action ceases to be authorised or endorsed with effect from the suspension date, and

(c)   the action is again authorised or endorsed with effect from a date which is not earlier than the resumption date or such later date as may be agreed between the union and the employer.'

(6)   In subsection (9) for 'subsection (7)' substitute 'subsections (7) to (7B)'.

Sections 7, 8 and 9   SCHEDULE 4
LEAVE FOR FAMILY REASONS ETC.

PART I
MATERNITY LEAVE AND PARENTAL LEAVE
NEW PART VIII OF EMPLOYMENT RIGHTS ACT 1996

'PART VIII

CHAPTER I
MATERNITY LEAVE

71.   Ordinary maternity leave

(1)   An employee may, provided that she satisfies any conditions which may be prescribed, be absent from work at any time during an ordinary maternity leave period.

(2)   An ordinary maternity leave period is a period calculated in accordance with regulations made by the Secretary of State.

(3)   Regulations under subsection (2)—

(a)   shall secure that no ordinary maternity leave period is less than 18 weeks;

(b)   may allow an employee to choose, subject to any prescribed restrictions, the date on which an ordinary maternity leave period starts.

(4) Subject to section 74, an employee who exercises her right under subsection (1)—

(a) is entitled to the benefit of the terms and conditions of employment which would have applied if she had not been absent,

(b) is bound by any obligations arising under those terms and conditions (except in so far as they are inconsistent with subsection (1)), and

(c) is entitled to return from leave to the job in which she was employed before her absence.

(5) In subsection (4)(a) 'terms and conditions of employment'—

(a) includes matters connected with an employee's employment whether or not they arise under her contract of employment, but

(b) does not include terms and conditions about remuneration.

(6) The Secretary of State may make regulations specifying matters which are, or are not, to be treated as remuneration for the purposes of this section.

(7) An employee's right to return under subsection (4)(c) is a right to return—

(a) with her seniority, pension rights and similar rights as they would have been if she had not been absent (subject to paragraph 5 of Schedule 5 to the Social Security Act 1989 (equal treatment under pension schemes: maternity)), and

(b) on terms and conditions not less favourable than those which would have applied if she had not been absent.

72. Compulsory maternity leave

(1) An employer shall not permit an employee who satisfies prescribed conditions to work during a compulsory maternity leave period.

(2) A compulsory maternity leave period is a period calculated in accordance with regulations made by the Secretary of State.

(3) Regulations under subsection (2) shall secure—

(a) that no compulsory leave period is less than two weeks, and

(b) that every compulsory maternity leave period falls within an ordinary maternity leave period.

(4) Subject to subsection (5), any provision of or made under the Health and Safety at Work etc. Act 1974 shall apply in relation to the prohibition under subsection (1) as if it were imposed by regulations under section 15 of that Act.

(5) Section 33(1)(c) of the 1974 Act shall not apply in relation to the prohibition under subsection (1); and an employer who contravenes that subsection shall be—

(a) guilty of an offence, and

(b) liable on summary conviction to a fine not exceeding level 2 on the standard scale.

73. Additional maternity leave

(1) An employee who satisfies prescribed conditions may be absent from work at any time during an additional maternity leave period.

(2) An additional maternity leave period is a period calculated in accordance with regulations made by the Secretary of State.

(3) Regulations under subsection (2) may allow an employee to choose, subject to prescribed restrictions, the date on which an additional maternity leave period ends.

(4) Subject to section 74, an employee who exercises her right under subsection (1)—

(a)   is entitled, for such purposes and to such extent as may be prescribed, to the benefit of the terms and conditions of employment which would have applied if she had not been absent,

(b)   is bound, for such purposes and to such extent as may be prescribed, by obligations arising under those terms and conditions (except in so far as they are inconsistent with subsection (1)), and

(c)   is entitled to return from leave to a job of a prescribed kind.

(5)   In subsection (4)(a) 'terms and conditions of employment'—

(a)   includes matters connected with an employee's employment whether or not they arise under her contract of employment, but

(b)   does not include terms and conditions about remuneration.

(6)   The Secretary of State may make regulations specifying matters which are, or are not, to be treated as remuneration for the purposes of this section.

(7)   The Secretary of State may make regulations making provision, in relation to the right to return under subsection (4)(c), about—

(a)   seniority, pension rights and similar rights;

(b)   terms and conditions of employment on return.

74.   Redundancy and dismissal

(1)   Regulations under section 71 or 73 may make provision about redundancy during an ordinary or additional maternity leave period.

(2)   Regulations under section 71 or 73 may make provision about dismissal (other than by reason of redundancy) during an ordinary or additional maternity leave period.

(3)   Regulations made by virtue of subsection (1) or (2) may include—

(a)   provision requiring an employer to offer alternative employment;

(b)   provision for the consequences of failure to comply with the regulations (which may include provision for a dismissal to be treated as unfair for the purposes of Part X).

(4)   Regulations under section 73 may make provision—

(a)   for section 73(4)(c) not to apply in specified cases, and

(b)   about dismissal at the conclusion of an additional maternity leave period.

75.   Sections 71 to 73: supplemental

(1)   Regulations under section 71, 72 or 73 may—

(a)   make provision about notices to be given, evidence to be produced and other procedures to be followed by employees and employers;

(b)   make provision for the consequences of failure to give notices, to produce evidence or to comply with other procedural requirements;

(c)   make provision for the consequences of failure to act in accordance with a notice given by virtue of paragraph (a);

(d)   make special provision for cases where an employee has a right which corresponds to a right under this Chapter and which arises under her contract of employment or otherwise;

(e)   make provision modifying the effect of Chapter II of Part XIV (calculation of a week's pay) in relation to an employee who is or has been absent from work on ordinary or additional maternity leave;

(f)   make provision applying, modifying or excluding an enactment, in such circumstances as may be specified and subject to any conditions specified, in relation to a person entitled to ordinary, compulsory or additional maternity leave;

(g)   make different provision for different cases or circumstances.

(2)   In sections 71 to 73 'prescribed' means prescribed by regulations made by the Secretary of State.

CHAPTER II
PARENTAL LEAVE

76.   Entitlement to parental leave

(1)   The Secretary of State shall make regulations entitling an employee who satisfies specified conditions—

(a)   as to duration of employment, and

(b)   as to having, or expecting to have, responsibility for a child,

to be absent from work on parental leave for the purpose of caring for a child.

(2)   The regulations shall include provision for determining—

(a)   the extent of an employee's entitlement to parental leave in respect of a child;

(b)   when parental leave may be taken.

(3)   Provision under subsection (2)(a) shall secure that where an employee is entitled to parental leave in respect of a child he is entitled to a period or total period of leave of at least three months; but this subsection is without prejudice to any provision which may be made by the regulations for cases in which—

(a)   a person ceases to satisfy conditions under subsection (1);

(b)   an entitlement to parental leave is transferred.

(4)   Provision under subsection (2)(b) may, in particular, refer to—

(a)   a child's age, or

(b)   a specified period of time starting from a specified event.

(5)   Regulations under subsection (1) may—

(a)   specify things which are, or are not, to be taken as done for the purpose of caring for a child;

(b)   require parental leave to be taken as a single period of absence in all cases or in specified cases;

(c)   require parental leave to be taken as a series of periods of absence in all cases or in specified cases;

(d)   require all or specified parts of a period of parental leave to be taken at or by specified times;

(e)   make provision about the postponement by an employer of a period of parental leave which an employee wishes to take;

(f)   specify a minimum or maximum period of absence which may be taken as part of a period of parental leave.

(g)   specify a maximum aggregate of periods of parental leave which may be taken during a specified period of time.

77.   Rights during and after parental leave

(1)   Regulations under section 76 shall provide—

(a)   that an employee who is absent on parental leave is entitled, for such purposes and to such extent as may be prescribed, to the benefit of the terms and conditions of employment which would have applied if he had not been absent,

(b)   that an employee who is absent on parental leave is bound, for such purposes and to such extent as may be prescribed, by any obligations arising under those terms and conditions (except in so far as they are inconsistent with section 76(1)), and

(c)   that an employee who is absent on parental leave is entitled, subject to section 78(1), to return from leave to a job of such kind as the regulations may specify.

(2) In subsection (1)(a) 'terms and conditions of employment'—

(a)   includes matters connected with an employee's employment whether or not they arise under a contract of employment, but

(b)   does not include terms and conditions about remuneration.

(3)   Regulations under section 76 may specify matters which are, or are not, to be treated as remuneration for the purposes of subsection (2)(b) above.

(4)   The regulations may make provision, in relation to the right to return mentioned in subsection (1)(c), about—

(a)   seniority, pension rights and similar rights;

(b)   terms and conditions of employment on return.

78.   Special cases

(1)   Regulations under section 76 may make provision—

(a)   about redundancy during a period of parental leave;

(b)   about dismissal (other than by reason of redundancy) during a period of parental leave.

(2)   Provision by virtue of subsection (1) may include—

(a)   provision requiring an employer to offer alternative employment;

(b)   provision for the consequences of failure to comply with the regulations (which may include provision for a dismissal to be treated as unfair for the purposes of Part X).

(3)   Regulations under section 76 may provide for an employee to be entitled to choose to exercise all or part of his entitlement to parental leave—

(a)   by varying the terms of his contract of employment as to hours of work, or

(b)   by varying his normal working practice as to hours of work,

in a way specified in or permitted by the regulations for a period specified in the regulations.

(4)   Provision by virtue of subsection (3)—

(a)   may restrict an entitlement to specified circumstances;

(b)   may make an entitlement subject to specified conditions (which may include conditions relating to obtaining the employer's consent);

(c)   may include consequential and incidental provision.

(5)   Regulations under section 76 may make provision permitting all or part of an employee's entitlement to parental leave in respect of a child to be transferred to another employee in specified circumstances.

(6)   The reference in section 77(1)(c) to absence on parental leave includes, where appropriate, a reference to a continuous period of absence attributable partly to maternity leave and partly to parental leave.

(7)   Regulations under section 76 may provide for specified provisions of the regulations not to apply in relation to an employee if any provision of his contract of employment—

(a)   confers an entitlement to absence from work for the purpose of caring for a child, and

(b)   incorporates or operates by reference to all or part of a collective agreement, or workforce agreement, of a kind specified in the regulations.

79.   Supplemental

(1)   Regulations under section 76 may, in particular—

(a)   make provision about notices to be given and evidence to be produced by employees to employers, by employers to employees, and by employers to other employers;

(b)   make provision requiring employers or employees to keep records;

(c)   make provision about other procedures to be followed by employees and employers;

(d)   make provision (including provision creating criminal offences) specifying the consequences of failure to give notices, to produce evidence, to keep records or to comply with other procedural requirements;

(e)   make provision specifying the consequences of failure to act in accordance with a notice given by virtue of paragraph (a);

(f)   make special provision for cases where an employee has a right which corresponds to a right conferred by the regulations and which arises under his contract of employment or otherwise;

(g)   make provision applying, modifying or excluding an enactment, in such circumstances as may be specified and subject to any conditions specified, in relation to a person entitled to parental leave;

(h)   make different provision for different cases or circumstances.

(2)   The regulations may make provision modifying the effect of Chapter II of Part XIV (calculation of a week's pay) in relation to an employee who is or has been absent from work on parental leave.

(3)   Without prejudice to the generality of section 76, the regulations may make any provision which appears to the Secretary of State to be necessary or expedient—

(a)   for the purpose of implementing Council Directive 96/34/EC on the framework agreement on parental leave, or

(b)   for the purpose of dealing with any matter arising out of or related to the United Kingdom's obligations under that Directive.

80.   Complaint to employment tribunal

(1)   An employee may present a complaint to an employment tribunal that his employer—

(a)   has unreasonably postponed a period of parental leave requested by the employee, or

(b)   has prevented or attempted to prevent the employee from taking parental leave.

(2)   An employment tribunal shall not consider a complaint under this section unless it is presented—

(a)   before the end of the period of three months beginning with the date (or last date) of the matters complained of, or

(b)   within such further period as the tribunal considers reasonable in a case where it is satisfied that it was not reasonably practicable for the complaint to be presented before the end of that period of three months.

(3)   Where an employment tribunal finds a complaint under this section well-founded it—

(a)   shall make a declaration to that effect, and

(b)   may make an award of compensation to be paid by the employer to the employee.

(4)   The amount of compensation shall be such as the tribunal considers just and equitable in all the circumstances having regard to—

(a)   the employer's behaviour, and

(b)   any loss sustained by the employee which is attributable to the matters complained of.'

PART II
TIME OFF FOR DEPENDANTS
PROVISIONS TO BE INSERTED AFTER SECTION 57 OF THE EMPLOYMENT RIGHTS ACT 1996

'Dependants

57A.   Time off for dependants

(1)   An employee is entitled to be permitted by his employer to take a reasonable amount of time off during the employee's working hours in order to take action which is necessary—

(a)   to provide assistance on an occasion when a dependant falls ill, gives birth or is injured or assaulted,

(b)   to make arrangements for the provision of care for a dependant who is ill or injured,

(c)   in consequence of the death of a dependant,

(d)   because of the unexpected disruption or termination of arrangements for the care of a dependant, or

(e)   to deal with an incident which involves a child of the employee and which occurs unexpectedly in a period during which an educational establishment which the child attends is responsible for him.

(2)   Subsection (1) does not apply unless the employee—

(a)   tells his employer the reason for his absence as soon as reasonably practicable, and

(b)   except where paragraph (a) cannot be complied with until after the employee has returned to work, tells his employer for how long he expects to be absent.

(3)   Subject to subsections (4) and (5), for the purposes of this section 'dependant' means, in relation to an employee—

(a)   a spouse,

(b)   a child,

(c)   a parent,

(d)   a person who lives in the same household as the employee, otherwise than by reason of being his employee, tenant, lodger or boarder.

(4)   For the purposes of subsection (1)(a) or (b) 'dependant' includes, in addition to the persons mentioned in subsection (3), any person who reasonably relies on the employee—

(a)   for assistance on an occasion when the person falls ill or is injured or assaulted, or

(b)   to make arrangements for the provision of care in the event of illness or injury.

(5)   For the purposes of subsection (1)(d) 'dependant' includes, in addition to the persons mentioned in subsection (3), any person who reasonably relies on the employee to make arrangements for the provision of care.

(6)   A reference in this section to illness or injury includes a reference to mental illness or injury.

57B.   Complaint to employment tribunal

(1)   An employee may present a complaint to an employment tribunal that his employer has unreasonably refused to permit him to take time off as required by section 57A.

(2)   An employment tribunal shall not consider a complaint under this section unless it is presented—

(a)   before the end of the period of three months beginning with the date when the refusal occurred, or

(b)   within such further period as the tribunal considers reasonable in a case where it is satisfied that it was not reasonably practicable for the complaint to be presented before the end of that period of three months.

(3) Where an employment tribunal finds a complaint under subsection (1) well-founded, it—

(a)   shall make a declaration to that effect, and

(b)   may make an award of compensation to be paid by the employer to the employee.

(4) The amount of compensation shall be such as the tribunal considers just and equitable in all the circumstances having regard to—

(a)   the employer's default in refusing to permit time off to be taken by the employee, and

(b)   any loss sustained by the employee which is attributable to the matters complained of.'

PART III
CONSEQUENTIAL AMENDMENTS

Trade Union and Labour Relations (Consolidation) Act 1992 (c. 52)

1.   The Trade Union and Labour Relations (Consolidation) Act 1992 shall be amended as follows.

2.   In section 237(1A) (dismissal of those taking part in unofficial industrial action)—

(a)   for the words from 'section 99(1) to (3)' to the end substitute 'or under—

(a)   section 99, 100, 101A(d), 103 or 103A of the Employment Rights Act 1996 (dismissal in family, health and safety, working time, employee representative and protected disclosure cases),

(b)   section 104 of that Act in its application in relation to time off under section 57A of that Act (dependants);' and

(b)   at the end insert '; and a reference to a specified reason for dismissal includes a reference to specified circumstances of dismissal'.

3.   In section 238(2A) (dismissal in connection with other industrial action)—
    (a)   for the words from 'section 99(1) to (3)' to the end substitute 'or under—
    (a)   section 99, 100, 101A(d) or 103 of the Employment Rights Act 1996
(dismissal in family, health and safety, working time and employee representative
cases),
    (b)   section 104 of that Act in its application in relation to time off under section
57A of that Act (dependants);' and
    (b)   at the end insert '; and a reference to a specified reason for dismissal
includes a reference to specified circumstances of dismissal'.

Employment Tribunals Act 1996 (c. 17)

4.   In section 13(2) of the Employment Tribunals Act 1996 (costs and expenses)
the following shall cease to have effect—
    (a)   the word 'or' after paragraph (a),
    (b)   paragraph (b), and
    (c)   the words ', or which she held before her absence,'.

Employment Rights Act 1996 (c. 18)

5.   The Employment Rights Act 1996 shall be amended as follows.

6.   In section 37 (contractual requirements for Sunday work: protected workers)
omit the following—
    (a)   subsection (4),
    (b)   the word 'and' after subsection (5)(a), and
    (c)   subsection (5)(b).

7.   In section 43 (contractual requirements relating to Sunday work: opting out)
omit the following—
    (a)   subsection (4),
    (b)   the word 'and' after subsection (5)(a), and
    (c)   subsection (5)(b).

8.   After section 47B (protection from detriment: disclosures) insert—

47C.   Leave for family and domestic reasons

    (1)   An employee has the right not to be subjected to any detriment by any act,
or any deliberate failure to act, by his employer done for a prescribed reason.

    (2)   A prescribed reason is one which is prescribed by regulations made by the
Secretary of State and which relates to—
    (a)   pregnancy, childbirth or maternity,
    (b)   ordinary, compulsory or additional maternity leave,
    (c)   parental leave, or
    (d)   time off under section 57A.

    (3)   A reason prescribed under this section in relation to parental leave may
relate to action which an employee takes, agrees to take or refuses to take under
or in respect of a collective or workforce agreement.

    (4)   Regulations under this section may make different provision for different
cases or circumstances.'

9.   In section 48(1) (detriment: complaints to employment tribunals) for 'or 47A'
substitute ', 47A or 47C'.

10.   In section 88(1)(c) (notice period: employment with normal working
hours) after 'childbirth' insert 'or on parental leave'.

11. In section 89(3)(b) (notice period: employment without normal working hours) after 'childbirth' insert 'or on parental leave'.

12. In section 92(4)(b) (right to written statement of reasons for dismissal) for 'maternity leave period' substitute 'ordinary or additional maternity leave period'.

13. Omit section 96 (failure to permit return after childbirth treated as dismissal).

14. Omit section 97(6) (effective date of termination: section 96).

15. In section 98 (fairness of dismissal)—

  (a) omit subsection (5), and

  (b) in subsection (6) for 'subsections (4) and (5)' substitute 'subsection (4)'.

16. For section 99 (unfair dismissal: pregnancy and childbirth) substitute—

99. Leave for family reasons

  (1) An employee who is dismissed shall be regarded for reasons. the purposes of this Part as unfairly dismissed if—

    (a) the reason or principal reason for the dismissal is of a prescribed kind, or

    (b) the dismissal takes place in prescribed circumstances.

  (2) In this section 'prescribed' means prescribed by regulations made by the Secretary of State.

  (3) A reason or set of circumstances prescribed under this section must relate to—

    (a) pregnancy, childbirth or maternity,

    (b) ordinary, compulsory or additional maternity leave,

    (c) parental leave, or

    (d) time off under section 57A;

and it may also relate to redundancy or other factors.

  (4) A reason or set of circumstances prescribed under subsection (1) satisfies subsection (3)(c) or (d) if it relates to action which an employee—

    (a) takes,

    (b) agrees to take, or

    (c) refuses to take,

under or in respect of a collective or workforce agreement which deals with parental leave.

  (5) Regulations under this section may—

    (a) make different provision for different cases or circumstances;

    (b) apply any enactment, in such circumstances as may be specified and subject to any conditions specified, in relation to persons regarded as unfairly dismissed by reason of this section.'

17. In section 105 (unfair dismissal: redundancy) omit subsection (2).

18. In section 108 (qualifying period of employment) omit subsection (3)(a).

19. In section 109 (upper age limit) omit subsection (2)(a).

20. In section 114 (order for reinstatement) omit subsection (5).

21. In section 115 (order for re-engagement) omit subsection (4).

22. In section 118(1)(b) (compensation: general) omit ', 127'.

23. In section 119 (compensation: basic award) omit subsection (6).

24. Omit section 127 (dismissal at or after end of maternity leave period).

25. Omit section 137 (failure to permit return after childbirth treated as dismissal).

26. In section 145 (redundancy payments: relevant date) omit subsection (7).

27. In section 146 (supplemental provisions) omit subsection (3).

28.   In section 156 (upper age limit) omit subsection (2).

29.   In section 157 (exemption orders) omit subsection (6).

30.   In section 162 (amount of redundancy payment) omit subsection (7).

31.   In section 192(2) (armed forces)—

  (a)   after paragraph (aa) insert—

        '(ab) section 47C,', and

  (b)   in paragraph (b) for '55 to 57' substitute '55 to 57B'.

32.   In section 194(2)(c) (House of Lords staff) for 'and 47' substitute ', 47 and 47C'.

33.   In section 195(2)(c) (House of Commons staff) for 'and 47' substitute ', 47 and 47C'.

34.   In section 199 (mariners)—

  (a)   in subsection (2) for '50 to 57' substitute '47C, 50 to 57B'.

  (b)   in subsection (2) omit the words '(subject to subsection (3))', and

  (c)   omit subsection (3).

35.   In section 200(1) (police officers)—

  (a)   after '47B,' insert '47C,',

  (b)   for 'to 57' substitute 'to 57B',

  (c)   after '93' insert 'and', and

  (d)   omit 'and section 137'.

36.   In section 202(2) (national security)—

  (a)   in paragraph (b) for 'and 47' substitute ', 47 and 47C',

  (b)   in paragraph (c) for '55 to 57' substitute '55 to 57B', and

  (c)   in paragraph (g) for sub-paragraph (i) substitute—

        '(i) by section 99, 100, 101A(d) or 103, or by section 104 in

its application in relation to time off under section 57A,'.

37.   In section 209 (power to amend Act) omit subsection (6).

38.—(1)   Section 212 (weeks counted in computing period of employment) is amended as follows.

  (2)   Omit subsection (2).

  (3)   In subsection (3)—

  (a)   insert 'or' after paragraph (b),

  (b)   omit 'or' after paragraph (c), and

  (c)   omit paragraph (d).

  (4)   In subsection (4) omit 'or (subject to subsection (2)) subsection (3)(d)'.

39.   In section 225(5)(b) (calculation date: rights during employment) for sub-paragraph (i) substitute—

        '(i)   where the day before that on which the suspension begins falls during a period of ordinary or additional maternity leave, the day before the beginning of that period,'.

40.   In section 226 (rights on termination) omit subsections (3)(a) and (5)(a).

41.   In section 235(1) (interpretation: other definitions) omit the definitions of 'maternity leave period' and 'notified day of return'.

42.—(1)   Section 236 (orders and regulations) shall be amended as follows.

  (2)   In subsection (2)(a) after 'order' insert 'or regulations'.

  (3)   In subsection (3)—

  (a)   after 'and no order' insert 'or regulations',

  (b)   for '72(3), 73(5), 79(3),' substitute '47C, 71, 72, 73, 76, 99,', and

(c)   for 'or order' substitute ', order or regulations'.

Section 16   SCHEDULE 5
UNFAIR DISMISSAL OF STRIKING WORKERS

Trade Union and Labour Relations (Consolidation) Act 1992 (c. 52)

1.   The Trade Union and Labour Relations (Consolidation) Act 1992 shall be amended as follows.

2.   In section 238 (dismissals in connection with industrial action) after subsection (2A) there shall be inserted—

'(2B)   Subsection (2) does not apply in relation to an employee who is regarded as unfairly dismissed by virtue of section 238A below.'

3.   The following shall be inserted after section 238—

'**238A. Participation in official industrial action**

(1)   For the purposes of this section an employee takes protected industrial action if he commits an act which, or a series of acts each of which, he is induced to commit by an act which by virtue of section 219 is not actionable in tort.

(2)   An employee who is dismissed shall be regarded for the purposes of Part X of the Employment Rights Act 1996 (unfair dismissal) as unfairly dismissed if—

(a)   the reason (or, if more than one, the principal reason) for the dismissal is that the employee took protected industrial action, and

(b)   subsection (3), (4) or (5) applies to the dismissal.

(3)   This subsection applies to a dismissal if it takes place within the period of eight weeks beginning with the day on which the employee started to take protected industrial action.

(4)   This subsection applies to a dismissal if—

(a)   it takes place after the end of that period, and

(b)   the employee had stopped taking protected industrial action before the end of that period.

(5)   This subsection applies to a dismissal if—

(a)   it takes place after the end of that period,

(b)   the employee had not stopped taking protected industrial action before the end of that period, and

(c)   the employer had not taken such procedural steps as would have been reasonable for the purposes of resolving the dispute to which the protected industrial action relates.

(6)   In determining whether an employer has taken those steps regard shall be had, in particular, to—

(a)   whether the employer or a union had complied with procedures established by any applicable collective or other agreement;

(b)   whether the employer or a union offered or agreed to commence or resume negotiations after the start of the protected industrial action;

(c)   whether the employer or a union unreasonably refused, after the start of the protected industrial action, a request that conciliation services be used;

(d)   whether the employer or a union unreasonably refused, after the start of the protected industrial action, a request that mediation services be used in relation to procedures to be adopted for the purposes of resolving the dispute.

(7)   In determining whether an employer has taken those steps no regard shall be had to the merits of the dispute.

(8)   For the purposes of this section no account shall be taken of the repudiation of any act by a trade union as mentioned in section 21 in relation to anything which occurs before the end of the next working day (within the meaning of section 237) after the day on which the repudiation takes place.'

4.—(1)   Section 239 (supplementary provisions relating to unfair dismissal) shall be amended as follows.

(2)   In subsection (1) for 'Sections 237 and 238' there shall be substituted 'Sections 237 to 238A'.

(3)   At the end of subsection (1) there shall be added '; but sections 108 and 109 of that Act (qualifying period and age limit) shall not apply in relation to section 238A of this Act.'

(4)   In subsection (2) after 'section 238' there shall be inserted 'or 238A'.

(5)   At the end there shall be added—

'(4)   In relation to a complaint under section 111 of the 1996 Act (unfair dismissal: complaint to employment tribunal) that a dismissal was unfair by virtue of section 238A of this Act—

(a)   no order shall be made under section 113 of the 1996 Act (reinstatement or re-engagement) until after the conclusion of protected industrial action by any employee in relation to the relevant dispute,

(b)   regulations under section 7 of the Employment Tribunals Act 1996 may make provision about the adjournment and renewal of applications (including provision requiring adjournment in specified circumstances), and

(c)   regulations under section 9 of that Act may require a pre-hearing review to be carried out in specified circumstances.'

Employment Rights Act 1996 (c. 18)

5.—(1)   Section 105 of the Employment Rights Act 1996 (redundancy) shall be amended as follows.

(2)   In subsection (1)(c) for 'subsections (2) to (7)' there shall be substituted 'subsections (2) to (7C).'.

(3)   After subsection (7B) (inserted by Schedule 3 to the Tax Credits Act 1999) there shall be inserted—

'(7C)   This subsection applies if—

(a)   the reason (or, if more than one, the principal reason) for which the employee was selected for dismissal was the reason mentioned in section 238A(2) of the Trade Union and Labour Relations (Consolidation) Act 1992 (participation in official industrial action), and

(b)   subsection (3), (4) or (5) of that section applies to the dismissal.'

Section 29   SCHEDULE 6
                    THE CERTIFICATION OFFICER

Introduction

1.   The Trade Union and Labour Relations (Consolidation) Act 1992 shall be amended as provided by this Schedule.

Register of members

2. In section 24 (duty to maintain register of members' names and addresses) the second sentence of subsection (6) (application to Certification Officer does not prevent application to court) shall be omitted.

3. In section 24A (securing confidentiality of register during ballots) the second sentence of subsection (6) (application to Certification Officer does not prevent application to court) shall be omitted.

4.—(1) Section 25 (application to Certification Officer for declaration of breach of duty regarding register of members' names and addresses) shall be amended as follows.

(2) In subsection (2)(b) (duty to give opportunity to be heard where Certification Officer considers it appropriate) omit 'where he considers it appropriate,'.

(3) After subsection (5) insert—

'(5A) Where the Certification Officer makes a declaration he shall also, unless he considers that to do so would be inappropriate, make an enforcement order, that is, an order imposing on the union one or both of the following requirements—

(a) to take such steps to remedy the declared failure, within such period, as may be specified in the order;

(b) to abstain from such acts as may be so specified with a view to securing that a failure of the same or a similar kind does not occur in future.

(5B) Where an enforcement order has been made, any person who is a member of the union and was a member at the time it was made is entitled to enforce obedience to the order as if he had made the application on which the order was made.'

(4) After subsection (8) insert—

'(9) A declaration made by the Certification Officer under this section may be relied on as if it were a declaration made by the court.

(10) An enforcement order made by the Certification Officer under this section may be enforced in the same way as an order of the court.

(11) The following paragraphs have effect if a person applies under section 26 in relation to an alleged failure—

(a) that person may not apply under this section in relation to that failure;

(b) on an application by a different person under this section in relation to that failure, the Certification Officer shall have due regard to any declaration, order, observations or reasons made or given by the court regarding that failure and brought to the Certification Officer's notice.'

5.—(1) Section 26 (application to court for declaration of breach of duty regarding register of members' names and addresses) shall be amended as follows.

(2) Omit subsection (2) (position where application in respect of the same matter has been made to Certification Officer).

(3) After subsection (7) insert—

'(8) The following paragraphs have effect if a person applies under section 25 in relation to an alleged failure—

(a) that person may not apply under this section in relation to that failure;

(b) on an application by a different person under this section in relation to that failure, the court shall have due regard to any declaration, order, observations or reasons made or given by the Certification Officer regarding that failure and brought to the court's notice.'

Accounting records

6.—(1)   Section 31 (remedy for failure to comply with request for access to accounting records) shall be amended as follows.

(2)   In subsection (1) after 'the court' insert 'or to the Certification Officer'.

(3)   In subsection (2) (court to make order if claim well-founded) after 'Where' insert 'on an application to it' and for 'that person' substitute 'the applicant'.

(4)   After subsection (2) insert—

'(2A)   On an application to him the Certification Officer shall—

(a)   make such enquiries as he thinks fit, and

(b)   give the applicant and the trade union an opportunity to be heard.

(2B)   Where the Certification Officer is satisfied that the claim is well-founded he shall make such order as he considers appropriate for ensuring that the applicant—

(a)   is allowed to inspect the records requested,

(b)   is allowed to be accompanied by an accountant when making the inspection of those records, and

(c)   is allowed to take, or is supplied with, such copies of, or of extracts from, the records as he may require.

(2C)   In exercising his functions under this section the Certification Officer shall ensure that, so far as is reasonably practicable, an application made to him is determined within six months of being made.'

(5)   In subsection (3) (court's power to grant interlocutory relief) after 'an application' insert 'to it'.

(6)   After subsection (3) insert—

'(4)   Where the Certification Officer requests a person to furnish information to him in connection with enquiries made by him under this section, he shall specify the date by which that information is to be furnished and, unless he considers that it would be inappropriate to do so, shall proceed with his determination of the application notwithstanding that the information has not been furnished to him by the specified date.

(5)   An order made by the Certification Officer under this section may be enforced in the same way as an order of the court.

(6)   If a person applies to the court under this section in relation to an alleged failure he may not apply to the Certification Officer under this section in relation to that failure.

(7)   If a person applies to the Certification Officer under this section in relation to an alleged failure he may not apply to the court under this section in relation to that failure.'

Offenders

7.—(1)   Section 45C (application to Certification Officer or court for declaration of breach of duty to secure positions not held by certain offenders) shall be amended as follows.

(2)   In subsection (2) (Certification Officer's powers and duties) insert before paragraph (a)—

'(aa) shall make such enquiries as he thinks fit,'

(3) In subsection (2)(a) (duty to give opportunity to be heard where Certification Officer considers it appropriate) omit ', where he considers it appropriate,'.

(4) Omit subsections (3) and (4) (different applications in respect of the same matter).

(5) After subsection (5) insert—

'(5A) Where the Certification Officer makes a declaration he shall also, unless he considers that it would be inappropriate, make an order imposing on the trade union a requirement to take within such period as may be specified in the order such steps to remedy the declared failure as may be so specified.

(5B) The following paragraphs have effect if a person applies to the Certification Officer under this section in relation to an alleged failure—

(a) that person may not apply to the court under this section in relation to that failure;

(b) on an application by a different person to the court under this section in relation to that failure, the court shall have due regard to any declaration, order, observations or reasons made or given by the Certification Officer regarding that failure and brought to the court's notice.

(5C) The following paragraphs have effect if a person applies to the court under this section in relation to an alleged failure—

(a) that person may not apply to the Certification Officer under this section in relation to that failure;

(b) on an application by a different person to the Certification Officer under this section in relation to that failure, the Certification Officer shall have regard to any declaration, order, observations or reasons made or given by the court regarding that failure and brought to the Certification Officer's notice.'

(6) In subsection (6) (entitlement to enforce order) after 'been made' insert under subsection (5) or (5A)'.

(7) After subsection (6) insert—

'(7) Where the Certification Officer requests a person to furnish information to him in connection with enquiries made by him under this section, he shall specify the date by which that information is to be furnished and, unless he considers that it would be inappropriate to do so, shall proceed with his determination of the application notwithstanding that the information has not been furnished to him by the specified date.

(8) A declaration made by the Certification Officer under this section may be relied on as if it were a declaration made by the court.

(9) An order made by the Certification Officer under this section may be enforced in the same way as an order of the court.'

Trade union administration: appeals

8. After section 45C there shall be inserted—

'45D. Appeals from Certification Officer

An appeal lies to the Employment Appeal Tribunal on any question of law arising in proceedings before or arising from any decision of the Certification Officer under section 25, 31 or 45C.'

Elections

9.　In section 54 (remedy for failure to comply with the duty regarding elections) the second sentence of subsection (1) (application to Certification Officer does not prevent application to court) shall be omitted.

10—(1)　Section 55 (application to Certification Officer for declaration of breach of duty regarding elections) shall be amended as follows.

(2)　In subsection (2)(b) (duty to give opportunity to be heard where Certification Officer considers it appropriate) omit 'where he considers it appropriate,'.

(3)　After subsection (5) insert—

'(5A)　Where the Certification Officer makes a declaration he shall also, unless he considers that to do so would be inappropriate, make an enforcement order, that is, an order imposing on the union one or more of the following requirements—

(a)　to secure the holding of an election in accordance with the order;

(b)　to take such other steps to remedy the declared failure as may be specified in the order;

(c)　to abstain from such acts as may be so specified with a view to securing that a failure of the same or a similar kind does not occur in future.

The Certification Officer shall in an order imposing any such requirement as is mentioned in paragraph (a) or (b) specify the period within which the union is to comply with the requirements of the order.

(5B)　Where the Certification Officer makes an order requiring the union to hold a fresh election, he shall (unless he considers that it would be inappropriate to do so in the particular circumstances of the case) require the election to be conducted in accordance with the requirements of this Chapter and such other provisions as may be made by the order.

(5C)　Where an enforcement order has been made—

(a)　any person who is a member of the union and was a member at the time the order was made, or

(b)　any person who is or was a candidate in the election in question,

is entitled to enforce obedience to the order as if he had made the application on which the order was made.'

(4)　After subsection (7) insert—

'(8)　A declaration made by the Certification Officer under this section may be relied on as if it were a declaration made by the court.

(9)　An enforcement order made by the Certification Officer under this section may be enforced in the same way as an order of the court.

(10)　The following paragraphs have effect if a person applies under section 56 in relation to an alleged failure—

(a)　that person may not apply under this section in relation to that failure;

(b)　on an application by a different person under this section in relation to that failure, the Certification Officer shall have due regard to any declaration, order, observations or reasons made or given by the court regarding that failure and brought to the Certification Officer's notice.'

11—(1)　Section 56 (application to court for declaration of failure to comply with requirements regarding elections) shall be amended as follows.

(2)　Omit subsection (2) (position where application in respect of the same matter has been made to the Certification Officer).

(3)   After subsection (7) insert—

'(8)   The following paragraphs have effect if a person applies under section 55 in relation to an alleged failure—

(a)   that person may not apply under this section in relation to that failure;

(b)   on an application by a different person under this section in relation to that failure, the court shall have due regard to any declaration, order, observations or reasons made or given by the Certification Officer regarding that failure and brought to the court's notice.'

12.   After section 56 there shall be inserted—

56A.   Appeals from Certification Officer

An appeal lies to the Employment Appeal Tribunal on any question of law arising in proceedings before or arising from any decision of the Certification Officer under section 55.'

Application of funds for political objects

13.   After section 72 there shall be inserted—

72A.   Application of funds in breach of section 71

(1)   A person who is a member of a trade union and of who claims that it has applied its funds in breach of section 71 may apply to the Certification Officer for a declaration that it has done so.

(2)   On an application under this section the Certification Officer—

(a)   shall make such enquiries as he thinks fit,

(b)   shall give the applicant and the union an opportunity to be heard,

(c)   shall ensure that, so far as is reasonably practicable, the application is determined within six months of being made,

(d)   may make or refuse the declaration asked for,

(e)   shall, whether he makes or refuses the declaration, give reasons for his decision in writing, and

(f)   may make written observations on any matter arising from, or connected with, the proceedings.

(3)   If he makes a declaration he shall specify in it—

(a)   the provisions of section 71 breached, and

(b)   the amount of the funds applied in breach.

(4)   If he makes a declaration and is satisfied that the union has taken or agreed to take steps with a view to—

(a)   remedying the declared breach, or

(b)   securing that a breach of the same or any similar kind does not occur in future,

he shall specify those steps in making the declaration.

(5)   If he makes a declaration he may make such order for remedying the breach as he thinks just under the circumstances.

(6)   Where the Certification Officer requests a person to furnish information to him in connection with enquiries made by him under this section, he shall specify the date by which that information is to be furnished and, unless he considers that it would be inappropriate to do so, shall proceed with his determination of the application notwithstanding that the information has not been furnished to him by the specified date.

(7)   A declaration made by the Certification Officer under this section may be relied on as if it were a declaration made by the court.

(8)   Where an order has been made under this section, any person who is a member of the union and was a member at the time it was made is entitled to enforce obedience to the order as if he had made the application on which the order was made.

(9)   An order made by the Certification Officer under this section may be enforced in the same way as an order of the court.

(10)   If a person applies to the Certification Officer under this section in relation to an alleged breach he may not apply to the court in relation to the breach; but nothing in this subsection shall prevent such a person from exercising any right to appeal against or challenge the Certification Officer's decision on the application to him.

(11)   If—

(a)   a person applies to the court in relation to an alleged breach, and

(b)   the breach is one in relation to which he could have made an application to the Certification Officer under this section,

he may not apply to the Certification Officer under this section in relation to the breach.'

Political ballot rules

14.   In section 79 (remedy for failure to comply with political ballot rules) the second sentence of subsection (1) (application to Certification Officer does not prevent application to court) shall be omitted.

15.—(1)   Section 80 (application to Certification Officer for declaration of failure to comply with political ballot rules) shall be amended as follows.

(2)   In subsection (2)(b) (duty to give opportunity to be heard where Certification Officer considers it appropriate) omit 'where he considers it appropriate,'.

(3)   After subsection (5) insert—

'(5A)   Where the Certification Officer makes a declaration he shall also, unless he considers that to do so would be inappropriate, make an enforcement order, that is, an order imposing on the union one or more of the following requirements—

(a)   to secure the holding of a ballot in accordance with the order;

(b)   to take such other steps to remedy the declared failure as may be specified in the order;

(c)   to abstain from such acts as may be so specified with a view to securing that a failure of the same or a similar kind does not occur in future.

The Certification Officer shall in an order imposing any such requirement as is mentioned in paragraph (a) or (b) specify the period within which the union must comply with the requirements of the order.

(5B)   Where the Certification Officer makes an order requiring the union to hold a fresh ballot, he shall (unless he considers that it would be inappropriate to do so in the particular circumstances of the case) require the ballot to be conducted in accordance with the union's political ballot rules and such other provisions as may be made by the order.

(5C)   Where an enforcement order has been made, any person who is a member of the union and was a member at the time the order was made is entitled to enforce obedience to the order as if he had made the application on which the order was made.'

(4)   After subsection (7) insert—

'(8)   A declaration made by the Certification Officer under this section may be relied on as if it were a declaration made by the court.

(9)   An enforcement order made by the Certffication Officer under this section may be enforced in the same way as an order of the court.

(10)   The following paragraphs have effect if a person applies under section 81 in relation to a matter—

(a)   that person may not apply under this section in relation to that matter;

(b)   on an application by a different person under this section in relation to that matter, the Certification Officer shall have due regard to any declaration, order, observations, or reasons made or given by the court regarding that matter and brought to the Certification Officer's notice.'

16.—(1)   Section 81 (application to court for declaration of failure to comply with political ballot rules) shall be amended as follows.

(2)   Omit subsection (2) (position where application in respect of the same matter has been made to Certification Officer).

(3)   After subsection (7) insert—

'(8)   The following paragraphs have effect if a person applies under section 80 in relation to a matter—

(a)   that person may not apply under this section in relation to that matter;

(b)   on an application by a different person under this section in relation to that matter, the court shall have due regard to any declaration, order, observations or reasons made or given by the Certification Officer regarding that matter and brought to the court's notice.'

Political fund

17—(1)   Section 82 (rules as to political fund) shall be amended as follows.

(2)   After subsection (2) insert—

'(2A)   On a complaint being made to him the Certification Officer shall make such enquiries as he thinks fit.'

(3)   After subsection (3) insert—

'(3A)   Where the Certification Officer requests a person to furnish information to him in connection with enquiries made by him under this section, he shall specify the date by which that information is to be furnished and, unless he considers that it would be inappropriate to do so, shall proceed with his determination of the application notwithstanding that the information has not been furnished to him by the specified date.'

Amalgamation or transfer of engagements

18.—(1)   Section 103 (complaints about procedure relating to amalgamation or transfer of engagements) shall be amended as follows.

(2)   After subsection (2) insert—

'(2A)   On a complaint being made to him the Certification Officer shall make such enquiries as he thinks fit.'

(3)   After subsection (5) insert—

'(6)   Where the Certification Officer requests a person to furnish information to him in connection with enquiries made by him under this section, he shall specify the date by which that information is to be furnished and, unless he considers that it would be inappropriate to do so, shall proceed with his determination of the application notwithstanding that the information has not been furnished to him by the specified date.

(7)   A declaration made by the Certification Officer under this section may be   relied on as if it were a declaration made by the court.

(8)   Where an order has been made under this section, any person who is a member of the union and was a member at the time it was made is entitled to enforce obedience to the order as if he had made the application on which the order was made.

(9)   An order made by the Certification Officer under this section may be enforced in the same way as an order of the court.'

Breach of union rules

19.   In Part I, after Chapter VII there shall be inserted—

'CHAPTER VIIA
BREACH OF RULES

108A.   Right to apply to Certification Officer

(1)   A person who claims that there has been a breach or threatened breach of the rules of a trade union relating to any of the matters mentioned in subsection (2) may apply to the Certification Officer for a declaration to that effect, subject to subsections (3) to (7).

(2)   The matters are—

(a)   the appointment or election of a person to, or the removal of a person from, any office;

(b)   disciplinary proceedings by the union (including expulsion);

(c)   the balloting of members on any issue other than industrial action;

(d)   the constitution or proceedings of any executive committee or of any decision-making meeting;

(e)   such other matters as may be specified in an order made by the Secretary of State.

(3)   The applicant must be a member of the union, or have been one at the time of the alleged breach or threatened breach.

(4)   A person may not apply under subsection (1) in relation to a claim if he is entitled to apply under section 80 in relation to the claim.

(5)   No application may be made regarding—

(a)   the dismissal of an employee of the union;

(b)   disciplinary proceedings against an employee of the union.

(6) An application must be made—

(a)   within the period of six months starting with the day on which the breach or threatened breach is alleged to have taken place, or

(b)   if within that period any internal complaints procedure of the union is invoked to resolve the claim, within the period of six months starting with the earlier of the days specified in subsection (7).

(7)   Those days are—

(a)   the day on which the procedure is concluded, and

(b)   the last day of the period of one year beginning with the day on which the procedure is invoked.

(8)   The reference in subsection (1) to the rules of a union includes references to the rules of any branch or section of the union.

(9)   In subsection (2)(c) 'industrial action' means a strike or other industrial action by persons employed under contracts of employment.

(10)   For the purposes of subsection (2)(d) a committee is an executive committee if—

(a)   it is a committee of the union concerned and has power to make executive decisions on behalf of the union or on behalf of a constituent body,

(b)   it is a committee of a major constituent body and has power to make executive decisions on behalf of that body, or

(c)   it is a sub-committee of a committee falling within paragraph (a) or (b).

(11) For the purposes of subsection (2)(d) a decision-making meeting is—

(a)   a meeting of members of the union concerned (or the representatives of such members) which has power to make a decision on any matter which, under the rules of the union, is final as regards the union or which, under the rules of the union or a constituent body, is final as regards that body, or

(b)   a meeting of members of a major constituent body (or the representatives of such members) which has power to make a decision on any matter which, under the rules of the union or the body, is final as regards that body.

(12)   For the purposes of subsections (10) and (11), in relation to the trade union concerned—

(a)   a constituent body is any body which forms part of the union, including a branch, group, section or region;

(b)   a major constituent body is such a body which has more than 1,000 members.

(13)   Any order under subsection (2)(e) shall be made by statutory instrument; and no such order shall be made unless a draft of it has been laid before and approved by resolution of each House of Parliament.

(14)   If a person applies to the Certification Officer under this section in relation to an alleged breach or threatened breach he may not apply to the court in relation to the breach or threatened breach; but nothing in this subsection shall prevent such a person from exercising any right to appeal against or challenge the Certification Officer's decision on the application to him.

(15) If—

(a)   a person applies to the court in relation to an alleged breach or threatened breach, and

(b)   the breach or threatened breach is one in relation to which he could have made an application to the Certification Officer under this section,
he may not apply to the Certification Officer under this section in relation to the breach or threatened breach.

108B.   Declarations and orders

(1)   The Certification Officer may refuse to accept an application under section 108A unless he is satisfied that the applicant has taken all reasonable steps to resolve the claim by the use of any internal complaints procedure of the union.

(2)   If he accepts an application under section 108A the Certification Officer—

(a)   shall make such enquiries as he thinks fit,

(b)   shall give the applicant and the union an opportunity to be heard,

(c) shall ensure that, so far as is reasonably practicable, the application is determined within six months of being made,

(d) may make or refuse the declaration asked for, and

(e) shall, whether he makes or refuses the declaration, give reasons for his decision in writing.

(3) Where the Certification Officer makes a declaration he shall also, unless he considers that to do so would be inappropriate, make an enforcement order, that is, an order imposing on the union one or both of the following requirements—

(a) to take such steps to remedy the breach, or withdraw the threat of a breach, as may be specified in the order;

(b) to abstain from such acts as may be so specified with a view to securing that a breach or threat of the same or a similar kind does not occur in future.

(4) The Certification Officer shall in an order imposing any such requirement as is mentioned in subsection (3)(a) specify the period within which the union is to comply with the requirement.

(5) Where the Certification Officer requests a person to furnish information to him in connection with enquiries made by him under this section, he shall specify the date by which that information is to be furnished and, unless he considers that it would be inappropriate to do so, shall proceed with his determination of the application notwithstanding that the information has not been furnished to him by the specified date.

(6) A declaration made by the Certification Officer under this section may be relied on as if it were a declaration made by the court.

(7) Where an enforcement order has been made, any person who is a member of the union and was a member at the time it was made is entitled to enforce obedience to the order as if he had made the application on which the order was made.

(8) An enforcement order made by the Certification Officer under this section may be enforced in the same way as an order of the court.

(9) An order under section 108A(2)(e) may provide that, in relation to an application under section 108A with regard to a prescribed matter, the preceding provisions of this section shall apply with such omissions or modifications as may be specified in the order; and a prescribed matter is such matter specified under section 108A(2)(e) as is prescribed under this subsection.

108C. Appeals from Certification Officer
An appeal lies to the Employment Appeal Tribunal on any question of law arising in proceedings before or arising from any decision of the Certification Officer under this Chapter.'

Employers' associations

20.—(1) Section 132 (provisions about application of funds for political objects to apply to unincorporated employers' associations) shall be amended as follows.

(2) For 'The' substitute '(1) Subject to subsections (2) to (5), the'.

(3) After subsection (1) (as created by sub-paragraph (2)) insert—

'(2) Subsection (1) does not apply to these provisions—

(a) section 72A;

(b) in section 80, subsections (5A) to (5C) and (8) to (10);

(c) in section 8 1, subsection (8).

(3) In its application to an unincorporated employers' association, section 79 shall have effect as if at the end of subsection (1) there were inserted—

'The making of an application to the Certification Officer does not prevent the applicant, or any other person, from making an application to the court in respect of the same matter.'

(4) In its application to an unincorporated employers' association, section 80(2)(b) shall have effect as if the words 'where he considers it appropriate,' were inserted at the beginning.

(5) In its application to an unincorporated employers' association, section 81 shall have effect as if after subsection (1) there were inserted—

'(2) If an application in respect of the same matter has been made to the Certification Officer, the court shall have due regard to any declaration, reasons or observations of his which are brought to its notice.'

21. In section 133 (provisions about amalgamations and similar matters to apply to unincorporated employers' associations) in subsection (2)(c) after '101(3)' there shall be inserted ', 103(2A) and (6) to (9)'.

Procedure before Certification officer

22. In section 256 (procedure before Certification Officer) for subsection (2) (provision for restricting disclosure of individual's identity) there shall be substituted—

'(2) He shall in particular make provision about the disclosure, and restriction of the disclosure, of the identity of an individual who has made or is proposing to make any such application or complaint.

(2A) Provision under subsection (2) shall be such that if the application or complaint relates to a trade union—

(a) the individual's identity is disclosed to the union unless the Certification Officer thinks the circumstances are such that it should not be so disclosed;

(b) the individual's identity is disclosed to such other persons (if any) as the Certification Officer thinks fit.'

23. After section 256 there shall be inserted—

'256A. Vexatious litigants

(1) The Certification Officer may refuse to entertain any application or complaint made to him under a provision of Chapters III to VIIA of Part I by a vexatious litigant.

(2) The Certification Officer must give reasons for such a refusal.

(3) Subsection (1) does not apply to a complaint under section 37E(1)(b) or to an application under section 41.

(4) For the purposes of subsection (1) a vexatious litigant is a person who is the subject of—

(a) an order which is made under section 33(1) of the Employment Tribunals Act 1996 and which remains in force,

(b) a civil proceedings order or an all proceedings order which is made under section 42(1) of the Supreme Court Act 1981 and which remains in force,

(c) an order which is made under section 1 of the Vexatious Actions (Scotland) Act 1898, or

(d) an order which is made under section 32 of the Judicature (Northern Ireland) Act 1978.

256B.   Vexatious litigants: applications disregarded

(1)   For the purposes of a relevant enactment an application to the Certification Officer shall be disregarded if—

(a)   it was made under a provision mentioned in the relevant enactment, and

(b)   it was refused by the Certification Officer under section 256A(1).

(2)   The relevant enactments are sections 26(8), 31(7), 45C(5B), 56(8), 72A(10), 81(8) and 108A(13).'

Annual report by Certification Officer

24.   In section 258(1) (Certification Officer: annual report) for 'calendar year' there shall be substituted 'financial year'.

Section 31   SCHEDULE 7
                    EMPLOYMENT AGENCIES

Introduction

1.   The Employment Agencies Act 1973 shall be amended as provided in this Schedule.

General regulations

2.—(1)   Section 5 (power to make general regulations) shall be amended as follows.

(2)   In subsection (1) there shall be substituted for paragraphs (f) and (g) and the proviso following paragraph (g)—

'(ea)   restricting the services which may be provided by persons carrying on such agencies and businesses;

(eb)   regulating the way in which and the terms on which services may be provided by persons carrying on such agencies and businesses;

(ec)   restricting or regulating the charging of fees by persons carrying on such agencies and businesses.'

(3)   After subsection (1) there shall be inserted—

'(1A)   A reference in subsection (1)(ea) to (ec) of this section to services includes a reference to services in respect of—

(a)   persons seeking employment outside the United Kingdom;

(b)   persons normally resident outside the United Kingdom seeking employment in the United Kingdom.'

Charges

3.   For section 6(1) (restriction on demand or receipt of fee for finding or seeking to find employment) there shall be substituted—

'(1)   Except in such cases or classes of case as the Secretary of State may prescribe—

(a)   a person carrying on an employment agency shall not request or directly or indirectly receive any fee from any person for providing services (whether by the provision of information or otherwise) for the purpose of finding him employment or seeking to find him employment;

(b)   a person carrying on an employment business shall not request or directly or indirectly receive any fee from an employee for providing services (whether by the provision of information or otherwise) for the purpose of finding or seeking to find another person, with a view to the employee acting for and under the control of that other person;

    (c) a person carrying on an employment business shall not request or directly or indirectly receive any fee from a second person for providing services (whether by the provision of information or otherwise) for the purpose of finding or seeking to find a third person, with a view to the second person becoming employed by the first person and acting for and under the control of the third person.'

Inspection

    4.—(1) Section 9 (inspection) shall be amended as follows.

    (2) In subsection (1) (power to inspect)—

        (a) for paragraph (a) there shall be substituted—

           '(a) enter any relevant business premises;', and

        (b) after paragraph (c) there shall be inserted—

           '; and

           (d) take copies of records and other documents inspected under paragraph (b).'.

    (3) After subsection (1) there shall be inserted—

    '(1A) If an officer seeks to inspect or acquire, in accordance with subsection (1)(b) or (c), a record or other document or information which is not kept at the premises being inspected, he may require any person on the premises—

        (a) to inform him where and by whom the record, other document or information is kept, and

        (b) to make arrangements, if it is reasonably practicable for the person to do so, for the record, other document or information to be inspected by or furnished to the officer at the premises at a time specified by the officer.

    (1B) In subsection (1) 'relevant business premises' means premises—

        (a) which are used, have been used or are to be used for or in connection with the carrying on of an employment agency or employment business,

        (b) which the officer has reasonable cause to believe are used or have been used for or in connection with the carrying on of an employment agency or employment business, or

        (c) which the officer has reasonable cause to believe are used for the carrying on of a business by a person who also carries on or has carried on an employment agency or employment business, if the officer also has reasonable cause to believe that records or other documents which relate to the employment agency or employment business are kept there.

    (1C) For the purposes of subsection (1)—

        (a) 'document' includes information recorded in any form, and

        (b) information is kept at premises if it is accessible from them.'

    (4) For subsection (2) (self-incrimination) there shall be substituted—

    '(2) Nothing in this section shall require a person to produce, provide access to or make arrangements for the production of anything which he could not be compelled to produce in civil proceedings before the High Court or (in Scotland) the Court of Session.

(2A)   Subject to subsection (2B), a statement made by a person in compliance with a requirement under this section may be used in evidence against him in criminal proceedings.

(2B)   Except in proceedings for an offence under section 5 of the Perjury Act 1911 (false statements made otherwise than on oath), no evidence relating to the statement may be adduced, and no question relating to it may be asked, by or on behalf of the prosecution unless—

(a)   evidence relating to it is adduced, or

(b)   a question relating to it is asked,

by or on behalf of the person who made the statement.'

(5)   In subsection (3) (offence)—

(a)   for 'or (b)' there shall be substituted ', (b) or (d)', and

(b)   after the words 'paragraph (c) of that subsection' there shall be inserted 'or under subsection (1A)'.

(6)   In subsection (4)(a) (restriction on disclosure of information) in sub-paragraph (iv) (exception for criminal proceedings pursuant to or arising out of the Act) the words 'pursuant to or arising out of this Act' shall be omitted.

Offences

5.   After section 11 there shall be inserted—

'11A.   Offences: extension of time limit

(1)   For the purposes of subsection (2) of this section a relevant offence is an offence under section 3B, 5(2), 6(2), 9(4)(b) or 10(2) of this Act for which proceedings are instituted by the Secretary of State.

(2)   Notwithstanding section 127(1) of the Magistrates' Courts Act 1980 (information to be laid within 6 months of offence) an information relating to a relevant offence which is triable by a magistrates' court in England and Wales may be so tried if it is laid at any time—

(a)   within 3 years after the date of the commission of the offence, and

(b)   within 6 months after the date on which evidence sufficient in the opinion of the Secretary of State to justify the proceedings came to his knowledge.

(3)   Notwithstanding section 136 of the Criminal Procedure (Scotland) Act 1995 (time limit for prosecuting certain statutory offences) in Scotland proceedings in respect of an offence under section 3B, 5(2), 6(2), 9(4)(b) or 10(2) of this Act may be commenced at any time—

(a)   within 3 years after the date of the commission of the offence, and

(b)   within 6 months after the date on which evidence sufficient in the opinion of the Lord Advocate to justify the proceedings came to his knowledge.

(4)   For the purposes of this section a certificate of the Secretary of State or Lord Advocate (as the case may be) as to the date on which evidence came to his knowledge is conclusive evidence.

11B.   Offences: cost of investigation

The court in which a person is convicted of an offence under this Act may order him to pay to the Secretary of State a sum which appears to the court not to exceed the costs of the investigation which resulted in the conviction.'

Regulations and orders

6. For section 12(5) (regulations and orders: procedure) there shall be substituted—

'(5) Regulations under section 5(1) or 6(1) of this Act shall not be made unless a draft has been laid before, and approved by resolution of, each House of Parliament.

(6) Regulations under section 13(7)(i) of this Act or an order under section 14(3) shall be subject to annulment in pursuance of a resolution of either House of Parliament.'

Interpretation

7. In section 13(2) (definition of employment agency) for 'workers' (in each place) there shall be substituted 'persons'.

Exemptions

8. For section 13(7)(i) there shall be substituted—

'(i)   any prescribed business or service, or prescribed class of business or service or business or service carried on or provided by prescribed persons or classes of person.'

Section 41   SCHEDULE 8
                          NATIONAL SECURITY

1. The following shall be substituted for section 193 of the Employment Rights Act 1996 (national security)—

'**193 National security.**
Part IVA and section 47B of this Act do not apply in security relation to employment for the purposes of—
    (a)   the Security Service,
    (b)   the Secret Intelligence Service, or
    (c)   the Government Communications Headquarters.'

2. Section 4(7) of the Employment Tribunals Act 1996 (composition of tribunal: national security) shall cease to have effect.

3. The following shall be substituted for section 10 of that Act (national security, &c.)—

'**10   National security**
    (1)   If on a complaint under—
        (a)   section 146 of the Trade Union and Labour Relations (Consolidation) Act 1992 (detriment: trade union membership), or
        (b)   section 111 of the Employment Rights Act 1996 (unfair dismissal),
it is shown that the action complained of was taken for the purpose of safeguarding national security, the employment tribunal shall dismiss the complaint.
    (2)   Employment tribunal procedure regulations may make provision about the composition of the tribunal (including provision disapplying or modifying section (4) for the purposes of proceedings in relation to which—
        (a)   a direction is given under subsection (3), or
        (b)   an order is made under subsection (4).

(3)   A direction may be given under this subsection by a Minister of the Crown if—

(a)   it relates to particular Crown employment proceedings, and

(b)   the Minister considers it expedient in the interests of national security.

(4)   An order may be made under this subsection by the President or a Regional Chairman in relation to particular proceedings if he considers it expedient in the interests of national security.

(5)   Employment tribunal procedure regulations may make provision enabling a Minister of the Crown, if he considers it expedient in the interests of national security—

(a)   to direct a tribunal to sit in private for all or part of particular Crown employment proceedings;

(b)   to direct a tribunal to exclude the applicant from all or part of particular Crown employment proceedings;

(c)   to direct a tribunal to exclude the applicant's representatives from all or part of particular Crown employment proceedings;

(d)   to direct a tribunal to take steps to conceal the identity of a particular witness in particular Crown employment proceedings;

(e)   to direct a tribunal to take steps to keep secret all or part of the reasons for its decision in particular Crown employment proceedings.

(6)   Employment tribunal procedure regulations may enable a tribunal, if it considers it expedient in the interests of national security, to do anything of a kind which a tribunal can be required to do by direction under subsection (5)(a) to (e).

(7)   In relation to cases where a person has been excluded by virtue of subsection (5)(b) or (c) or (6), employment tribunal procedure regulations may make provision—

(a)   for the appointment by the Attorney General, or by the Advocate General for Scotland, of a person to represent the interests of the applicant;

(b)   about the publication and registration of reasons for the tribunal's decision;

(c)   permitting an excluded person to make a statement to the tribunal before the commencement of the proceedings, or the part of the proceedings, from which he is excluded.

(8)   Proceedings are Crown employment proceedings for the purposes of this section if the employment to which the complaint relates—

(a)   is Crown employment, or

(b)   is connected with the performance of functions on behalf of the Crown.

(9)   The reference in subsection (4) to the President or a Regional Chairman is to a person appointed in accordance with regulations under section 1(1) as—

(a)   a Regional Chairman,

(b)   President of the Employment Tribunals (England and Wales), or

(c)   President of the Employment Tribunals (Scotland).

10A   Confidential information

(1)   Employment tribunal procedure regulations may enable an employment tribunal to sit in private for the purpose of hearing evidence from any person which in the opinion of the tribunal is likely to consist of—

(a)   information which he could not disclose without contravening a prohibition imposed by or by virtue of any enactment,

(b) information which has been communicated to him in confidence or which he has otherwise obtained in consequence of the confidence reposed in him by another person, or

(c) information the disclosure of which would, for reasons other than its effect on negotiations with respect to any of the matters mentioned in section 178(2) of the Trade Union and Labour Relations (Consolidation) Act 1992, cause substantial injury to any undertaking of his or in which he works.

(2) The reference in subsection (1)(c) to any undertaking of person or in which he works shall be construed—

(a) in relation to a person in Crown employment, as a reference to the national interest,

(b) in relation to a person who is a relevant member of the House of Lords staff, as a reference to the national interest or (if the case so requires) the interests of the House of Lords, and

(c) in relation to a person who is a relevant member of the House of Commons staff, as a reference to the national interest or (if the case so requires) the interests of the House of Commons.

10B   Restriction of publicity in cases involving national security

(1) This section applies where a tribunal has been directed under section 10(5) or has determined under section 10(6)—

(a) to take steps to conceal the identity of a particular witness, or

(b) to take steps to keep secret all or part of the reasons for its decision.

(2) It is an offence to publish—

(a) anything likely to lead to the identification of the witness, or

(b) the reasons for the tribunal's decision or the part of its reasons which it is directed or has determined to keep secret.

(3) A person guilty of an offence under this section is liable on summary conviction to a fine not exceeding level 5 on the standard scale.

(4) Where a person is charged with an offence under this section it is a defence to prove that at the time of the alleged offence he was not aware, and neither suspected nor had reason to suspect, that the publication in question was of, or included, the matter in question.

(5) Where an offence under this section committed by a body corporate is proved to have been committed with the consent or connivance of, or to be attributable to any neglect on the part of—

(a) a director, manager, secretary or other similar officer of the body corporate, or

(b) a person purporting to act in any such capacity,

he as well as the body corporate is guilty of the offence and liable to be proceeded against and punished accordingly.

(6) A reference in this section to publication includes a reference to inclusion in a programme which is included in a programme service, within the meaning of the Broadcasting Act 1990.'

4. Section 28(5) of the Employment Tribunals Act 1996 (composition of Appeal Tribunal: national security) shall cease to have effect.

5.—(1) Section 30 of that Act (Appeal Tribunal Procedure rules) shall be amended as follows.

(2)   In subsection (2)(d) for 'section 10' substitute 'section 10A'.

(3)   After subsection (2) insert—

'(2A)   Appeal Tribunal procedure rules may make provision of a kind which may be made by employment tribunal procedure regulations under section 10(2), (5), (6) or (7).

(2B)   For the purposes of subsection (2A)—

(a)   the reference in section 10(2) to section 4 shall be treated as a reference to section 28, and

(b)   the reference in section 10(4) to the President or a Regional Chairman shall be treated as a reference to a judge of the Appeal Tribunal.

(2C)   Section 10B shall have effect in relation to a direction to or determination of the Appeal Tribunal as it has effect in relation to a direction to or determination of an employment tribunal.'

6.   After section 69(2) of the Race Relations Act 1976 (evidence: Minister's certificate as to national security, &c.) there shall be inserted—

'(2A) Subsection (2)(b) shall not have effect for the purposes of proceedings on a complaint under section 54.'

7.   Paragraph 4(1)(b) of Schedule 3 to the Disability Discrimination Act 1995 (evidence: Minister's certificate as to national security, &c.) shall cease to have effect.

Section 44

SCHEDULE 9
REPEALS

1. BALLOTS AND NOTICES

Chapter	Short title	Extent of repeal
1992 c. 52.	Trade Union and Labour Relations (Consolidation) Act 1992.	In section 226(2) the word 'and' at the end of paragraph (b). Section 227(2). In section 234A(7)(a) the words 'otherwise than to enable the union to comply with a court order or an undertaking given to a court'.

2. LEAVE FOR FAMILY REASONS ETC

Chapter	Short title	Extent of repeal
1996 c. 17.	Employment Tribunals Act 1996.	In section 13(2)— the word 'or' after paragraph (a), paragraph (b), and the words ', or which she held before her absence,'.
1996 c. 18.	Employment Rights Act 1996.	In section 37, subsection (4), the word 'and' after subsection (5)(a), and subsection (5)(b). In section 43, subsection (4), the word 'and' after subsection (5)(a), and subsection (5)(b). Section 96. Section 97(6). Section 98(5). Section 105(2). Section 108(3)(a). Section 109(2)(a). Section 114(5). Section 115(4). In section 118(1)(b), the word ', 127'. Section 119(6). Section 127. Section 137. Section 145(7). Section 146(3). Section 156(2). Section 157(6). Section 162(7).

Chapter	Short title	Extent of repeal
		In section 199, the words '(subject to subsection (3)' in subsection (2), and subsection (3). In section 200(1), the words 'and section 137'. Section 209(6). In section 212— subsection (2), in subsection (3), the word 'or' after paragraph (c), and paragraph (d), in subsection (4) the words 'or (subject to subsection (2)) subsection (3)(d)'. Section 226(3)(a) and (5)(a). In section 235(1), the definitions of 'maternity leave period' and 'notified day of return'.
SI 1994/2479.	Maternity (Compulsory Leave) Regulations 1994.	The whole instrument.

3. AGREEMENT TO EXCLUDE DISMISSAL RIGHTS

Chapter	Short title	Extent of repeal
1992 c. 52.	Trade Union and Labour Relations (Consolidation) Act 1992.	In Schedule A1, paragraph 163
1996 c. 18.	Employment Rights Act	In section 44(4) the words from the beginning to 'the dismissal,'. In section 45A(4) the words from ', unless' to the end. In section 46(2) the words from the beginning to 'the dismissal,'. In section 47(2) the words from the beginning to 'the dismissal,'. In section 47A(2) the words from the beginning to 'the dismissal,'. In section 47B(2) the words from the beginning to 'the dismissal,'. Section 197(1) and (2). In section 197(4) the words '(1) or'.

Chapter	Short title	Extent of repeal
		In section 203(2)(d) the words '(1) or'. In section 209(2)(g) the words 'and 197(1)'.
1999 c. 26.	Employment Relations Act 1999.	Section 18(6).

4. POWER TO CONFER RIGHTS ON INDIVIDUALS

Chapter	Short title	Extent of repeal
1996 c. 18.	Employment Rights Act 1996.	Section 209(7).

5. ACAS: GENERAL DUTY

Chapter	Short title	Extent of repeal
1992 c. 52.	Trade Union and Labour Relations (Consolidation) Act 1992.	In section 209 the words from ', in particular' to the end.
1993 c. 19.	Trade Union Reform and Employment Rights Act 1993	Section 43(1)

6. COMMISSIONERS

Chapter	Short title	Extent of repeal
1967 c. 13.	Parliamentary Commissioner Act 1967.	In Schedule 2, the entries relating to— the Office of the Commissioner for Protection Against Unlawful Industrial Action, and the Office of the Commissioner for the Rights of Trade Union Members.
1975 c. 24.	House of Commons Disqualification Act 1975.	In Part III of Schedule 1, the entries relating to— the Commissioner for Protection Against Unlawful Industrial Action, and the Commissioner for the Rights of Trade Union Members.

Chapter	Short title	Extent of repeal
1975 c. 25.	Northern Ireland Assembly Disqualification Act 1975.	In Part III of Schedule 1, the entries relating to— the Commissioner for Protection Against Unlawful Industrial Action, and the Commissioner for the Rights of Trade Union Members.
1992 c. 52.	Trade Union and Labour Relations (Consolidation) Act 1992.	In section 65(3) the words 'the Commissioner for the Rights of Trade Union Members or'. In Part I, Chapter VII. Sections 235B and 235C. Section 266 (and the heading immediately proceeding it) and sections 267 to 271. In Schedule 7, paragraphs 1 and 4(4).
1993 c. 19.	Trade Union Reform and Employment Rights Act 1993.	In Schedule 7, paragraphs 20. In Schedule 8, paragraphs 2, 6, 7, 58 to 60 and 79 to 84.

7. THE CERTIFICATION OFFICER

Chapter	Short title	Extent of repeal
1992 c. 52.	Trade Union and Labour Relations (Consolidation) Act 1992.	In section 24(6), the second sentence. In section 24A(6), the second sentence. In section 25(2)(b) the words 'where he considers it appropriate,'. Section 26(2). In section 45C(2)(a) the words ', where he considers it appropriate,' and section 45C(3) and (4). In section 54(1), the second sentence. In section 55(2)(b) the words 'where he considers it appropriate,'. Section 56(2). In section 79(1), the second sentence. In section 80(2)(b) the words 'where he considers it appropriate,'. Section 81(2).

8. EMPLOYMENT AGENCIES

Chapter	Short title	Extent of repeal
1973 c. 35.	Employment Agencies Act 1973.	In section 9(4)(a)(iv) the words words 'pursuant to or arising out of this Act'.

9.　EMPLOYMENT RIGHTS: EMPLOYMENT OUTSIDE GREAT BRITAIN

Chapter	Short title	Extent of repeal
1996 c. 18.	Employment Rights Act 1996.	Section 196, In section 199(6), the words 'Section 196(6) does not apply to an employee, and'. In section 201(3)(g), the word '196,'. Section 204(2). In section 209(2)(g), the words '196(1) and'. In section 209(5), the words ', 196(2), (3) and (5)'.

10. SECTIONS 33 TO 36

Chapter	Short title	Extent of repeal
1992 c. 52.	Trade Union and Labour Relations (Consolidation) Act 1992.	Section 157. Section 158. Section 159. Section 176(7) and (8).
1996 c. 18.	Employment Rights Act 1996.	In section 117, subsection (4)(b) and the word 'or' before it, and subsections (5) and (6). Section 118(2) and (3). Section 120(2). Section 124(2). Section 125. Section 186(2). Section 208. Section 227(2) to (4). Section 236(2)(c). In section 236(3) the words '120(2), 124(2)'. In Schedule 1, paragraph 56(10) and (11).
1998 c. 8.	Employment Rights (Dispute Resolution) Act 1998.	Section 14(1).

11. COMPENSATORY AWARD: REMOVAL OF LIMIT IN CERTAIN CASES

Chapter	Short title	Extent of repeal
1996 c. 18.	Employment Rights Act 1996.	In section 112(4), the words 'or in accordance with regulations under section 127B'. In section 117(2) and (3), the words 'and to regulations under section 127B'. In section 118(1), the words 'Subject to regulations under section 127B,'. Section 127B.
1998 c. 23.	Public Interest Disclosure Act 1998.	Section 8. Section 18(4)(b).

12. NATIONAL SECURITY

Chapter	Short title	Extent of repeal
1995 c. 50.	Disablity Discrimination Act 1995.	Paragraph 4(1)(b) of Schedule Schedule 3, and the word 'or' immediately before it.
1996 c. 17.	Employment Tribunals Act 1996.	Section 4(7). Section 28(5).
1998 c. 23.	Public Interest Disclosure Act 1998.	Section 11.

Appendix 2
Maternity and Parental Leave etc. Regulations 1999

PART I
GENERAL

1. Citation and commencement

These Regulations may be cited as the Maternity and Parental Leave etc. Regulations 1999 and shall come into force on 15 December 1999.

2. Interpretation

(1) In these Regulations—

'the 1996 Act' means the Employment Rights Act 1996;

'additional maternity leave' means leave under section 73 of the 1996 Act;

'business' includes a trade or profession and includes any activity carried on by a body of persons (whether corporate or unincorporated);

'child' means a person under the age of eighteen;

'childbirth' means the birth of a living child or the birth of a child whether living or dead after 24 weeks of pregnancy;

'collective agreement' means a collective agreement within the meaning of section 178 of the Trade Union and Labour Relations (Consolidation) Act 1992, the trade union parties to which are independent trade unions within the meaning of section 5 of that Act;

'contract of employment' means a contract of service or apprenticeship, whether express or implied, and (if it is express) whether oral or in writing;

'disability living allowance' means the disability living allowance provided for in Part III of the Social Security Contributions and Benefits Act 1992;

'employee' means an individual who has entered into or works under (or, where the employment has ceased, worked under) a contract of employment;

'employer' means the person by whom an employee is (or, where the employment has ceased, was) employed;

'expected week of childbirth' means the week, beginning with midnight between Saturday and Sunday, in which it is expected that childbirth will occur, and 'week of childbirth' means the week, beginning with midnight between Saturday and Sunday, in which childbirth occurs;

'job', in relation to an employee returning after additional maternity leave or parental leave, means the nature of the work which she is employed to do in accordance with her contract and the capacity and place in which she is so employed;

'ordinary maternity leave' means leave under section 71 of the 1996 Act;

'parental leave' means leave under regulation 13(1);

'parental responsibility' has the meaning given by section 3 of the Children Act 1989, and 'parental responsibilities' has the meaning given by section 1(3) of the Children (Scotland) Act 1995;

'workforce agreement' means an agreement between an employer and his employees or their representatives in respect of which the conditions set out in Schedule 1 to these Regulations are satisfied.

(2)   A reference in any provision of these Regulations to a period of continuous employment is to a period computed in accordance with Chapter I of Part XIV of the 1996 Act, as if that provision were a provision of that Act.

(3)   For the purposes of these Regulations any two employers shall be treated as associated if—

(a)   one is a company of which the other (directly or indirectly) has control; or

(b)   both are companies of which a third person (directly or indirectly) has control;

and 'associated employer' shall be construed accordingly.

(4)   In these Regulations, unless the context otherwise requires—

(a)   a reference to a numbered regulation or schedule is to the regulation or schedule in these Regulations bearing that number;

(b)   a reference in a regulation or schedule to a numbered paragraph is to the paragraph in that regulation or schedule bearing that number, and

(a)   a reference in a paragraph to a lettered sub-paragraph is to the sub-paragraph in that paragraph bearing that letter.

3.   Application

(1)   The provisions of Part II of these Regulations have effect only in relation to employees whose expected week of childbirth begins on or after 30 April 2000.

(2)   Regulation 19 (protection from detriment) has effect only in relation to an act or failure to act which takes place on or after 15 December 1999.

(3)   For the purposes of paragraph (2)—

(a)   where an act extends over a period, the reference to the date of the act is a reference to the last day of that period, and

(b)   a failure to act is to be treated as done when it was decided on.

(4)   For the purposes of paragraph (3), in the absence of evidence establishing the contrary an employer shall be taken to decide on a failure to act—

(a)   when he does an act inconsistent with doing the failed act, or

(b)   if he has done no such inconsistent act, when the period expires within which he might reasonably have been expected to do the failed act if it was to be done.

(5)   Regulation 20 (unfair dismissal) has effect only in relation to dismissals where the effetive date of termination (within the meaning of section 97 of the 1996 Act) falls on or after 15 December 1999.

PART II
MATERNITY LEAVE

4.   Entitlement to ordinary maternity leave

(1)   An employee is entitled to ordinary maternity leave provided that she satisfies the following conditions—

(a)   at least 21 days before the date on which she intends her ordinary maternity leave period to start, or, if that is not reasonably practicable, as soon as is reasonably practicable, she notifies her employer of—

    (i)   her pregnancy;

    (ii)   the expected week of childbirth, and

    (iii)   the date on which she intends her ordinary maternity leave period to start,

and

(b)   if requested to do so by her employer, she produces for his inspection a certificate from—

    (i)   a registered medical practitioner, or

    (ii)   a registered midwife,

stating the expected week of childbirth.

(2)   The notification provided for in paragraph (1)(a)(iii)—

(a)   shall be given in writing, if the employer so requests, and

(b)   shall not specify a date earlier than the beginning of the eleventh week before the expected week of childbirth.

(3)   Where, by virtue of regulation 6(1)(b), an employee's ordinary maternity leave period commences with the first day after the beginning of the sixth week before the expected week of childbirth on which she is absent from work wholly or partly because of pregnancy—

(a)   paragraph (1) does not require her to notify her employer of the date specified in that paragraph, but

(b)   (whether or not she has notified him of that date) she is not entitled to ordinary maternity leave unless she notifies him as soon as is reasonably practicable that she is absent from work wholly or partly because of pregnancy.

(4)   Where, by virtue of regulation 6(2), an employee's ordinary maternity leave period commences with the day on which childbirth occurs—

(a)   paragraph (1) does not require her to notify her employer of the date specified in that paragraph, but

(b)   (whether or not she has notified him of that date) she is not entitled to ordinary maternity leave unless she notifies him as soon as is reasonably practicable after the birth that she has given birth.

(5)   The notification provided for in paragraphs (3)(b) and (4)(b) shall be given in writing, if the employer so requests.

5.   Entitlement to additional maternity leave

An employee who satisfies the following conditions is entitled to additional maternity leave—

(a)   she is entitled to ordinary maternity leave, and

(b)   she has, at the beginning of the eleventh week before the expected week of childbirth, been continuously employed for a period of not less than a year.

6.   Commencement of maternity leave periods

(1)   Subject to paragraph (2), an employee's ordinary maternity leave period commences with the earlier of—

(a)   the date which, in accordance with regulation 4(1)(a)(iii), she notifies to her employer as the date on which she intends her ordinary maternity leave period to start, and

(b)   the first day after the beginning of the sixth week before the expected week of childbirth on which she is absent from work wholly or partly because of pregnancy.

(2)   Where the employee's ordinary maternity leave period has not commenced by virtue of paragraph (1) when childbirth occurs, her ordinary maternity leave period commences with the day on which childbirth occurs.

(3)   An employee's additional maternity leave period commences on the day after the last day of her ordinary maternity leave period.

7.   Duration of maternity leave periods

(1)   Subject to paragraphs (2) and (5), an employee's ordinary maternity leave period continues for the period of eighteen weeks from its commencement, or until the end of the compulsory maternity leave period provided for in regulation 8 if later.

(2)   Subject to paragraph (5), where any requirement imposed by or under any relevant statutory provision prohibits the employee from working for any period after the end of the period determined under paragraph (1) by reason of her having recently given birth, her ordinary maternity leave period continues until the end of that later period.

(3)   In paragraph (2), 'relevant statutory provision' means a provision of—

(a)   an enactment, or

(b)   an instrument under an enactment,

other than a provision for the time being specified in an order under section 66(2) of the 1996 Act.

(4)   Subject to paragraph (5), where an employee is entitled to additional maternity leave her additional maternity leave period continues until the end of the period of 29 weeks beginning with the week of childbirth.

(5)   Where the employee is dismissed after the commencement of an ordinary or additional maternity leave period but before the time when (apart from this paragraph) that period would end, the period ends at the time of the dismissal.

8.   Compulsory maternity leave

The prohibition in section 72 of the 1996 Act, against permitting an employee who satisfies prescribed conditions to work during a particular period (referred to as a 'compulsory maternity leave period'), applies—

(a)   in relation to an employee who is entitled to ordinary maternity leave, and

(b)   in respect of the period of two weeks which commences with the day on which childbirth occurs.

9.   Exclusion of entitlement to remuneration during ordinary maternity leave

For the purposes of section 71 of the 1996 Act, which includes provision excluding the entitlement of an employee who exercises her right to ordinary maternity leave to the benefit of terms and conditions of employment about remuneration, only sums payable to an employee by way of wages or salary are to be treated as remuneration.

10.   Redundancy during maternity leave

(1)   This regulation applies where, during an employee's ordinary or additional maternity leave period, it is not practicable by reason of redundancy for her employer to continue to employ her under her existing contract of employment.

(2)   Where there is a suitable available vacancy, the employee is entitled to be offered (before the end of her employment under her existing contract) alternative employment with her employer or his successor, or an associated employer, under a

new contract of employment which complies with paragraph (3) (and takes effect immediately on the ending of her employment under the previous contract).

(3)   The new contract of employment must be such that—

(a)   the work to be done under it is of a kind which is both suitable in relation to the employee and appropriate for her to do in the circumstances, and

(b)   its provisions as to the capacity and place in which she is to be employed, and as to the other terms and conditions of her employment, are not substantially less favourable to her than if she had continued to be employed under the previous contract.

11.   Requirement to notify intention to return during a maternity leave period

(1)   An employee who intends to return to work earlier than the end of her ordinary maternity leave period or, where she is entitled to additional maternity leave, the end of her additional maternity leave period, shall give to her employer not less than 21 days' notice of the date on which she intends to return.

(2)   If an employee attempts to return to work earlier than the end of a maternity leave period without complying with paragraph (1), her employer is entitled to postpone her return to a date such as will secure, subject to paragraph (3), that he has 21 days' notice of her return.

(3)   An employer is not entitled under paragraph (2) to postpone an employee's return to work to a date after the end of the relevant maternity leave period.

(4)   If an employee whose return to work has been postponed under paragraph (2) has been notified that she is not to return to work before the date to which her return was postponed, the employer is under no contractual obligation to pay her remuneration until the date to which her return was postponed if she returns to work before that date.

12.   Requirement to notify intention to return after additional maternity leave

(1)   Where, not earlier than 21 days before the end of her ordinary maternity leave period, an employee who is entitled to additional maternity leave is requested in accordance with paragraph (3) by her employer to notify him in writing of—

(a)   the date on which childbirth occurred, and

(b)   whether she intends to return to work at the end of her additional maternity leave period,

the employee shall give the requested notification within 21 days of receiving the request.

(2)   The provisions of regulations 19 and 20, in so far as they protect an employee against detriment or dismissal for the reason that she took additional maternity leave, do not apply in relation to an employee who has failed to notify her employer in accordance with paragraph (1).

(3)   A request under paragraph (1) shall be—

(a)   made in writing, and

(b)   accompanied by a written statement—

(i)   explaining how the employee may determine, in accordance with regulation 7(4), the date on which her additional maternity leave period will end, and

(ii)   warning of the consequence, under paragraph (2), of failure to respond to the employer's request within 21 days of receiving it.

PART III
PARENTAL LEAVE

13. Entitlement to parental leave

(1)   An employee who—

(a)   has been continuously employed for a period of not less than a year; and

(b)   has, or expects to have, responsibility for a child,

is entitled, in accordance with these Regulations, to be absent from work on parental leave for the purpose of caring for that child.

(2)   An employee has responsibility for a child, for the purposes of paragraph (1), if—

(a)   he has parental responsibility or, in Scotland, parental responsibilities for the child; or

(b)   he has been registered as the child's father under any provision of section 10(1) or 10A(1) of the Births and Deaths Registration Act 1953 or of section 18(1) or (2) of the Registration of Births, Deaths and Marriages (Scotland) Act 1965.

(3)   An employee is not entitled to parental leave in respect of a child born before 15 December 1999, except for a child who is adopted by the employee, or placed with the employee for adoption by him, on or after that date.

14. Extent of entitlement

(1)   An employee is entitled to thirteen weeks' leave in respect of any individual child.

(2)   Where the period for which an employee is normally required, under his contract of employment, to work in the course of a week does not vary, a week's leave for the employee is a period of absence from work which is equal in duration to the period for which he is normally required to work.

(3)   Where the period for which an employee is normally required, under his contract of employment, to work in the course of a week varies from week to week or over a longer period, or where he is normally required under his contract to work in some weeks but not in others a week's leave for the employee is a period of absence from work which is equal in duration to the period calculated by dividing the total of the periods for which he is normally required to work in a year by 52.

(4)   Where an employee takes leave in periods shorter than the period which constitutes, for him, a week's leave under whichever of paragraphs (2) and (3) is applicable in his case, he completes a week's leave when the aggregate of the periods of leave he has taken equals the period constituting a week's leave for him under the applicable paragraph.

15. When parental leave may be taken

An employee may not exercise any entitlement to parental leave in respect of a child—

(a)   except in the cases referred to in paragraphs (b) to (d), after the date of the child's fifth birthday;

(b)   in a case where the child is entitled to a disability living allowance, after the date of the child's eighteenth birthday;

(c)   in a case where the child was placed with the employee for adoption by him (other than a case where paragraph (b) applies), after—

(i)   the fifth anniversary of the date on which the placement began, or

(ii)   the date of the child's eighteenth birthday,
whichever is the earlier.
    (d)   in a case where—
        (i)   the provisions set out in Schedule 2 apply, and
        (ii)   the employee would have taken leave on or before a date or anniversary
referred to in paragraphs (a) to (c) but for the fact that the employer postponed it under
paragraph 6 of that Schedule,
after the end of the period to which the leave was postponed.

16.   Default provisions in respect of parental leave

The provisions set out in Schedule 2 apply in relation to parental leave in the case of
an employee whose contract of employment does not include a provision which—
    (a)   confers an entitlement to absence from work for the purpose of caring for
a child, and
    (b)   incorporates or operates by reference to all or part of a collective agreement
or workforce agreement.

PART IV
PROVISIONS APPLICABLE IN RELATION TO MORE THAN ONE KIND OF ABSENCE

17.   Application of terms and conditions during periods of leave

An employee who takes additional maternity leave or parental leave—
    (a)   is entitled, during the period of leave, to the benefit of her employer's
implied obligation to her of trust and confidence and any terms and conditions of her
employment relating to—
        (i)   notice of the termination of the employment contract by her employer;
        (ii)   compensation in the event of redundancy, or
        (iii)   disciplinary or grievance procedures;
    (b)   is bound, during that period, by her implied obligation to her employer of
good faith and any terms and conditions of her employment relating to—
        (i)   notice of the termination of the employment contract by her;
        (ii)   the disclosure of confidential information;
        (iii)   the acceptance of gifts or other benefits, or
        (iv)   the employee's participation in any other business.

18.   Right to return after additional maternity leave or parental leave

    (1)   An employee who takes parental leave for a period of four weeks or less, other
than immediately after taking additional maternity leave, is entitled to return from
leave to the job in which she was employed before her absence.
    (2)   An employee who takes additional maternity leave, or parental leave for a
period of more than four weeks, is entitled to return from leave to the job in which
she was employed before her absence, or, if it is not reasonably practicable for the
employer to permit her to return to that job, to another job which is both suitable for
her and appropriate for her to do in the circumstances.
    (3)   An employee who takes parental leave for a period of four weeks or less
immediately after additional maternity leave is entitled to return from leave to the job
in which she was employed before her absence unless—

(a)   it would not have been reasonably practicable for her to return to that job if she had returned at the end of her additional maternity leave period, and

(b)   it is not reasonably practicable for the employer to permit her to return to that job at the end of her period of parental leave;

otherwise, she is entitled to return to another job which is both suitable for her and appropriate for her to do in the circumstances.

(4)   Paragraphs (2) and (3) do not apply where regulation 10 applies.

(5)   An employee's right to return under paragraph (1), (2) or (3) is to return—

(a)   on terms and conditions as to remuneration not less favourable than those which would have been applicable to her had she not been absent from work at any time since—

(i)   in the case of an employee returning from additional maternity leave (or parental leave taken immediately after additional maternity leave), the commencement of the ordinary maternity leave period which preceded her additional maternity leave period, or

(ii)   in the case of an employee returning from parental leave (other than parental leave taken immediately after additional maternity leave), the commencement of the period of parental leave;

(b)   with her seniority, pension rights and similar rights as they would have been if the period or periods of her employment prior to her additional maternity leave period, or (as the case may be) her period of parental leave, were continuous with her employment following her return to work (but subject, in the case of an employee returning from additional maternity leave, to the requirements of paragraph 5 of Schedule 5 to the Social Security Act 1989 (equal treatment under pension schemes: maternity)), and

(c)   otherwise on terms and conditions not less favourable than those which would have been applicable to her had she not been absent from work after the end of her ordinary maternity leave period or (as the case may be) during her period of parental leave.

19.   Protection from detriment

(1)   An employee is entitled under section 47C of the 1996 Act not to be subjected to any detriment by any act, or any deliberate failure to act, by her employer done for any of the reasons specified in paragraph (2).

(2)   The reasons referred to in paragraph (1) are that the employee—

(a)   is pregnant;

(b)   has given birth to a child;

(c)   is the subject of a relevant requirement, or a relevant recommendation, as defined by section 66(2) of the 1996 Act;

(d)   took, sought to take or availed herself of the benefits of, ordinary maternity leave;

(e)   took or sought to take—

(i)   additional maternity leave;

(ii)   parental leave, or

(iii)   time off under section 57A of the 1996 Act;

(f)   declined to sign a workforce agreement for the purpose of these Regulations, or

(g)   being—

(i)   a representative of members of the workforce for the purposes of Schedule 1, or

(ii)   a candidate in an election in which any person elected will, on being elected, become such a representative,

performed (or proposed to perform) any functions or activities as such a representative or candidate.

(3)   For the purposes of paragraph (2)(d), a woman avails herself of the benefits of ordinary maternity leave if, during her ordinary maternity leave period, she avails herself of the benefit of any of the terms and conditions of her employment preserved by section 71 of the 1996 Act during that period.

(4)   Paragraph (1) does not apply in a case where the detriment in question amounts to dismissal within the meaning of Part X of the 1996 Act.

(5)   Paragraph (2)(b) only applies where the act or failure to act takes place during the employee's ordinary or additional maternity leave period.

(6)   For the purposes of paragraph (5)—

(a)   where an act extends over a period, the reference to the date of the act is a reference to the last day of that period, and

(b)   a failure to act is to be treated as done when it was decided on.

(7)   For the purposes of paragraph (6), in the absence of evidence establishing the contrary an employer shall be taken to decide on a failure to act—

(a)   when he does an act inconsistent with doing the failed act, or

(b)   if he has done no such inconsistent act, when the period expires within which he might reasonably have been expected to do the failed act if it were to be done.

20.   Unfair dismissal

(1)   An employee who is dismissed is entitled under section 99 of the 1996 Act to be regarded for the purposes of Part X of that Act as unfairly dismissed if—

(a)   the reason or principal reason for the dismissal is of a kind specified in paragraph (3), or

(b)   the reason or principal reason for the dismissal is that the employee is redundant, and regulation 10 has not been complied with.

(2)   An employee who is dismissed shall also be regarded for the purposes of Part X of the 1996 Act as unfairly dismissed if—

(a)   the reason (or, if more than one, the principal reason) for the dismissal is that the employee was redundant;

(b)   it is shown that the circumstances constituting the redundancy applied equally to one or more employees in the same undertaking who held positions similar to that held by the employee and who have not been dismissed by the employer, and

(c)   it is shown that the reason (or, if more than one, the principal reason) for which the employee was selected for dismissal was a reason of a kind specified in paragraph (3).

(3)   The kinds of reason referred to in paragraphs (1) and (2) are reasons connected with—

(a)   the pregnancy of the employee;

(b)   the fact that the employee has given birth to a child;

(c)   the application of a relevant requirement, or a relevant recommendation, as defined by section 66(2) of the 1996 Act;

(d)   the fact that she took, sought to take or availed herself of the benefits of, ordinary maternity leave;

(e)   the fact that she took or sought to take—

(i)   additional maternity leave;

(ii)   parental leave, or

(iii)   time off under section 57A of the 1996 Act;

(f)   the fact that she declined to sign a workforce agreement for the purposes of these Regulations, or

(g)   the fact that the employee, being—

(i)   a representative of members of the workforce for the purposes of Schedule 1, or

(ii)   a candidate in an election in which any person elected will, on being elected, become such a representative,

performed (or proposed to perform) any functions or activities as such a representative or candidate.

(4)   Paragraphs (1)(b) and (3)(b) only apply where the dismissal ends the employee's ordinary or additional maternity leave period.

(5)   Paragraph (3) of regulation 19 applies for the purposes of paragraph (3)(d) as it applies for the purpose of paragraph (2)(d) of that regulation.

(6)   Paragraph (1) does not apply in relation to an employee if—

(a)   immediately before the end of her additional maternity leave period (or, if it ends by reason of dismissal, immediately before the dismissal) the number of employees employed by her employer, added to the number employed by any associated employer of his, did not exceed five, and

(b)   it is not reasonably practicable for the employer (who may be the same employer or a successor of his) to permit her to return to a job which is both suitable for her and appropriate for her to do in the circumstances or for an associated employer to offer her a job of that kind.

(7)   Paragraph (1) does not apply in relation to an employee if—

(a)   it is not reasonably practicable for a reason other than redundancy for the employer (who may be the same employer or a successor of his) to permit her to return to a job which is both suitable for her and appropriate for her to do in the circumstances;

(b)   an associated employer offers her a job of that kind, and

(c)   she accepts or unreasonably refuses that offer.

(8)   Where on a complaint of unfair dismissal any question arises as to whether the operation of paragraph (1) is excluded by the provisions of paragraph (6) or (7), it is for the employer to show that the provisions in question were satisfied in relation to the complainant.

21.   Contractual rights to maternity or parental leave

(1)   This regulation applies where an employee is entitled to—

(a)   ordinary maternity leave;

(b)   additional maternity leave, or

(c)   parental leave,

(referred to in paragraph (2) as a 'statutory right') and also to a right which corresponds to that right and which arises under the employee's contract of employment or otherwise.

(2)　In a case where this regulation applies—

(a)　the employee may not exercise the statutory right and the corresponding right separately but may, in taking the leave for which the two rights provide, take advantage of whichever right is, in any particular respect, the more favourable, and

(b)　the provisions of the 1996 Act and of these Regulations relating to the statutory right apply, subject to any modifications necessary to give effect to any more favourable contractual terms, to the exercise of the composite right described in sub-paragraph (a) as they apply to the exercise of the statutory right.

22.　Calculation of a week's pay

Where—

(a)　under Chapter II of part XIV of the 1996 Act, the amount of a week's pay of an employee falls to be calculated by reference to the average rate of remuneration, or the average amount of remuneration, payable to the employee in respect of a period of twelve weeks ending on a particular date (referred to as 'the calculation date');

(b)　during a week in that period, the employee was absent from work on ordinary or additional maternity leave or parental leave, and

(c)　remuneration is payable to the employee in respect of that week under her contract of employment, but the amount payable is less than the amount that would be payable if she were working,

that week shall be disregarded for the purpose of the calculation and account shall be taken of remuneration in earlier weeks so as to bring up to twelve the number of weeks of which account is taken.

Stephen Byers
Secretary of State for Trade and Industry
10 December 1999

Regulation 2(1)　　　　　SCHEDULE 1
WORKFORCE AGREEMENTS

1.　An agreement is a workforce agreement for the purposes of these Regulations if the following conditions are satisfied—

(a)　the agreement is in writing;

(b)　it has effect for a specified period not exceeding five years;

(c)　it applies either—

(i)　to all of the relevant members of the workforce, or

(ii)　to all of the relevant members of the workforce who belong to a particular group;

(d)　the agreement is signed—

(i)　in the case of an agreement of the kind referred to in sub-paragraph (c)(i), by the representatives of the workforce, and in the case of an agreement of the kind referred to in sub-paragraph (c)(ii), by the representatives of the group to which the agreement applies (excluding, in either case, any representative not a relevant member of the workforce on the date on which the agreement was first made available for signature), or

(ii)　if the employer employed 20 or fewer employees on the date referred to in sub-paragraph (d)(i), either by the appropriate representatives in accordance with that sub-paragraph or by the majority of the employees employed by him; and (e)　before the agreement was made available for signature, the employer provided all the employees to whom it was intended to apply on the date on which it came into effect with copies of the text of the agreement and such guidance as those employees might reasonably require in order to understand it in full.

2.　For the purposes of this Schedule—

'a particular group' is a group of the relevant members of a workforce who undertake a particular function, work at a particular workplace or belong to a particular department or unit within their employer's business;

'relevant members of the workforce' are all of the employees employed by a particular employer, excluding any employee whose terms and conditions of employment are provided for, wholly or in part, in a collective agreement;

'representatives of the workforce' are employees duly elected to represent the relevant members of the workforce, 'representatives of the group' are employees duly elected to represent the members of a particular group, and representatives are 'duly elected' if the election at which they were elected satisfied the requirements of paragraph 3 of this Schedule.

3.　The requirements concerning elections referred to in paragraph 2 are that—

(a)　the number of representatives to be elected is determined by the employer;

(b)　the candidates for election as representatives of the workforce are relevant members of the workforce, and the candidates for election as representatives of a group are members of the group;

(c)　no employee who is eligible to be a candidate is unreasonably excluded from standing for election;

(d)　all the relevant members of the workforce are entitled to vote for representatives of the workforce, and all the members of a particular group are entitled to vote for representatives of the group;

(e)　the employees entitled to vote may vote for as many candidates as there are representatives to be elected, and

(f)　the election is conducted so as to secure that—

(i)　so far as is reasonably practicable, those voting do so in secret, and

(ii)　the votes given at the election are fairly and accurately counted.

Regulation 16　　　　　　　SCHEDULE 2
DEFAULT PROVISIONS IN RESPECT OF PARENTAL LEAVE

Conditions of entitlement

1.　An employee may not exercise any entitlement to parental leave unless—

(a)　he has complied with any request made by his employer to produce for the employer's inspection evidence of his entitlement, of the kind described in paragraph 2;

(b)　he has given his employer notice, in accordance with whichever of paragraphs 3 to 5 is applicable, of the period of leave he proposes to take, and

(c)　in a case where paragraph 6 applies, his employer has not postponed the period of leave in accordance with that paragraph.

2.　The evidence to be produced for the purpose of paragraph 1(a) is such evidence as may reasonably be required of—

(a)　the employee's responsibility or expected responsibility for the child in respect of whom the employee proposes to take parental leave;

(b)   the child's date of birth or, in the case of a child who was placed with the employee for adoption, the date on which the placement began, and

(c)   in a case where the employee's right to exercise an entitlement to parental leave under regulation 15, or to take a particular period of leave under paragraph 7, depends upon whether the child is entitled to a disability living allowance, the child's entitlement to that allowance.

Notice to be given to employer

3.   Except in a case where paragraph 4 or 5 applies, the notice required for the purpose of paragraph 1(b) is notice which—

(a)   specifies the dates on which the period of leave is to begin and end, and

(b)   is given to the employer at least 21 days before the date on which that period is to begin.

4.   Where the employee is the father of the child in respect of whom the leave is to be taken, and the period of leave is to begin on the date on which the child is born, the notice required for the purpose of paragraph 1(b) is notice which—

(a)   specifies the expected week of childbirth and the duration of the period of leave, and

(b)   is given to the employer at least 21 days before the beginning of the expected week of childbirth.

5.   Where the child in respect of whom the leave is to be taken is to be placed with the employee for adoption by him and the leave is to begin on the date of the placement, the notice required for the purpose of paragraph 1(b) is notice which—

(a)   specifies the week in which the placement is expected to occur and the duration of the period of leave, and

(b)   is given to the employer at least 21 days before the beginning of that week, or, if that is not reasonably practicable, as soon as is reasonably practicable.

Postponement of leave

6.   An employer may postpone a period of parental leave where—

(a)   neither paragraph 4 nor paragraph 5 applies, and the employee has accordingly given the employer notice in accordance with paragraph 3;

(b)   the employer considers that the operation of his business would be unduly disrupted if the employee took leave during the period identified in his notice;

(c)   the employer agrees to permit the employee to take a period of leave—

(i)   of the same duration as the period identified in the employee's notice, and

(ii)   beginning on a date determined by the employer after consulting the employee, which is no later than six months after the commencement of that period;

(d)   the employer gives the employee notice in writing of the postponement which—

(i)   states the reason for it, and

(ii)   specifies the dates on which the period of leave the employer agrees to permit the employee to take will begin and end, and

(e)   that notice is given to the employee not more than seven days after the employee's notice was given to the employer.

Minimum periods of leave

7.   An employee may not take parental leave in a period other than the period which constitutes a week's leave for him under regulation 14 or a multiple of that period, except in a case where the child in respect of whom leave is taken is entitled to a disability living allowance.

Maximum annual leave allowance

8.   An employee may not take more than four weeks' leave in respect of any individual child during a particular year.

9.   For the purposes of paragraph 8, a year is the period of twelve months beginning—

(a)   except where sub-paragraph (b) applies, on the date on which the employee first became entitled to take parental leave in respect of the child in question, or

(b)   in a case where the employee's entitlement has been interrupted at the end of a period of continuous employment, on the date on which the employee most recently became entitled to take parental leave in respect of that child,

and each successive period of twelve months beginning on the anniversary of that date.

Appendix 3
Part-time Workers (Prevention of Less Favourable Treatment) Regulations 2000

PART I
GENERAL AND INTERPRETATION

1. Citation, commencement and interpretation

(1)   These Regulations may be cited as the Part-time Workers (Prevention of Less Favourable Treatment) Regulations 2000 and shall come into force on 1 July 2000.

(2)   In these Regulations—

'the 1996 Act' means the Employment Rights Act 1996;

'contract of employment' means a contract of service or of apprenticeship, whether express or implied, and (if it is express) whether oral or in writing;

'employee' means an individual who has entered into or works under or (except where a provision of these Regulations otherwise requires) where the employment has ceased, worked under a contract of employment;

'employer', in relation to any employee or worker, means the person by whom the employee or worker is or (except where a provision of these Regulations otherwise requires) where the employment has ceased, was employed;

'pro rata principle' means that where a comparable full-time worker receives or is entitled to receive pay or any other benefit, a part-time worker is to receive or be entitled to receive not less than the proportion of that pay or other benefit that the number of his weekly hours bears to the number of weekly hours of the comparable full-time worker;

'worker' means an individual who has entered into or works under or (except where a provision of these Regulations otherwise requires) where the employment has ceased, worked under—

(a)   a contract of employment; or

(b)   any other contract, whether express or implied and (if it is express) whether oral or in writing, whereby the individual undertakes to do or perform personally any work or services for another party to the contract whose status is not by virtue of the contract that of a client or customer of any profession or business undertaking carried on by the individual.

(3)   In the definition of the pro rata principle and in regulations 3 and 4 'weekly hours' means the number of hours a worker is required to work under his contract of employment in a week in which he has no absences from work and does not work

any overtime or, where the number of such hours varies according to a cycle, the average number of such hours.

2.   Meaning of full-time worker, part-time worker and comparable full-time worker

(1)   A worker is a full-time worker for the purpose of these Regulations if he is paid wholly or in part by reference to the time he works and, having regard to the custom and practice of the employer in relation to workers employed by the worker's employer under the same type of contract, is identifiable as a full-time worker.

(2)   A worker is a part-time worker for the purpose of these Regulations if he is paid wholly or in part by reference to the time he works and, having regard to the custom and practice of the employer in relation to workers employed by the worker's employer under the same type of contract, is not identifiable as a full-time worker.

(3)   For the purposes of paragraphs (1), (2) and (4), the following shall be regarded as being employed under different types of contract—

(a)   employees employed under a contract that is neither for a fixed term nor a contract of apprenticeship;

(b)   employees employed under a contract for a fixed term that is not a contract of apprenticeship;

(c)   employees employed under a contract of apprenticeship;

(d)   workers who are neither employees nor employed under a contract for a fixed term;

(e)   workers who are not employees but are employed under a contract for a fixed term;

(f)   any other description of worker that it is reasonable for the employer to treat differently from other workers on the ground that workers of that description have a different type of contract.

(4)   A full-time worker is a comparable full-time worker in relation to a part-time worker if, at the time when the treatment that is alleged to be less favourable to the part-time worker takes place—

(a)   both workers are—

(i)   employed by the same employer under the same type of contract, and

(ii)   engaged in the same or broadly similar work having regard, where relevant, to whether they have a similar level of qualification, skills and experience; and

(b)   the full-time worker works or is based at the same establishment as the part-time worker or, where there is no full-time worker working or based at that establishment who satisfies the requirements of sub-paragraph (a), works or is based at a different establishment and satisfies those requirements.

3.   Workers becoming part-time

(1)   This regulation applies to a worker who—

(a)   was identifiable as a full-time worker in accordance with regulation 2(1); and

(b)   following a termination or variation of his contract, continues to work under a new or varied contract, whether of the same type or not, that requires him to work for a number of weekly hours that is lower than the number he was required to work immediately before the termination or variation.

(2)   Notwithstanding regulation 2(4), regulation 5 shall apply to a worker to whom this regulation applies as if he were a part-time worker and as if there were a

comparable full-time worker employed under the terms that applied to him immediately before the variation or termination.

(3)　The fact that this regulation applies to a worker does not affect any right he may have under these Regulations by virtue of regulation 2(4).

4.　Workers returning part-time after absence

(1)　This regulation applies to a worker who—

(a)　was identifiable as a full-time worker in accordance with regulation 2(1) immediately before a period of absence (whether the absence followed a termination of the worker's contract or not);

(b)　returns to work for the same employer within a period of less than twelve months beginning with the day on which the period of absence started;

(c)　returns to the same job or to a job at the same level under a contract, whether it is a different contract or a varied contract and regardless of whether it is of the same type, under which he is required to work for a number of weekly hours that is lower than the number he was required to work immediately before the period of absence.

(2)　Notwithstanding regulation 2(4), regulation 5 shall apply to a worker to whom this regulation applies ('the returning worker') as if he were a part-time worker and as if there were a comparable full-time worker employed under—

(a)　the contract under which the returning worker was employed immediately before the period of absence; or

(b)　where it is shown that, had the returning worker continued to work under the contract mentioned in sub-paragraph (a) a variation would have been made to its term during the period of absence, the contract mentioned in that sub-paragraph including that variation.

(3)　The fact that this regulation applies to a worker does not affect any right he may have under these Regulations by virtue of regulation 2(4).

PART II
RIGHTS AND REMEDIES

5.　Less favourable treatment of part-time workers

(1)　A part-time worker has the right not to be treated by his employer less favourably than the employer treats a comparable full-time worker—

(a)　as regards the terms of his contract; or

(b)　by being subjected to any other detriment by any act, or deliberate failure to act, of his employer.

(2)　The right conferred by paragraph (1) applies only if—

(a)　the treatment is on the ground that the worker is a part-time worker, and

(b)　the treatment is not justified on objective grounds.

(3)　In determining whether a part-time worker has been treated less favourably than a comparable full-time worker the pro rata principle shall be applied unless it is inappropriate.

(4)　A part-time worker paid at a lower rate for overtime worked by him in a period than a comparable full-time worker is or would be paid for overtime worked by him in the same period shall not, for that reason, be regarded as treated less favourably than the comparable full-time worker where, or to the extent that, the total number of hours worked by the part-time worker in the period, including overtime, does not exceed the number of hours the comparable full-time worker is required to work in the period, disregarding absences from work and overtime.

6.   Right to receive a written statement of reasons for less favourable treatment

(1)   If a worker who considers that his employer may have treated him in a manner which infringes a right conferred on him by regulation 5 requests in writing from his employer a written statement giving particulars of the reasons for the treatment, the worker is entitled to be provided with such a statement within twenty-one days of his request.

(2)   A written statement under this regulation is admissible as evidence in any proceedings under these Regulations.

(3)   If it appears to the tribunal in any proceedings under these Regulations—

(a)   that the employer deliberately, and without reasonable excuse, omitted to provide a written statement, or

(b)   that the written statement is evasive or equivocal,

it may draw any inference which it considers it just and equitable to draw, including an inference that the employer has infringed the right in question.

(4)   This regulation does not apply where the treatment in question consists of the dismissal of an employee, and the employee is entitled to a written statement of reasons for his dismissal under section 92 of the 1996 Act.

7.   Unfair dismissal and the right not to be subjected to detriment

(1)   An employee who is dismissed shall be regarded as unfairly dismissed for the purposes of Part X of the 1996 Act if the reason (or, if more than one, the principal reason) for the dismissal is a reason specified in paragraph (3).

(2)   A worker has the right not to be subjected to any detriment by any act, or any deliberate failure to act, by his employer done on a ground specified in paragraph (3).

(3)   The reasons or, as the case may be, grounds are—

(a)   that the worker has—

(i)   brought proceedings against the employer under these Regulations;

(ii)   requested from his employer a written statement of reasons under regulation 6;

(iii)   given evidence or information in connection with such proceedings brought by any worker;

(iv)   otherwise done anything under these Regulations in relation to the employer or any other person;

(v)   alleged that the employer had infringed these Regulations; or

(vi)   refused (or proposed to refuse) to forgo a right conferred on him by these Regulations, or

(b)   that the employer believes or suspects that the worker has done or intends to do any of the things mentioned in sub-paragraph (a).

(4)   Where the reason or principal reason for dismissal or, as the case may be, ground for subjection to any act or deliberate failure to act, is that mentioned in paragraph (3)(a)(v), or (b) so far as it relates thereto, neither paragraph (1) nor paragraph (2) applies if the allegation made by the worker is false and not made in good faith.

(5)   Paragraph (2) does not apply where the detriment in question amounts to the dismissal of an employee within the meaning of Part X of the 1996 Act.

8.   Complaints to employment tribunals etc.

(1)   Subject to regulation 7(5), a worker may present a complaint to an employment tribunal that his employer has infringed a right conferred on him by regulation 5 or 7(2).

(2)   Subject to paragraph (3), an employment tribunal shall not consider a complaint under this regulation unless it is presented before the end of the period of three months (or, in a case to which regulation 13 applies, six months) beginning with the date of the less favourable treatment or detriment to which the complaint relates or, where an act or failure to act is part of a series of similar acts or failures comprising the less favourable treatment or detriment, the last of them.

(3)   A tribunal may consider any such complaint which is out of time if, in all the circumstances of the case, it considers that it is just and equitable to do so.

(4)   For the purposes of calculating the date of the less favourable treatment or detriment under paragraph (2)—

(a)   where a term in a contract is less favourable, that treatment shall be treated, subject to paragraph (b), as taking place on each day of the period during which the term is less favourable;

(b)   where an application relies on regulation 3 or 4 the less favourable treatment shall be treated as occurring on, and only on, in the case of regulation 3, the first day on which the applicant worked under the new or varied contract and, in the case of regulation 4, the day on which the applicant returned; and

(c)   a deliberate failure to act contrary to regulation 5 or 7(2) shall be treated as done when it was decided on.

(5)   In the absence of evidence establishing the contrary, a person shall be taken for the purposes of paragraph (4)(c) to decide not to act—

(a)   when he does an act inconsistent with doing the failed act; or

(b)   if he has done no such inconsistent act, when the period expires within which he might reasonably have been expected to have done the failed act if it was to be done.

(6)   Where a worker presents a complaint under this regulation it is for the employer to identify the ground for the less favourable treatment or detriment.

(7)   Where an employment tribunal finds that a complaint presented to it under this regulation is well founded, it shall take such of the following steps as it considers just and equitable—

(a)   making a declaration as to the rights of the complainant and the employer in relation to the matters to which the complaint relates;

(b)   ordering the employer to pay compensation to the complainant;

(c)   recommending that the employer take, within a specified period, action appearing to the tribunal to be reasonable, in all the circumstances of the case, for the purpose of obviating or reducing the adverse effect on the complainant of any matter to which the complaint relates.

(8)   Where a tribunal finds a complaint to be well founded on the ground that the complainant has been treated less favourably in respect of either the terms on which he is afforded access to membership of an occupational pension scheme or his treatment under the rules of such a scheme, the steps taken by a tribunal under paragraph (7) as regards that less favourable treatment shall not relate to a period earlier than two years before the date on which the complaint was presented.

(9)   Where a tribunal orders compensation under paragraph (7)(b), the amount of the compensation awarded shall be such as the tribunal considers just and equitable in all the circumstances (subject to paragraph (8)) having regard to—

(a)   the infringement to which the complaint relates, and

(b)   any loss which is attributable to the infringement having regard, in the case of an infringement of the right conferred by regulation 5, to the pro rata principle except where it is inappropriate to do so.

(10)   The loss shall be taken to include—

(a)   any expenses reasonably incurred by the complainant in consequence of the infringement, and

(b)   loss of any benefit which he might reasonably be expected to have had but for the infringement.

(11)   Compensation in respect of treating a worker in a manner which infringes the right conferred on him by regulation 5 shall not include compensation for injury to feelings.

(12)   In ascertaining the loss the tribunal shall apply the same rule concerning the duty of a person to mitigate his loss as applies to damages recoverable under the common law of England and Wales or (as the case may be) Scotland.

(13)   Where the tribunal finds that the act, or failure to act, to which the complaint relates was to any extent caused or contributed to by action of the complainant, it shall reduce the amount of the compensation by such proportion as it considers just and equitable having regard to that finding.

(14)   If the employer fails, without reasonable justification, to comply with a recommendation made by an employment tribunal under paragraph (7)(c) the tribunal may, if it thinks it just and equitable to do so—

(a)   increase the amount of compensation required to be paid to the complainant in respect of the complaint, where an order was made under paragraph (7)(b); or

(b)   make an order under paragraph (7)(b).

9.   Restrictions on contracting out

Section 203 of the 1996 Act (restrictions on contracting out) shall apply in relation to these Regulations as if they were contained in that Act.

PART III
MISCELLANEOUS

10.   Amendments to primary legislation

The amendments in the Schedule to these Regulations shall have effect.

11.   Liability of employers and principals

(1)   Anything done by a person in the course of his employment shall be treated for the purposes of these Regulations as also done by his employer, whether or not it was done with the employer's knowledge or approval.

(2)   Anything done by a person as agent for the employer with the authority of the employer shall be treated for the purposes of these Regulations as also done by the employer.

(3)   In proceedings under these Regulations against any person in respect of an act alleged to have been done by a worker of his, it shall be a defence for that person to prove that he took such steps as were reasonably practicable to prevent the worker from—

    (a)   doing that act; or

    (b)   doing, in the course of his employment, acts of that discription.

PART IV
SPECIAL CLASSES OF PERSON

12. Crown employment

(1)   Subject to regulation 13, these Regulations have effect in relation to Crown employment and persons in Crown employment as they have effect in relation to other employment and other employees and workers.

(2)   In paragraph (1) 'Crown employment' means employment under or for the purposes of a government department or any officer or body exercising on behalf of the Crown functions conferred by a statutory provision.

(3)   For the purposes of the application of the provisions of these Regulations in relation to Crown employment in accordance with paragraph (1)—

    (a)   references to an employee and references to a worker shall be construed as references to a person in Crown employment to whom the definition of employee or, as the case may be, worker is appropriate; and

    (b)   references to a contract in relation to an employee and references to a contract in relation to a worker shall be construed as references to the terms of employment of a person in Crown employment to whom the definition of employee or, as the case may be, worker is appropriate.

13. Armed forces

(1)   These Regulations, shall have effect in relation—

    (a)   subject to paragraphs (2) and (3) and apart from regulation 7(1), to service as a member of the armed forces, and

    (b)   to employment by an association established for the purposes of Part XI of the Reserve Forces Act 1996.

(2)   These Regulations shall not have effect in relation to service as a member of the reserve forces in so far as that service consists in undertaking training obligations—

    (a)   under section 38, 40 or 41 of the Reserve Forces Act 1980,

    (b)   under section 22 of the Reserve Forces Act 1996,

    (c)   pursuant to regulations made under section 4 of the Reserve Forces Act 1996,

or consists in undertaking voluntary training or duties under section 27 of the Reserve Forces Act 1996.

(3)   No complaint concerning the service of any person as a member of the armed forces may be presented to an employment tribunal under regulation 8 unless—

    (a)   that person has made a complaint in respect of the same matter to an officer under the service redress procedures, and

    (b)   that complaint has not been withdrawn.

(4)   For the purposes of paragraph (3)(b), a person shall be treated as having withdrawn his complaint if, having made a complaint to an officer under the service redress procedures, he fails to submit the complaint to the Defence Council under those procedures.

(5)   Where a complaint of the kind referred to in paragraph (3) is presented to an employment tribunal, the service redress procedures may continue after the complaint is presented.

(6)   In this regulation, 'the service redress procedures' means the procedures, excluding those which relate to the making of a report to Her Majesty, referred to in section 180 of the Army Act 1955, section 180 of the Air Force Act 1955 and section 130 of the Naval Discipline Act 1957.

14.   House of Lords staff

(1)   These Regulations have effect in relation to employment as a relevant member of the House of Lords staff as they have effect in relation to other employment.

(2)   In this regulation 'relevant member of the House of Lords staff' means any person who is employed under a contract with the Corporate Officer of the House of Lords by virtue of which he is a worker.

15.   House of Commons staff

(1)   These Regulations have effect in relation to employment as a relevant member of the House of Commons staff as they have effect in relation to other employment.

(2)   In this regulation 'relevant member of the House of Commons staff' means any person—

    (a)   who was appointed by the House of Commons Commission; or

    (b)   who is a member of the Speaker's personal staff.

16.   Police service

(1)   For the purposes of these Regulations, the holding, otherwise than under a contract of employment, of the office of constable or an appointment as a police cadet shall be treated as employment, under a contract of employment, by the relevant officer.

(2)   In this regulation 'the relevant officer' means—

    (a)   in relation to a member of a police force or a special constable or police cadet appointed for a police area, the chief officer of police (or, in Scotland, the chief constable);

    (b)   in relation to a person holding office under section 9(1)(b) or 55(1)(b) of the Police Act 1997 (police members of the National Criminal Intelligence Service and the National Crime Squad), the Director General of the National Criminal Intelligence Service or, as the case may be, the Director General of the National Crime Squad; and

    (c)   in relation to any other person holding the office of constable or an appointment as a police cadet, the person who has the direction and control of the body of constables or cadets in question.

17.   Holders of judicial offices

These Regulations do not apply to any individual in his capacity as the holder of a judicial office if he is remunerated on a daily fee-paid basis.

Alan Johnson,
Parliamentary Under Secretary of State for Competitiveness, Department of Trade and Industry
8th June 2000

Regulation 10   SCHEDULE
AMENDMENTS TO PRIMARY LEGISLATION

1. The Employment Tribunals Act 1996 shall be amended as follows—

   (a) In section 18(1) (cases where conciliation provisions apply)—

     (i) at the end of paragraph (ff), the word 'or' shall be omitted, and

     (ii) after paragraph (g), there shall be inserted—

'or

     (h) arising out of a contravention, or alleged contravention of regulation 7(2) of the Part-time Workers (Prevention of Less Favourable Treatment) Regulations 2000.'.

   (b) In section 21 (jurisdiction of the Employment Appeal Tribunal) in subsection (1) (which specifies the proceedings and claims to which the section applies)—

     (i) at the end of paragraph (h), the word 'or' shall be omitted,

     (ii) after paragraph (i) there shall be inserted—

'or

     (j) the Part-time Workers (Prevention of Less Favourable Treatment) Regulations 2000.'.

2.—(1) In section 105 of the 1996 Act (redundancy as unfair dismissal) in subsection (1)(c) (which requires one of a specified group of subsections to apply for a person to be treated as unfairly dismissed) for '(7D)' there shall be substituted '(7E)' and after subsection (7D) there shall be inserted—

'(7E) This subsection applies if the reason (or, if more than one, the principal reason) for which the employee was selected for dismissal was one specified in paragraph (3) of regulation 7 of the Part-time Workers (Prevention of Less Favourable Treatment) Regulations 2000 (unless the case is one to which paragraph (4) of that regulation applies).'.

(2) In section 108 of the 1996 Act (exclusion of right: qualifying period of employment) in subsection (3) (cases where no qualifying period of employment is required) the word 'or' at the end of paragraph (h) shall be omitted and after paragraph (hh) there shall be inserted—

'or

     (i) paragraph (1) of regulation 7 of the Part-time Workers (Prevention of Less Favourable Treatment) Regulations 2000 applies.'.

(3) In section 109 of the 1996 Act (exclusion of right: upper age limit) in subsection (2) (cases where upper age limit does not apply) the word 'or' at the end of paragraph (h) shall be omitted and after paragraph (hh) there shall be inserted—

'or

     (i) paragraph (1) of regulation 7 of the Part-time Workers (Prevention of Less Favourable Treatment) Regulations 2000 applies.'.

Appendix 4
Code of Practice
Disciplinary and Grievance Procedures

Section 3 — The statutory right to be accompanied at disciplinary and grievance hearings

What is the right?

50. Workers have a statutory right to be accompanied by a fellow worker or trade union official where they are requried or invited by their employer to attend certain disciplinary or grievance hearings and when they make a reasonable request to be so accompanied. This right is additional to any contractual rights.

To whom does the right apply?

51. The statutory right to be accompanied applies to all workers, not just employees working under a contract of employment. 'Worker' is defined in the legislation and includes anyone who performs work personally for someone else, but is not genuinely self-employed, as well as agency workers and home workers, workers in Parliament and Crown employees other than members of the armed forces. There are no exclusions for part-time or casual workers, those on short term contracts or for people who work overseas (subject to any jurisdictional rules).

Application of the statutory right

52. The statutory right applies where a worker:
- (i)   is required or invited to attend a disciplinary or grievance hearing, and
- (ii) reasonably requests to be accompanied at the hearing.

What is a disciplinary hearing?

53. Whether a worker has a statutory right to be accompanied at a disciplinary hearing will depend on the nature of the hearing. Employers often choose to deal with disciplinary problems in the first instance by means of an informal interview or counselling session. So long as the informal interview or counselling session does not result in a formal warning or some other action it would not generally be good practice for the worker to be accompanied as matters at this informal stage are best resolved directly by the worker and manager concerned. Equally, employers should not allow an investigation into the facts surrounding a disciplinary case to extend into a disciplinary hearing. If it becomes clear during the course of the informal or investigative interview that formal disciplinary action may be needed then the interview should be terminated and a formal hearing convened at which the worker should be afforded the statutory right to be accompanied.

54. The statutory right to be accompanied applies specifically to hearings which could result in:

(i) the administration of a formal warning to a worker by his employer (i.e., a warning, whether about conduct or capability, that will be placed on the worker's record);

(ii) the taking of some other action in respect of a worker by his employer (e.g., suspension without pay, demotion or dismissal); or

(iii) the confirmation of a warning issued or some other action taken.

What is a grievance hearing?

55. The statutory right to accompaniment applies only to grievance hearings which concern the performance of a 'duty by an employer in relation to a worker'. This means a legal duty arising from statute or common law (e.g., contractual commitments). Ultimately, only the courts can decide what sort of grievances fall within the statutory definition but the individual circumstances of each case will always be relevant. For instance:

(i) An individual's request for a pay rise is unlikely to fall within the definition unless specifically provided for in the contract. On the other hand a grievance about equal pay would be included as this is covered by a statutory duty imposed on employers.

(ii) Grievances about the application of a grading or promotion exercise are likely to be included if they arise out of the contract but not grievances arising out of requests for new terms and conditions of employment, for instance a request for subsidised health care or travel loans where these are not already provided for in the contract.

(iii) Equally an employer may be under no duty to provide car parking facilities and thus a grievance on the issue would not attract the right to be accompanied. However, if the worker was disabled and needed parking facilities in order to attend work the employer's duty of care becomes relevant and the worker is likely to have a statutory right to be accompanied.

(iv) Grievance arising out of day to day friction between fellow workers may not involve the breach of a legal duty unless the friction develops into incidents of bullying or harassment which would be included as they arise out of the employer's duty of care.

What is a reasonable request?

56. In order for workers to exercise their statutory right to be accompanied they must make a reasonable request to their employer. It will be for the Courts to decide what is reasonable in all the circumstances. There is no test of reasonableness associated with the choice of companion and workers are therefore free to choose any one fellow worker or trade union official (within the limitations of paragraph 57). However, in making their choice workers should bear in mind that it would not be appropriate to insist on being accompanied by a colleague whose presence would prejudice the hearing or who might have a conflict of interest. Nor would it be sensible for a worker to request accompaniment by a colleague from a geographically remote location when someone suitably qualified was available on site. The request to be accompanied need not be in writing.

The accompanying person

57.   A worker has a statutory right to be accompanied at a disciplinary or grievance hearing by a single companion who is either a:

(i)   Fellow worker, ie, another of the employer's workers;

(ii)   A full-time official employed by a trade union; or a lay trade union official, so long as they have been reasonably certified in writing by their union as having experience of, or as having received training in, acting as a worker's companion at disciplinary or grievance hearings. Such certification may take the form of a card or letter.

Workers may, however, have contractual rights to be accompanied by persons other than those listed above, for instance a partner, spouse or legal representative.

58.   Workers are free to choose an official from any trade union to accompany them at a disciplinary or grievance hearing regardless of whether the union is recognised or not. However where a trade union is recognised in a workplace it is good practice for an official from that union to accompany the worker at a hearing.

59.   There is no duty on a fellow worker or trade union official to accept a request to accompany a worker and no pressure should be brought to bear on a person if they do not wish to act as a companion.

60.   Accompanying a worker at a disciplinary or grievance hearing is a serious responsibility and it is important therefore that trade unions ensure their officials are trained in the role. Even where a trade union official has experience of acting in the role there may still be a need for periodic refresher training.

61.   A worker who has been requested to accompany a colleague employed by the same employer and has agreed to do so is entitled to take a reasonable amount of paid time off to fulfil this responsibility. The time off should not only cover the hearing but should also allow a reasonable amount of time off for the accompanying person to familiarise themselves with the case and confer with the worker before and after the hearing. A lay trade union official is permitted to take a reasonable amount of paid time off to accompany a worker at a hearing so long as the worker is employed by the same employer.

The statutory right in operation

62.   It is good practice for an employer to try to agree a mutually convenient date for the disciplinary or grievance hearing with the worker and their companion. This is to ensure that hearings do not have to be delayed or postponed at the last minute. Where the chosen companion cannot attend on the date proposed the worker can offer an alternative time and date so long as it is reasonable and falls before the end of the period of five working days beginning with the first working day after the day proposed by the employer. In proposing an alternative date the worker should have regard to the availability of the relevant manager. For instance it would not normally be reasonable to ask for a new date for the hearing where it was known the manager was going be absent on business or on leave unless it was possible for someone else to act for the manager at the hearing. The location and timing of any alternative hearing should be convenient to both worker and employer.

63.   Both the employer and worker should prepare carefully for the hearing. The employer should ensure that a suitable venue is available and that, where necessary, arrangements are made to cater for any disability the worker or their companion may have. Where English is not the worker's first language there may also be a need for translation facilities. The worker should think carefully about what is to be said at the hearing and should discuss with their chosen companion their respective roles at the meeting. Before the hearing the worker should inform the employer of the identity of their chosen companion. In certain circumstances, for instance where the chosen companion is an official of a non-recognised trade union, it might also be helpful for the employer and chosen companion to make contact with each other before the hearing.

64.   The chosen companion has a statutory right to address the hearing but no statutory right to answer questions on the worker's behalf. Companions have an important role to play in supporting a worker and to this end should be allowed to ask questions and should, with the agreement of the employer, be allowed to participate as fully as possible in the hearing. The companion should also be permitted reasonable time to confer privately with the worker, either in the hearing room or outside.

What if the right to be accompanied is infringed?

65.   If an employer fails to allow a worker to be accompanied at a disciplinary or grievance hearing or fails to re-arrange a hearing to a reasonable date proposed by the worker when a companion cannot attend on the date originally proposed, the worker may present a complaint to an employment tribunal. If the tribunal finds in favour of the worker the employer may be liable to pay compensation of up to two weeks' pay as defined in statute. Where the failure leads to a finding of unfair dismissal greater legal remedies might be involved.

66.   Employers must be careful not to place any worker at a disadvantage for exercising or seeking to exercise their right to be accompanied as such detriment is unlawful and may lead to a claim to an employment tribunal. Equally employers must not place at a disadvantage those who act or seek to act as the accompanying person.

Appendix 5
Code of Practice
Industrial Action Ballots and Notice to Employers

PREAMBLE

The legal framework for the operation of this Code is explained in **Annex 1** and in its main text. While every effort has been made to ensure that explanations included in the Code are accurate, only the courts can give authoritative interpretations of the law.

The Code's provisions apply equally to men and to women, but for simplicity the masculine pronoun is used throughout. Wherever it appears in the Code the word 'court' is used to mean the High Court in England and Wales and the Court of Session in Scotland, but without prejudice to the Code's relevance to any proceedings before any other court.

Passages in this Code which are printed in bold are re-statements of provisions in primary legislation.

SECTION A
INTRODUCTION

1.   This Code provides practical guidance to trade unions and employers to promote the improvement of industrial relations and good practice in the conduct of trade union industrial action ballots.

2.   A union is legally responsible for organising industrial action only if it 'authorises or endorses' the action. Authorisation would take place before the industrial action starts, and endorsement after it has previously started as unofficial action.

3.   Apart from certain small accidental failures that are unlikely to affect the result, a failure to satisfy the statutory requirements relating to the ballot or giving employers notice of industrial action will give grounds for proceedings against a union by an employer, a customer or supplier of an employer, or an individual member of the public claiming that an effect or likely effect of the industrial action would be to prevent or delay the supply of goods or services to him or to reduce the quality of goods or services so supplied. With the exception of failures to comply with the requirements to give notice to employers, these will also give grounds for action by the union's members.

4.   The Code does not deal with other matters which may affect a union's liability in respect of industrial action. For example, the law will give no protection against proceedings to a union which organises secondary action, intimidatory or violent picketing, industrial action which is not 'in contemplation or furtherance of a trade dispute', industrial action to establish or maintain any closed shop practice or in supporter a worker dismissed while taking part in unofficial industrial action. Nor does it apply to union election ballots, ballots on union political funds or ballots on union recognition or derecognition arranged for by the Central Arbitration Committee under section 70A of and Schedule A1 to the Trade Union and Labour Relations (Consolidation) Act 1992 ('the 1992 Act'). These are subject to separate statutory requirements.

Legal status
5.   The Code itself imposes no legal obligations and failure to observe it does not by itself render anyone liable to proceedings. But section 207 of the 1992 Act provides that any provisions of the Code are to be admissible in evidence and are to be taken into account in proceedings before any court where it considers them relevant.

SECTION B
WHETHER A BALLOT IS APPROPRIATE

Observing procedural agreements
6.   An industrial action ballot should not take place until any agreed procedures, whether formal or otherwise, which might lead to the resolution of a dispute without the need for industrial action have been completed and consideration has been given to resolving the dispute by other means, including seeking assistance from the Advisory, Conciliation and Arbitration Service (ACAS). A union should hold a ballot on industrial action only if it is contemplating the organisation of industrial action.

Balloting by more than one union
7.   Where more than one union decides that it wishes to ballot members working for the same employer in connection with the same dispute, the arrangements for the different ballots should be co-ordinated so that, as far as practicable, they are held at the same time and the results are announced simultaneously.

SECTION C
PREPARING FOR AN INDUSTRIAL ACTION BALLOT

Arranging for independent scrutiny of the ballot
8.   For a ballot where more than 50 members are given entitlement to vote (see *paragraph 21* below), the union must appoint a qualified person as the scrutineer of the ballot. For a person to be qualified for appointment as scrutineer of an industrial action ballot, he must be among those specified in an order made by the Secretary of State and the union must not have grounds for believing that he will carry out the functions which the law requires other than competently or that his independence in relation to the union might reasonably be called into question.
9.   The scrutineer's terms of appointment must require him to take such steps as appear appropriate to him for the purpose of enabling him to make a report to the union as soon as reasonably practicable after the date of the ballot (i.e. the last day on which votes may be cast, if they may be cast on more than one day), and in any event not later than four weeks after that date.

10.   The union must ensure that the scrutineer carries out the functions required to be part of his terms of appointment, and that there is no interference with this from the union, or any of its members, officials or employees; and comply with all reasonable requests made by the scrutineer for the purpose of carrying out those functions.

11.   It may be desirable to appoint the scrutineer before steps are taken to satisfy any of the other requirements of the law to make it easier for the scrutineer to satisfy himself whether what is done conforms to the legal requirements.

12.   In some circumstances, it may help ensure adequate standards for the conduct of the ballot or simplify the balloting process if a union gives the scrutineer additional tasks to carry out on the union's behalf, such as—

● supervising the production and distribution of voting papers;
● being the person to whom the voting papers are returned by those voting in the ballot, and
● retaining custody of all returned voting papers for a set period after the ballot.

13.   Although the scrutiny requirement does not apply to ballots where 50 or fewer members are entitled to vote, a union may want to consider whether the appointment of a scrutineer would still be of benefit in enabling it to demonstrate compliance with the statutory requirements more easily.

Providing ballot notice to employers

14.   The union must take such steps as are reasonably necessary to ensure that any employer who it is reasonable for the union to believe will be the employer of any of its members who will be given entitlement to vote receives written notice of the ballot not later than the seventh day before the intended opening day of the ballot (i.e. the first day on which a voting paper is sent to any person entitled to vote). That notice must—

● state that the union intends to hold the ballot;
● specify the date which the union reasonably believes will be the opening day of the ballot; and
● contain such information in the union's possession as would help the employer to make plans (for example, as appropriate, to enable him to warn his customers of the possibility of disruption so that they can make alternative arrangements or to take steps to ensure the health and safety of his employees or the public or to safeguard equipment which might otherwise suffer damage from being shut down or left without supervision) and bring information to the attention of those of his employees who it is reasonable for the union to believe (at that time) will be entitled to vote. In particular, the union must provide as a minimum any information which it possesses as to the number, category or workplace of the employees concerned. But a notice will not fail to satisfy the requirements simply because it does not name any employees.

15.   To avoid the risk of legal action, the union should allow sufficient time for delivery, use a suitable means of transmission (such as first class post, courier, fax, email or hand delivery) and consider obtaining confirmation that the employer has received the notice, by using recorded delivery or otherwise.

16.   It may also reduce the risk of litigation for a union to check that an employer accepts that the information provided complies with the requirements of section 226A(2)(c) of the 1992 Act. Similarly, it would be in the interests of good industrial

relations for an employer who believes the notice he has received does not contain sufficient information to comply with the statutory requirements to raise that with the union promptly before pursuing the matter in the court.

17.   It is for the union to satisfy the requirement to provide sufficient notice. In reaching a decision on what information needs to be provided, the union may find it helpful to consider what information an employer is likely to have available, apart from that in the notice itself, which could help it make plans and bring information to those entitled to vote. Depending on the circumstances, factors such as the size and turnover rate of the employer's workforce; the variety of work done for the employer; the number of locations at which it is carried out; and any previous experience of ballot notifications concerning the same employer may be relevant to a decision about how much detail needs to be included.

18.   In some circumstances the requirement is likely to be satisfied by indicating to the employer that entitlement to vote will be given to all of the union's members engaged on, for example, a specified kind of work activity, or in a certain grade, or at a particular location. In some cases, if the employer would otherwise be left in doubt, more specific information, such as a combination of these items of information, may be needed, but in no case will a union be required to give employees' names. Ultimately, it will always be a question on the facts of a particular case whether the notice gives an employer the required details.

Providing sample voting paper(s) to employers

19.   The union must take such steps as are reasonably necessary to ensure that any employer who it is reasonable for the union to believe will be the employer of any of its members who will be given entitlement to vote receives a sample voting paper (and a sample of any variant of that voting paper) not later than the third day before the opening day of the ballot. Where more than one employer's workers are being balloted, it is sufficient to send each employer only the voting paper or papers which will be sent to his employees.

20.   If the sample voting paper is available in time, the union may wish to include it with the notice of intention to ballot. As with the ballot notice, the risk of non-compliance can be reduced by allowing enough time, using appropriate means of transmission and, possibly, by obtaining confirmation of receipt.

Establishing entitlement to vote (the 'balloting constituency')

21.   Entitlement to vote in the ballot must be given to all the union's members who it is reasonable at the time of the ballot for the union to believe will be induced (whether that inducement will be successful or not) to take part in or continue with the industrial action, and to no other members.

22.   The validity of the ballot will not however be affected if the union subsequently induces members to take part in or continue with industrial action who at the time of the ballot—

●   were not members; or
●   were members but who it was not reasonable to expect would be induced to take action (for example because they changed jobs after the ballot).

23.   It should also be noted that accidental failures to comply with the requirements on—

●   who is given entitlement to vote,
●   the dispatch of voting papers,

- giving members the opportunity to vote conveniently by post, and
- balloting merchant seamen employed in a ship at sea or outside Great Britain at some time during the voting period

will be disregarded if, taken together, they are on a scale unlikely to affect the ballot's result.

Balloting members at more than one workplace

24.   Where the members of a union with different workplaces are to be balloted, a separate ballot will be necessary for each workplace unless one of the conditions set out below is met. It will be unlawful for the union to organise industrial action at any such workplace where a majority of those voting in the ballot for that workplace have not voted 'Yes' in response to the relevant required question (or questions) (see *paragraph 30* below). (If an employee works at or from a single set of premises, his workplace is those premises. If not, it is the premises with which his employment has the closest connection.)

25.   In summary, the conditions for holding a single ballot for more than one workplace are—

- at each of the workplaces covered by the single ballot there is at least one member of the union affected by the dispute; or
- entitlement to vote in the single ballot is given, and limited, to all of a union's members who, according to the union's reasonable belief, are employed in a particular occupation or occupations by one employer or any of a number of employers with whom the union is in dispute; or
- entitlement to vote in the single ballot is given, and limited, to all of a union's members who are employed by a particular employer or any of a number of employers with whom the union is in dispute.

It is possible for a union to hold more than one ballot on a dispute at a single workplace. If the conditions above are met, some or all of those ballots may also cover members in other workplaces.

The balloting method

26.   Votes must be recorded by the individual voter marking a voting paper. Voting papers must be sent out by post and members must be enabled conveniently to return them by post at no direct expense to themselves. In practice, this means that those properly entitled to vote should be supplied with pre-paid reply envelopes in which to return the voting paper.

27.   The period between sending out voting papers (i.e. the opening day of the ballot) and the date by which completed voting papers should be returned should be long enough for the voting papers to be distributed and returned and for the members concerned to consider their vote. The appropriate period may vary according to such factors as the geographical dispersion of the workforce, their familiarity or otherwise with the issues in the dispute, the class of post used and whether the ballot is being held at a time of year when members are more than usually likely to be away from home or the workplace, for example during the summer holidays. Generally, seven days should be the minimum period where voting papers are sent out and returned by first class post and fourteen days where second class post is used, although — very exceptionally — shorter periods may be possible for ballots with very small, concentrated constituencies who can be expected to be familiar with the terms of the dispute.

28.   In order to reduce the likelihood of dispute over whether or not sufficient time has been allowed, the union may wish to consider obtaining one or more certificates of posting to confirm the date when voting papers were actually put into the post, and the number sent out.

Voting papers

29.   The voting paper must—
- where applicable, state the name of the independent scrutineer;
- clearly specify the address to which, and the date by which, it is to be returned;
- be marked with a number, which is one of series of consecutive numbers used to give a different number to each voting paper;
- make clear whether voters are being asked if they are prepared to take part in industrial action which consists of a strike, or in industrial action short of a strike, which for this purpose includes overtime bans and call-out bans; and
- specify the person or persons (and/or class or classes of person/s) who the union intends to have authority to make the first call for industrial action to which the ballot relates, in the event of a vote in favour of industrial action.

30.   While the question (or questions) may be framed in different ways, the voter must be asked to say by answering 'Yes' or 'No' whether he is willing to take part in or continue with the industrial action. If the union has not decided whether the industrial action would consist of a strike or action short of a strike (including overtime bans or call-out bans), separate questions in respect of each type of action must appear on the voting paper.

31.   The relevant required question (or questions) should be simply expressed. Neither they, nor anything else which appears on the voting paper, should be presented in such a way as to encourage a voter to answer one way rather than another as a result of that presentation. It is not in general good practice for the union to include additional questions on the voting paper (for example, asking if voters agree with the union's opinion on the merits of the dispute or are prepared to 'support' industrial action), but if it chooses to do so they should be clearly separate from the required question(s).

32. The following words must appear on every voting paper—
'If you take part in a strike or other industrial action, you may be in breach of your contract of employment. However, if you are dismissed for taking part in a strike or other industrial action which is called officially and is otherwise lawful, the dismissal will be unfair if it takes place fewer than eight weeks after you started taking part in the action, and depending on the circumstances may be unfair if it takes place later.'
This statement must not be qualified or commented upon by anything else on the voting paper.

33.   An example voting paper containing the information required by law and other useful information is set out in **Annex 2** to this Code. Factual information as indicated would appear in the square brackets and either or both questions could be used as appropriate.

Printing and distribution of the voting papers

34.   The union will wish to ensure that arrangements for producing and distributing voting papers will prevent mistakes which might invalidate the ballot. If in doubt, the independent scrutineer may be able to provide useful advice.

35. If there is no independent scrutineer, or if a union decides that it cannot follow the advice offered by the scrutineer, it should consider—
- printing the voting papers on a security background to prevent duplication;
- whether the arrangements proposed for printing (or otherwise producing) the voting papers, and for their distribution to those entitled to vote in the ballot, offer all concerned sufficient assurance of security.

Communication with members

36. A union should give relevant information to its members entitled to vote in the ballot, including (so far as practicable)—
- the background to the ballot and the issues to which the dispute relates,
- the nature and timing of the industrial action the union proposes to organise if a majority vote 'Yes';
- any considerations in respect of turnout or size of the majority vote in the ballot that will be taken into account in deciding whether to call for industrial action; and
- the possible consequences for workers if they take industrial action.

In doing so, the union should ensure that any information it gives to members in connection with the ballot is accurate and not misleading.

SECTION D
HOLDING AN INDUSTRIAL ACTION BALLOT

37. In an industrial action ballot—
- every person entitled to vote must be allowed to do so without interference from, or constraint imposed by, the union or any of its members, officials or employees;
- as far as reasonably practicable, every person entitled to vote must be—
  — sent a voting paper by post to his home address, or another address which he has asked the union (in writing) to treat as his postal address;
  — given a convenient opportunity to vote; and
  — allowed to do so without incurring any direct cost to himself (see also *paragraph 26*); and
- as far as reasonably practicable, the ballot must be conducted in such a way as to ensure that those voting do so in secret.

Checks on number of voting papers for return

38. In order to reduce the risk of failures to satisfy the statutory requirements and invalidating the ballot, the union should establish an appropriate checking system so that—
- no-one properly entitled to vote is accidentally disenfranchised, for example through the use of an out of date or otherwise inaccurate membership list; and
- votes from anyone not properly entitled to vote are excluded.

The independent scrutineer may provide advice on this.

Ensuring secrecy of voting

39. Any list of those entitled to vote should be compiled, and the voting papers themselves handled, so as to preserve the anonymity of the voter so far as this is consistent with the proper conduct of the ballot.

40. Steps should be taken to ensure that a voter's anonymity is preserved when a voting paper is returned. This means, for example, that—

- envelopes in which voting papers are to be posted should have no distinguishing marks from which the identity of the voter could be established, and
- the procedures for counting voting papers should not prejudice the statutory requirement for secret voting.

SECTION E
FOLLOWING AN INDUSTRIAL ACTION BALLOT

41.   The union must—
- ensure that the votes given in an industrial action ballot are fairly and accurately counted;
- observe its obligations in connection with the notification of details of the result of an industrial action ballot to all those entitled to vote in the ballot and their employers; and
- provide a copy of the scrutineer's report on the ballot to anyone entitled to receive it.

An inaccuracy in the counting of the votes is to be disregarded if it is both accidental and on a scale which could not affect the result of the ballot. Whether an accidental inaccuracy meets this test in practice will depend on the closeness of the ballot result.

Counting votes accurately and fairly
42.   Where the union itself is conducting the ballot, it may wish to apply some or all of the following procedures to secure that the statutory requirements have been complied with—
- ensuring all unused or unissued voting papers are retained only for so long as is necessary after the time allowed for voting has passed to allow the necessary information for checking the number of voting papers issued and used to be prepared, and that a record is kept of such voting papers when they are destroyed;
- rejection of completed voting papers received after the official close of voting or the time set for receipt of voting papers;
- settlement well in advance of the actual ballot of the organisational arrangements for conducting the count of votes cast, and making available equipment or facilities needed in the conduct of the count to those concerned;
- storage of all voting papers received at the counting location under secure conditions from when they arrive until they are counted;
- setting clear criteria to enable those counting the votes to decide which voting papers are to be rejected as 'spoiled', and designating someone who is neither directly affected by the dispute to which the ballot relates nor a union official who regularly represents any of those entitled to vote in the ballot to adjudicate on any borderline cases;
- locking and securing the counting room during the period during which votes are to be counted whenever counting staff are not actually at work; and
- storage of voting papers, once counted, under secure conditions (i.e. so that they cannot be tampered with in any way and are available for checking if necessary) for at least 6 months after the ballot.

The union may wish to consider putting the counting exercise as a whole into the hands of the independent scrutineer.

Announcing details of the result of a ballot

43.   A union must, as soon as reasonably practicable after holding an industrial action ballot, take steps to inform all those entitled to vote, and their employer(s), of the number of—

- votes cast in the ballot;
- individuals answering 'Yes' to the required question (or questions);
- individuals answering 'No' to the required question (or questions); and
- spoiled voting papers.

Where separate workplace ballots are required (see *paragraphs 24* and *25* above), these details must be notified separately for each such workplace to those entitled to vote there.

44.   To help ensure that its result can be notified as required, the union may wish to consider, for example—

- designating a 'Returning Officer' for the centralised count of votes cast in the ballot (or separate 'Returning Officers' for counts conducted at different locations) to whom the results will be notified in the form required prior to their announcement
- organising the counting of votes in such a way that the information required to satisfy the relevant statutory requirements can be easily obtained after the counting process is over;
- using its own journals, local communications news-sheets, company or union branch noticeboards to publicise the details of the ballot result to its members; and
- checking with relevant employers that the ballot result details notified to them have arrived.

45.   Before giving the seven-day notice to employers of intended industrial action, the union must have taken the required steps to notify the relevant employer(s) of the ballot result details. Where the employees of more than one employer have been balloted, a failure to provide the required ballot result details to a particular employer or employers will mean that if the union organises industrial action by the workers of that employer or those employers it will not have the support of a ballot.

46.   If the inducement of industrial action to which the ballot relates is to be capable of being protected by the law, some part of the action must be induced and start to take place within four weeks from the date of the ballot (i.e. the last day on which votes may be cast in the ballot) or such longer period not exceeding eight weeks as the union and employer may agree. (To reduce the risk of misunderstanding, both parties may find it helpful for such agreements to be in writing.) If a ballot results in a 'Yes' vote for both a strike and action short of a strike and action short of a strike is induced and starts to take place within the relevant period, the ballot would also continue to protect strike action subsequently, and vice versa.

Obtaining, and providing copies of, the scrutineer's report

47.   Where more than 50 members are given entitlement to vote, a union must appoint an independent scrutineer, whose terms of appointment must include the production of a report on the conduct of the ballot. This report must be produced as soon as reasonably practicable after the date of the ballot, and in any event not later than four weeks after that date.

48.   The union must provide a copy of the scrutineer's report to any union member who was entitled to vote in the ballot, or any employer of such a member,

who requests one within six months of the date of the ballot. The copy must be supplied as soon as reasonably practicable, and free of charge (or on payment of a reasonable fee specified by the union).

49.   In order to reduce the risk of challenge to a ballot's compliance with the statutory requirements, a union may wish to delay any call for industrial action, following a ballot, until it has obtained the scrutineers report on the ballot.

If the union decides to authorise or endorse industrial action

50.   If the union decides to authorise or endorse industrial action following a ballot, it must take such steps as are reasonably necessary to ensure that any employer who it is reasonable for the union to believe employs workers who will be, or have been, called upon to take part in the action receives no less than seven days before the day specified in the notice as the date on which workers are intended to begin to take part in continuous action or as the first date on which they are intended to take part in discontinuous action a written notice from the union which—

- is given by any officer, official or committee of the union for whose act of inducing industrial action the union is responsible in law (an indication of whom this might cover is given in **Annex 1** to this Code);
- specifies: (i) whether the union intends the action to be 'continuous' or 'discontinuous'; and (ii) the date on which any of the workers concerned are intended to begin to take part in the action (where it is continuous action), or all the dates on which any of them are intended to take part (where it is discontinuous action);
- contains such information in the union's possession as would help the employer to make plans and bring information to the attention of those of his employees who the union intends should take part in the action; and
- states that it is a notice given for the purposes of section 234A of the 1992 Act.

Changes in the union's intentions, for example as to the dates on which action is to be taken, require further notices to be given accordingly.

51.   With the exception of the requirements relating to continuous and discontinuous action and to the need to give further notices in the event of changes in the union's intentions, the statutory requirements applying to notice of industrial action are for the most part the same as those applying to notice of industrial action ballots and the guidance in paragraphs 15–18 will be of relevance, taking account of the different circumstances.

52.   Where continuous industrial action is suspended, for example for further negotiations between the employer and union, the union must normally give the employer a further notice as in paragraphs 50 and 51 above before resuming the action. There is an exception to this requirement to give further notice, however, where the union agrees with the employer that the industrial action will cease to be authorised or endorsed with effect from a date specified in the agreement but may be authorised or endorsed again on or after another date specified in the agreement and the union—

- ceases to authorise or endorse the action with effect from the specified date; and
- subsequently re-authorises or re-endorses the action from a date on or after the originally specified date or such later date as may be agreed with the employer.

For this exception to apply, the resumed industrial action must be of the same kind as covered in the original notice. That will not be so if, for example, the later action is taken by different or additional descriptions of workers. In order to avoid misunderstanding, both parties may find it helpful for such agreements to be in writing.

Seeking union members' views after a union has authorised or endorsed industrial action

53.   There is no statutory obligation on a union to ballot, or otherwise consult, its members before it decides to call off industrial action. However, if a union decides to seek its members' views about continuing with industrial action, it may wish to apply the same standards to the process of seeking their views as are set out in this Code.

ANNEX 1
TRADE UNION LIABILITY

1.   Section 20 of the Trade Union and Labour Relations (Consolidation) Act 1992 lays down when a union is to be held responsible for the act of inducing, or threatening, a breach or interference with a contract when there is no immunity. The union will be held liable for any such act which is done, authorised or endorsed by—
- its Executive Committee, General Secretary, President;
- any person given power under the union's rules to do, authorise or endorse acts of the kind in question; or
- any committee or official of the union (whether employed by it or not).

A union will be held responsible for such an act by such a body or person regardless of any term or condition to the contrary in its own rules, or in any other contractual provision or rule of law.

2.   For these purposes—
- a 'committee of the union' is any group of persons constituted in accordance with the rules of the union;
- an 'official of the union' is any person who is an officer of the union or of a branch or section of the union or any person who is elected or appointed in accordance with the union's own rules to be a representative of its members, including any person so elected or appointed who is an employee of the same employer as the members, or one or more of the members, he is elected to represent (e.g. a shop steward); and
- an act will be treated to have been done (or authorised or endorsed) by an official if it was so done (or authorised or endorsed) by a group of persons, or any member of a group, to which an official belonged at the relevant time if the group's purposes included organising or co-ordinating industrial action.

3.   A union will not be held liable for such an act of any of its committees or officials, however, if its Executive Committee, President or General Secretary repudiates the act as soon as reasonably practicable after it has come to the attention of any of them, and the union takes the steps which the law requires to make that repudiation effective. But the union will not be considered to have 'effectively repudiated' an act if the Executive Committee, President or General Secretary subsequently behave in a manner which is inconsistent with the repudiation.

4.   The fact that a union is responsible for organising industhal action to which immunity does not apply does not prevent legal action also being taken against the individual organisers of that action.

'Immunity'

5.   A trade union which organises (i.e. authorises or endorses) industrial action without satisfying the requirements of section 226 (for balloting on industrial action), or 234A (for notice to employers of official industrial action), of the 1992 Act will have no 'immunity'. Without immunity the trade union will be at risk of legal action by (i) an employer (and/or a customer or supplier of such an employer) who suffers (or may suffer) damage as a consequence of the trade union's unlawful inducement to his workers to break or interfere with the performance of contracts; and/or (ii) any individual who is (or is likely to be) deprived of goods or services because of the industrial action. Such legal proceedings might result in a court order requiring the trade union not to proceed with, andlor desist from, the unlawful inducement of its members to take part or continue with the action, and that no member does anything after the order is made as a result of unlawful inducement prior to the making of the order.

6.   Under section 62 of the 1992 Act, a member of a trade union who claims that members of the union, including himself, are likely to be or have been induced by the union to take industrial action which does not have the support of a ballot may apply to the court for an order, which may require the trade union to take steps to ensure that there is no, or no further, unlawful inducement to members to take part or continue to take part in the action, and that no member does anything after the order is made as a result of unlawful inducement prior to the making of the order.

Contempt and other proceedings

7.   If a court order issued following legal proceedings as described in paragraphs 5 and 6 above is not obeyed, anyone who sought it can go back to court and ask that those concerned be declared in contempt of court. A union found in contempt of court may face heavy fines, or other penalties which the court may consider appropriate.

8.   In addition, any member of the union may have grounds for legal action against the union's trustees if they have caused or permitted the unlawful application of union funds or property.

ANNEX 2
EXAMPLE OF VOTING PAPER FOR BALLOT ON TAKING
INDUSTRIAL ACTION

[VOTING PAPER NUMBER]
[NAME OF THE TRADE UNION]
ARE YOU PREPARED TO TAKE PART IN INDUSTRIAL ACTION CONSIST-
ING OF A STRIKE?

YES [   ]   NO [   ]

ARE YOU PREPARED TO TAKE PART IN INDUSTRIAL ACTION SHORT OF A STRIKE (which for this purpose is defined to include overtime and call-out bans)?

YES [   ]   NO [   ]

Your union intends the following to have authority to make the call for industrial action to which this ballot relates: [DETAILS OF RELEVANT PERSON, PERSONS, AND/OR CLASS OR CLASSES OF PERSONS]

If your vote is to count, this voting paper must be returned to [FULL ADDRESS OF LOCATION TO WHICH THE VOTING PAPER IS TO BE RETURNED] by [FULL DATE AND TIME AS APPROPRIATE]. Please use the enclosed pre-paid envelope provided for this purpose.

The independent scrutineer for this ballot is [DETAILS OF RELEVANT PERSON].

The law requires your union to ensure that your vote is accurately and fairly counted and that you are able to vote without interference from the union or any of its members, officials or employees and, so far as is reasonably practicable, in secret.

If you take part in a strike or other industrial action, you may be in breach of your contract of employment. However, if you are dismissed for taking part in a strike or other industrial action which is called officially and is otherwise lawful, the dismissal will be unfair if it takes place fewer than eight weeks after you started taking part in the action, and depending on the circumstances may be unfair if it takes place later.

ANNEX 3
INFORMATION TO BE GIVEN TO EMPLOYERS

The following paragraphs of the Code deal with requirements to provide information to employers—

	Paragraphs
Ballot notice	14–18
Sample voting papers	19–20
Results of the ballot	43–45
Scrutineer's report on the conduct of the ballot	48
Notice of intention to authorise or endorse industrial action or resume suspended industrial action	50–51

Appendix 6
Code of Practice
Access to Workers during Recognition
and Derecognition Ballots

PREAMBLE

The legal framework within which this Code will operate is explained in its text. While every effort has been made to ensure that explanations included in the Code are accurate, only the courts can give authoritative interpretations of the law.

The Code's provisions apply equally to men and to women, but for simplicity the masculine pronoun is used throughout.

Unless the text specifies otherwise, (i) the term 'union' should be read to mean 'unions' in cases where two or more unions are seeking to be jointly recognised; (ii) the term 'workplace' should be read to mean 'workplaces' in cases where a recognition application covers more than one workplace, and (iii) the term 'working day' should be read to mean any day other than a Saturday or a Sunday, Christmas Day or Good Friday, or a day which is a bank holiday.

Passages in this Code which appear in italics are extracts from, or re-statements of, provisions in primary legislation.

SECTION A
INTRODUCTION

Background

1. Schedule A1 of the Trade Union and Labour Relations (Consolidation) Act 1992, inserted by the Employment Relations Act 1999, sets out the statutory procedure for the recognition and derecognition of trade unions for the purpose of collective bargaining.

Recognition

2. Where an employer and a trade union fail to reach agreement on recognition voluntarily, the statute provides for the union to apply to the Central Arbitration Committee (CAC) to decide whether it should be recognised for collective bargaining purposes. in certain cases, the CAC may award recognition, or dismiss the application, without a ballot. In other cases, the CAC will be obliged to hold a secret ballot of members of the bargaining unit to determine the issue. If a ballot takes place, the CAC will decide whether it should be held at the workplace, by post, or, if special

factors make it appropriate, by a combination of the two methods. The ballot must be conducted by a qualified independent person appointed by the CAC.

3.   Paragraph 26(2) of Schedule A1 places a duty on the employer *to co-operate generally, in connection with the ballot, with the union and the independent person appointed to conduct the ballot.*

4.   Paragraph 26(3) of Schedule A1 places a duty on the employer to give a union applying for recognition *such access to the workers constituting the bargaining unit as is reasonable to enable the union to inform the workers of the object of the ballot and to seek their support and their opinions on the issues involved.*

5.   Section 203(1)(a) of the Trade Union and Labour Relations (Consolidation) Act 1992 gives a general power to the Secretary of State to issue Codes of Practice containing practical guidance for the purpose of promoting the improvement of industrial relations. Paragraph 26(8)(b) of Schedule A1 specifies that this general power includes the particular power to issue a Code of Practice giving practical guidance about reasonable access during recognition ballots for the purposes of paragraph 26(3).

Derecognition

6.   The CAC can also call a derecognition ballot in cases where an employer, or his workers, are seeking to end recognition arrangements with a union. Paragraph 118(3) of Schedule A1 contains identical wording to paragraph 26(3) of Schedule A1, placing a duty on the employer to give the recognised union reasonable access to the workers comprising the bargaining unit where the CAC is holding a ballot on derecognition. Paragraph 118(8)(b) contains a similar provision to paragraph 26(8)(b) enabling the Secretary of State to issue a Code of Practice giving practical guidance about reasonable access during derecognition ballots.

7.   The guidance contained in this Code applies equally to cases where the ballot is about recognition or derecognition.

General purpose of the Code

8.   This Code gives practical guidance about the issues which arise when an employer receives a request by a union to be granted access to his workers at their workplace and/or during their working time. It does not cover other forms of access outside the employer's control away from the workplace or outside working hours. For example, it does not discuss how the union might use other means, such as local newspapers or media, to put across its message to the workers involved. This Code deals with the specific circumstances of access during the period of recognition or derecognition ballots. It does not provide guidance on access at other times.

9.   Access can take many and varied forms depending largely on the type of workplace involved and the characteristics of the balloted workforce. The overall aim is to ensure that the union can reach the workers involved, but local circumstances will need to be taken into account when deciding what form the access should take. Each case should be looked at on the facts. This Code therefore aims to help the employer and the union arrive at agreed arrangements for access, which can take full account of the circumstances of each individual case.

10.   This Code also aims to encourage reasonable and responsible behaviour by both the employer and the union. This should ensure that acrimony between the parties is avoided and individual workers are not exposed to intimidation or threat.

As regards the treatment of individuals, both parties should note that the law provides protections against dismissal or detriment for workers who campaign either for or against recognition.

11.   In order for a ballot to take place, the union must have satisfied the CAC that at least 10 per cent of the proposed bargaining unit are already members of the union, and that a majority of the workers in the proposed bargaining unit would be likely to favour recognition. There is therefore a good chance that recognition will be granted to the union, and that a working relationship between the parties will have to be sustained after the ballot. This longer term perspective should encourage both the employer and the union to behave responsibly and in a co-operative spirit during the balloting period.

Legal status of the Code

12.   *Under paragraphs 27 and 119 of Schedule A1 to the Trade Union and Labour Relations (Consolidation) Act 1992, the CAC may order employers who are breaching their duty to allow reasonable access, to take specified, reasonable steps to do so, and can award recognition without a ballot, or can refuse to award derecognition where applied for by the employer, if an employer fails to abide by its orders to remedy a breach.*

13.   *This Code itself imposes no legal obligations and failure to observe it does not in itself render anyone liable to proceedings. But section 207 of the Trade Union and Labour Relations (Consolidation) Act 1992 provides that any provisions of this Code are to be admissible in evidence and are to be taken into account in proceedings before any court, tribunal or the CAC where they consider them relevant.*

SECTION B
PREPARING FOR ACCESS

When should preparations for access begin?

14.   Preparations for access should begin as soon as possible. The CAC is required to give notice to the employer and the union that it intends to arrange for the holding of a ballot. There then follows a period of ten working days before the CAC proceeds with arrangements for the ballot. The parties should make full use of this notification period to prepare for access. The union should request an early meeting with the employer in this period to discuss access arrangements. The employer should agree to arrange the meeting on an early date and at a mutually convenient time. The employer and the union should ensure that the individual or individuals representing them at the meeting are expressly authorised by them to take all relevant decisions regarding access, or are authorised to make recommendations directly to those who take such decisions.

Joint applications by two or more unions

15.   Where there is a joint application for recognition by two or more unions acting together, the unions should act jointly in preparing and implementing the access arrangements. Therefore, unless the employer and the unions agree otherwise, the unions should have common access arrangements. The amount of time needed for access would normally be the same for single or joint applications.

Establishing an access agreement

16.   It would be reasonable for the employer to want to give his prior permission before allowing a full time union official to enter his workplace and talk to his

workers. In particular, the employer may have security and health and safety issues to consider. The parties should discuss practical arrangements for the union's activities at the workplace, in advance of the period of access actually beginning.

17.   Consideration should be given to establishing an agreement, preferably in written form, on access arrangements. Such an agreement could include:
• the union's programme for where, when and how it will access the workers on site and/or during their working time; and
• a mechanism for resolving disagreements, if any arise, about implementing the agreed programme of access.

18.   In seeking to reach an agreement, the union should put its proposals for accessing the workers to the employer. The employer should not dismiss the proposals unless he considers the union's requirements to be unreasonable in the circumstances. If the employer rejects the proposals, he should offer alternative arrangements to the union at the earliest opportunity, preferably within three working days of receiving the union's initial proposals. In the course of this dialogue the union will need to reveal its plans for on-site access.

19.   It is reasonable for the union to request information from the employer to help it formulate and refine its access proposals. In particular, the employer should disclose to the union information about his typical methods of communicating with his workforce and provide such other practical information as may be needed about, say, workplace premises or patterns of work. Where relevant to the union in framing its plans, the employer should also disclose information about his own plans to put across his views, directly or indirectly, to the workers about the recognition (or derecognition) of the union. The employer should not, however, disclose to the union the names or addresses (postal or e-mail) of the workers who will be balloted, unless the workers concerned have authorised the disclosure.

Amending the access agreement

20.   Every effort should be made to ensure access agreements are faithfully implemented. However, in some cases, the agreement may need to be changed if circumstances alter. For example, a union official selected to enter the workplace may be unexpectedly called away by his union on other urgent business. Likewise, the employer might wish to re-arrange an event if the selected meeting-room is unexpectedly and unavoidably needed for other important business purposes. If such circumstances arise, the union, or the employer if his situation changes, should notify the other party at the earliest opportunity that a change will need to be made to the agreed access arrangements, and offer alternative suggestions. The other party should generally accept the alternative arrangements, if they are of an equivalent nature to those already agreed.

Resolving differences about agreeing access arrangements

21.   Where the employer and the union fail to agree access arrangements voluntarily, either party, acting separately or together, may ask the Advisory, Conciliation and Arbitration Service (ACAS) to conciliate. Given the limited time available, ACAS will respond to the conciliation request as soon as possible, and preferably within one working day of receiving the request. Both parties should give all reasonable assistance to ACAS to enable it to help the parties overcome their difficulties through conciliation.

22.   Every effort should be made to resolve any procedural difficulties remaining, but, ultimately, where it remains deadlocked, the CAC may be asked to assist. The CAC could, in appropriate circumstances, consider delaying the arrangement of the ballot for a limited period to give extra time for the parties to settle their differences. However, where no agreement is forthcoming, the CAC may be asked to adjudicate and to make an order.

SECTION C
ACCESS IN OPERATION

What is the access period?

23.   *Following the notification period, and providing it does not receive a contrary request from the trade union, the CAC will be required to arrange the holding of the ballot. As soon as is reasonably practicable, the CAC must inform the parties of the fact that it is arranging the ballot, the name of the qualified independent person appointed to conduct the ballot, and the period within which the ballot must be conducted. The ballot must be held within 20 working days from the day after the appointment of the independent person, or longer if the CAC should so decide.*

24.   The period of access will begin as soon as the parties have been informed of the arrangements for the ballot as in paragraph 23 above. The CAC will endeavour to inform both parties as soon as the independent person has been appointed. This may be achieved by a telephone call to both parties, followed by a letter of confirmation.

25.   If the ballot is to be conducted by post, the period of access will come to an end on the closing date of the balloting period. If the ballot is to be conducted at the workplace, access will continue until the ballot has closed. However, where the ballot is to be conducted at the workplace, and where the union has already had adequate access opportunities, both the employer and the union should largely confine their activities during the actual hours of balloting to the encouragement of workers to vote. They should reduce or cease other campaigning activity at this time. For example, both the employer and the union should avoid scheduling large meetings at such times. This should ensure that the ballot is conducted in a calm and orderly fashion, with minimum disruption to the normal functioning of the workplace.

Who may be granted access?

26.   The access agreement should specify who should be given access to the workers who will be balloted. Employers should be prepared to give access to:

(a)   individual union members employed by the employer, who are nominated by the union as the lead representative of their members at workplaces where the bargaining unit is situated;

(b)   individual union members employed by the employer, who are nominated by the union as the lead representative of their members at other workplaces in the employer's business, provided that it is practicable for them to attend events at workplaces where the bargaining unit is situated. The costs of travelling from other workplaces should be met by the individuals or the union; and

(c)   'full-time' union officials. (That is, individuals employed by the union, who are officials of the union within the meaning of the sections 1 and 119 of the Trade Union and Labour Relations (Consolidation) Act 1992).

The number of union representatives entitled to gain access should be proportionate to the scale and nature of the activities or events organised within the agreed access programme.

Where will the access take place?

27.   Where practicable in the circumstances, a union should be granted access to the workers at their actual workplace. However, each case will depend largely on the type of workplace concerned, and the union will need to take account of the wide variety of circumstances and operational requirements that are likely to be involved. In particular, consideration will need to be given to the employer's responsibility for health and safety and security issues. In other words, access arrangements should reflect local circumstances and each case should be examined on the facts.

28.   Where they are suitable for the purpose, the employer's typical methods of communicating with his workforce should be used as a benchmark for determining how the union should communicate with members of the same workforce during the access period. If the employer follows the custom and practice of holding large workforce meetings in, for example, a meeting room or a canteen, then the employer should make the same facilities available to the union. However, in cases where the workplace is more confined, and it is therefore the employer's custom and practice to hold only small meetings at the workplace, then the union will also be limited to holding similar small meetings at that workplace. In exceptional circumstances, due to the nature of the business or severe space limitations, access may need to be restricted to meetings away from the workplace premises, and the union will need to consider finding facilities off-site at its own expense unless it agrees otherwise with the employer. In these circumstances, the employer should give all reasonable assistance to the union in notifying the workers in advance of where and when such off-site events are to take place. Where such exceptional circumstances exist, it would normally be expected that the employer would not hold similar events at the workplace.

When will the access take place?

29.   The union should ensure that disruption to the business is minimised, especially for small businesses which might find it more difficult to organise cover for absent workers. The union's access to the workers should usually take place during normal working hours but at times which minimise any possible disruption to the activities of the employer. This will ensure that the union is able to communicate with as large a number of the workers as possible. Again, the arrangements should reflect the circumstances of each individual case. Consideration should be given to holding events, particularly those involving a large proportion of the workers in the bargaining unit, during rest periods or towards the end of a shift. In deciding the timing of meetings and other events, the union and the employer should be guided by the employer's custom and practice when communicating with his workforce. If, due to exceptional circumstances, access must be arranged away from the workplace, it might be practicable to arrange events in work time if they are held nearby, within easy walking distance. Otherwise, off-site events should normally occur outside work time.

The frequency and duration of union activities

30.   The parties will need to establish agreed limits on the duration and frequency of the union's activities during the access period. Subject to the circumstances

discussed in paragraphs 27–29 above, the employer should allow the union to hold one meeting of at least 30 minutes in duration for every 10 days of the access period, or part thereof, which all workers or a substantial proportion of them are given the opportunity to attend. In circumstances where the employer or others organise similar large-scale meetings in work time against the recognition application (or in favour of derecognition), then it would be reasonable for the union to hold additional meetings, if necessary, to ensure that in total it has the same number of large-scale meetings as the employer and his supporters.

31. Where they would be appropriate having regard to all the circumstances, union 'surgeries' could be organised at the workplace during working hours at which each worker would have the opportunity, if they wish, to meet a union representative for fifteen minutes on an individual basis or in small groups of two or three. The circumstances would include whether there was a demand from the workforce for surgeries, whether the surgeries could be arranged off-site as effectively, whether the holding of surgeries would lead to an unacceptable increase in tension at the workplace and whether the employer, line managers or others use similar one-to-one or small meetings to put across the employer's case. The union should organise surgeries in a systematic way, ensuring that workers attend meetings at pre-determined times, thereby avoiding delays before workers are seen and ensuring that they promptly return to their work stations afterwards. Wherever practicable, the union should seek to arrange surgeries during periods of down-time such as rest or meal breaks. Where surgeries do not take place, the minimum time allowed for each larger scale meeting should be 45 minutes.

32. An employer should ensure that workers who attend a meeting or a 'surgery' organised by the union with his agreement during work time, should be paid, in full, for the duration of their absence from work. The employer will not be expected to pay the worker if the meeting or surgery takes place when the worker would not otherwise have been at work, and would not have been receiving payment from the employer.

33. Where the union wishes one of the employer's workers within the meaning of paragraphs 26(a) and 26(b) above to conduct a surgery, the employer should normally give time off with pay to the worker concerned. The worker should ensure that he provides the employer with as much notice as possible, giving details about the timing and location of the surgery. Exceptionally, it may be reasonable for the employer to refuse time off. This will apply if unavoidable situations arise where there is no adequate cover for the workep. s absence from the workplace and the production process, or the provision of a service cannot otherwise be maintained. Before refusing permission, the employer should discuss the matter with the union and the worker to explore alternative arrangements.

What about written communication?

34. The union may want to display written material at the place of work. Employers, where practicable, should provide a notice board for the union's use. This notice board should be in a prominent location in the workplace and the union should be able to display material, including references to off-site meetings, without interference from the employer. Often, an existing notice-board could be used for this purpose. The union should also be able to place additional material near to the notice-board including, for example, copies of explanatory leaflets, which the

workers may read or take away with them. If there are no union representatives within the meaning of paragraphs 26(a) and 26(b) above present at the workplace, the employer should allow access to a full time official of the union to display the material.

35.   The union may also wish to make use of its web-site pages on the internet for campaigning purposes. An employer should allow his workers access to the union's material in the same way that he explicitly, or tacitly, allows his workers to down-load information in connection with activities not directly related to the performance of their job. If an employer generally disallows all such internet use, he should consider giving permission to one of his workers nominated by the union to down-load the material, and it would be this person's responsibility to disseminate it more widely among other workers.

36.   A nominated union representative employed by the employer may also want to make use of internal electronic communication, such as electronic mail or intranets, for campaigning purposes. For example, he may want to remind workers of forthcoming union meetings or surgeries. The employer should allow the representative to make reasonable use of these systems if the employer explicitly, or tacitly, allows his workers to use them for matters which are not directly related to the performance of their job. In cases where such use is disallowed, it would still be reasonable for the representative to use them, if the employer uses such forms of communication to send to the workers information against the union's case. When sending messages in this capacity, the representative should make it clear that the advice comes from the union and not the employer.

What about small businesses?

37.   Access arrangements for small businesses need not necessarily create difficulties. For example, it may be easier to arrange for a smaller number of workers to meet together. On the other hand, there may be difficulties providing cover for workers in smaller organisations, or in finding accommodation for meetings. In such cases, the employer and the union should try to reach an understanding about how access arrangements can be organised to ensure minimum disruption. Agreements may need to be flexible to accommodate any particular needs of the employer.

Arrangements for non-typical workers

38.   Many, or sometimes most, workers in a bargaining unit may not work full time in a standard Monday–Friday working week. Others might rarely visit the employer's premises. The employer should bear in mind the difficulties faced by unions in communicating with—

- shift workers
- part-time workers
- homeworkers
- a dispersed or peripatetic workforce
- those on maternity or parental leave
- those on sick leave.

39.   The employer should be receptive to a union's suggestions for securing reasonable access to such 'non-typical workers', and allow them, where practicable, to achieve a broadly equivalent level of access to those workers as to typical workers. It would be reasonable for the union to organise its meetings or surgery arrangements

on a more flexible basis to cover shift workers or part-time workers. An employer should agree to the maximum flexibility of arrangements, where reasonable in the circumstances. This would not extend to an employer being obliged to meet the travel costs of his workers attending meetings arranged by the union.

40.   In addition, the union will be able to make use of the independent person to distribute information to home addresses via the postal service. This will ensure that literature will be received by any workers who are not likely to attend the workplace during the access period, for example those on maternity or sick leave. The CAC will supply the name, address and telephone number of the independent person to both the union and the employer.

What about joint employer/union activities?

41.   There may be scope for the union and the employer to undertake joint activities where they both put across their respective views about recognition or derecognition in a non-confrontational way. Such joint activities can be an efficient method of providing information, minimising business disruption and costs. For example, the parties may wish to consider—
- the arrangement of joint meetings with each party allocated a period of thirty minutes to address the workers; and
- the use of a joint notice-board where an equal amount of space is devoted to the employer and the union.

SECTION D
GENERAL RESPONSIBILITIES OF EMPLOYERS AND TRADE UNIONS

Observing an access agreement

42.   Both parties should ensure they keep to agreements about access arrangements. For example, if the parties agree to hold a meeting lasting 30 minutes in duration, every effort should be made to ensure that the meeting does not over-run its allocated time. Likewise, neither party should remove, or tamper with, material placed on a notice board by the other party, unless they are obliged to do so for legal reasons.

Avoiding acrimonious situations

43.   Both parties should endeavour to ensure that, wherever possible, potentially acrimonious situations are avoided throughout the period of access. In particular, the parties should avoid—
- using defamatory material or provocative propaganda,
- personal attacks or personalised negative campaigning against individuals;
- the harassment or intimidation of individuals,
- issuing threats,
- placing pressure on workers to reveal their voting intentions; and
- behaviour likely to cause unnecessary offence.

44.   The employer and the union should also dissociate themselves from material containing personal attacks or allegations which is circulated on an anonymous basis. The party whose case appears to be favoured by the anonymous material should formally repudiate it, informing all workers in the bargaining unit accordingly.

Behaving responsibly

45.   For access arrangements to work satisfactorily, the employer and the union should behave responsibly, and give due consideration to the requirements of the

other party throughout the access period. For example, neither the union nor the employer should seek to disrupt or interfere with meetings being held by the other party. If one party is holding a large meeting, the other should avoid the scheduling of other conflicting meetings or events, and should not attempt to distract attention from the business of the meeting.

46.   Where it is practicable to hold meetings or surgeries at the workplace, the employer should provide appropriate accommodation, fit for the purpose, which should include adequate heating and lighting, and arrangements to ensure that the meeting is held in private. In turn, the union should ensure that business costs and business disruption are minimised. Unions should be aware of the needs of the employer to maintain the production process, to maintain a level of service, and to ensure safety and security at all times.

SECTION E
NON-COMPLIANCE WITH ACCESS PROVISIONS

Intervention by the CAC

47.   Disputes may arise between the parties during the access period about the failure to allow reasonable access or to implement access agreements. If these disputes cannot be resolved, the union may ask the CAC to decide whether the employer has failed to perform his statutory duties in relation to the ballot.

48.   *If the CAC is satisfied that the employer has failed to perform one or more of its three duties:*

(a)   *to co-operate generally with the union and the independent person on the ballot,*

(b)   to give the union such access to the workers constituting the bargaining unit as is reasonable to inform them of the object of the ballot and to seek their support and opinions, and

(c)   *to provide the CAC with the names and home addresses of those workers, and the ballot has not been held, the CAC may order the employer to take such steps to remedy the failure as the CAC considers reasonable, and within a time that the CAC considers reasonable.* Where the CAC is asked to make an order very shortly before the end of the access period, it may be impracticable for the CAC to consider the request and for the employer and the union to remedy any failure in the short time before the ballot is held. In such circumstances, the CAC may extend the access period by ordering the ballot to be rescheduled for a later date to ensure that access is achieved.

49.   *If the employer fails to comply with the CAC's order within the time specified, and the ballot has still not been held, the CAC may issue a declaration that the union is recognised, or that the union is not derecognised.*

50.   The law does not provide for employers to complain to the CAC about the union's behaviour in relation to access. However, in deciding whether the employer has complied with his duty to give the union access, the CAC may take into account all relevant circumstances. This may include the behaviour of the union. The CAC may therefore decide that the employer has complied with the duty in circumstances where, because the union has acted unreasonably, he denies the union access or refuses to implement agreed access arrangements.

Minor disputes

51. Some disputes may be minor by nature. For example, the employer may be aggrieved that a meeting has over-run somewhat. On the other hand, a union might have cause to complain if it regards the meeting room provided by the employer as being too small to accommodate everyone in comfort. In such cases, both parties should avoid taking hasty action which might prejudice the implementation of other access arrangements. The union should generally avoid taking minor complaints to the CAC as a first course of action.

52. Instead, the parties should make every effort to resolve the dispute between themselves. They should make full use of any mechanism to resolve such disputes which they may have established in the access agreement, and consider the use of ACAS's conciliation services. It would generally be a good practice if both the employer and the union nominated a person to act as their lead contact if disagreements or questions arose about the implementation of access arrangements.

53. The period of access will be limited in duration, given that the balloting period will normally be a maximum of 20 working days, and the parties should therefore ensure that disputes are swiftly resolved. The parties should endeavour to inform each other immediately if a dispute arises, and should seek to resolve any disputes as a matter of priority, preferably within one working day of their occurrence.

The independent person

54. The prime duties of the independent person are to ensure that—
- the names and addresses of the workers comprising the balloting constituency are accurate;
- the ballot is conducted properly and in secret; and
- the CAC is promptly informed of the ballot result.

It is not the function of the independent person to adjudicate disputes about access. That is the CAC's role. However, the independent person may have wide experience and knowledge of balloting arrangements in different settings. The parties might consider informing the independent person about their problems and draw on his experience to identify possible options to resolve their difficulties.

Appendix 7
Trade Union Recognition (Method of Collective Bargaining) Order 2000

TERMS AND CONDITIONS OF EMPLOYMENT

Whereas—

(1) under paragraph 168(1) of Schedule A1 to the Trade Union and Labour Relations (Consolidation) Act 1992 the Secretary of State, after consulting the Advisory Conciliation and Arbitration Service, may by order specify for the purposes of paragraphs 31(3) and 63(2) of that Schedule a method by which collective bargaining might be conducted; and

(2) in accordance with the said paragraph 168(1), the Secretary of State consulted the Advisory, Conciliation and Arbitration Service on a draft containing proposals for the said method;

Now, therefore, the Secretary of State, in exercise of the powers conferred on him by paragraph 168(1) of Schedule A1 to the Trade Union and Labour Relations (Consolidation) Act 1992, hereby makes the following Order:

1. Citation and Commencement

This Order may be cited as the Trade Union Recognition (Method of Collective Bargaining) Order 2000 and comes into force on 6 June 2000.

2. Specification of method

The method specified for the purposes of paragraphs 31(3) and 63(2) of Schedule A1 to the Trade Union and Labour Relations (Consolidation) Act 1992 is the method set out under the heading 'the specified method' in the Schedule to this Order.

Article 2   THE SCHEDULE
                                   PREAMBLE

The method specified below ('the specified method') is one by which collective bargaining might be conducted in the particular, and possibly rare, circumstances discussed in the following paragraph. The specified method is not designed to be applied as a model for voluntary procedural agreements between employers and unions. Because most voluntary agreements are not legally binding and are usually concluded in a climate of trust and co-operation, they do not need to be as prescriptive as the specified method. However, the Central Arbitration Committee ('CAC') must take the specified method into account when exercising its powers to impose a method of collective bargaining under paragraphs 31(3) and 63(2) of Schedule A1 to the Trade Union and Labour Relations (Consolidation) Act 1992. In exercising those powers the CAC may depart from the specified method to such extent as it thinks appropriate in the circumstances of individual cases.

Paragraph 31(3) provides for the CAC to impose a method of collective bargaining in cases where a union (or unions, where two or more unions act jointly) has been recognised by an employer by means of an award of the CAC under Part I of Schedule A1, but the employer and union(s) have been unable to agree a method of bargaining between themselves, or have failed to follow an agreed method. Paragraph 63(2) provides for the CAC to impose a bargaining method in cases where an employer and a union (or unions) have entered an agreement for recognition, as defined by paragraph 52 of Part II of Schedule A1, but cannot agree a method of bargaining, or have failed to follow the agreed method.

The bargaining method imposed by the CAC has effect as if it were a legally binding contract between the employer and the union(s). If one party believes the other is failing to respect the method, the first party may apply to the court for an order of specific performance, ordering the other party to comply with the method. Failure to comply with such an order could constitute contempt of court.

Once the CAC has imposed a bargaining method, the parties can vary it, including the fact that it is legally binding, by agreement provided that they do so in writing.

The fact that the CAC has imposed a method does not affect the rights of individual workers under either statute or their contracts of employment. For example, it does not prevent or limit the rights of individual workers to discuss, negotiate or agree with their employer terms of their contract of employment, which differ from the terms of any collective agreement into which the employer and the union may enter as a result of collective bargaining conducted by this method. Nor does the imposed method affect an individual's statutory entitlement to time off for trade union activities or duties.

In cases where the CAC imposes a bargaining method on the parties, the employer is separately obliged, in accordance with Section 70B of the Trade Union and Labour Relations (Consolidation) Act 1992 (as inserted by section 5 of the Employment Relations Act 1999), to consult union representatives periodically on his policy, actions and plans on training. The specified method does not discuss how such consultations should be organised.

The law confers certain entitlements on independent trade unions which are recognised for collective bargaining purposes. For example, employers must disclose, on request, certain types of information to the representatives of the recognised unions. The fact that the CAC has imposed a bargaining method does not affect these existing statutory entitlements.

THE SPECIFIED METHOD

The Parties

1.   The method shall apply in each case to two parties, who are referred to here as the 'employer' and the 'union'. Unless the text specifies otherwise, the term 'union' should be read to mean 'unions' in cases where two or more unions are jointly recognised.

The Purpose

2.   The purpose is to specify a method by which the employer and the union conduct collective bargaining concerning the pay, hours and holidays of the workers comprising the bargaining unit.

3.   The employer shall not grant the right to negotiate pay, hours and holidays to any other union in respect of the workers covered by this method.

The Joint Negotiating Body

4.   The employer and the union shall establish a Joint Negotiating Body (JNB) to discuss and negotiate the pay, hours and holidays of the workers comprising the bargaining unit. No other body or group shall undertake collective bargaining on the pay, hours and holidays of these workers, unless the employer and the union so agree.

JNB Membership

5.   The membership of the JNB shall usually comprise three employer representatives (who together shall constitute the Employer Side of the JNB) and three union representatives (who together shall constitute the Union Side of the JNB). Each union recognised by the employer in respect of the bargaining unit shall be entitled to one seat at least. To meet this requirement, the Union Side may need to be larger than three and in this eventuality the employer shall be entitled to increase his representation on the JNB by the same number, if he wishes.

6.   The employer shall select those individuals who comprise the Employer Side. The individuals must either be those who take the final decisions within the employer's organisation in respect of the pay, hours and holidays of the workers in the bargaining unit or who are expressly authorised by the employer to make recommendations directly to those who take such final decisions. Unless it would be unreasonable to do so, the employer shall select as a representative the most senior person responsible for employment relations in the bargaining unit.

7.   The union shall select those individuals who comprise the Union Side in accordance with its own rules and procedures. The representatives must either be individuals employed by the employer or individuals employed by the union who are officials of the union within the meaning of sections 1 and 119 of the Trade Union and Labour Relations (Consolidation) Act 1992 ('the 1992 Act').

8.   The JNB shall determine their own rules in respect of the attendance at JNB meetings of observers and substitutes who deputise for JNB members.

Officers

9.   The Employer Side shall select one of its members to act as its Chairman and one to act as its Secretary. The Union Side shall select one of its members to act as its Chairman and one to act as its Secretary. The same person may perform the roles of Chairman and Secretary of a Side.

10.   For the twelve months from the date of the JNB's first meeting, meetings of the JNB shall be chaired by the Chairman of the Employer Side. The Chairman of the Union Side shall chair the JNB's meetings for the following twelve months. The chairmanship of JNB meetings will alternate in the same way thereafter at intervals of twelve months. In the absence of the person who should chair JNB meetings, a JNB meeting shall be chaired by another member of that person's Side.

11. The Secretary of the Employer Side shall act as Secretary to the JNB. He shall circulate documentation and agendas in advance of JNB meetings, arrange suitable accommodation for meetings, notify members of meetings and draft the written record of JNB meetings. The Secretary of the Employer Side shall work closely with the Secretary of the Union Side in the discharge of these duties, disclosing full information about his performance of these tasks.

JNB Organisation

12. Draft agendas shall be circulated at least three working days in advance of JNB meetings. The draft record of JNB meetings shall be circulated within ten working days of the holding of meetings for approval at the next JNB meeting. The record does not need to be a verbatim account, but should fully describe the conclusions reached and the actions to be taken.

13. Subject to the timetable of meetings stipulated in paragraphs 15, 17, 20 and 28 below, the date, timing and location of meetings shall be arranged by the JNB's Secretary, in full consultation with the Secretary of the Union Side, to ensure maximum attendance at meetings. A meeting of the JNB shall be quorate if 50 per cent or more of each Side's members (or, where applicable, their substitutes) are in attendance.

Bargaining Procedure

14. The union's proposals for adjustments to pay, hours and holidays shall be dealt with on an annual basis, unless the two Sides agree a different bargaining period.

15. The JNB shall conduct these negotiations for each bargaining round according to the following staged procedure.

Step 1 — The union shall set out in writing, and send to the employer, its proposals (the 'claim') to vary the pay, hours and holidays, specifying which aspects it wants to change. In its claim, the union shall set out the reasons for its proposals, together with the main supporting evidence at its disposal at the time. In cases where there is no established annual date when the employer reviews the pay, hours and holidays of all the workers in the bargaining unit, the union shall put forward its first claim within three months of this method being imposed (and by the same date in subsequent rounds). Where such a common review date is established, the union shall submit its first claim at least a month in advance of that date (and by the same date in subsequent rounds). In either case, the employer and the union may agree a different date by which the claim should be submitted each year. If the union fails to submit its claim by this date, then the procedure shall be ended for the bargaining round in question. Exceptionally, the union may submit a late claim without this penalty if its work on the claim was delayed while the Central Arbitration Committee considered a relevant complaint by the union of failure by the employer to disclose information for collective bargaining purposes.

Step 2 — Within ten working days of the Employer Side's receipt of the union's letter, a quorate meeting of the JNB shall be held to discuss the claim. At this meeting, the Union Side shall explain its claim and answer any reasonable questions arising to the best of its ability.

Step 3 —

(a)   Within fifteen working days immediately following the Step 2 meeting, the employer shall either accept the claim in full or write to the union responding to its claim. If the Employer Side requests it, a quorate meeting of the JNB shall be held within the fifteen day period to enable the employer to present this written response directly to the Union Side. In explaining the basis of his response, the employer shall set out in this written communication all relevant information in his possession. In particular, the written communication shall contain information costing each element of the claim and describing the business consequences, particularly any staffing implications, unless the employer is not required to disclose such information for any of the reasons specified in section 182(1) of the 1992 Act. The basis of these estimated costs and effects, including the main assumptions that the employer has used, shall be set out in the communication. In determining what information is disclosed as relevant, the employer shall be under no greater obligation that he is under the general duty imposed on him by sections 181 and 182 of the 1992 Act to disclose information for the purposes of collective bargaining.

(b)   If the response contains any counter-proposals, the written communication shall set out the reasons for making them, together with the supporting evidence. The letter shall provide information estimating the costs and staffing consequences of implementing each element of the counter proposals, unless the employer is not required to disclose such information for any of the reasons specified in section 182(1) of the 1992 Act.

Step 4 — Within ten working days of the Union Side's receipt of the employer's written communication, a further quorate meeting of the JNB shall be held to discuss the employer's response. At this meeting, the Employer Side shall explain its response and answer any reasonable questions arising to the best of its ability.

Step 5 — If no agreement is reached at the Step 4 meeting (or the last of such meetings if more than one is held at that stage in the procedure), another quorate meeting of the JNB shall be held within ten working days. The union may bring to this meeting a maximum of two other individuals employed by the union who are officials within the meaning of the sections 1 and 119 of the 1992 Act. The employer may bring to the meeting a maximum of two other individuals who are employees or officials of an employer's organisation to which the employer belongs. These additional persons shall be allowed to contribute to the meeting, as if they were JNB members.

Step 6 — If no agreement is reached at the Step 5 meeting (or the last of such meetings if more than one meeting is held at that stage in the procedure), within five working days the employer and the union shall consider, separately or jointly, consulting ACAS about the prospect of ACAS helping them to find a settlement of their differences through conciliation. In the event that both parties agree to invite ACAS to conciliate, both parties shall give such assistance to ACAS as is necessary to enable it to carry out the conciliation efficiently and effectively.

16.   The parties shall set aside half a working day for each JNB meeting, unless the Employer Side Chairman and the Union Side Chairman agree a different length of time for the meeting. Unless it is essential to do otherwise, meetings shall be held during the normal working time of most union members of the JNB. Meetings may be adjourned, if both Sides agree. Additional meetings at any point in the procedure may be arranged, if both Sides agree. In addition, if the Employer Side requests it, a meeting of the JNB shall be held before the union has submitted its claim or before the employer is required to respond, enabling the Employer Side to explain the business context within which the employer shall assess the claim.

17.   The employer shall not vary the contractual terms affecting the pay, hours or holidays of workers in the bargaining unit, unless he has first discussed his proposals with the union. Such proposals shall normally be made by the employer in the context of his consideration of the union's claim at Steps 3 or 4. If, however, the employer has not tabled his proposals during that process and he wishes to make proposals before the next bargaining round commences, he must write to the union setting out his proposals and the reasons for making them, together with the supporting evidence. The letter shall provide information estimating the costs and staffing consequences of implementing each element of the proposals, unless the employer is not required to disclose such information for any of the reasons specified in section 182(1) of the 1992 Act. A quorate meeting of the JNB shall be held within five working days of the Union Side's receipt of the letter. If there is a failure to resolve the issue at that meeting, then meetings shall be arranged, and steps shall be taken, in accordance with Steps 5 and 6 of the above procedure.

18.   Paragraph 17 does not apply to terms in the contract of an individual worker where that worker has agreed that the terms may be altered only by direct negotiation between the worker and the employer.

Collective Agreements

19.   Any agreements affecting the pay, hours and holidays of workers in the bargaining unit, which the employer and the union enter following negotiations, shall be set down in writing and signed by the Chairman of the Employer Side and by the Chairman of the Union Side or, in their absence, by another JNB member on their respective Sides.

20.   If either the employer or union consider that there has been a failure to implement the agreement, then that party can request in writing a meeting of the JNB to discuss the alleged failure. A quorate meeting shall be held within five working days of the receipt of the request by the JNB Secretary. If there is a failure to resolve the issue at that meeting, then meetings shall be arranged, and steps shall be taken, in accordance with Steps 5 and 6 of the above procedure.

Facilities and Time Off

21.   If they are employed by the employer, union members of the JNB:
— shall be given paid time off by the employer to attend JNB meetings;
— shall be given paid time off by the employer to attend a two hour pre-meeting of the Union Side before each JNB meeting; and
— shall be given paid time off by the employer to hold a day-long meeting to prepare the claim at Step 1 in the bargaining procedure.
The union members of the JNB shall schedule such meetings at times which minimise the effect on production and services. In arranging these meetings, the union members of the JNB shall provide the employer and their line management with as much notice as possible and give details of the purpose of the time off, the intended location of the meeting and the timing and duration of the time off. The employer shall provide adequate heating and lighting for these meetings, and ensure that they are held in private.

22.   If they are not employed by the employer, union members of the JNB or other union officials attending JNB meetings shall be given sufficient access to the employer's premises to allow them to attend Union Side pre-meetings, JNB meetings and meetings of the bargaining unit as specified in paragraph 23.

23.   The employer shall agree to the union's reasonable request to hold meetings with members of the bargaining unit on company premises to discuss the Step 1 claim, the employer's offer or revisions to either. The request shall be made at least three working days in advance of the proposed meeting. However, the employer is not required to provide such facilities, if the employer does not possess available premises which can be used for meetings on the scale suggested by the union. The employer shall provide adequate heating and lighting for meetings, and ensure that the meeting is held in private. Where such meetings are held in working time, the employer is under no obligation to pay individuals for the time off. Where meetings take place outside normal working hours, they should be arranged at a time which is otherwise convenient for the workers.

24.   Where resources permit, the employer shall make available to the Union Side of the JNB such typing, copying and word-processing facilities as it needs to conduct its business in private.

25.   Where resources permit, the employer shall set aside a room for the exclusive use of the Union Side of the JNB. The room shall possess a secure cabinet and a telephone.

26.   In respect of issues which are not otherwise specified in this method, the employer and the union shall have regard to the guidance issued in the ACAS Code of Practice on Time Off for Trade Union Duties and Activities and ensure that there is no unwarranted or unjustified failure to abide by it.

Disclosure of Information

27.   The employer and the union shall have regard to the ACAS Code of Practice on the Disclosure of Information to Trade Unions for Collective Bargaining Purposes and ensure that there is no unwarranted or unjustified failure to abide by it in relation to the bargaining arrangements specified by this method.

Revision of the Method

28.   The employer or the union may request in writing a meeting of the JNB to discuss revising any element of this method, including its status as a legally binding contract. A quorate meeting of the JNB shall be held within ten working days of the receipt of the request by the JNB Secretary. This meeting shall be held in accordance with the same arrangements for the holding of other JNB meetings.

General

29.   The employer and the union shall take all reasonable steps to ensure that this method to conduct collective bargaining is applied efficiently and effectively.

30.   The definition of a 'working day' used in this method is any day other than a Saturday or a Sunday, Christmas Day or Good Friday, or a day which is a bank holiday.

31.   All time limits mentioned in this method may be varied on any occasion, if both the employer and the union agree.

Index